DESIGNING

MO
THER
HOO
D

MICHELLE MILLAR FISHER
AMBER WINICK

The MIT Press
Cambridge, Massachusetts
London, England

For our mothers, Ellie, Terry, and
Pooa. And to those we care for, and
who care for us, Austin, Daniel,
Alice, and Cosima, and someone
so new they are yet unnamed

Withdrawn

AUTHORS——
Michelle Millar Fisher and Amber
Winick in community with esteemed
contributors
CONTRIBUTING CURATORS——
Juliana Rowen Barton and Zoë Greggs
EDITOR——
Kathleen Krattenmaker
MIT PRESS——
    COMMISSIONING EDITOR
    Victoria Hindley
    PRODUCTION
    Janet Rossi, Gabriela Bueno Gibbs

BOOK DESIGN——
Lana Cavar and Natasha Chandani
(Clanada)
TYPEFACE——
GT America by Grillitype
PAPER——
Favini Burano Rosa 90 g/m;
MaxiGloss 90 g/m
PREPRESS——
Miho Karolyi (Kaligraf), Croatia
PRINTED AND BOUND——
KershOffset, Croatia

First edition (edition of 3,000)

LIBRARY OF CONGRESS
CONTROL NUMBER——
2021931308
ISBN——
978-0-262-04489-9

DESIGNING MOTHERHOOD
Things That Make and Break Our Births
supported by The Pew Center for Arts
& Heritage.

The project is conceived in collaboration
with Maternity Care Coalition of
Philadelphia, an organization that works
daily to ensure families can birth with
dignity, parent with autonomy, and
raise babies who are healthy, growing,
and thriving. The project's Maternity
Care Coalition Advisors are Adrianne
Edwards, Tekara Gainey, Porsche
Holland, Gabriella Nelson, Karen
Pollack, and Sabrina Taylor.

The *Designing Motherhood* exhibition
partners are the Mütter Museum and
the Center for Architecture, both in
Philadelphia, and the academic partner
is the Weitzman School of Design
at The University of Pennsylvania.

Across Midwife Luz Argueta-Vogel tenderly wraps a mother's postpartum belly
with a faja just hours after a home birth in Oakland, California, 2018
p. 12 Nurses attending to a baby in the maternity ward of the University
Children's Hospital, Vienna, Austria, 1921

In my early days as a doula and health educator, long before LOOM was even an idea, I looked around at our culture and realized that sexual and reproductive health experiences were shrouded in shame, discomfort, and, most critically, confusion.

I cofounded LOOM, a platform for sexual and reproductive well-being, to offer empowered education on everything from periods and sex to pregnancy and menopause because we are incomplete without this knowledge. Most people operate from a knowledge deficit about the dynamism, beauty, and profundity of how our bodies work. The focus of LOOM was to help reduce that deficit and educate people about the lived experiences of sexual and reproductive health.

At my core, I believe education is alchemic. Education is power. Education is healing. Education is elemental.

All reproductive experiences are part of a continuum. They are inextricably linked. Fertility and birth control, periods and menopause, pregnancy and postpartum, sex and pleasure. They're all capable of existing inside a single person, whether through their own direct encounters or through bearing witness to those of a friend, family member, or lover. It's crucial that people—whether they identify as women, as nonbinary, or as allies— have access to culturally sensitive and emotionally calibrated education that makes room for the elasticity of their lived experience.

Design is integral to the arc of human reproduction because design can enhance, simplify, soften, and excite whatever it touches. Creating better designs to support our reproductive capacities can lower barriers to access, particularly psychic barriers heightened by the oppression of patriarchy.

Those marginalized or unheard because of their lived and embodied experiences need and deserve support at every juncture, and support of their reproduction is no exception. As we continue to innovate around design and reproduction, including economic accessibility, and to make better systems for us all to live in and with, we must also acknowledge the impact of trauma and foreground reproductive justice. Such considerations must be built into the roadmap.

I care about this conversation because I care about humanity, and our reproductive arcs are central to the preservation and the extension of humanity. In a very literal sense, uteruses give life and welcome people onto the planet. Yet some of the primary physical needs of people with uteruses—their reproductive well-being and agency—are not centered or valued by the wider culture. Helping people push back against that and cultivate reproductive sovereignty and power is what gets me out of bed in the morning.

When there is a crisis, these issues are often forgotten. This is why the coronavirus pandemic, with the deep pain it has caused, is also an opportunity for us all to turn inward, learn our histories,

and invest in our bodies and in body literacy. Periods, pregnancy, abortions, and menopause don't stop even when the world is burning and transforming. Our bodies contain infinite power. By knowing them, and by making better designs for them, we can create the new worlds we all need.

My work, and the work of this book, is to create a gentle, tangible, and visual invitation for people to reclaim, explore, and celebrate their bodies. Join us.

——Erica Chidi

"There is nobody against this—NOBODY, NOBODY, NOBODY but a bunch of…a bunch of MOTHERS!" Waiting for his turn to speak at a hearing about the city's plans to run a divided roadway through Washington Square Park in New York, parks commissioner Robert Moses had heard enough. Although Jane Jacobs and Shirley Hayes, the chief organizers of the Greenwich Village group that had arranged photogenic picket lines of children opposing the loss of their play space, had yet to have their say, Moses was incredulous that they might prevail. Despite his close study of the levers of power, he had failed to consider how those traditionally considered the weakest—women and children—might win a public relations battle. They did so by transforming a subject, motherhood, that women were by their nature supposed to know best from a private concern to a public one, moving it from the home to the streets.

Their protest described an arc that is repeated again and again in the design objects whose stories are told in *Designing Motherhood*. This arc connects the personal to the political, the interior to the city, and transforms us versus them to, in the end, simply us—because we all arrive here via some process of birth and, at some point and in some way, we all mother. The designs in this book go beyond binaries and biology.

Maternity clothes and baby carriers, because of their temporary use and identification with the domestic sphere, have received little attention in histories of design, a reality I found in my own research on toys. I was among the first followers of the *Designing Motherhood* Instagram account, which for the last

two years has served as a teaser and research lead for this project. In multiple ways, I have already learned as much from the account as from many scholarly books. This approach of research-in-public, a terrific symbol of the energy and fresh ideas the organizers bring to bear on the subject, is significant. Design history today must go beyond the physical walls of the museum or the printed page to consider, as this project does, the social, scientific, and political implications of objects.

Here, euphemisms like "in an interesting condition" and "up the duff" and the French *enceinte* are replaced with focused looks at online fertility trackers, gender-reveal parties, and day-by-day social media updates. Written and edited by Michelle Millar Fisher and Amber Winick, but embracing a plurality of voices and experiences in the form of interviews, contributor essays, and visual materials, *Designing Motherhood* underlines just how many design fields contribute to the lifelong project of motherhood. Books, fashion, and industrial, automotive, and medical designs each have a role to play from preconception (and contraception) to death, from the ritualistic taking of prenatal vitamins to the poignant memorials of pregnancy-loss tattoos.

The reason for the scatteration of fields responsible for the products of motherhood becomes clear through the examples collected in this volume. Motherhood was a field hiding in plain sight, obscured by its own ubiquity and sidelined by everyday sexism. The famous innovators of motherhood were more often medical men than people who parented, including Dr. Benjamin Spock, whose 1946 *Common Sense*

Book of Baby and Child Care defined the post–World War II middle-class childrearing experience, and the earlier and more sinister Dr. J. Marion Sims, considered the father of modern gynecology, who only achieved that renown by testing his unproven surgical methods on enslaved Black women. In *Designing Motherhood* they are given equal billing with Elsie Frankfurt, the mother of modern maternity wear, who created the tie-waist skirt so that her pregnant sister would not look like a "beach ball in an unmade bed."

I wrote this foreword during at-home quarantine in Brooklyn in June 2020, witnessing the simultaneous pandemics of COVID-19 and structural racism collide. Zoom meetings and video calls have put family life on display at work as never before: the desktop picture of the kids is now a live show. But while both parents may be at home, the burden of homeschooling has disproportionately fallen on mothers, according to a *New York Times* poll, setting up potentially disastrous long-term consequences for their careers. And for some, even a successful career is no protection. As Dr. Khiara Bridges points out in the interview titled "#ListenToBlackWomen," Black college-educated, economically stable women in the United States are still three to four times more likely to die during or immediately after childbirth than White women with less than a high school education and rockier financial foundations. The authors demonstrate the many ways our struggles as women, people of color, and non-gender-conforming persons are designed into society, and how we can—how we must—design our way out. They have been guided throughout the project by thought partners and longtime grassroots advocates at Philadelphia's Maternity Care Coalition.

The focus on the design of systems is woven throughout the book and the wider project. It animates graduate student Alexis Hope's first-person account of the "Make the Breast Pump Not Suck" hackathon at MIT, organized by Hope and a fellow graduate student (now professor), Catherine D'Ignazio. After the hackathon, both women realized that it wasn't so much the device that sucked (though it does), but the circumstances pushing women toward a return to work long before the pediatrician-recommended six months of breastfeeding (also controversial and covered in the essay on formula, p. 263). Hope writes, "Framing breast-feeding as an individual choice, without reflecting on the circumstances that guide people's ability to make a choice (for example, going back to work may be the only economically feasible choice; many don't have the time or a place to pump at work; and so on), is misguided." What she and D'Ignaizio ultimately decided to hack was not the breast pump but America's lack of a federal family leave policy.

There is also room for joy in *Designing Motherhood*, perhaps best expressed by Fisher's essay on "model, singer, actor, provocateur" Grace Jones's 1979 performance wardrobe of a "maternity mega-dress," designed by Antonio Lopez and expectant father Jean-Paul Goude. Outfitted in the mega-dress, with its bright colors, empire waist, ceinture of spiky cardboard triangles, and tricorne hat with an exclamation point, Jones's image was a far cry from the porcelain Mother and Child figurines of the past, or even the girdled conformity of the postwar era, when a mother's clothes often matched her brand new kitchen. Jones capped her successful album launch with a disco baby shower, complete with runway. "Show us the stomach, honey!" someone in the crowd chanted, and Jones showed them why no one should underestimate the power of a bunch of mothers.

——**Alexandra Lange**

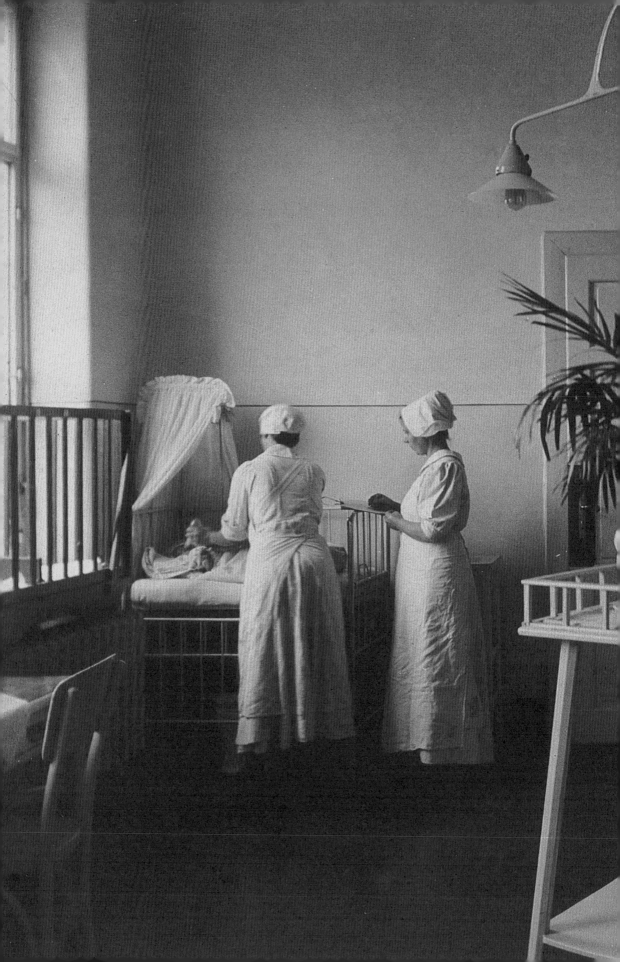

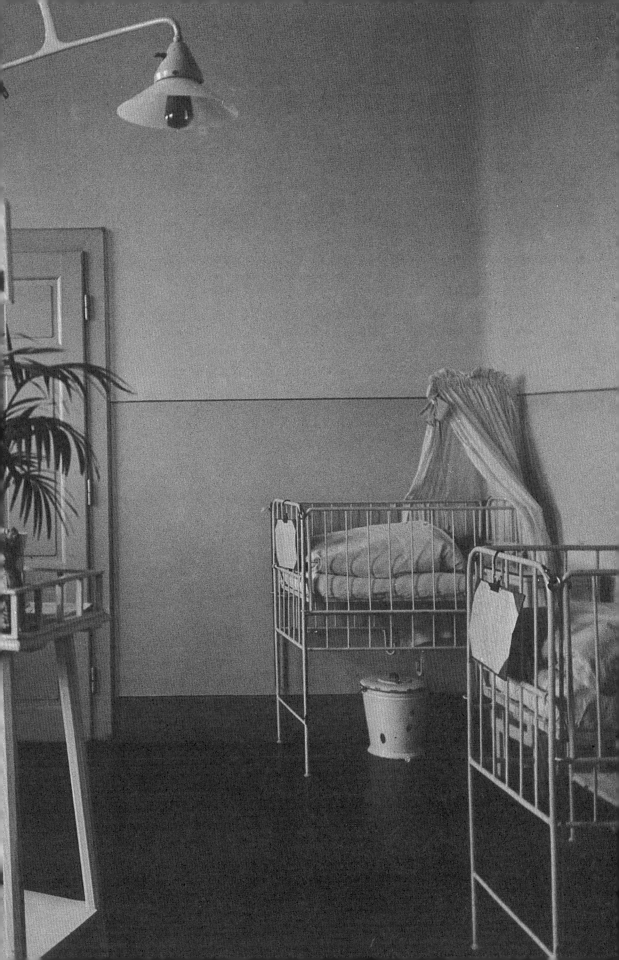

"We Don't Have to Put Up With This," ran the headline of an October 2020 *New York Times* interview on the social taboos around pregnancy-induced incontinence and postpartum hemorrhoids.[1] In their discussion, Mara Altman and Luce Brett engage in a sometimes funny, often harrowing conversation about their years of research into two subjects that almost no one talks about in polite company. As they make clear, the embarrassment of describing the inability to sneeze without peeing a little, or of revealing swollen and painful nether regions (and anything else related to genital health, for that matter) to health providers is often so great, it eclipses the desire to seek help.[2] Yet if you know these things, *you know*.

While the headline articulated the way sufferers might feel about such bodily trials, it also was a riposte to the cultural consensus that such issues are too unsavory for public discussion. As Altman put it, even she—someone who "wrote a whole chapter about anuses"—had difficulty asking her doctor to "take a good close gander back there when mine felt unwieldy and questionable" after the birth of her twins. She added that the shame around female reproductive health at any age and stage runs so deep that it is etymological. *Pudenda*, the Latin word for external genitalia, and usually applied specifically to the vulva, means "to be ashamed of."[3] Through the making of *Designing Motherhood*, we learned that this kind of suppression is not experienced just by women. In our chapter on masculine birth, Thomas Beatie, an American author and activist who gave birth to the first of his four children in 2008, talks about his painful struggle to be recognized for what he is—their father—on his children's birth certificates.

Designing Motherhood affirms that there is no monolithic experience of birth for any of the humans involved in the equation. The same goes for the experiences and circumstances of reproductive health, conception, pregnancy, the postpartum period, menopause, and any of the other knotty aspects that make up motherhood, here expansively understood as noun, verb, and beyond the confines of biology and gender. Yet one common thread in these unique experiences is that the designs governing them are too often kept out of sight and out of mind unless they are required (or until there is a public flare-up about accessibility or impact). Because they are sequestered behind the scenes, it is more difficult to widely share and refine successful systems, do-it-yourself hacks, medical tools, or objects that mediate the arc of human reproduction. And when such designs fail those who use them, it is easier for these fraught experiences to be denied or erased.

But, as the headline says, we don't have to put up with this.

The material culture of human reproduction matters. It should matter to everyone. We all share the universal circumstance of having been born. So we embarked on the journey of writing *Designing Motherhood* as a public reckoning with the designs that, for better or worse, shape experiences for all of us. In this book we cast a critical eye on the designs that govern the choice (or lack of choice) to give birth, that mold motherhood across intersections, that ensure that people can remain childfree, and ultimately that shape every living person. Here, we gather wildly different—and sometimes totally contradictory—histories around many designs, including contraceptives, breast pumps, labor and delivery wards, menstrual products, obstetric stirrups, at-home abortion kits, pain-relief methods, maternity garments, mass media depictions of reproductive milestones, home birth, postpartum underwear, family leave, culturally appropriate care, and baby monitors, to name just a few.

Such objects, spaces, and ideas define life and death and the parameters of autonomy over body and mind. They should occupy a central place in canons of visual culture. They should be among the most well-considered design solutions. Yet these tools, techniques, systems, and speculations receive almost no attention in design history classrooms, or in the collections and exhibitions we pored over in the cultural institutions we visit and work within, or in the studios of designers and architects whose work receives wide acclaim.[4] Despite the fervent public interest in a topic that touches us all—literally—at least once in our lives, museum collections, fashion and design exhibitions, the mainstream of design scholarship, and many public forums have yet to fully embrace maternity as a topic worthy of serious inquiry. Instead, the subject is treated furtively or as unimportant—as something beneath debate or lacking in intellectual content. This gap inspired the book you now hold.

It provokes a wry laugh whenever we remember the moment four years ago when we first started sending out book and exhibition proposals for consideration. We thought it was such a fascinating topic that we would have to fend off a crowd of eager respondents. Instead, the opposite was true. We had to knock hard on many doors before arriving at the constellation of brilliant partners who helped midwife *Designing Motherhood* into existence. Why have the designs we explore in this book remained so hidden even as they define the everyday experiences of so many? One answer is that most heads of publishing houses, museum directors, chairs of exhibition proposal committees, and chief curators we encountered have not, and never will, directly use these things. Indeed, one of the wonderful artists we met along the way, Philadelphia-based Aimee Gilmore, recounted the time in graduate school that her professor, glancing at her desk during a studio visit, mistook her breast pump for an air horn. Suffice it to say, she had a hard time getting faculty to take seriously her desire to make art about motherhood.

In this light, a key aspect of our project became the inclusion of living and archival anecdotes of as many people as possible who *have* experienced the designs we interrogate. We heeded historian Sarah Knott's description of the value of anecdote to history, especially in unearthing narratives that have been consistently sidelined, disenfranchised, or undervalued by socially dominant groups (in her case, she was referring specifically to stories of maternity within a patriarchy). This approach is explicitly feminist and anti-racist. As Knott states in her book *Mother Is a Verb*:

> The telling of anecdotes…is a particularly powerful means
> of moving between History with a capital H…and the
> mundane stuff of living with an infant. Anecdotes offer
> the rare opportunity to interpret different kinds of scenes,
> remarks, or objects that illuminate [a subject], even where
> there is no continuous record, and the tiny archival traces
> that are left usually appear minor or inconsequential. They
> are the only means to keep asking "What was it like?"[5]

In seeking to weave oral histories into our chapters as often as possible, we were inspired by the many before us who have honored storytelling as a valuable form of knowledge sharing. They include the matriarchs in our lives, who over decades shared with us their reproductive experiences, and the people who wrote their own stories of sexual pleasure, violence, and perplexity, for example, in the seminal *Our Bodies, Ourselves*. They also include contemporary historians such as Knott; Shannon Withycombe, author of *Lost: Miscarriage in Nineteenth-Century America*; and Ann Fessler, who wrote *The Girls Who Went Away: The Hidden History of Women Who Surrendered Children for Adoption in the Decades Before Roe v. Wade*. Each combed over diaries, receipts, and other ephemera to understand individual experiences—of everything from infant loss to unwilling adoption to a first milk letdown—that would otherwise be absent in the historical record. We have approached design expansively, using interdisciplinary tools from the medical and social sciences and visual histories outside the mainstream, a necessary approach, since existing canons have not welcomed many of the objects and ideas we selected for interrogation. These are the things that fall between the cracks of disciplinary boundaries as well as social mores.

This book explores over a hundred designs—iconic, profound, archaic, titillating, emotionally charged, or just plain odd—that have defined the relationships between people, reproductive capacities, and babies over the last century. We have foregrounded designs across four categories: reproduction, pregnancy, birth, and postpartum. You will most likely find in these pages designs you have used: the tampons you unwrap every month, the abortion you underwent, or the pill blister pack whose day you consulted before you popped and swallowed, perhaps. These designs often live in very embedded ways in our memories and our bodies. We don't just remember our first period, but also the technologies that first collected the blood. We don't just remember the way babies arrive, but also what they were wrapped in when they finally reached our arms. We might recall what it feels like to have a breast pump stretch and suck us dry, or feel our muscles tense in response to reminders of a cold and uncomfortable speculum, or relive the long, heart-pounding minutes spent waiting to read the result on a pregnancy test.

Many of the designs in this book have been used by millions of people and have altered the course of human experience. A great many crisscross the globe to play roles in radically different lives. Some are or have been complicit in the subjugation of people. They are the things that, as our subtitle states, "make and break our births"—as birthing people and as people who have been given birth to.

We have written the majority of the chapters in the book, and our viewpoints are wholly subjective. We are two White women—one Scottish, the other American, one with children, the other without—in our late thirties. No book could ever comprehensively address the wide topic set out in our title. We have instead tried to represent a range of different experiences, inviting over fifty different contributors to share their perspectives through interviews, artwork, or their own writing. There are vastly different experiences of gender and racial dynamics and identities reflected in the essays in this book.

We have used "women" in most historical instances, for example to denote specific experiences of gender discrimination. However, we have deferred to gender neutral pronouns when speaking in the present or future tense. We have capitalized when a color is used to describe a race, for example Black, Brown, and White, to emphasize the constructed nature of racial identities, a fact that has greatly impacted the shape and effect of the majority of the designs included in this book. While we recognize proponents of white supremacy have taken to the capitalization of White, we feel strongly that the grammatical gesture emphasizes White people as racialized subjects.

There will no doubt be designs explored in the following chapters that are entirely new to you, and also omissions of things that figured hugely in your past, or still figure in your present. We have been able to tackle only a fraction of the evocative and emotionally charged objects and spaces that relate to motherhood. In addressing designs and subjects that we felt were in urgent need of greater attention, we hope we allow readers to move toward a sense of playfulness and joy when it comes to our bodies and the designs that interact with them, without ignoring the many racist, misogynistic motivations that have frequently been woven into them.

Designing Motherhood acts as a prompt for future scholars, curators, architects, designers, and audiences to tackle, as part of design history, the political and material considerations of having a reproductive body, including—we hope prioritizing—empowerment, body autonomy, and better outcomes for everyone involved. At stake is a centering of subject matter, designs, and ideas that rarely if ever get airtime in cultural institutions, yet are to be found everywhere in daily life. Beyond this, the histories presented in *Designing Motherhood* often reposition women-identifying people as the locus of design—as creators and as users—elevating their concerns as relevant and necessary.

Reframing the design history we were taught—and once bought into—is a large part of our project. Nothing runs quite so deep in our discipline as the history of modern design. In 1934 the Museum of Modern Art in New York held its first exhibition of design, *Machine Art*, which followed on the heels of its inaugural exhibition of contemporary architecture extolling the International Style. Curated by Philip Johnson, the museum's first chair of architecture and design, and Alfred Barr Jr., the museum's director, *Machine Art* celebrated innovations in engineering and technology, including a self-aligning ball bearing, scientific beakers made by Corning Glass, and industrial springs. The objects were elevated, both literally and metaphorically, on white pedestals. This exhibition was the genesis of the MoMA canon of design, which in turn went on to indelibly shape public and scholarly attitudes about what counts as design, as well similar museum collections and their commercial derivations, and many a classroom textbook.[6]

In the twenty-first century this genealogy gave birth to *Humble Masterpieces*, an exhibition organized by Paola Antonelli at MoMA in 2004 that similarly pilfered from the everyday, presenting over a hundred objects, including the condom, the Chupa Chup, and the Post-it note.[7] Fertile forays into speculative and critical design—Sputniko!'s *Menstruation Machine*, which promised wearers the feeling of a period—and biodesign followed. But while design now seemed more expansive in its purview, museum galleries still did not reflect motherhood (nor did the museum's human resource policies, mirroring a wider US workforce culture inhospitable to working parents).[8] Nowhere in the nearly nine decades during which MoMA has been collecting and displaying design in its most innovative forms have any designs related to human reproduction, pregnancy, or birth from the perspectives of women-identifying or trans people been included. For that, one must visit the Smithsonian Institution in Washington, DC, with its more encyclopedic remit, or medical collections such as the Mütter Museum in Philadelphia or the Dittrick Medical History Center at Case Western Reserve University in Ohio.

From the very earliest moments of our project we saw the breast pump as a technology that could (and should) have been included in *Machine Art* or *Humble Masterpieces*.[9] Although Johnson could not have come across the portable breast pump developed in the 1950s by the Swedish civil engineer Einar Egnell and Sister Maja Kindberg in Stockholm, he might have included one of its precursors. None would have looked out of place among his industrial marvels. The pump typology fits the canon of labor-saving devices aimed specifically at women. It also looks the part.

The breast pump, in its portable incarnation, connects human milk production to the larger capital structures of the global, industrial workplace. Millions of people today rely on the speculum—another design fit for a MoMA pedestal, and one which pinpoints the foundation of modern gynecology—undergoing routine cervical examinations completely unaware of the torture and suffering of enslaved women in the early nineteenth century who served as unwilling test subjects for the technology. The Del-Em Menstrual Evacuation Kit speaks to a history of feminist, do-it-yourself technologies designed to give people with ovaries and uteruses self-control of their reproductive destinies. The tie-waist skirt helps to tell the story of the public coming out of pregnancy, on national television.[10]

Yet museums and other spaces that produce (or design) culture are still grappling with how to do so in ways that truly honor a wide and diverse range of human experience. For the designs we explore in this book, and others like them, we argue that it is not ignorance or ambivalence that has caused scholarly lacunae, but rather the systematic disenfranchisement of reproductive experiences, which are too often gendered and feminized. This happens not in some abstract, theoretical research space but at the tables where museum professionals make decisions about which exhibitions to greenlight, publishers decide which books to support, and administrators and board members allocate research funding and determine school curricula. At its most potent, design is a lens onto wider conversations that intersect with a broad swath of human experience, and the objects, systems, and spaces described within these pages unearth many that have for too long remained hidden because decision makers don't reflect this diversity.

If it takes a village to raise a child, it also takes a village to change prevailing attitudes toward maternity within the wider culture—and to change the status of design within the fine arts. In the last few years there has been a particular efflorescence of writing and visual-arts practices centering on the stages of life that are sometimes collectively called motherhood.[11] This blossoming has, to our delight, only increased during the course of our own research and has reached the national stage. In February 2019, Stacey Abrams, then a Georgia state representative and the first Black woman to deliver a State of the Union rebuttal, addressed Black maternal mortality as an issue of national importance and contextualized it within deep histories of racism and lack of access to health care. Just over a year later, a coalition of advocates and activists took out a full-page advertisement in the *New York Times* that unequivocally stated that "racism, not race" was responsible for high maternal mortality in the United States, under a headline that asked bluntly, "How Many Black, Brown, & Indigenous People Have To Die Giving Birth?"

It is thus wrong to say that histories of human reproduction are completely absent from the cultural universe. Of course they're not. The robust "Selected Readings" section at the back of this book is testament to the many thinkers whose work we relied on over the course of this project. But we could not find such stories reflected in the vehicles and platforms that promulgate the histories of *design*.

One of the recent books that lodged in our consciousness came from the young Australian writer Jessica Friedmann. Her collection of autobiographical stories, *Things That Helped* (2017), describes the birth of her first child, Owen, and the postnatal depression that followed. In her subsequent essay of 2019, "Motherhood Is a Political Category," she invokes the term *matrescence* to describe the psychological process of becoming a mother that she and her literary peers mine.[12] Friedmann writes:

> Motherhood is a political category.... We are told it is something we must cherish and excel at. Motherhood is janitorial work. It is health care. It is elder care. It is care for the environment, rapidly choking under industrialization. It is working against the carceral system as it rips families apart.... It is an exquisite pleasure and a wonder and a privilege. It is also, by every metric, just a fucking raw deal.[13]

Conjuring the work of the anthropologist Dana Raphael and the psychologist Aurélie Athan, Friedmann also writes of the need to construct an identity separate from her child. As described in one passage of her postpartum diary, she achieves this at the very threshold of preparing to deliver her son, while dressed in the uniform of the cesarean birth—blue hairnet, hospital gown, divested of all her own clothes, jewelry, and nail polish. She asks the attending nurse if she can retain her shock of red lipstick: "'I don't see why not,' [the nurse] says, laughing at me a little.... I don't laugh.... My lips stand out like flames on an otherwise pale face—the last visible sign of any choices I have made on my own behalf."[14]

Design needs similar stories. Many existing products and systems actively undermine the circumstances of different ethnic, social, and cultural groups and promote heteronormative White values as "standards."[15] The history of

——INTRODUCTION

design for the arc of human reproduction is full of incidents in which designers imposed their values, beliefs, and convictions onto their viewers, users, and consumers in the name of finding solutions or solving problems "for them," many times without informed—or any—consent.

The writing of the histories collected in this book reflects, much like Friedmann's lipstick, our determined choice to shape disciplinary boundaries and bend them to our will, even when there was only a small purchase to cling to. It is also our intent to construct an identity separate from the essentialized and biological understanding of motherhood as involving women-identifying people and a uterus—to expand the vocabulary we use when speaking of design's intersection with human reproduction. So much of the language is gendered, as are so many of the expectations, socially and culturally. We struggled with using the word *motherhood* in the title of the book. But it is shorthand for acts that go beyond a gender binary and beyond people who have been pregnant or given birth. It is a word that can be embodied, deferred, refused, taken on as a duty or expectation, or otherwise engaged with, in all its knotty contours. Motherhood is myriad.

Birth is universal, but social location shapes each experience of human reproduction in sometimes achingly unique ways. While our research was expansive, it was also indelibly influenced by the very particular geography we write from. The United States is a place where it is especially difficult to be in control of one's uterus, gender identity, pregnancy, parturition, or postpartum period. One in four postpartum people here return to the workplace within two weeks of giving birth. The United States is the only country in the so-called developed world without a national statutory paid parental leave, and it is ranked last for paid family leave provisions.[16] It is a place where reproductive health is a political debate rather than a personal choice, where maternal mortality has doubled since 1991, and where culturally appropriate care is often in tension with mass medicalization and Big Pharma.

The centrality of the United States to this project was confirmed through the close partnership we formed with a truly inspiring organization, the Philadelphia-based Maternity Care Coalition.[17] Since 1980, MCC has worked in southeastern Pennsylvania to improve the health and well-being of pregnant people and parenting families, focusing particularly on neighborhoods with high rates of poverty, infant mortality, health disparities, and changing immigration patterns. MCC's work focuses on programs that anticipate and address community needs through a continuum of maternal and family health home-visit interventions.

We crossed paths with MCC at a time when they wanted to make their work more widely known and ensure its support in the future. We hoped that by spearheading *Designing Motherhood* together, it would give MCC stakeholders a voice, bring new audiences to the organization, and foreground stories of reproductive rights and motherhood from the perspective of—*and with*—their clients, whose stories and voices are often left out of mainstream discussions. Though they are internationally recognized for their important work, this work is still often siloed as a "women's issue" rather than understood as the foundation of healthy citizens, societies, and culture at large. As Gabriella Nelson, associate director of policy at MCC, and a trained urban planner, puts it:

> We advocate for a wide range of things, but that's what motherhood is. Motherhood is housing, it is food security, it's public education, it's health care systems, it's public transportation. We're trying to make sure that we live under that reproductive justice framework and always center it back on mom and baby. This means policy making for any number of issues.[18]

One such policy is the provision of community-based doulas, which MCC has pioneered for the last forty years—as one of the first centers in the United States to emphasize the positive impact of culturally appropriate care on maternal and infant outcomes. A century ago, birthing people in labor would have been attended at home by folks from their own communities. In Minnesota, Dr. Katy B. Kozhimannil, a health services researcher, found that doula support for Medicaid enrollees in the state was associated with a 40.9 percent reduction in cesarean deliveries, indicating potential state Medicaid savings from covering doula services in excess of $2 million. This work directly informed the 2013 legislation and subsequent passage of Minnesota's "doula bill," now a national model for establishing Medicaid coverage of doula care, which is associated with better maternal health outcomes and a reduction in racial inequities. Dr. Kozhimannil speaks truth to power:

> Maternal and infant mortality has salience because it has relevance to all of us, but at the time I was beginning my work,

I had to fight conventional wisdom about what was an important research question. I had this "pat on my head" experience so many times from people who would say, "It's just so nice that you're studying birth. Is that because you're a mom?" No, I'm studying birth because it matters. To everyone.[19]

We see *Designing Motherhood* as part of this larger conversation on design development, activism, and policy change, as well as a source of reclaimed joy, body literacy, and reproductive agency. We hope the images and words throughout this book will allow readers to see themselves represented in a public forum and will normalize truth-telling about the ways motherhood has been designed until now—and the ways in which it might be different in the future. We want readers to laugh, bristle with indignation, or sigh with disbelief at the things individually or collectively endured—and that are begging to be addressed by designers, and by us all.

1 Mara Altman and Luce Brett, "'We Don't Have to Put Up With This': A Candid Conversation about Bodies," *New York Times*, October 26, 2020 (in the In Her Words section), nytimes.com.
2 A conservative global estimate of postpartum incontinence sufferers alone stands at four hundred million.
3 Altman and Brett, "We Don't Have to Put Up With This."
4 As one way to combat this lacuna, we have been testing out curriculum interventions centered on design histories featured in this book, in collaboration with design students and Professor Orkan Telhan at the University of Pennsylvania in Philadelphia, beginning in the fall 2020 semester.
5 Sarah Knott, *Mother Is a Verb* (New York: Farrar, Straus, and Giroux, 2019), 85. Knott lays out her methodology in an epilogue (263–65), pointing to three further reasons for using anecdote as part of her historical method: the precedent of "historical writing that emerged in the seventeenth century and took anecdote as a means of exploring private lives and inner worlds...in contrast to conventional preoccupations

with the doings of important men"; of unearthing fragmented histories that have not been privileged, using "small shards and occasional nuggets" left in the records but previously passed over; and the notion of honoring histories "interrupted by care work." We are compelled by her explanation that "historical interpretation can reside in the slow accumulation of a trellis of detail. Juxtaposing, contrasting, pausing over, and serializing anecdote can make for a full historical interpretation by comparison and accretion."
6 We should note here that we worship the design historians and curators from whom we learned much of this material—and much more that is off the beaten path, too. Our book is not a critique but a retelling of sorts, and one fully encouraged by our teachers and mentors.
7 The exhibition took place at MoMA's offsite location in Queens during the building of the museum's Tanaguchi extension, perhaps accounting for its permissiveness. See also *Strangely Familiar: Design and Everyday Life* (Minneapolis: Walker Art Center, 2003) and *Items: Is Fashion Modern?* (New York: MoMA, 2017).

8 See Michelle Millar Fisher, "Parenting and Labor in the Art World: A Call to Arms," *Hyperallergic*, May 6, 2019. During the course of researching this book, a landmark pregnancy discrimination case was brought—and won—by curator Nikki Columbus against MoMA PS1 in Queens, New York.
9 When one of us did suggest that the breast pump be included in an exhibition while working at MoMA, and then again at the Philadelphia Museum of Art, she was unsuccessful (we ultimately sent our pumps to the Art Institute of Chicago, which put them in their design galleries).
10 The tie-waist skirt did make it into MoMA's hallowed halls, in the 2017 exhibition *Items: Is Fashion Modern?* which one of us coorganized. Carmen Winant's powerful *My Birth* installation in MoMA's photography galleries in 2018 finally tipped the scales, inviting audiences to contemplate the ways in which they enter the world.
11 It includes the photographer Heji Shin's 2017 *Baby* series, displayed as part of the last Whitney Biennial (2019), and the work of various writers, including Maggie Nelson (*The Argonauts*, 2015), Sheila Heti (*Motherhood: A Novel*,

2018), Lena Dunham (who wrote of her hysterectomy at age thirty-one in 2018), Angela Garbes (*Like a Mother: A Feminist Journey through the Science and Culture of Pregnancy*, 2018), and Dani McClain (*We Live for the We: The Political Power of Black Motherhood*, 2019). In March 2019 the *New York Times* debuted its Parenting section, a formalization of similar online forums that stretched back decades, one of the most widely known and used being the UK-based Mumsnet, founded in 2000.
12 This word has been having a renaissance over the last year or so—it's almost a trend. Type it into an online search engine to witness its recent explosion.
13 Jessica Friedmann, "Motherhood Is a Political Category," *Human Parts* at *Medium*, May 10, 2019, humanparts.medium.com.
14 Jessica Friedmann, *Things That Helped: On Postpartum Depression* (New York: Farrar, Straus, and Giroux, 2017), 29.
15 Surprisingly, there are relatively few published books and no major museum exhibitions about designs made for reproduction, pregnancy, birth, and motherhood. Academic

publications that touch on these types of designs (see "Selected Readings") are often under-illustrated.
16 Only eight states have passed their own paid family leave laws. As a country, the United States spends the most per capita globally on maternal health care, yet maternal mortality has grown alarmingly in recent decades. The US Family and Medical Leave Act (FMLA) only covers 60 percent of workers for up to twelve weeks of unpaid leave.
17 The project is thus a first-of-its-kind exploration of the arc of human reproduction through the lens of architecture and design that will manifest not just as this book, but also as an exhibition and a series of public programs at sites across Philadelphia.
18 Presentation to the first Designing Motherhood design class at Penn Design, University of Pennsylvania, Philadelphia, October 12, 2020.
19 In October 2020, the Heinz Family Foundation named Dr. Kozhimannil the recipient of the prestigious 25th Heinz Award in the public policy category. This quote is taken from their press release announcing the award.

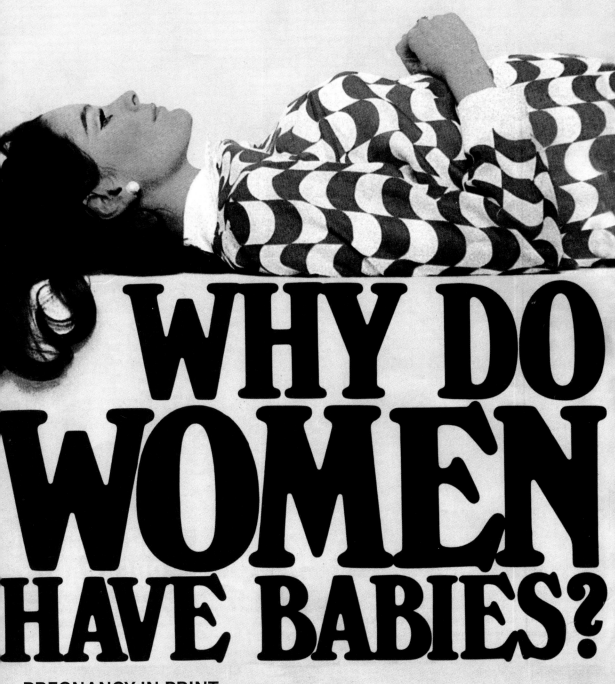

MAY 1967 THREE SHILLINGS

NOVA

STARTING
LEN DEIGHTON'S
NEW SPY BOOK.
ALSO DAVID FROST,
MOREAU, BROPHY,
SHRIMPTON, PROOPS,
LADY CHICHESTER

WHY DO WOMEN HAVE BABIES?

PREGNANCY IN PRINT

PREGNANCY IN PRINT Print publications—especially their front covers—are places of public reckoning for many controversial topics in the realm of human reproduction, as well as spaces for the cultural construction of womanhood and motherhood through graphics and advertising. The print materials here probe a range of expectations and idealizations of reproductive bodies, often framed by rhetorical questions that call attention to urgent issues while simultaneously essentializing overlapping experiences or, through lack of diverse representation, erasing them entirely.

1—— "Why Do Women Have Babies?," *Nova*, cover of May 1967. Photograph by Terence Donovan, art direction by Harry Peccinotti
2—— "The New Magazine for Women," *Ms.*, cover of July 1972
3—— "Fashion magazine for smart young mothers-to-be," cover of Page Boy Maternity Company's catalog for fall/winter 1952
4—— "Where Are the Mothers?," *Nieman Reports*, summer 2017. Designed by Pentagram
5—— "High School Pregnancy," *Life*, cover of April 2, 1971
6—— *The Practicing Midwife*, cover of issue 12 (winter/spring 1981)

Nieman

To attract and retain millennial journalists, news outlets must better meet the needs of parents with young children

WHERE ARE THE MOTHERS?

THE PRACTICING MIDWIFE

Winter/Spring 1984

No. 12

CELL——How did life begin on this planet? How did it evolve into humans? Such questions have motivated scientists—and many others—over centuries. Today, they help us not only trace different origins for motherhood but also locate it on a continuum and reimagine it within a diverse set of new beginnings.

A membrane around a center. A tiny little droplet that encapsulates all of chemistry and that can give birth to anything from bacteria to plants. The cell is often the smallest metaphor we use to describe the origins of life. Myriad narratives exist to explain why cells themselves came into being, what motivated these little droplets to form membranes, to isolate themselves from their environment, and then, even more interestingly, to divide.

Cells mother differently across different species, but what unites them all is the motivation to make copies of themselves. We call it growth. Some split and make identical copies, and some merge with others and give birth to a hybrid that mixes chemistry, information, and appearance from two parent cells. François Jacob, the scientist who shared the Nobel Prize in 1965 for his work on genetics, famously said, "the dream of every bacterial cell is to become two cells."

But why?

According to one theory, when cells started to get too big it became harder for them survive in their environment. Their growth slowed. So splitting was a matter of housekeeping. Others theorize that splitting contributes to survival under dire conditions; it is a mechanism of adaptability.

But cells don't just split into two. They also make identical copies of their genetic material so that each copy has an equal chance of surviving. This is a lot of extra work for an individual cell. Instead of focusing on using all of its resources for itself, it projects itself into an unknown future with a copy.

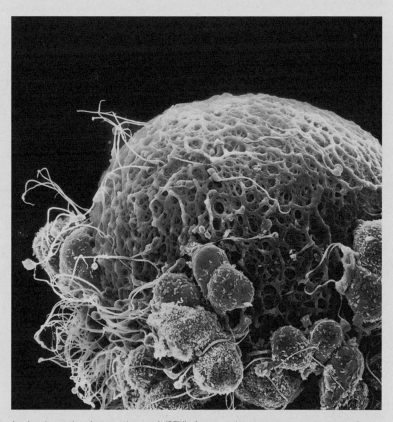

A colored scanning electron micrograph (SEM) of sperm trying to penetrate an egg, captured by Lennart Nilsson in 1965. About six days after fertilization, an embryo in the blastocyst stage will be in the process of "hatching" just before implanting in the wall of the uterus

——REPRODUCTION

But why?

It is a desire for "connectivity," according to the microbiologist Vic Norris, who, focusing on bacteria cells, defines life as a "relationship" that happens among chemicals. It gets harder for these chemicals to stay connected and for cells to maintain their "identity" as they get bigger.[1] As they gain mass through incorporating other ingredients, they become fundamentally different. Their motility and ability to survive decreases. So they divide. In each daughter cell the relationships among the components—and therefore life— is restored.

The dream is to remain connected internally but also to exist on a different level. Each new cell becomes a new possibility to encounter others. Mothering, in cellular terms, is both a desire for survival and a curiosity manifesting in an external connection that expands the idea of self. In Norris's terms this allows the bacteria cells he studies to live as both individuals and species. Each clone—a copy, an offspring—is another opportunity to seek connections within and beyond the self and brings value to the multitude. Cells become communities, and organize into more complex species in which life further interconnects.

Becoming human took longer. After cells began to divide billions of years ago, they did not immediately start to form complex species. And when they did, these were very different from the species we encounter now. Across land and sea, cells grouped, sedimented, and piled up as multitudes that benefited from the existence of each of the others. One

such particular collective is stromatolites, aggregates of cyanobacteria, which formed mound-like formations within lakes or riverbeds. Stromatolites were the dominant life-form on the planet around 1.25 billion years ago. As they peaked in numbers, they slowly transformed the world around them and paved the way for more novel and complex species.

Cyanobacteria are the first organisms that used photosynthesis, the well-known chemical reaction that turns sunlight into energy—a niche cellular activity back then. Then, a large number of simultaneously photosynthesizing organisms contributed to the accumulation of atmospheric oxygen, precipitating a major extinction of many anaerobe, or oxygen-free, organisms. The new atmosphere selected and mothered certain species. Plants and roaming animals began to prevail.

Other life forms developed different chemical strategies. Some turned to the newly available fruits in their environment and used their sugar as an energy source. One particular species, Saccharomyces cerevisiae, known as baker's yeast, excelled at turning sugars into alcohols and carbon dioxide. The alcohol helped them kill the bacteria in their environment and increased their chances of survival.[2] What we refer to today as fermentation shaped entire civilizations—defined trade routes, caused wars, set colonial practices—in the name of getting hold of wine, cheese, bread, and other such resources.[3] While many types of fungus disappeared along the timeline of evolution, Saccharomyces formed a deep connection with humans

and rose to power as a similarly prevalent species on the planet. Understanding the chemical and biological beginnings of these very first mothers, these pioneering cells, is fundamental to design's histories. Today, designers grow cells to make all kinds of things, from new materials to medicine. Photosynthetic algae are now designed to grow so that they respire and make biodegradable plastics. Baker's yeast is genetically transformed to ferment insulin, saving the lives of millions of people whose bodies cannot produce it on their own. A field known as cellular agriculture defines new paths for growing food alternatives—milk proteins without cows, egg yolk without chickens. In labs cells divide, grow, replicate, and substitute.

Design becomes the domain where many definitions of motherhood are reinterpreted. For Hélène Cixous, a poet, writer, and daughter of a midwife, motherhood amounts to *the* generative force behind writing, making, resisting, and actualizing oneself in the space of the other: "Writing…to give birth to myself and to nurse myself, too. Life summons life."[3]

As the son of an ob-gyn, I lived Cixous's words through my father's stories of his work. Motherhoods kindle across bodies and forms. As our cellular beginnings continue to evolve through the making of new connections, motherhood restores, reinterprets, and repurposes life—as a form of curiosity and generosity toward what else may begin, again, through our cellular selves.

—Orkan Telhan

1 Vic Norris, "Why Do Bacteria Divide?," *Frontiers in Microbiology* 6, no. 322 (2015), doi.org/10.3389/ fmicb.2015.00322. 2 Sofia Dashko et al., "Why, When, and How Did Yeast Evolve Alcoholic Fermentation?," *FEMS Yeast Research* 14, no. 6 (2014): 826–32, doi.org/ 10.1111/1567-1364.12161. 3 Nané Jordan, "Daughter of Writing Mother Writ Large with Hélène Cixous," *Journal of the Motherhood Initiative for Research and Community Involvement* 7, no. 2 (2016): 98.

OUR BODIES, OURSELVES——The latest edition of *Our Bodies, Ourselves*, published in 2011 and over nine hundred pages long, is a doorstop of a book, far weightier in size and reach than its originating documents. Those were a Xeroxed sheaf of handwritten notes passed between women in Boston after a 1969 women's liberation conference at the city's Emmanuel College.[1]

Yet, despite the radical shift in scale, the project's ethos has remained fairly steady over the past five decades: know yourselves, women, for knowledge of your own bodies is power that enables stewardship of health, reproduction, and personal destiny. As the opening sentence of the latest edition exhorts, "Learning about our sexual anatomy and observing and exploring our bodies are good ways to become more comfortable with ourselves and our sexuality." And, the book goes on to explain, makes us empowered advocates rather than passive recipients of the health care we need.

Originally titled *Women and Their Bodies*, the text was collaboratively written by a group of White middle-class women, the Boston Women's Health Collective. Developed for a class, which ran only once, it was self-published for wider distribution in 1970. The original 193-page newsprint booklet cost seventy-five cents and was refined through a series of consciousness-raising workshops held between 1969 and 1970.[2]

Handwritten in a neat cursive, the first table of contents listed the course outline—from an introductory essay on the intersection of women, medicine, and capitalism through chapters on basic anatomy, sexuality, and sexually-transmitted diseases, to birth control (including abortion), pregnancy, childbirth, and postpartum care. The text was picked up by a publisher in 1971, the New England Free Press, and graduated to Simon & Schuster in 1973. Its first revised edition appeared in 1984, undertaken by the same core group of women who had been meeting weekly for over a decade. Like so

Published by the New England Free Press first as *Women and Their Bodies* (1970), and then as *Our Bodies, Ourselves* (1971), the 193-page, hand-stapled booklet sold more than 250,000 copies, mainly through distribution by hand and word of mouth

many US-based women's groups of that era—including DIY abortion groups that, pre–Roe v. Wade, taught themselves to perform medical procedures—they focused on self-education (see Del-Em Device, p. 47). They made the personal political through consciousness raising, speaking out in public about their own experiences and encouraging others to do so. These first-person testimonials formed the core of the book, overriding predominantly male doctors to place trust in women's own embodied experiences.

What became Our Bodies, Ourselves opened up a world of information about women's reproductive health and emotional well-being that had previously only been whispered, if spoken at all. Susan Wells, author of a comprehensive reflection on the OBO project, notes that it was "a labor of language, creating vocabulary in which women could talk about their bodies, forging discursive styles and modes of argument, and inventing narrative forms that, by building authority and solidarity, could establish health work as a field of practice for the women's movement."[3] It is unsurprising that its birth was contemporaneous with Meg Crane's design for the at-home pregnancy test (see p. 81) and with Jane, a Chicago-based underground abortion service. The need for the book was decided, in part, when the group tried to create a list of physicians who treated women with respect and came up short—the same factor that precipitated the formation of Jane.[4] Whether objects or networks, these designs put information about reproductive health into the hands of women who operated outside the male-dominated realms of the doctor's office, the hospital, or public policy.

As the editions developed, the number of forthright illustrations and photographs depicting self-examination and what to expect within and outside the health care system grew, in many cases providing women with their first sight of their own biological parts.[5] The book's twelve original authors, who ranged in age from twenty-four to forty, used the word we throughout as a gesture of sisterhood, though the founding group's homogeneity placed the question of inclusivity at the heart of subsequent revisions of the book and its wider adoption worldwide.

In 2007, the feminist scholar Kathy Davis characterized the book's numerous translations as acts of "faithless appropriation" rather than a "faithful copy" of the original.[6] The Spanish-language edition was published in 1977, primarily for a US audience, as Nuestros Cuerpos, Nuestras Vidas. Editions in other countries and cultural contexts grapple with a range of issues that affect women, while recognizing that exporting any feminist project beyond its original boundaries—whether of geography, language, class, or race— is a fraught proposition. In Egypt, after heated discussion, consensus ultimately was reached around the text on female circumcision, which, controversially to some readers, "explained the cultural context allowing the continuation of the practice and…offered objective information on the drawbacks of the practice to women readers."[7] Same-sex love and sex were omitted in the same book (citing religious censure), but a new chapter was included on violence by women against other women.[8] As illiteracy was an issue, the book was recorded on tape in Arabic. In the United States, the 2011 edition explores the needs of intersex and trans people—a precursor to the stand-alone Trans Bodies, Trans Selves published in 2014.[9]

Critics, reviewers, and readers have continued to contribute to shaping Our Bodies, Ourselves, too. A 1973 reviewer in the seminal radical feminist journal off our backs publicly criticized the changes they perceived when the book moved from the New England Press to Simon & Schuster, claiming that the new edition was "less angry."[10] Contemporary reviewers of the revised 1984 edition accused the tome of a bias toward charting fertility over taking the pill or using an IUD. These criticisms are complex and call for historical context. Unbiased contraceptive information is key to body autonomy, but in an era in which medical abuses over the testing of the pill and infertility caused by the Dalkon Shield were just coming to light (see p. 43), the OBO collective's suspicion of for-profit pharmaceutical companies and racist medical systems was reasonable.

Ultimately, the text of Our Bodies, Ourselves synthesized real-life experiences and medical knowledge using colloquial language to promote women's body sovereignty. Today, it is the one of the most frequently translated (thirty-one languages and counting) and best-selling feminist books worldwide.[11]

1 For full author credits across editions, see "Our Bodies, Ourselves: The Nine US Editions," ourbodiesourselves.org.
2 Jane Pincus, one of the women who would go on to coauthor the first edition of Our Bodies, Ourselves, recalls that there were about fifty women in the room and a "tremendous feeling of sexuality, freedom, and excitement. A lot of women for the first time talked about themselves, their experiences, how they felt…. People just had a sense…that what we learned would give us a lot of control, a lot of power."

See Susan Wells, "Our Bodies, Ourselves" and the Work of Writing (Stanford, CA: Stanford University Press, 2010), n. 54.
3 Wells, "Our Bodies, Ourselves" and the Work of Writing, 698.
4 See Jennifer J. Yanco, "Our Bodies, Ourselves in Beijing: Breaking the Silences," Feminist Studies 22, no. 3 (Autumn 1996): 512.
5 Hunger for this information is not a thing of the past. In 2019, I put a copy of the second edition of OBO out for public use in a museum exhibition; the copy fell apart from

use within four months, the spine breaking at the two-page spread depicting the stages of labor, birth, and immediate postpartum—images still so rarely seen in public today.
6 Kathy Davis, The Making of "Our Bodies, Ourselves": How Feminism Travels across Borders (Durham, NC: Duke University Press, 2007), 192.
7 Nadia Farah, "Our Bodies, Ourselves: The Egyptian Women's Health Book Collective," in "Gender and Politics," special issue, Middle East Report 173

(November–December 1991): 17.
8 Farah, "Our Bodies, Ourselves," 17.
9 In the 1973 reprint, the chapter title had morphed into the more evocative "In Amerika They Call Us Dykes"; in 1984 it was "Loving Women: Lesbian Life and Relationships"; and in 1998 it became "Relationships with Women."
10 It continued, "and contains fewer mentions of 'capitalism,' 'imperialism,' 'revolution' and 'male chauvinism.' 'Pee' was changed to 'urinate,' and 'communal funcking [sic],' became

'communal lovemaking.'" The journal conceded that the book was "honest, supportive and self-accepting. It encourages women to share their feelings and knowledge, to control their own bodies and lives, to become whole people." Chris Hobbs, "Our Bodies, Ourselves," off our backs 3, no. 8 (May 1973): 29.
11 See Jill Bystydzienski, review of The Making of "Our Bodies, Ourselves": How Feminism Travels across Borders, by Kathy Davis, in Journal of Sociology 114, no. 6 (May 2009): 1901.

THE PILL——"Dear Participants, We wish to ascertain your priorities," read the start of a survey distributed to half the attendees at the US Agency for International Development World Population Conference in 1976. The survey was handed out during a coffee break and asked participants to choose from six snack options, placing check marks next to those they desired. Only 13 percent of those in the half of the room given a choice indicated that they wanted a cookie. Those in the other half of the room were offered only cookies and 96 percent of them took one or more.

The cookies stood in for contraception, specifically the pill. Devised by Reimert Ravenholt, then director of the USAID Office of Population, the experiment was a proof of concept for his organization's strategy that posited women around the world as consumers, and the contraceptive pill as an "unmet need" fulfilling their unarticulated desire. In Ravenholt's estimation, women didn't need choice; they needed easy access. This was a simpler solution than other forms of contraception that involved larger commitments to health care infrastructure, and it followed the logic of other globally successful US brands like McDonald's and Coca-Cola, whose widespread availability and low cost precipitated a massive increase in sales. By 1979 USAID had produced 780 million cycles of its own Blue Lady brand of oral contraceptive pills for around fifteen cents a packet. It was one of the most widely circulated oral contraceptives of the era.[1]

Millions worldwide take the oral contraceptive pill, often a default choice when understanding of the range of alternatives is lacking. Few know how it affects their bodies' biochemistry, let alone the forces that shaped its design and debut in the pharmaceutical market in the mid-twentieth century and that continue to shape how it is administered today. Different brands contain varying synthetic forms of the hormones estrogen and progestin, blocking the release of gonadotropins in the pituitary gland that stimulate ovulation. This not only prevents ovulation but also thickens cervical mucus, both of which result in sperm being unable to connect with an egg.

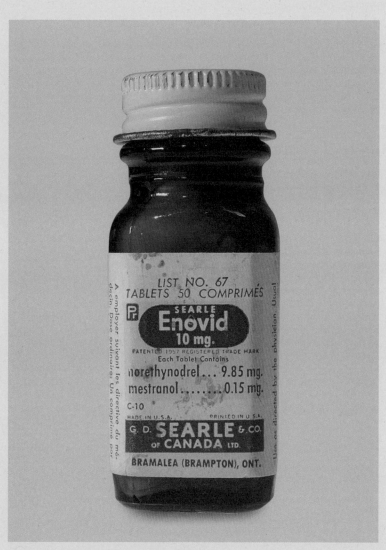

An early bottle for G. D. Searle's Enovid, approved by the US Food and Drug Administration for contraceptive use in 1960

——REPRODUCTION

Five protagonists are at the heart of the pill's inception. First came Margaret Sanger, the American public health nurse who popularized the term *birth control*, crusaded to make sex as consequence free for women as it is for men, and formed what would become Planned Parenthood, an organization that has since renounced her for her eugenicist beliefs.

Also central to the story is Gregory Goodwin Pincus, the scientist who—denied tenure at Harvard for undertaking what were then considered outlandishly provocative experiments, such as attempting to grow rabbits in Petri dishes—set up his own Foundation for Experimental Biology in Worcester, Massachusetts (with neuroendocrinologist Hudson Hoagland). His collaborators were Chang Min-Chueh, a reproductive biologist, and John Rock, an obstetrician-gynecologist and devout Catholic who was convinced that family planning and God's work were not incompatible. Katharine Dexter McCormick, a wealthy philanthropist, bankrolled their years of experiments and agitations in pursuit of the magic pill.

Building on earlier tests with animal- and plant-derived steroid hormones in the 1930s, the team of Pincus, Rock, and Chang screened hundreds of chemical compounds with progestogenic activity between 1951 and 1955. They settled on a combination—eventually given the proprietary name Enovid by its manufacturer, G. D. Searle & Company—that went into an initial human trial phase in 1956 in Puerto Rico. The location was chosen because of Puerto Rico's looser laws governing contraceptive use and, as writer Jonathan Eig points out bluntly, because Pincus thought there would be less pushback from participants in case of side effects, which were expected and could be severe.[2]

Female medical students of a colleague of Pincus's in Puerto Rico were also told that they were required to enroll in the clinical trial and submit to urine tests and pelvic exams as part of their coursework—or it would be held against them "when considering grades."[3] As a fail-safe, he found yet another group of women (and men) to test—patients being treated for various mental illnesses at the Worcester State Hospital. "You could do experiments there you would never think of doing these days," said one doctor who was then on staff. "You never asked the patients for permission. Nobody supervised."[4] Little wonder, given this and other horrifying patient abuse stories—including those involving thalidomide and the Dalkon Shield—that not everyone trusted the pill, either at its inception or today, a history often glossed over in favor of the narrative of medical miracle.

Enovid came to market in 1958 as a treatment for irregular menses and was approved by the FDA in 1960 as an oral contraceptive. Although unmarried women could not access it until some time later (in 1965, in the US), and it took time to reach other countries (Ireland put up a fight until 1979), it is often credited—too simplistically—as the catalyst for the subsequent free-loving sexual revolution of the 1960s and the record numbers of women entering the workforce in the 1970s.[5]

Rock and Pincus determined that three weeks of taking hormones and one week without, the latter often managed in the form of a benign placebo pill, would simulate the "natural" menstrual cycle. This was an extension of the careful consideration that Rock had given to framing the pill as simply an expansion of the body's own production of progestin rather than an artificial intervention (ultimately, the Vatican disagreed, rather vehemently).[6] Although it is not the most popular form of birth control, either globally or in the US (that honor goes to female sterilization in both cases), the United Nations estimates that around 151 million people took the pill in 2019.[7]

When it first came to market, the pill retailed in a jar, much like ibuprofen or vitamins. And just like the latter, it was easy to forget whether you'd taken your daily dose. Enter David P. Wagner, an Illinois engineer, and his wife, Doris, who started taking the pill in 1962 after the birth of their fourth child. Wagner invented the round DialPak dispenser arranged in four sets of seven days as a memory aid, leading to a slew of similar designs.[8]

"No woman can call herself free who does not own and control her own body," wrote Margaret Sanger in 1922.[9] A century later, the Ukrainian-born physiologist Polina Lishko won a 2020 MacArthur "genius" award for her work at the University of California, Berkeley, on non-hormonal contraceptives that could offer unisex application.[10] Finally, "cookies" for anyone and everyone who wants them—and hormone-free.

1   For an excellent overview of the "supply side" history and politics of the US government's entry into the contraceptive market in the mid to late twentieth century, see Michelle Murphy, *Seizing the Means of Reproduction: Entanglements of Feminism, Health, and Technoscience* (Durham, NC: Duke University Press, 2012), esp. 163–67. USAID also distributed menstrual extraction kits in countries like Bangladesh until Christian senators got wind of the program and put a stop to it (see Del-Em Device, p. 47).
2   At its inception, the pill contained many times higher hormonal loads than contemporary medications.

In the early years this induced nausea, bloating, weight gain, and depression, as well as blood clots and strokes, all of which were—surprise!—discounted by the manufacturer when reported by doctors and patients.
3   Jonathan Eig, *The Birth of the Pill: How Four Crusaders Reinvented Sex and Launched a Revolution* (New York: W. W. Norton, 2014), 201.
4   Dr. Enoch Calloway, quoted in Eig, *The Birth of the Pill*, 178.
5   See Claudia Goldin and Lawrence F. Katz, "The Power of the Pill: Oral Contraceptives and Women's Career and Marriage Decisions," *Journal of Political Economy* 110, no. 4 (August 2002): 730–70.
6   "In 1951, for example, Pope Pius XII had sanctioned the rhythm method for Catholics because he deemed it a 'natural' method of regulating procreation…. But how did the rhythm method work? It worked by limiting sex to the safe period that progestin created." Per Rock, if the pill operated in the same fashion, it was "'no more than 'an adjunct to nature.'" See Malcolm Gladwell, "John Rock's Error," *New Yorker*, March 6, 2000, newyorker.com. The papal encyclical titled *Humanae Vitae* (Of Human Life), issued in July 1968 by Pope Pius XII, made it a mortal sin to use oral contraceptives.
7   "The pill is used by over 20 per cent of women of reproductive age in 27 countries worldwide, with the highest prevalence in European countries." United Nations Department of Economic and Social Affairs, "Contraceptive Use by Method, 2019," Data Booklet 9, un.org.
8   Wagner took his invention to the director of advertising at G. D. Searle in 1962 and applied for a patent for his design; when they expressed no interest, he sent it to Ortho Pharmaceuticals, which stole the design to launch their pill in February 1963. Searle copied Wagner's design for Enovid-E, released in 1964. Wagner sued both companies and won a handsome settlement in each case.
9   Quoted in Susan C. M. Scrimshaw, "Women and the Pill: From Panacea to Catalyst," *Family Planning Perspectives* 13, no. 6 (November–December 1981): 254.
10   Lishko is developing what she terms "molecular condoms" for sperm that target its motility and render it incapable of penetrating an egg. See Proceedings of the National Academy of Sciences of the United States of America, "Podcast Interview: Polina Lishko," Science Sessions Podcast, transcript, 1, pnas.org/sites/default/files/mp3s/podcasttranscript1.pdf.

MENSTRUAL CUP——The improbable first-known design for a menstrual cup resembled something the Three Stooges might have invented. The "Catamenial Sack" (*catamenial* referring to menstruation) was the invention of the American S. L. Hockert in 1867. His device, a kind of deflated balloon attached to a wire that "passes down the vagina" and is kept in place with a belt, unsurprisingly never made it to market.[1] But slipshod as the design was, the idea had a certain genius.

What if a design could enable menstrual blood to be comfortably collected internally, rather than absorbed as it leaked out?

For most of human history menstrual devices have had two main goals: absorb the blood and stay in place. The Egyptians, it seems, made tampons from papyrus or other grasses, while the Romans may have used cotton, and menstruating people later made pads from sheep's wool or rags.[2] Indonesians and Hawaiians have traditions of using various local plants. Around the world, people have been purchasing or adapting readily available materials, whether store-bought or homemade, to help absorb their menstrual fluid once it has exited the body. This means that, for most, using a menstrual cup for the first time takes a leap of faith. The design asks us to reimagine, if not jettison entirely, our preconceived notions about how best to manage our periods, and how we touch and care for our vaginas. Though it may seem radical, from a commercial design perspective the cup is one of the oldest period products; that first-ever patent in 1867 predates the first commercial pads by a decade and the first commercial tampons by more than a half century.

The modern menstrual cup—a flexible, bell-shaped device that folds easily for inserting into the vagina—was designed in several iterations. The midwifery group McGlasson and Perkins designed a "bullet-shaped" rubber prototype in 1932.[3] The first commercially available cup was designed in 1935 by Leona Watson Chalmers, a former Broadway actress who cites her costumes of white silk as inspirations for the design.

A menstrual cup from the Danish company OrganiCup, founded in 2012

——REPRODUCTION

Chalmers's "catamenial appliance" was made from pliable vulcanized rubber that "fit snugly within the vulvo-uterine canal…without causing uncomfortableness or consciousness of its presence."[4] At the time, comfort and ease of movement were qualities promoted by the ready-to-wear fashion industry, and Chalmers positioned her invention as an extension of such sartorial freedoms—as a fashion accessory in and of itself. In her words, the device "permit[s] thin, light, close-fitting clothing to be worn during the menstrual periods" by removing the need for "telltale straps, belts, pins and buckles …which form ridges and bulges on the otherwise smooth rounded contours of the feminine figure."

These benefits aside, the cup required touching one's labia, vagina, and menstrual fluid, a widespread cultural inhibition that the nascent commercial tampon industry was also trying to circumvent with its applicators, or "inner and outer tubes," as Tampax's inventor Earle Haas called them in 1933.[5] As women became more physically active during World War II, especially outside of the domestic sphere, the popularity of tampons surged, while rubber shortages ended the production of menstrual cups. In 1959, Chalmers partnered with Robert Oreck to revive the idea, calling the product Tassette (*tasse* is "cup" in French, and the diminutive

-*ette* was added to indicate "little cup"). They advertised widely and gave cups to nurses in the hope that word would spread. In 1961, Oreck even promoted Tassette (pictured as a tulip) on a thirty-by-forty-foot billboard in the heart of Times Square. Despite these efforts, Tassette Inc. never made a profit and dissolved in 1963. But Oreck and Chalmers laid important groundwork for alternative period designs and challenged the many stigmas associated with periods and menstrual products.

The first profitable menstrual cup was the Keeper, an American brand that introduced a latex version in 1987. Though softer than previous designs, it lacked durability and wasn't hypoallergenic, and it never caught on. In 2002, the British company Mooncup made a breakthrough when they recreated the cup in medical-grade silicone. Mooncup and its American equivalent, DivaCup, dominated a small but devoted market in the first two decades of the twenty-first century.

Today's menstrual cup is made of flexible silicone, latex, or rubber; collects menstrual fluid rather than absorbs it; and can be worn for up to twelve hours. After taking it out, one simply tips the blood out, rinses the cup, and reinserts it (deeper cleans of the cup are done between periods). Because cups last for about ten years,

they are significantly more affordable and environmentally friendly than disposable alternatives. For low-income women who experience period poverty (a lack of access to period products, menstrual hygiene education, toilets, or handwashing facilities) the cup can be a game changer, and in many cases can mean the difference between participating in school, work, and society—or not.

Globally, an estimated 1.9 billion people—around 26 percent of the population—were of menstruating age in 2017, underscoring the need for effective, safe, affordable menstrual products.[6] As more menstruating people explore alternatives, the market is responding. In 2018, the behemoth Tampax added menstrual cups to its line of products, claiming that its years of industry research had enabled improvements to the design.

At this stage there is no real need to gild the lily. Everyone, from global public-health researchers to large-scale companies, has championed the efficacy, comfort, affordability, and sustainability of menstrual cups, making them more accessible than ever before. For all its slapdash beginnings, today's menstrual cup is a design feat, proving that some period products are simply better than others. That is, as long as we're willing to take the plunge.

1 S. L. Hockert, US Patent 70,843, issued November 12, 1867.
2 Petra Habiger, "Early History: Menstruation, Menstrual Hygiene, and Women's Health

in Ancient Egypt," A Note from Germany, 1998, mum.org/germnt5.htm.
3 L. J. Goddard, US Patent 1,891,761, filed October 6, 1932, issued December 20, 1932.

4 L. W. Chalmers, US Patent 2,089,113, filed July 11, 1935, issued August 3, 1937.
5 Dr. Earle Haas, US Patent 1926900, filed November 19, 1931, issued

September 12, 1933.
6 Anna Maria van Eijk et al., "Menstrual Cup Use, Leakage, Acceptability, Safety, and Availability: A Systematic Review and Meta-Analysis," *The Lancet*

4, no. 8 (August 1, 2019): e377–93, doi.org/10.1016/S2468-2667(19)30111-2.

What's the secret of the fresh-dressed woman?

Fresh panties all the time.

Carefree
Panty Shields®

When you're fresh and clean right down to your pretty underwear—you feel wonderful! One little way to have that feeling is with Carefree Panty Shields. Use them every day—it's like having fresh panties all the time.

Between-period discharge is normal but can be uncomfortable. Why put up with this kind of discomfort when it's so easy to feel dry and comfortable with Carefree Panty Shields. They're so light and soft you hardly feel them.

Light, small and comfortable enough for every day. No wonder so many women make Carefree Panty Shields part of getting dressed.

Certain contraceptives can cause problems. If you're wearing an I.U.D. you may have spotting—and the pill can increase vaginal moisture. Carefree Panty Shields keep your panties fresh and you secure.

Ovulation or hormonal changes can cause stains. Carefree Panty Shields are the comfortable answer.

At the end of your period or to back up your tampon. Use Carefree Panty Shields. Pretty panties are expensive so why not keep them new-looking longer with Carefree Panty Shields.

Deodorant Carefree Panty Shields are for extra freshness.

The secret of the fresh-dressed woman!

CAREFREE PANTY SHIELDS is a trademark of Personal Products Company, Milltown N.J 08850 © PPC 1984

BLOOD

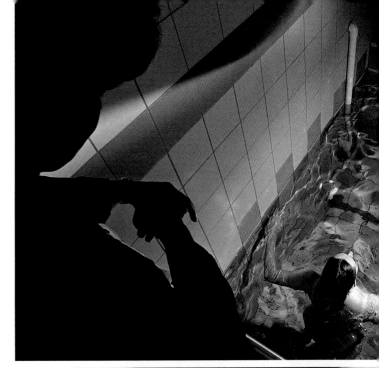

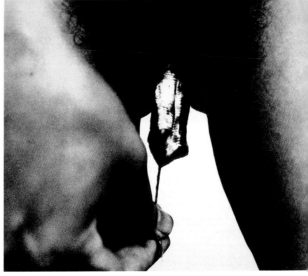

BLOOD "So what would happen if suddenly, magically, men could menstruate and women could not?" wrote Gloria Steinem in "If Men Could Menstruate" in the October 1978 issue of *Ms.* magazine. "Clearly, menstruation would become an enviable, worthy, masculine event…. Gifts, religious ceremonies, family dinners, and stag parties would mark the day." Contemporary activists have expanded such calls for menstrual equity to include an end to period poverty (the lack of access to menstrual hygiene products) and to note that not all menstruators are women, not all women menstruate, and some people miss periods (termed *amenorrhea*) due to a range of factors. Some progress has been made since the days when the advertising trope for menstrual emissions was an inoffensive blue liquid. Yet even in 2015, Thinx, a maker of period underwear, had a hard time getting the word *period* on their NYC subway advertisements.

1——Advertisement for Carefree Panty Shields, c. 1983
2——A woman in a mikvah, a ritual bath for post-menstrual married observant Jewish women, and a mikvah attendant, from *The Mikvah Project*, 2000. Photograph by Janice Rubin
3——The subway marketing campaign for Thinx period underwear, New York, c. 2015
4——Judy Chicago's *Red Flag*, 1971. Photolithograph
5——T-shirts for Ulta, a gender-neutral menstrual cup
6——An 18th-century engraving illustrating the Jewish mikvah
7——Protesters demand an end to menstrual products being taxed as "luxury items" in London, 2015
8——Lee Miller in a Kotex advertisement in *McCall's* magazine, July 1928. Photograph by Edward Steichen

2   3
4   5   6
7

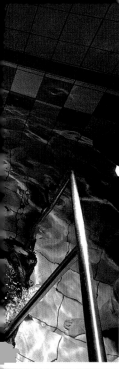

THINX

hellothinx.com

IDENTIFIES AS
BLEEDING

IDENTIFIES AS
BLEEDING

END TAMPON TAX

STOP TAXING PERIODS PERIOD.

"It has women's enthusiastic approval!"

The
IMPROVED
KOTEX

combining correct appearance and hygienic comfort

H OW many times you hear women say — indeed, how many times you, yourself, say: "What did we ever do without Kotex?"

This famous sanitary convenience is now presented with truly amazing perfections. And already women are expressing delighted approval.

"It is cut so that you can wear it under the sheerest, most clinging frocks," they tell one another. "The corners are rounded, the pad fits snugly — it doesn't reveal any awkward bulkiness. You can have complete peace of mind now."

The downy filler is even softer than before. The gauze is finer and smoother. Chafing and binding no longer cause annoyance and discomfort.

Positively Deodorizes While Worn

Kotex is now deodorized by a patented process (U. S. Patent No. 1,670,587), the only sanitary pad using a Government-patented treatment to assure absolutely safe deodorization. Ten layers of filler in each pad are treated by a perfect neutralizer to end all your fear of offending in this way again.

Women like the fact that they can adjust Kotex filler—add or remove layers as needed. And they like all the other special advantages, none of which has been altered: disposability is instant; protective area is just as large; absorption quick and thorough.

Buy a box today and you will realize why doctors and nurses endorse it so heartily—45c for a box of twelve. On sale at all drug, dry goods and department stores; supplied, also, in rest-rooms, by West Disinfecting Co. Kotex Company, 180 N. Michigan Avenue, Chicago, Illinois.

8 Superiorities of Improved Kotex

1 — *Softer*—by an exclusive process—no chafing.

2 — *Corners rounded* and tapered for perfect fit.

3 — *Deodorizes* actively when worn.

4 — *Adjustable*. Make it any thickness desired.

5 — *Light and cool* when worn.

6 — *Proper absorbency.*

7 — *Pliable*—soft and resilient.

8 — *Disposable* without embarrassment.

KOTEX

CHARTING THE MENSTRUAL CYCLE——Some bodily functions loom larger in the popular imagination than others. Take the menstrual cycle: more than just a monthly bleed, it is an intricate cascade of hormonal signals that are sent back and forth between the brain, ovaries, and uterus. When it comes to body literacy (the self-knowledge gained by learning to observe and chart the signs of fertility and infertility),Western culture has historically set a low bar, but people from every culture and epoch have created ways to help us visualize the inner workings of our bodies.[1]

Though we can't confirm it, a Paleolithic artifact found near the modern border of Uganda and the Democratic Republic of Congo—a carved baboon fibula to be precise—appears to chart a menstrual cycle, suggesting that women have been finding ways to represent themselves for at least thirteen thousand years. Visualizations of our bodies orient us, unite us, sell us ideas and things; they empower us to build literacy, resilience, and self-compassion around our bodies; and they reveal the deepest held beliefs and values of a given time and place.[2]

In the twentieth century, designers and thinkers refined their understanding of the body in the midst of massive cultural shifts. Explorations into the possibilities offered by science and artistic expression were especially useful to those looking to envision female anatomy. So, too, was the rise of the pharmaceutical industry, industrialized medicine, feminism, and new ideas surrounding labor and work. In the 1920s, artists and designers at the Bauhaus—the German art school famous for elevating and integrating art, craft, and design into daily life—believed in art as a vehicle for social transformation and understanding. In 1939, Herbert Bayer, a promising young Austrian-born designer, tried his hand at envisioning the menstrual cycle after receiving a commission by the pharmaceutical company Schering AG, which had just developed Progynon-B and Progynon-DH, a new form of estrogen, good for "correcting menstrual disturbances," as Bayer's brochure would declare. In his wider practice, Bayer loved incorporating colorful illustrations within his photomontage—splicing, dicing,

THE MENSTRUAL CYCLE

A brochure illustrating the menstrual cycle, designed by Herbert Bayer for the Schering Corporation in 1939 to promote hormone-based drugs to doctors

and reassembling photographs and adding gouache, to make new kinds of graphic compositions. Bayer's brochure, *The Menstrual Cycle*, is full of anatomical detail as well as cosmic reverence.[3] The black background evokes a night sky, and a uterus at the center of the image appears to radiate out into the universe. Bordered by phases of the moon, an ova circles the page, its satellite journey proceeding from ovary to fallopian tube to uterus and beyond.In this idealized view, the uterus is in perfect harmony with the cosmos. It has a twenty-eight day cycle and on the fourteenth day is ripe for fertilization.

The understanding of the menstrual cycle as a standard twenty-eight days ushered in a number of modern designs, and is foundational for everything from the pill to the rhythm method (tracking your menstrual history to predict when you'll ovulate). Using a standard-length menstrual cycle as the basis for her design, the Austrian gynecologist Dr. Maria Hengstberger developed the Baby Necklace in 1989. Hengstberger worked closely with an Ethiopian community, finally settling on a necklace of color-coded beads to help people visualize their cycles. This necklace was instrumental in the later development of CycleBeads (patented in 2002) and its "Standard Days Method," a similar design for family planning that helps people identify their potentially fertile windows.

Of course, our cycles can deviate, stretch out over much longer periods, or not come at all. Many of us want to know more about ourselves than which days we are fertile or when we will next bleed. In 1996, Toni Weschler published *Taking Charge of Your Fertility*, popularizing the Fertility Awareness Method (FAM) and ushering in a more nuanced and agile model of body literacy. Weschler sets out comprehensive explanations of the phases of the menstrual cycle and identifies the three primary signs of fertility: waking (basal body) temperature, cervical fluid, and cervical positioning. Beyond observing these signs, Weschler makes room for different cycle lengths and instructs readers in how to "chart" on ready-made templates, always framing the knowledge gained from the process as an elucidating privilege rather than an onerous task.

The charts themselves are simple and geometric. Throughout a monthly cycle, FAM followers are instructed to circle and link together thermal shifts to plot their preovulatory, fertile, and infertile phases. In older editions of the book readers simply take pen to paper, but in newer editions charting can be done digitally, making it easy to sync with a partner's calendar (for timed intercourse, of course).

In a similar vein, the mobile app Clue, designed in Berlin, employs simple, graphic language to calculate and predict a user's period, fertility window, and premenstrual syndrome based on user-generated information. This generation of cycle visualizations gives people the tools to better understand their menstrual cycles without the involvement of doctors or pharmaceuticals.

Beyond their practical value, though, these designs ask us to participate in visualizing our cycles, and to know ourselves deeply. And when you know your body, you will not only marvel at your own internal wisdom and capacities, but also make informed and empowered decisions.

1 The term *body literacy* was coined in 2005 by the Canadian women's health activists Laura Wershler, Geraldine Matus, and Megan Lalonde.
2 Perhaps one reason why so many of us lack self-knowledge when it comes to our menstrual cycles is the fact that, for centuries, our bodies have been explained to us by men. Medical scholars—from Galen in second-century Greece to William Harvey in seventeenth-century Britain—all assumed that women's internal organs were structurally analogous to their own external ones, and they made the prints and drawings to prove it. As Nemesius, bishop of Emesa, Syria, in the fourth century put it, "Women have the same genitals as men, except theirs are inside the body and not outside it." Nemesius of Emesa, *On the Nature of Man*, ed. William Tefler (Philadelphia: Westminster Press, 1955), 369.
3 For more about Bayer and his brochure *The Menstrual Cycle*, see Ellen Lupton's excellent essay "Herbert Bayer, Master of the Universe," Cooper Hewitt, Smithsonian Design Museum, November 25, 2019, cooperhewitt.org.

DALKON SHIELD INTRAUTERINE DEVICE——Loretta J. Ross
is a pioneer of the women's movement, having begun her career
in the 1970s at the DC Rape Crisis Center, and then moving on to
the National Organization for Women, the National Black Women's
Health Project, and the SisterSong Women of Color Reproductive
Justice Collective. She is one of the co-creators of the reproductive
justice framework and has tirelessly shared her own reproductive
experiences to prevent future generations from suffering forced
sterilization as she did.

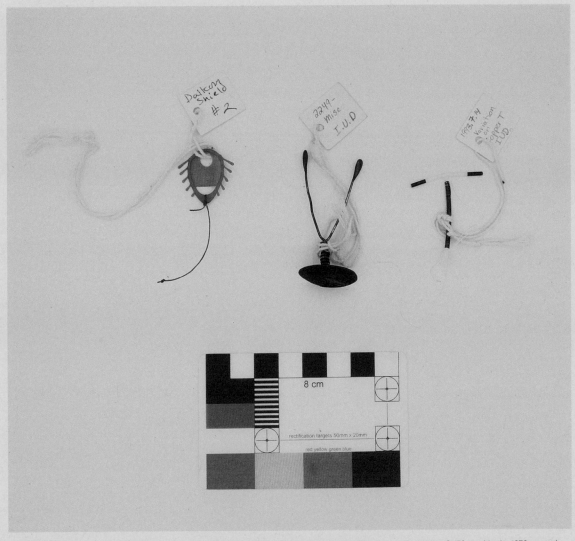

The tail of the Dalkon Shield, a contraceptive intrauterine device (IUD) used in the 1970s, acted
as a wick for bacteria, leading to infections that caused severe injury and even death for a large
percentage of its users

——REPRODUCTION

DESIGNING MOTHERHOOD——Small and variously shaped, and usually made of polyethylene or copper, intrauterine devices (or IUDs) come in hormonal and nonhormonal forms.[1] Once inserted in the uterus by a medical professional, they disrupt the process of insemination and implantation of an egg, offering a reliable and usually safe method of contraception. Their design is highly regulated because of one device in particular, the Dalkon Shield.

It was administered to around 2.5 million women in the United States and Puerto Rico in the early 1970s—including you, Professor Ross, and precipitated your life's work in the field of reproductive justice. It caused widespread pelvic inflammatory disease and infertility. How did the Dalkon Shield alter the course of your life?

LORETTA ROSS——I had a Dalkon Shield implanted at Howard University Health Services [in Washington, DC] in 1973. I had unsuccessful-ly tried to use other contraceptives, and this was offered to me as a problem-free method. My body adapted to it very well until three years later, in 1976, when I developed acute pelvic inflammatory disease. The design flaw was the wick, the string the doctor was supposed to use to remove it. It had no other medical purpose than to serve the doctor's convenience, and it introduced bacteria into the womb through the cervix. That caused an infection that then caused me to lapse into a coma, and I underwent a total hysterecto-my at the age of twenty-three.

It ended my fertility prematurely. By age twenty-five I was experiencing menopausal symptoms because my ovaries had been removed in the hysterectomy. The doctor tried to persuade me to take hormone replacement therapy until my natural menopause would have occurred. I remember telling him that I wouldn't even take aspirin for forty years without fear of consequences, much less Premarin.

DM——And can I clarify—because you were in a coma when you reached the hospital you...

LR——I couldn't give permission. I wasn't able to give permission for the hysterectomy; there was no informed consent. My boyfriend at the time was in medical school, and when I passed out he called an ambulance. I did not wake up until the doctor who had performed my hysterectomy—who was the head of OB-GYN services at the George Washington University Hospital—was standing by my bedside. I remember that he and four or five other doctors standing there were congratulating themselves on the surgery they had done on me. He said, "Well, it's a good thing you already had a baby, because I think I did a good job saving your life."

He was the same doctor who for six months had been misdiagnosing my symptoms. I kept coming back to him with this growing infection that he kept misdiagnosing as a venereal disease, or what we call an STD today. He didn't remove the Dalkon Shield until my fallopian tubes erupted. It was a teaching hospital, so I'm persuaded that part of the motivation for doing the hysterectomy was to do it as a demon-stration for the medical students that he was training.

DM——Were any of the doctors women?
LR——No.

DM——What was your experience after that?
LR——I ended up enduring forty years of menopausal symptoms: hot flashes, weight gain. All the symptoms that women in their sixties get, I got in my twenties. It also made me a reproductive justice activist, because I had already had a full-term pregnancy due to incest, an abortion, a miscarriage, and now sterilization. So in a short, seven-year period I felt like I had been through the reproductive mill. I hadn't planned on being a reproductive justice activist. The doctor's sense of self-satisfaction is what caused me to launch the lawsuit against him and [Dalkon manufacturer] A. H. Robins. I just thought that this was an injustice that was unsupportable. So those are the ways it changed my life.

DM——It was, I believe, the largest civil legal case since those filed against manufacturers of asbestos. Hundreds of thousands of women reported issues after using the Dalkon Shield.[2] Do you think this is something that could happen today in the US medical system?

LR— I think the public is still at risk of companies putting profits over safety when it comes to drugs and devices. The Dalkon Shield was evidence of that. The A. H. Robins Company had evidence that this was a problematic design, but they suppressed it, which is why we prevailed in our lawsuit. This flawed design helped precipitate the 1976 Medical Device Regulation Act. We still need a cure for people pursuing profits over patient well-being.

DM— How would you define reproductive justice, a term that you helped coin?

LR— The best way to describe reproductive justice is to see it as a fusion between the terms *reproductive rights* and *social justice*. We created it in 1994—"we" being twelve African American women—because we didn't like the fact that abortion rights were isolated from the other social justice issues that affected women's decision-making when it came to an unplanned pregnancy.[3] Any time a woman is facing an unplanned pregnancy, she has to worry about whether she has adequate health care, whether she has freedom from violence, whether she can stay in school or keep her job or have a bedroom to put this child in. All of these are social justice and human rights issues that both the pro-choice and the pro-life movements undervalue and understate. They are things that we have to fight for as Black women. We're subjected to strategies of population control, and our children are blamed for every ill in society, whether it's crime or terrorism or environmental degradation. We also join with the pro-choice movement in fighting for the right not to have children, which is about the right to use birth control, including abortion. We fight for the right to raise our children in safe and healthy environments, which includes things like quality schools, gun control, safe neighborhoods, and no environmental contaminants in drinking water. Reproductive justice is concerned with a whole host of issues, both biological and nonbiological, that affect people's reproductive decision-making.

DM— Health care has been a focus for feminist groups and others since at least the 1960s, as women recognized that body autonomy was a way of reclaiming rights often denied to them in the United States and elsewhere. While there's a shared desire to raise consciousness, White voices often drown out those of people of color, especially Black women.

LR— Well, no one who is acculturated in US society is going to be free of the internalization of white supremacy, not even people of color. I find that some of what White women do toward women of color is a product of racism and white supremacy. But to be honest, some of what they do toward women of color is just the normal brutality with which they treat each other, because they're acculturated in a very competitive, atomistic, individualized world where they're taught to be competitive and brutal toward each other.

Black women and White women have been subjected to different reproductive management strategies. For example, as a Black woman, I was subjected to sterilization abuse because white supremacist thinking assumes Black and other women of color have too many babies. While we were fighting to maintain our fertility, a different story was happening among White women fighting to limit their fertility. If a White woman wanted to have a voluntary sterilization, she had to go through committees of doctors to be certified that she was sane for not wanting to have more White babies. Rather than just simply believing in an angel/devil theory of Black women versus White women, our focus should be about women's autonomy and self-determination and decision-making power, and the power of believing women—that we know what's best for ourselves. It's really Black women and White women and all women together against a patriarchal system that is racially delineated.

—REPRODUCTION

DM — How do you see the landscape of women's health today? What has changed and what has not changed since the late sixties or early seventies, and what is the most pressing issue that needs our attention?

LR — The things that I would like to see strengthened are organizations like the National Women's Health Network, because we need consumer watchdog agencies. We need someone who is sufficiently funded and empowered to pay attention to adequate testing of drugs and devices and manipulation through pharmaceutical and other types of advertising. For example, even something as basic as the fact that we're being told our vaginas are not supposed to smell a certain way, so companies create a product and sell us vagina deodorant. We are bombarded with so much of this; it's a natural output of capitalism. And so if there's anything that I would urgently want shored up, it is the ability of women to have protective watchdog agencies. Without those, we're very vulnerable.

I also think that there is a growing problem with assisted reproductive technologies, where science has outpaced our morality. The tenet of reproductive justice around the right to have children can collide with people's determination to have children by exploiting more vulnerable people. We really need to have intentional, protracted conversations about what the human right to reproduce actually looks like.

1 Patricia A. Lohr, Richard Lyus, and Sarah Prager. "Clinical Guidelines: Use of Intrauterine Devices in Nulliparous Women," *Contraception: An International Reproductive Health Journal* 95, no. 6 (June 1, 2017): 529–37, doi.org/10.1016/j. contraception.2016.08.011.
2 Gina Kolata, "The Sad Legacy of the Dalkon Shield," *New York Times*, December 6, 1987, sec. 6, 120, nytimes.com.
3 The twelve women who became the founding mothers of the concept of reproductive justice, and their affiliations at the time, are Toni M. Bond (Chicago Abortion Fund), Reverend Alma Crawford (Religious Coalition for Reproductive Choice), Evelyn S. Field (National Council of Negro Women), Terri James (American Civil Liberties Union of Illinois), Bisola Marignay (National Black Women's Health Project, Chicago Chapter), Cassandra McConnell (Planned Parenthood of Greater Cleveland), Cynthia Newbille (National Black Women's Health Project, now Black Women's Health Imperative), Loretta J. Ross (Center for Democratic Renewal), Elizabeth Terry (National Abortion Rights Action League of Pennsylvania), Mabel Thomas (Pro-Choice Resource Center, Inc.), Winnette P. Willis (Chicago Abortion Fund), Kim Youngblood (National Black Women's Health Project); see Loretta J. Ross, "Reproductive Justice as Intersectional Feminist Activism," *Souls* 19, no. 3 (2017): 286–314, tandfonline.com/doi/full/10.1080/10999949.2017.1389634.

DEL-EM DEVICE——At first glance, the Del-Em device might easily be mistaken for a domestic gadget of the sort used for baking or making jam. Indeed, at its inception in 1971 its design was deliberately homespun, made from components readily available in a hardware store, a grocery store, or—without too much digging—a medical supply retailer.

It consists of a glass jar with two thin plastic tubes sprouting from its lid. One tube connects the jar to a valved syringe, while the other joins the jar, via an adapter, to a flexible, smaller bore cannula, the end of which is fed through the cervix and into the uterus. Once inserted (along with a speculum), the syringe plunger is extended to create a vacuum, and this extracts menstrual matter through the cannula into the jar. The apparatus was specifically developed in this form as an abortive device to be used in the early weeks of pregnancy.

The design emerged from a consciousness-raising meeting of the Los Angeles–based Self-Help Clinic that was held at the Everywoman's Bookstore in Venice Beach on April 7, 1971. Carol Downer, author of *A New View of a Woman's Body* (1981), and later acclaimed as a "founding mother" of the self-help movement, climbed up on a table during the gathering and showed the group how to self-insert a speculum to examine usually unseen internal anatomy. Another member passed around a simple kit—a syringe, cannula, and jar—for manual vacuum evacuation of the uterus. She had seen it used at an underground abortion clinic in Santa Monica run by Harvey Karman. (Although Karman trained as a psychologist, he had been performing abortions since the 1950s, had once served jail time for doing so, and pioneered other controversial abortion methods in the 1970s.) Less invasive than dilation and curettage, the method could be less painful during illegal abortions, which often took place unanesthetized to enable a quick departure afterward (or during a police raid).

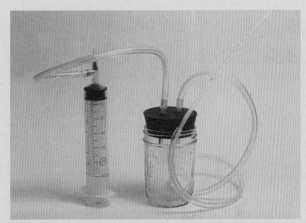

The Del-Em device, also known as a menstrual extraction kit, was pioneered by Lorraine Rothman and Carol Downer. Downer, an abortion rights activist and pioneer of menstrual extraction, is pictured here holding a Del-Em kit and her cat, Red

——REPRODUCTION

Lorraine Rothman, a public school teacher and mother of four, took Karman's device home from the Everywoman's event and substantially improved it using components bought at various retailers, including an aquarium shop. Crucially, she attached a valve that prevented air from being accidentally pushed back into the uterus, where it could then enter the bloodstream and cause a fatal embolism. Another central component was a mirror propped or held in a location that allowed the person undergoing the procedure to watch if they wished, and to be in control of and guide its speed and movement. As Downer recounted, "Usually the woman can tell us when the cannula has touched the back wall of the uterus if they can feel it…. She may either feel pain or suggest the angle needed to be changed. [Women] actively participated in this…. They could say, 'Hey, let's stop for a while.'" A group of early self-helpers named the device the Del Em, claiming "it grew out of a humerous situation … it just struck our funny bone (its meaning remains a well-kept group secret)."[1]

The LA Self-Help Clinic was part of a heterogenous wave of localized activist groups across the United States and beyond that recognized women's health as a battleground for their broader political rights. These groups shared common goals: to engender greater familiarity with one's own anatomy rather than cede body autonomy to physicians, and to challenge the "fear and shame of our bodies that society has taught us….

We learn to see our bodies in a new way … expand[ing] a range of what is 'normal.'"[2] While the Del Em has sometimes been incorrectly referred to as a do-it-yourself design, Downer and Rothman were unequivocal that a committed collective of people specializing in and serious about its careful deployment was essential.[3]

Self-help group members across the country practiced with the device on each other, sometimes for months, before taking on real-world cases. They often used it without their clients taking a pregnancy test—for plausible deniability if caught. At the National Organization for Women (NOW) conference in Santa Monica in August 1971, Del Em demonstrations were sequestered in a hotel room, deemed too shocking to occupy the main exhibit space. Rothman and Downer subsequently traveled across the United States to share the Del Em, visiting twenty-three cities in six weeks and meeting with various collectives, including the women-run underground abortion service Jane in Chicago.[4]

Rothman patented the Del Em design for commercial distribution in 1974, though collectives were empowered to purchase components and assemble their own. Ready-made "menstrual regulation" kits were also commercially produced by other organizations, including the World Population Council and the pro-abortion International Project Assistance Services (IPAS). Such kits are still used, for example in Bangladesh, where abortion remains illegal but

where, since 1979, vacuum evacuation soon after a missed period is politically palatable and thus permitted.[5]

Rothman's design—and Kalman's suction device before it—built on existing technologies of vacuum aspiration that had been in use in various settings for decades. Dorothea Kerslake, a British consultant obstetrician and gynecologist at the Freeman Hospital in Newcastle-upon-Tyne, produced a didactic film, *Pregnancy Termination by Vacuum Aspiration*, in 1966 and published her work (with Donn Casey, an agricultural scientist and population control advocate) in *Obstetrics and Gynecology* in July 1967.[6] A decade prior to that, two Shanghai obstetricians, Yuantai Wu and Xianzhen Wu, described similar methods in the *Chinese Journal of Obstetrics and Gynecology*, though their paper was not translated into English until 2008. The human reproductive scientist Malcolm Potts dates the first manual vacuum aspiration to the Scottish gynecologist James Young Simpson (1811–1870), who attended, among others, Queen Victoria.

Designed in direct response to federal and state restrictions on abortion, the Del Em is part of a long history of collective struggle over control of the uterus. Potts pointed to this knotty history when he wryly remarked in 2008, "Only in a field as controversial as abortion would the same idea need to be discovered three times, each independently."[7]

1   Carol Downer, interview with the author, March 25, 2020.
2   Debra Brody, Sara Grusky, and Patricia Logan, "Self-Help Health," *off our backs* 12, no. 7 (July 1982): 14.
3   See the detailed, definitive, chapters-long description in Downer's and Rebecca Chalker's *A Woman's Book of Choices: Abortion, Menstrual Extraction, and RU-486* (New York: Four Walls Eight Windows, 1992).
4   See Laura Kaplan, *Jane: The Legendary Underground Abortion Service* (Chicago: University of Chicago Press, 1995).
5   Vengadasalam D. Fortney, "Disposable Menstrual Regulation Kits in a Non-Throw-Away Economy," *Contraception* 21, no. 3 (March 1980): 235–44; Population Council, "Menstrual Regulation: The Method and the Issues," *Studies in Family Planning* 8, no. 10 (October 1977): 253–56.
6   Kerslake and Casey, "Abortion Induced by Means of the Uterine Aspirator," *Obstetrics and Gynecology* 30, no. 1 (July 1967): 35–45.
7   Rebecca Coombes, "Obstetricians Seek Recognition for Chinese Pioneers of Safe Abortion," *British Medical Journal* 336, no. 7657 (June 14, 2008): 1332–33.

STOP VIOLENCE AGAINST WOMEN

Pornography is not healthy for women, children other living things

PLAYBY

STOP SEXIST VIOLENCE AGAINST WOMEN

A MUJER

take back the night

JOAN E. BIREN

JOAN E. BIREN Joan E. Biren, or JEB, is an internationally known photographer and documentary filmmaker who has chronicled social justice movements and the lives of lesbians for more than four decades, making visible the often hidden histories of women and other marginalized people. Biren came out in the 1960s and realized the need for self-expression and affirming images of lesbian culture, beyond traditional and patriarchal visual languages. In the 1970s, Biren toured the United States, photographing lesbians at women's events like the Michigan Womyn's Music Festival, anti–Ku Klux Klan demonstrations, and gay and lesbian pride marches. Her ground-breaking images are intimate portraits of daily life and documents of the emerging women's health movement.

1— Dessie Woods (later Rashida Muhammad Mustafa) at a Take Back the Night March, Washington, DC, 1981

2— A lesbian mothers' group at the pro-choice March for Women's Lives, Washington, DC, 1986

3— The pro-choice march and rally Mobilize for Women's Lives/Women's Equality, Washington, DC, 1989

4— A mother and daughter marching in the Gay Freedom Day parade, San Francisco, 1980

5— Dr. Susan Love and her daughter, 1990

6— Darquita with her mother, Denyeta, 1979

7— Jan Dixon (later Jamilah Ali) and Barbara Lewis doing a cervical examination, 1979

2 3
4 5
    6

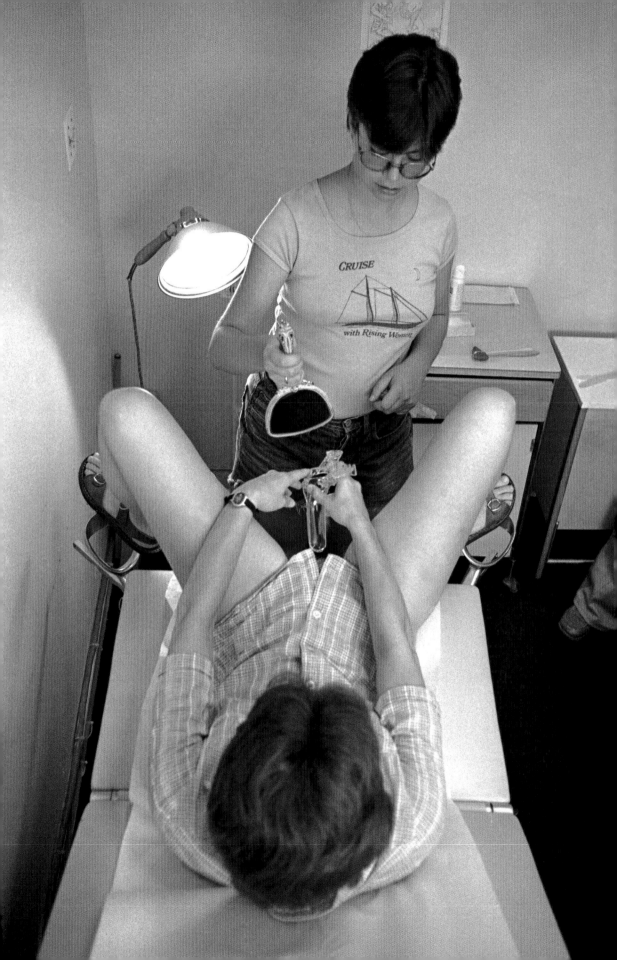

CLOMID——Millions of children born over the past six decades owe their lives to a man they've never met and likely never heard of: Frank Palopoli, an American chemist born to Italian immigrants. Palopoli led the research team that in 1956 synthesized clomiphene citrate, a cheap, effective oral medication known by its many brand names, but perhaps most widely as Clomid. It's often called a wonder drug by the many who ingest it.

Introduced as a fertility medication in 1967, Palopoli's design ushered in the modern era of assisted reproduction. Clomid is often a physician's first intervention in treating infertility.[1] Its strong follicular stimulation has also been held responsible for a spike in multiple births in the ensuing decades.

The fact that Clomid is a synthetic, human-made compound underscores that drugs, too, are designed. It is composed of a triphenylethylene core (a simple hydrocarbon that possesses estrogenic activity) substituted with a chloride anion, an aminoalkoxy side chain, and dihydrogen citrate. As a series of endocrinologists, embryologists, and biochemists—some working for the Population Council—found in preclinical trials in the 1960s, this elemental compound works on the pituitary gland's production of gonadotropins, the sex hormones that control ovulation.[2] In people who do not release an egg during their menstrual cycle (termed *anovulatory*), Clomid triggers higher levels of these hormones, which in turn stimulates the ovarian follicles, causing ripe eggs to be released into the fallopian tubes.[3]

All told, the arc from initial discovery of clomiphene citrate through patent, US Food and Drug Administration (FDA) trials, and delivery to market took eleven years. The first results of clinical trials were released in 1961 by a team from the Medical College of Georgia led by Dr. Robert B. Greenblatt, who declared in the pages of the *Journal of the American Medical Association* that the drug (code named MRL/41) had restored ovulation in twenty-eight of thirty-six participants, four of whom subsequently became pregnant while

The structural formula for clomifene, commonly known as Clomid and used to treat infertility

participating in the project. Palopoli's lab was part of the Cincinnati-based pharmaceutical giant William S. Merrell Company, and it was through Merrell that the drug first became available for prescription in 1967 as a radical new tool in the fertility arsenal.

However, some of the first patients prescribed Clomid were rightly cautious, if not downright suspicious, in the wake of the veritable tsunami of pharmaceutical innovations aimed at regulating their reproductive systems that also emerged in the 1960s. In a 1979 issue of the radical feminist journal *off our backs*, Clomid was regarded warily and assessed alongside the pill (see p. 33), estrogen-replacement therapy, and the report of a hysterectomy undergone without patient consent as ways in which menstruating people's bodies were acted upon using drugs and techniques that were not adequately vetted.[4]

Though Clomid offered a lifeline to those desperate to carry their own biological child, Merrell was also the company that, not even a decade earlier, had released the sedative thalidomide (see p. 235) to US patients, including to treat morning sickness in pregnant people, without waiting for full FDA approval. Although the drug was subsequently recalled, its side effects left thousands of babies with severe birth defects. Moreover, the triphenylethylenes within Clomid are derived from diethylstilbestrol

(DES), a synthetic estrogen given to pregnant people in the United States between 1938 and 1971 to prevent miscarriage and early labor. DES was banned in the US (though international use continued for some years afterward) when it was found to produce birth defects in female children, such as T-shaped uteruses that impaired or completely foreclosed their ability to bear children, and also to cause a rare form of cancer.

Some have decried the focus on individual issues of fertility that drugs like Clomid address in the face of larger environmental factors that have changed contemporary patterns of conception, especially in industrialized countries. Writing a decade ago, the ecofeminist scholar Greta Gaard noted that in countries where Big Pharma rules, drugs like Clomid have been used to "medicalize and thus depoliticize the contemporary phenomenon of decreased fertility…personalizing and privatizing both the problem and the solution when the root of this phenomenon may be more usefully addressed as a problem of…toxic by-products of industrialized culture that are degrading our personal and environmental health."[5] Gaard frames these medical interventions within the rhetoric of choice developed by second-wave feminism in the 1970s, including the right to choose abortion as health care and contraception as family planning. She (and others) argue that such hard-won agency over one's body is now

being commodified and sold back to people with uteruses as a medical panacea—the choice to access fertility interventions, including drugs like Clomid whose profits go back to the medical industry, rather than treat the root causes of infertility, such as inflexible work environments and endocrine-disrupting ecosystems.

Despite these legitimate structural and social causes for critique, Clomid is regarded as a highly beneficial drug design and is considered so indispensable that the World Health Organization lists it among the most essential medicines. It has changed so very many lives—for those who have used it, they would argue, for the better—enabling longed-for births and biological families to be formed the world over. Palopoli himself, by his family's account, was a modest and hardworking professional delighted that his design did so much good for so many.

When the *New York Times* announced Palopoli's death at age ninety-four in 2016, one of his sons shared the family anecdote that, during a meal at a restaurant to mark their endowment of a university professorship in honor of their father, their server asked them what they were celebrating. "When she was told about Mr. Palopoli's accomplishments, according to the family account, she rushed to her office and returned with photographs of her two daughters. 'These are my Clomid babies,' she said."[6]

1   In 1968 the *British Medical Journal* reported that the basic cost to the National Health Service of thirty 50-mg clomiphene citrate tablets under the brand name Clomid was 30 shillings—about $35 today. "Today's Drugs: Clomiphene Citrate," *British Medical Journal* 1, no. 5588 (February 10, 1968): 363–64.
2   "Leading contributors to this initial functional characterization included R. K. Meyer, Ph.D. (University of Wisconsin), as well as Warren O. Nelson, Ph.D., and Sheldon J. Segal, Ph.D. (Population Council), to name a few"; Eli Y. Adashi, "Clomiphene Citrate at 50: The Dawning of Assisted Reproduction," *Fertility and Sterility* 108, no. 4 (October 2017): 592, doi.org/10.1016/j.fertnstert.2017.08.002.
3   Barbara J. Culliton, "Fertility Drug for Single Births," *Science News* 90, no. 26 (December 24, 1966): 539.
4   "Drugs: Clomid; Estrogen Replacement; the Pill," *off our backs* 9, no. 8 (August–September 1979): 7.
5   Greta Gaard, "Reproductive Technology, or Reproductive Justice?: An Ecofeminist, Environmental Justice Perspective on the Rhetoric of Choice," *Ethics and the Environment* 15, no. 2 (Fall 2010): 103. See also Margaret Marsh and Wanda Ronner, *The Empty Cradle: Infertility from Colonial Times to the Present* (Baltimore: Johns Hopkins University Press, 1996).
6   Sam Roberts, "Frank Palopoli, Inventor of Fertility Drug Used by Millions, Dies at 94," *New York Times*, August 12, 2016, sec. A, 17.

SPECULUM——It began with fingers and a spoon. Childbearing and associated maladies that afflict women have required a midwife, shaman, or doctor to open the vagina. Closed fingers made a cone-shaped probe. Inserted in the body, fingers opened to dilate the birth canal. Healers inspected for anomalies by feel and sight. This operation of the hand suggested a tool, leading to perhaps the earliest diagnostic instrument in medicine: the vaginal speculum.[1]

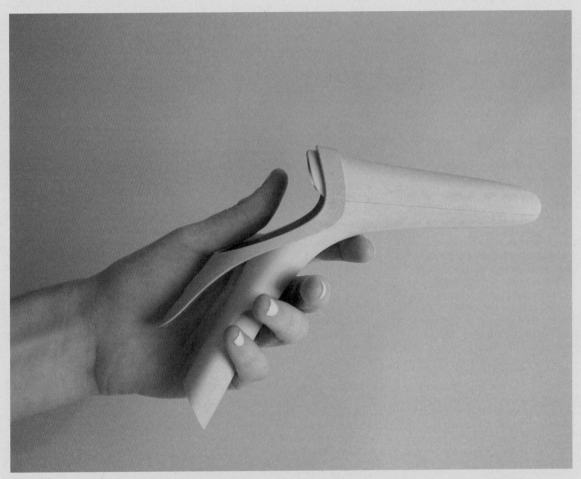

The designers of the Yona speculum hope their prototype design will be a step toward realizing their vision of a patient-centered pelvic exam

The etymology of *speculum* denotes a mirror: one needs light to see what is going on. Engineering geniuses, the Romans created a speculum with four prongs that opened by a screw mechanism, thus illuminating the vagina. The ruins of Pompeii yielded one of these, as well as obstetrical spoons. Inserting a spoon into the vagina similarly dilated the passage to facilitate a view within. During the nineteenth century, J. Marion Sims, a doctor from South Carolina, elaborated the spoon into a snake-shaped device and pronounced it a speculum. Little changed from Roman times until now, the ur-speculum has simply exchanged four blades for three and taken on the appearance of a duck bill.

That the speculum has continued in use essentially unchanged from Roman times says much about how Western societies have perceived bodies with uteruses. In the European medical tradition, anatomical atlases presented male bodies as the reference; women's bodies were aberrant. Further, tampering with female genitalia was believed to modify—or control—behavior. The history of the speculum mirrors these notions. Although centuries ago some midwives may have employed specula, when male doctors began to usurp midwives as birth managers they appropriated obstetrical tools as privileged to their profession (see Forceps, p. 161). Hysterical behavior—nineteenth-century medical code for troubles believed to originate in the female reproductive organs—was thought to be triggered by use of the speculum. Women who seemed over-nervous or suffered a loss of sex drive were suspected of having a speculum-induced injury such as *furor uterinus*, or mania of the uterus. The speculum might lead a woman to misbehave and therefore became linked to sexual deviancy. Deviant or not, the speculum threatened women's modesty.

The speculum underwent adaptation and elaboration during the late nineteenth century as gynecology became a medical specialty—almost exclusively of male doctors. Through such instruments gynecology became a vehicle for the political control of people with uteruses. As the medical historian Charles Rosenberg observed, illness—and particularly women's illnesses of the reproductive parts—have never been "a value-free enterprise."[2]

Nevertheless, Sharp & Smith, a prominent manufacturer of gynecological tools in the late nineteenth century, included in its catalogue a description of what constitutes a successful speculum design. According to Dr. John Blake White, writing in the catalogue, the ideal instrument featured "facility of introduction … readiness of adaptability and perfect command of the parts to be examined and treated."[3] There is no mention of pain control, nor any mention of women's opinions on the instruments advertised. Enter the supposed father of American gynecology, J. Marion Sims. Sims doubtless improved the health of women by inventing a method of repairing the vesicovaginal fistula, the tearing of the birth canal during childbirth, which results in the bladder emptying into the vaginal canal and discharging urine through the vagina. But he achieved success with his method only after four years of experimental surgery on enslaved Black women in the 1840s—without anesthesia, even when available.[4] The enslaved patients whose names are known—Betsey, Anarcha, and Lucy—endured many surgeries to fix their distressing condition. By virtue of their enslavement, they were incapable of consenting to these excruciating surgeries. Sims shared racist medical ideas about women's physiology that were lamentably common at the time and persist today, such as that Black women's pain threshold was higher than that of White women and that they were more lascivious, with larger vaginal labia. Sims went on to become a medical entrepreneur and affixed his name to a range of tools still in use, including specula. In 2020 the New York-based obstetrician and gynecologist Dr. Kameelah Phillips shared a story on Instagram that she had renamed the Sims speculum "Lucy" in recognition of one of the enslaved women subjected to his surgeries. When the story was picked up by news outlets, Dr. Phillips noted, "I wasn't going to give honor to a man who operated and developed instruments on the backs of women who looked like me."

Today, more than sixty million pelvic examinations with specula take place in the United States annually. At the San Francisco design firm Frog, four women—Rachel Hobart, Sahana Kumar, Hailey Stewart, and Fran Wang—investigated a range of specula and interviewed medical personnel and many people who expressed a wish for a new speculum design.[5] The designers questioned why the speculum has not changed to better serve those who, in the twenty-first century, have also used the instrument for self-examination. To develop the new instrument, which they have called Yona (from the Hindu *yoni*, or the life force symbolized by the vulva), the design team evaluated materials, efficiency, ergonomics, and even auditory phenomena. Yona features surgical-grade silicone that eliminates the feel of cold steel, diminishes the metallic sounds of early specula, and modifies the angle of the handle to improve comfort. Ultimately, Yona may lead to shorter pelvic exams with less stress and discomfort. For two millennia, people have had no voice in the design of tools that entered their bodies to manage their reproduction. Now a new speculum has appeared that, as Frog puts it, is designed "for people with vaginas" by people with vaginas.

—**Robert D. Hicks**

1 Elisabeth Bennion, *Antique Medical Instruments* (Los Angeles: University of California Press, 1979), 127–24.
2 Charles E. Rosenberg, "Framing Disease," introduction to *Framing Disease: Studies in Cultural History*, ed. Charles E. Rosenberg and Janet Golden (New Brunswick, NJ: Rutgers University Press, 1992), xiv.
3 John Blake White, "Gynaecological—Specula," in *Catalogue of Sharp & Smith, … Surgical Instruments, Deformity Apparatus, Artificial Limbs, Artificial Eyes, Elastic Stockings, Trusses, Crutches, Supporters, Galvanic and Faradic Batteries, Etc.; Surgeons' Appliances of Every Description* (Chicago, 1889), 630.
4 Deirdre Cooper Owens, *Medical Bondage: Race, Gender, and the Origins of American Gynecology* (Athens: University of Georgia Press, 2017).
5 Daniela Blei, "Women Are Reinventing the Long-Despised Speculum," *The Atlantic*, March 8, 2018, theatlantic.com.

CHILDFREE——"Obituary: Motherhood" was the deliberately direct—and consequently incendiary—headline of Ellen Peck's 1972 op-ed in the *New York Times*. "Died, as a symbol, a life role, a sacred institution, sometime in the early nineteen-seventies," the writer, activist, and high school teacher announced.[1] In her op-ed, she pointed a finger at rising awareness of environmental catastrophe and patriarchal social attitudes as reasons to remain—in a term coined in that moment—"childfree."

My mum in the 1960s, and then later, pregnant with my brother, holding my hand and carrying my sister in 1984

——REPRODUCTION

A year earlier, along with the sexologist William Granzig, Peck had written *The Baby Trap*, one of the first books about the emerging childfree movement. She went on to found the National Organization for Non-Parents, or N.O.N.—always spoken, in my mind, in an arch, insouciant tone as the French *non!*—an advocacy organization for people who choose not to have children. (Later known as the National Alliance for Optional Parenthood, it dissolved in the early 1980s.) Her partner in this venture was Shirley Radl, a writer and mother whose own provocative tome, *Mother's Day Is Over* (1973), featured on its front cover a diaper pin bent beyond repair. Just in case anyone missed the analogous connection to the mental state of mothers everywhere, the cover blurb was blunt: "Until now, millions of women have secretly shared, and silently endured, a profound guilt: they love their children, but they do not love being mothers. This book will end their solitude and reduce their guilt and make them more dignified human beings."[2]

The reprint edition spelled it out even more bleakly, referencing a poll in which 70 percent of mothers said that if they could start over, they wouldn't have children. Given that the triple whammy of the pill, the home pregnancy test, and Roe v. Wade had all emerged within the last decade, the opportunity to contemplate a childfree life was on the table in ways impossible for previous generations. As the historian Sarah Knott put it, "somewhere between the fecund past and parsimonious present, mothering as a dilemma replaced mothering as destiny."[3]

The movement term *childfree*—as opposed to *childless*, which implies a thwarted desire to procreate—was (and still is) often followed by the qualifier "by choice" or "by circumstance," the former denoting deliberate agency and the latter reflecting context, such as widespread periods of financial precarity that make having a child a risky proposition. In reality, these factors are so inextricable as to render the two qualifiers synonymous. Choice, and its absence, is never divorced from the environment in which we live. While the neologism of being *childfree* emerged from second-wave feminist consciousness-raising and access to increasingly reliable forms of contraception, it was women of color forming the vocabulary of the reproductive justice movement who gave it nuance. They recognized that, far from signifying just an individual choice, this adjective and the state it describes are bound to systemic and interconnected social and cultural factors that determine who gets to procreate, and how.[4] Regardless of who utters it, *childfree* has been, since its inception, received as an extremely gendered term almost always reserved for women, and sometimes substituted with spiteful terms ranging from *barren* and *deviant* to *selfish*.

It is crucial to note that the choice or circumstance of childbearing and child-rearing has often been violently withheld. The foundational literature of the childfree movement makes no reference to the racialized historical experiences of enslaved people whose children were considered not their own to raise and tend but the property of others, or to generations of women, predominately of color, who were sterilized without their consent and consequently unable to conceive (see p. 65). When anti-natalists invoked the environment in the 1960s and 1970s, it was in the form of cries to save the planet, without mention of the debilitating effects of pollutants on human endocrine systems that can lead to devastating infertility for those who do want babies. The postwar baby boom also included "the girls who went away" to places like the Florence Crittenton Homes to live out their pregnancies, give birth, and hand over their babies for adoption. In a hundred oral interviews collected by the artist Ann Fessler, these women spoke in their later years of the widespread coercion, social shaming, and guilt they experienced as they were legally divested of their children.[5]

In the twenty-first century, when the choice exists to opt out of childbearing on environmental and anti-capitalist grounds, it is now bound up with increasing access to education (one of the most predictive factors for fertility; when education rises, birth rates fall) and the right to access family planning without political interference and with governmental support. Almost fifty years after Peck and Radl wrote their texts, Anna Louie Sussman mined this millennial zeitgeist in her 2019 *New York Times* opinion piece "The End of Babies?": "Something is stopping us from creating the families we claim to desire. But what?"[6] (Her answer: late capitalism.)

Rebecca Solnit's self-described "rabbinical approach" is my favorite response to what she calls this "mother of all questions" that inevitably hounds women—and almost never men. Recalling a talk she once gave on Virginia Woolf that devolved into numerous questions from the audience about why Woolf never had children, Solnit reminds us to be vigilant when we talk about the lack of children: "Why are we asking that?"[7] A fascination with the productive capacity of a uterus is so often a deflection from other types of creation: "Many people make babies; only one made *To The Lighthouse*," she says.[8] Yet Solnit still sticks to a binary—babies or books. Many have before her, too. Doris Lessing chose to be childfree *after* giving birth and despairing over the "Himalayas of tedium" of young motherhood (she left her marriage and children to write). As she explained, "no one can write with a child around."[9]

And yet, as other writers and workers prove, there is no one-size-fits-all. Toni Morrison framed motherhood, in her books and her life, not in terms of the millennial struggle to retain work-life balance or the need to choose one over the other, but as part of the powerful and multidimensional whole of Black female identity. For Morrison, mothering is part of knowing "how to be complete human beings…it's not a question, it's not a conflict. You don't have to give up anything. You choose your responsibilities."[10]

Whether childfree or not, it is the right to shape reproductive destiny that reimagines social power relations not as inevitable inheritance but as paradigms ripe for resistance and rethinking.

While I can't speak for Sussman, or anyone else who is currently childfree, I know exactly what led me to stifle my ovaries during their reproductive prime: watching my own mother. "You were my miracle baby, Shell," she would always say on my birthday, before describing her struggles with miscarriage and her unalloyed delight at my arrival. In the same year I was born, 1982, a poet that my mum never knew, Adrienne Rich, wrote that her own "experience of motherhood was eventually to radicalize me."[11] She gave birth to her three sons in the 1950s, thirty years before my mother's own pregnancies. I have not had to wait to procreate for my own awakening. Watching the immediate aftereffects of my mother's natal acts radicalized me even as—perhaps especially as—a child.

Her marriage lasted almost fifteen years, and by the time I turned up five years into it, my father had turned out to be a domestic abuser. We watched him hit her so hard she became partially deaf. My sister and brother and I grew up knowing we children were the trap that kept her financially tied to a situation everyone wanted to escape. Her other albatross was our wonderful grandfather, who watched the screaming rows, physical bouts, and simmering animosity from a wheelchair in his waning years, the aftereffects of strokes having rendered him incapable of protecting his daughter. Shortly after he died, my mother moved us to Scotland, to the countryside. It was such a radical new beginning it felt as if we were reborn. We never looked back.

Rich was describing my mother and me—and every mother and every child—when she opened her ground-breaking 1976 text, *Of Woman Born: Motherhood as Experience and Institution*, with the reminder that because those who bear and suckle children are also tasked disproportionately with the responsibility for their raising, "most of us first know both love and disappointment, power and tenderness, in the person of a woman. We carry the imprint of this experience for life."[12] Steeped in the same women's liberation stew of the 1970s as Peck, but transcendent in her lucid, lyrical capacity to write about womanhood, Rich put words to the difference between one's individual relationship with the "powers of reproduction" and the institution-alized and essentialized notion of motherhood that, she argued, "alien-ated women from our bodies by incarcerating us in them."[13]

Opting out of human reproduction is, for some, a deliberate refusal with intended secondary effects. Inspired by reading Paul Erhlich's 1968 classic, *The Population Bomb*, Les Knight of Oregon got a vasectomy at age twenty-five (he got a discount for be-ing a student doctor's first try at the procedure) and founded the Voluntary Human Extinction Movement in 1991. With a slogan—"May we live long and die out"—that turns Star Trek's Vulcan salute on its head, the organization

aims to persuade others to forgo having any children at all. Knight claims that "procreation today is the moral equivalent of selling berths on a sinking ship."[14] For the author Jenny Brown, the imperative to be childfree is part of a conscious "birth strike," responding to "bad labor conditions" in the twenty-first century. The move-ment she describes holds hostage current global governmental anxieties around falling birth rates by with-holding individual fertility until legislation and policy—especially in the United States—adequately value and compensate gestational labor and child-rearing work.

Following in the footsteps of the feminist activists Silvia Federici and Barbara Ehrenreich, Brown sums up the contraceptive effects of modern life through interviews with a range of women who describe the lived realities of inadequate, racist, and ex-orbitant prenatal medical care in the United States, the lack of universal childcare, and personal and cultural reasons for remaining childfree.[15]

I interpreted having kids and being married as limiting my mother's potential, so I was not going to do it either.... There were too many material obstacles.
—Bernadette

What if it's more tasks and not enough joy?
—Bernice

We could either afford to buy a house or we could afford to have a child, and I picked the house.
—Nona

In 1975, Adrienne Rich highlighted the power of sharing such experi-ences widely: "Women have often felt insane when cleaving to the truth of our experience. Our future depends on the sanity of each of us, and we have a profound stake, beyond the personal, in the project of describing our reality as candidly and fully as we can to each other."[16]

I often wonder to whom my mother could speak candidly in an era when a Saturday night "domestic" was loud enough to be heard down the street but never mentioned the next day. She was a devotee of bake sales, Women's Institute meets, and craft guilds all her life. I know she found

community in these places. When she died, her home was strewn with so many exquisite handmade cushions and cashmere jumpers scored on years of Saturday morning adven-tures across the Scottish Borders where we lived that we gave them away as favors at her funeral.

Little did we know until we reached her attic that she had simultaneously amassed a veritable grandmother's trousseau of hand-knitted woolens for babies.

Neatly folded and boxed were tiny white baby bootees, russet-red toddler sweaters, bobbled blankets, a cardigan with mother-of-pearl buttons—we could almost smell the traybakes and cups of milky coffee that would have accompanied these purchases. Not one of her three chil-dren, all of us in our mid-thirties, had our own children by the time she left us. We are part of the generation jammed between the gig economy and the Great Recession (and, now, a pandemic). Unlike mum, who left school at sixteen to train as a secre-tary, and who trusted her spouse with her savings, we got the education she told us to strive for and concentrated on careers and financial indepen-dence. We each picked out our favorite knits and filed them away in our childfree homes.

Mothering transcends biological ties. I know this from years of nannying. It also wells up as a way to cope when those bonds are broken. Queenie, our septuagenarian neighbor from two doors down when we were kids, was our "adopted grandmother" in the absence of our dead ones. She was a Londoner who had made it through the wartime Blitz, and who cackled and chain-smoked her way through daytime TV by the time we knew her. Her house was a haven of pear drops, backyard plum trees, and small yapping dogs. A profoundly accomplished knitter, she made us three children a seemingly endless supply of perfect woolen cardigans and jumpers that presaged our own mum's stash. In the eulogy she delivered at Queenie's funeral, our mum called her a "second mum." I never considered why Queenie had no children of her own, until I learned one day that in fact she *did*. Three of them—Gerard, Yvonne, and Robert—who she lost along with her

——REPRODUCTION

marriage in the 1950s. In service from her teens, she worked in hotels and as a housekeeper. Her boys became two of the tens of thousands of "Home Children" sent off to various Commonwealth countries (in their case, to Australia) because Queenie was a single parent piecing it together, just like our mum. Three children were beyond her means. She never saw Gerard again—he died on duty in the Australian Navy. She was reunited with Yvonne forty-seven years later. And I remember the summer I was nine, when Robert came all the way from Australia, with an accent to match, and picked the sun-ripened plums with us in Queenie's garden like we'd done with her all our lives. Mum used her plastic Nikon camera to take a photo of Robert with his mother. I wonder now—was it their first? It was given pride of place on Queenie's sideboard, alongside ours.

In her 2018 book *Making Kin Not Population: Reconceiving Generations*, Donna Haraway—born in 1944, the same year as my mum—exhorts us to "make flourishing and generous lives ... without making more babies."[17] What did that blossoming look like for those whose generations were reconceived without their permission, or because of their class, or because the feminist revolution was, for them, a foreign sound dimly heard in the distance?

My mother finalized her divorce when we were still small. We asked her never to bring a man home. She never did. She never had so much as a temporary lover. She had a brain aneurysm when we were still teens and afterwards, when she regained use of language and relearned she had three children, it was as if all her past traumas melted away, leaving only us. We were the uncontested center of her universe, secure in a kind of unconditional love that bordered on obsessive and remains an indelible tie even after her death. And yet, from time to time, when a terrifying, unpayable utility bill arrived or her tiredness got the better of her, she would sit and sob at the kitchen table and wonder aloud what might have been if she had not had us. At the time, I wondered about that too, with a curiosity separate from my own stake in it; sometimes I still wonder, in the way magical thinking allows us all to inhabit quantum lives.

I don't believe in the binary of books or babies. There may be a point in my life when I have both. But until that time, I have ensured that my printed offspring represent their matrilineage clearly. On an overcast, gray day almost a decade ago, exactly three weeks before I got married, I walked into a small notary's office on East 23rd Street in New York and legally changed my surname to my mum's maiden name: Millar. It is a name that traces back to generations in Glasgow, to Scottish stock, to a part of me that connects to the memories of all the people who made their families—my family—before me, and who paved the path for my own adventure. Every book I publish, every exhibition I make, every time my name is logged in the annals of the internet, every time someone introduces me at a public lecture—they are there. *She* is there.

Today I am not ambivalent about loving children or being currently childfree, nor about the choices and circumstances I am privileged to occupy. I just am, and always will be, my mother's daughter.

1   Ellen Peck, "Obituary: Motherhood," *New York Times*, May 13, 1972, 31, nytimes.com.
2   Shirley Radl, *Mother's Day Is Over* (New York: Charterhouse, 1973), front cover blurb.
3   Sarah Knott, *Mother Is a Verb: An Unconventional History* (New York: Picador, 2019), 15.
4   See the work of Loretta Ross, among others, whose book *Reproductive Justice: An Introduction*, edited in collaboration with Rickie Solinger (Oakland: University of California Press, 2017), is a great place to start. See also Adele E. Clarke and Donna J. Haraway, eds., *Making Kin Not Population* (Chicago: Prickly Paradigm Press, 2018), 20–22: "Who—which women and which mothers—get to own and control their bodies and their children was and remains very highly stratified by class and race.... Reproduction is always and relentlessly individual *and* social *and* biological *and* cultural *and* political in complexly entangled ways" (original emphasis).
5   Ann Fessler, *The Girls Who Went Away: The Hidden History of Women Who Surrendered Children for Adoption in the Decades Before Roe v. Wade* (New York: Penguin Books, 2014). These girls and women were conditioned to pretend their motherhood was "invisible" —the "little wet ink across a piece of [adoption] paper made me *not* a mother" (53)—in order that they return home carefree and childfree.
6   Anna Louie Sussman, "The End of Babies?," *New York Times*, November 16, 2019, nytimes.com.
7   Rebecca Solnit, *The Mother of All Questions* (Chicago: Haymarket Books, 2017), 6.
8   Solnit, *The Mother of All Questions*, 4. Virginia Woolf's description of "killing" the mirage of the domestic "Angel in the House" (1931) is echoed in countless similar pronouncements, perhaps most famously by the writer Cyril Connolly: "There is no more sombre enemy of good art than the pram in the hall"; quoted in Shane Jones, "The Pram in the Hall," *Paris Review*, January 29, 2014.
9   Nigel Farndale, "Doris Lessing: Prize Fighter," *The Telegraph*, April 21, 2008, telegraph.co.uk.
10 See Andrea O' Reilly, *Toni Morrison and Motherhood: A Politics of the Heart* (Albany: State University of New York Press, 2004), 42. See also Ruha Benjamin, "Black AfterLives Matter: Cultivating Kinfulness as Reproductive Justice," in Clarke and Haraway, eds., *Making Kin Not Population*, 41–66.
11 Adrienne Rich, "Split at the Root: An Essay on Jewish Identity (1982)," in *Blood, Bread, and Poetry: Selected Prose, 1979–1985* (New York: W. W. Norton, 1986), 117.
12 Adrienne Rich, *Of Woman Born: Motherhood as Experience and Institution* (New York: W. W. Norton, 1985), 11.
13 Rich, *Of Woman Born*, 13.
14 Les Knight, "Experience: I Campaign for the Extinction of the Human Race," *The Guardian*, Life and Style section, January 10, 2020, theguardian.com.
15 This is what Sussman describes in "The End of Babies" too: "What we have come to think of as 'late capitalism'—that is, not just the economic system, but all its attendant inequalities, indignities, opportunities and absurdities— has become hostile to reproduction. Around the world, economic, social and environmental conditions function as a diffuse, barely perceptible contraceptive." *New York Times*, November 16, 2019, nytimes.com.
16 Adrienne Rich, "Women and Honor: Some Notes on Lying (1975)," in *On Lies, Secrets, and Silence: Selected Prose, 1966–1978* (New York: W. W. Norton, 1979). In *The Mother of All Questions*, the book recommended to me by countless people who believe I require some help deciding on my currently childfree state, Rebecca Solnit quotes Ursula K. Le Guin in this vein too (18), a quote worth repeating here: "We are volcanoes. When we women offer our experience as our truth, as human truth, all the maps change. There are new mountains." Originally from Le Guin's 1986 Bryn Mawr College commencement address, first published in a collection of her essays, *Dancing at the Edge of the World: Thoughts on Words, Women*, Places (New York: Grove Press, 1988), 160.
17 Clarke and Haraway, eds., *Making Kin Not Population*, 94.

CUTBACK THE
MILITARY BUDGET
NOT DAYCARE
WOMEN UNITE
FOR ACTION
58 WEST 25 ST
10010
212-989-1252

PROTEST Autonomy over one's reproductive agency and protection from gender-based discrimination should be enshrined as human rights but instead are battled over worldwide, both individually and communally. These marches, gatherings, and solo pickets have taken various forms though history, and the opinions expressed—often via signs, buttons, and symbols—are neither monolithic nor all-inclusive. Demands for wages for housework or the right to abortion as a form of family planning have divided stakeholders as often as they have united them, while issues such as high rates of femicide in certain locales or skyrocketing maternal mortality for women of color have often been ignored by protesters who don't yet understand the necessity of intersectionality.

1—— Children participating in a demonstration for affordable childcare in New York, August 20, 1974. Photograph by Bettye Lane

2—— A young girl holding a placard reading "Stop Period Stigma" during a fundraising race in Kyotera, Uganda, on March 7, 2020

3—— Barbara Smith, founding member of the Combahee River Collective, protesting unsolved murders of women of color in Boston, 1979

4—— An activist in Krakow, Poland, protesting an effort to tighten the country's abortion rules, April 2020

5—— People braving snow and hail for the first women's liberation march held in London, when four thousand marched for equal pay and education, free contraception and abortion care, 24-hour state-funded nurseries, and the right to live free from coercion and to form families without risk of poverty, March 6, 1971

6—— A member of Wages for Housework at the International Women's Day march on March 12, 1977. Photograph by Bettye Lane

7—— A street stencil that states "My Body My Choice" in six languages, December 2018

8—— The artist Maggie Preston protesting Trump's 2016 inauguration from home in a T-shirt she made, having broken her ankle the day before

2 3
4 5 6
7

STERILIZATION ABUSE——"Sterilization is a terrible thing to do to a woman. They had no right to do that to me. They never ask you about it. They told me that it was just for my appendix and then they did that to me." —Unnamed eugenic sterilization survivor[1]

"What they did to me they shouldn't do it. They should never do it. No matter if the welfare is supporting them, no matter if they're on Medi-Cal. I don't care. That's one of the personal rights that we, as a woman, have to defend." —Consuelo Hermosillo[2]

Sterilized in a California state institution for the so-called feebleminded, the unnamed woman quoted above was one of some sixty thousand people sterilized under eugenic laws established in the United States between the 1910s and 1960s. These laws, passed in thirty-two states, reflected a widespread belief in eugenics and a willingness among US legislators to make reproductive oppression a facet of public policy. A popular science in the early twentieth century, eugenics combined theories of heredity with biological determinism. Believing that reproductive control was paramount to social progress, eugenicists sought to prevent the "unfit" from reproducing while encouraging reproduction among the "fit." Eugenicists asserted that social issues such as poverty and crime were caused by the biologically "unfit," who required reproductive constraint to stem the social consequences of their supposed defects. Framed in the language of science, eugenics obscured the structural causes of poverty and crime, tying social inequalities to individual inferiority. Notions of eugenic fitness reflected racist, ableist, and sexist ideologies, and physicians, social workers, and other state authorities used sterilization laws to diminish the reproductive rights of already marginalized groups. In California, state authorities targeted working-class, Mexican-origin, and disabled people for sterilization.[3] In North Carolina, social workers disproportionately referred Black women receiving public assistance to the Eugenics Board for sterilization.[4] In more racially homogeneous states like Minnesota and Indiana, state authorities targeted working-class women and women

Poster for a 1977 rally against forced sterilization in San Francisco, designed by Rachael Romero

who challenged social norms—namely unwed mothers and women engaging in nonmarital sex.[5] As the eugenic sterilization survivor describes in the opening paragraph, these operations were often mired in deception and performed without consent. The design and implementation of eugenic sterilization laws represent one of the most violent ways that state authorities in the United States worked to reserve parenthood as a privilege bound by ideologies of race, class, and disability.

Eugenic sterilization helped set the stage for what happened to Consuelo Hermosillo. Coerced into signing a consent form in the midst of giving birth, Hermosillo was one of about two hundred women sterilized at a Los Angeles County hospital in the early 1970s.[6] By that time eugenics had been discredited, and many eugenic sterilization laws had been repealed. Nevertheless, the notion that certain groups required sterilization remained part of public policy, albeit in less explicit ways. In the 1960s, concerns over poverty and overpopulation converged in confounding ways with the broadening access to birth control. As part of his "war on poverty," President Lyndon Johnson increased federal funding for family planning, giving low-income women greater access to birth control. But minimal regulations and a lack of oversight resulted in continued widespread sterilization abuse, particularly of women of color. Viewing themselves as arbiters of social policy, and low-income women of color as irresponsible breeders,

many physicians and social workers drew on federal funds to coerce or outright force women into unwanted sterilizations. According to them, these women were incapable and undeserving of motherhood because they relied on welfare or other social programs. As a result, low-income Mexican-origin women like Hermosillo were sterilized at county hospitals in California; Puerto Rican women were sterilized at public hospitals in New York;[7] Native American women were sterilized at Indian Health Service facilities;[8] and Black women were subjected to the "Mississippi appendectomy" in the South.[9] That physicians and social workers used family-planning funds to sterilize low-income women of color reflects how eugenic ideologies persisted into the second half of the twentieth century. In practice, diminishing the right to parenthood became a legitimate component of poverty management. As is too often the case, poverty was characterized as an individual failure resulting from irresponsibility and inherent inferiority, a framework that placed these women outside the bounds of "legitimate" motherhood.

In 1975, Hermosillo joined other Latina sterilization survivors in Madrigal v. Quilligan, a civil rights lawsuit asserting that physicians at the Los Angeles County hospital violated their constitutional right to bear children. In a shocking decision, the presiding judge ruled against the women. Yet their efforts and those of reproductive-rights organizers across the country exposed rampant sterilization abuse and forced the federal

government to establish regulations and guidelines for informed consent.

The experiences of the women quoted at the beginning of this essay, sterilized in two different eras and under different state policies, highlight state authorities' persistent use of sterilization to prevent access to motherhood. Their statements drawing connections between the individual harms they experienced and broader issues of social inequality and reproductive rights also represent an antecedent to the modern reproductive justice movement. Unfortunately, their experiences remain relevant today. In 2013, investigative reporting revealed that 150 women confined to California prisons were sterilized between 2006 and 2010.[10] In 2017, a Tennessee judge sought to coerce defendants into sterilization in exchange for reduced sentences.[11] In 2020, immigrant testimony and a whistleblower complaint exposed a Georgia doctor for performing unnecessary hysterectomies on women confined to an Immigration and Customs Enforcement detention center without their consent.[12] Listening to sterilization-abuse survivors broadens our understanding of how access to motherhood has been designed in exclusionary ways. Their experiences compel us to consider what reproductive freedom means for communities that have historically been targeted for reproductive constraint. Perhaps most importantly, these stories inspire us to work toward the conditions necessary for all people to be free from state violence.

—**Natalie Lira**

1   Sterilized in the late 1940s, this woman was recorded and her statement published by two researchers. Very few studies on how survivors of eugenic sterilization felt about the practice exist, so her testimony, while brief and anonymous, is important. See G. Sabagh and Robert B. Edgerton, "Sterilized Mental Defectives Look at Eugenic Sterilization," *Eugenics Quarterly* 9, no. 4 (December 4, 1962): 221.
2   Rene Tajima-Peña, *No Más Bebés* (documentary), 2015.
3   Natalie Lira and Alexandra Minna Stern, "Mexican Americans and Eugenic Sterilization: Resisting Reproductive Justice in California,

1920–1950," *Aztlán: A Journal of Chicano Studies* 39, no. 2 (Fall 2014): 9–34; Nicole L. Novak et al., "Disproportionate Sterilization of Latinos under California's Eugenic Sterilization Program, 1920–1945," *American Journal of Public Health* 108, no. 5 (May 2018): 611–13.
4   Johanna Schoen, *Choice and Coercion: Birth Control, Sterilization, and Abortion in Public Health and Welfare* (Chapel Hill: University of North Carolina Press, 2005).
5   Molly Ladd-Taylor, "The 'Sociological Advantages' of Sterilization: Fiscal Policies and Feebleminded Women in Interwar Minnesota," in *Mental Retardation in America: A Historical

Reader*, ed. Steven Noll and James W. Trent (New York: New York University Press, 2004), 281–302; Alexandra Minna Stern, "'We Cannot Make a Silk Purse Out of a Sow's Ear': Eugenics in the Hoosier Heartland," *Indiana Magazine of History* 103, no. 1 (March 1, 2007): 3–38.
6   Elena R. Gutiérrez, *Fertile Matters: The Politics of Mexican-Origin Women's Reproduction* (Austin: University of Texas Press, 2008); Tajima-Peña, *No Más Bebés.*
7   Ana María García, *La Operación* (documentary), 1982; Iris Lopez, *Matters of Choice: Puerto Rican Women's Struggle for Reproductive Freedom* (New Brunswick, NJ: Rutgers University Press, 2008).

8   Andrea Smith, *Conquest: Sexual Violence and American Indian Genocide* (Cambridge, MA: South End Press, 2005); Barbara Gurr, *Reproductive Justice: The Politics of Health Care for Native American Women* (New Brunswick, NJ: Rutgers University Press, 2014).
9   Dorothy Roberts, *Killing the Black Body: Race, Reproduction, and the Meaning of Liberty* (New York: Vintage, 1998); Loretta Ross, "Trust Black Women: Reproductive Justice and Eugenics," in *Radical Reproductive Justice: Foundations, Theory, Practice, Critique*, ed. Loretta Ross et al. (New York: Feminist Press, 2017), 58–85.
10   Corey G. Johnson,

"Female Inmates Sterilized in California Prisons without Approval," *Reveal: From the Center for Investigative Reporting*, July 7, 2013, revealnews.org.
11   "Tennessee Judge Who Offered Inmates Reduced Sentences for Sterilization Rebuked," *CBS News*, November 22, 2017, cbsnews.com.
12   Tina Vasquez, "Exclusive: Georgia Doctor Who Forcibly Sterilized Detained Women Has Been Identified," *Prism*, September 15, 2020, prismreports.org; Vasquez, "Immigrants Allege Mistreatment by Georgia Doctor and Whistleblower," *Prism*, September 17, 2020, prismreports.org.

POPULATION POLICY POSTERS——Policies designed to control population growth, whether by contracting or expanding birth rates, have long existed, including policies such as coordinated mass sterilization, pursued in the United States, for example, through legislation and its subsequent applications that effectively dressed up eugenics in economic terms.[1] But in the twentieth century one country became the poster child—literally and figuratively—for these programs as a result of the visual propaganda it produced in pursuit of population control: the People's Republic of China.

From the founding of the People's Republic of China (PRC) in 1949 to present-day life under President Xi Jinping, a very particular type of visual propaganda has come to permeate everyday experience in China. Posters, electronic screens, murals, billboards, and even development hoardings have all been used by the country's ruling Communist Party to promote changing state ideals—enlisting the language of graphic design in service to often far-reaching public policy.

Chubby infants have long been a persistent feature of such campaigns, appearing on posters about family planning and population management as well as health, education, and the future of "the mother country." Posters created to reinforce China's one-child policy, implemented in 1979 to curb exponential population growth, especially glorified happy, plump babies with beaming smiles and rosy cheeks to demonstrate that one child is best.[2] Usually prominently placed within the composition, these babies are frequently shown surrounded by goldfish or luscious peaches, both symbols of good fortune.

The graphic language of these posters points to the influence of *nianhua*—popular New Year pictures widely associated with the countryside—on PRC visual propaganda. *Nianhua* were customarily hung in households at the start of the New Year to bid goodbye to the past and welcome the future. Many depicted chubby baby boys (*pang wawa*) holding carp, an image that represented ideals such as happiness, longevity, and wealth in addition to the culturally preferred gender. Party-commissioned posters accordingly appropriated this design

A Chinese propaganda poster c. 1974, shortly before the one child policy was introduced, illustrating a birth control campaign with scenes of happy family life. It reads *Jihua shengyu haochu duo* (Family planning has many advantages) which chimed with the slogan of the day: "one's not too few, two will do, and three are too many for you"

typology to fit state messages, culminating in hybrid images that blended cultural traditions (rooted in patriarchal lineage and Confucianism) with the politics of socialism.[3]

Communist China's early propaganda campaigns were ostensibly designed to promote equality between the biological sexes. Posters referencing the one-child policy, for instance, featured baby girls and boys alike, while illustrations of nuclear families depicted a single (baby) girl to emphasize their importance. Yet, in practice, enduring preferences for male heirs throughout China resulted in countless newborn baby girls being abandoned by their families—either forsaken in public spaces for others to discover or left to die. A large percentage of baby girls consequently ended up at orphanages, were discreetly put up for adoption, or became victims of human trafficking.[4] Numerous others were "hidden" by relatives.[5]

Whereas population control posters painted a picture of a solo happy child, graphic banners, also conspicuously displayed in public spaces, could take a more sinister tone, conveying messages such as "Anyone who refuses to sterilize will be arrested on sight."[6] Procedures like forced sterilization and involuntary abortion were systematically imposed on people under the one-child policy. Usually brutally enforced, these measures were overseen by provincial-level family-planning committees—local bodies tasked with meeting policy guidelines outlined by the central government, and left to administer penalties when families were found to have exceeded the quota. This decentralized system resulted in varied practices, both in how policies were implemented by officials and how top-down directives were negotiated, covertly evaded (as with *heihaizi*), or sometimes openly challenged by people in rural areas.

It is impossible to objectively assess the numerous tolls of the one-child policy, but personal accounts recorded in several recent investigations reveal some of the most overlooked consequences of this complex social-engineering experiment: the human and emotional costs associated with policing women's bodies.[7] Wang Peng, a Beijing-based visual artist, has been working to bring these issues to public attention. His 2010 photographic series *Ruins*, for example, captures sobering scenes of aborted fetuses discarded in local rubbish dumps. In Nanfu Wang's excellent 2019 documentary, *One Child Nation*, enforced late-term abortions of infants that would cause a family to exceed the one-child policy, as well as infanticide of newborns, are recalled matter-of-factly by Chinese health professionals and officials as they reflect on the policy's legacy. These harrowing, poignant stories are a stark contrast to the cheerful, plump babies immortalized in PRC poster propaganda.

In 2015, the Chinese government officially replaced its longstanding one-child policy with a two-child policy. Crafted to address state anxieties about an aging population, this new mandate encourages women in heterosexual marriages to have two babies.[8] Digital platforms such as Weibo provide a glimpse into its reception: "The person who was forced to have an abortion then, is the same person who is pressured to have a baby now," commented one woman in 2018. "They do not treat us as humans.... They're treating us as 'fertility resources,'" observed another.[9]

Population control measures like these are not unique to China, of course. In 2019, India's ruling Bharatiya Janata Party initiated discussions around introducing a two-child limit to tackle surging population growth, an approach that has historically been accompanied by punitive measures to ensure compliance. Other countries facing demographic deficits similar to China's, such as South Korea and Finland, are encouraging new births via financial incentives. Whatever the method, the (rhetorical) questions to be asked of such policies remain the same: Where do we draw the line between people's bodily integrity and contributing to "the greater good" of a nation; and who should ultimately be the one(s) to decide?

—**Zara Arshad**

1 See Lisa Ko, "Unwanted Sterilizations and Eugenics Programs in the United States," *Independent Lens* (blog), PBS, January 29, 2016, pbs.org.
2 When first introduced, the one-child policy directed that Han Chinese, the ethnic majority in China, could have only one child (the directive was more relaxed for ethnic minorities). By the mid-1980s, however, the Chinese government realized that it was too difficult to enforce the one-child mandate in rural areas, and so the policy was adjusted.
3 For more on *nianhua* and the PRC, see Xiaobing Tang, *Visual Culture in Contemporary China: Paradigms and Shifts* (Cambridge: Cambridge University Press, 2015).
4 See Sten Johansson and Ola Nygren, "The Missing Girls of China: A New Demographic Account," *Population and Development Review* 17, no. 1 (March 1991): 35–51; Yuyu Chen, Avraham Ebenstein, Lena Edlund, and Hongbin Li, "Girl Adoption in China—A Less-Known Side of Son Preference,"
Population Studies 69, no. 2 (July 2015): 161–78.
5 Unregistered people in China lack *hukou*, a record linking them to the governmental household registration system, required to gain access to education, employment, health services, and so on.
6 Nanfu Wang, 'What It Was Like to Grow Up under China's One-Child Policy," *TED2019*, April 2019, ted.com.
7 See, for example, Mei Fong, *One Child: The Story of China's Most Radical Experiment* (London: Oneworld, 2016); Jiaoming
Pang, *The Orphans of Shao: A True Account of the Blood and Tears of the One-Child Policy in China* (New York: Women's Rights in China Organization, 2014); Kay Ann Johnson, *China's Hidden Children: Abandonment, Adoption, and the Human Costs of the One-Child Policy* (Chicago: University of Chicago Press, 2016); John James Kennedy and Yaojiang Shi, *Lost and Found: The "Missing Girls" in Rural China* (New York: Oxford University Press, 2019); and *One Child Nation* (documentary),
directed by Nanfu Wang and Jialing Zhang (Culver City, CA: Amazon Studios, 2019).
8 For more on the nuances of this policy, see Leta Hong Fincher, *Betraying Big Brother: The Feminist Awakening in China* (London: Verso, 2018), 159–86.
9 Gabi Verberg, Manya Koetse, and Miranda Barnes, "China's Proposed 'No Child Tax' Stirs Controversy: 'First Forced Abortions, Now Pressured Into Pregnancy,'" *What's on Weibo*, August 18, 2018, whatsonweibo.com.

TEST-TUBE BABY——It was a birth announcement that echoed around the world. On July 25, 1978, Louise Joy Brown was born at 5 pounds, 12 ounces at Oldham and District General Hospital in the north of Manchester. The world's first "test-tube baby" (that is, the first baby conceived via in vitro fertilization, or IVF), the birth was a highly public and closely watched event. Reporters representing news outlets from every continent descended on the small British hospital, all determined to bear witness to what *Time* magazine called "the most awaited birth in perhaps 2,000 years."[1]

The term *test-tube baby* came into being in part because of how the international media portrayed it—as a sci-fi fantasy writ large. Numerous newspapers and magazines of the time showed illustrations of glowing embryos in test tubes being passed from gloved hand to gloved hand in a lab. The Latin term *in vitro*, meaning "in glass," is used because early biological experiments involving cultivation of tissues outside living organisms were carried out in glass containers, such as beakers, test tubes, or Petri dishes. In cases of IVF, the egg and the sperm are fertilized in a Petri dish, hence *in vitro*, meaning within the glass culture dish, as opposed to *in vivo*, or inside the living body.

Nine months before Louise's birth, a team of three fertility specialists— Robert Edwards, a physiologist; Jean Purdy, a nurse and embryologist; and Patrick Steptoe, a gynecologist—became the first group to successfully carry out IVF by extracting an egg from Lesley Brown, impregnating it with Peter Brown's sperm, and planting the resulting embryo in Lesley's uterus.

In 1978, the British press grabbed hold of the story and fiercely reshaped it. Headlines presented Lesley's pregnancy and Louise's birth as both a British success story and a source of hope and future happiness for infertile people everywhere. But in this version of the story there was only ever room for a dual set of "parents": Steptoe and Edwards (representing British science) and Lesley and John Brown (standing in for infertile couples). Steptoe and Edwards were celebrated as "the men who made the breakthrough" and lauded for

Jean Purdy established Bourn Hall Clinic with Patrick C. Steptoe and Robert Edwards as the world's first in vitro fertilization (IVF) clinic

——REPRODUCTION

embodying British values of perseverance, industriousness, altruism, and ingenuity.[2] Then as now, Jean Purdy was routinely omitted from the story.

Purdy, who was initially hired as a lab technician by Edwards, was the first person to witness the successful cell division of the embryo that would eventually become Louise Brown. During her career she coauthored twenty-six academic papers about IVF and helped found the Bourn Hall fertility clinic in Cambridgeshire. Purdy was so integral to the development of the first successful IVF that when she took leave to care for her ill mother, the project was halted until her return.[3]

Edwards was awarded a Nobel prize in 2010 for the development of IVF and was knighted in 2011.[4] Neither award can be made posthumously, and because Purdy died in 1985 at age thirty-nine, and Steptoe died in 1988 at age seventy-four (both of cancer), her acknowledgment in particular came too late. In 2019, Louise Brown visited the grave of Jean Purdy to recognize and raise awareness about Purdy's significant contributions to reproductive science.

The second successful IVF baby was born in India just sixty-seven days after Louise's birth, but Britain had won an international race of sorts, at least according to British television and newspapers.[5] After these initial successes, the number of women undergoing IVF grew rapidly: the first IVF baby in Scotland was born in 1979; in Australia, in 1980; in the United States, in 1981; and in Sweden, in 1982. The fortieth IVF baby, born in 1982, was Louise's sister, Natalie.

To date, well over eight million babies have been born via IVF.[6] Yet since the earliest days, IVF was—and in many circles, still is—shadowed by dismissal, fear, confusion, and sexism.[7] On the one hand, IVF has offered hope to infertile people; on the other, it smacks of Aldous Huxley's *Brave New World*.[8] In the late 1970s and 1980s, ethical debates over so-called artificial or medicalized pregnancy added to a growing divide over who gets to claim "natural" forms of motherhood. That Louise was so often described as a Frankenbaby, and indeed that "test-tube baby" became, for a time, the default descriptor for IVF babies, reflects the way media still shapes public perceptions of Assisted Reproductive Technology (ART).

Though IVF is now considered mainstream, factors such as high cost, geography, and punitive laws keep it out of reach for many infertile, gay, and single people throughout the world. In the United States, the average cost of IVF per cycle is over $10,000, and most must pay that fully out of pocket, as fertility treatment is not a benefit that many health insurance plans cover. In Sub-Saharan Africa, the high cost of treatments has resulted in fewer than one-third of countries even having an IVF clinic.[9] In France, by contrast, the national health system routinely pays for IVF for heterosexual couples, but the country has some of Europe's most restrictive laws on access to fertility treatments as a result of its Catholic heritage, conservative bioethics, and intensely complex debates about kinship.[10] As is the case for LGBTQ and unmarried people in many countries throughout the world, French lesbians and single mothers who can afford it must travel to more accepting countries to get fertility treatments.

Today, as a result of ART, definitions of motherhood have never been more expansive.[11] ART now includes in vitro fertilization and embryo transfer (IVF-ET), gamete intrafallopian transfer (GIFT), zygote intrafallopian transfer (ZIFT), frozen embryo transfer (FET), egg and sperm donation, and gestational carriers or surrogates. Yet, even as we increasingly use ART and expand its frontiers with stem cell research, reformed surrogacy laws, and gene-editing technologies like CRISPR, we are still coming to terms with what these technologies mean for humanity and our larger relationships with childbearing, kinship, nature, creation, religion, national and financial responsibility, and each other. And until reproductive policies are designed to serve individuals rather than political interests, fertility treatments will remain out of reach for millions, and new technologies will be accessible only to those privileged enough to be able to afford them.[12]

1 "Medicine: Test-Tube Baby: It's a Girl," *Time*, August 7, 1978.
2 See Katherine Dow, "'The Men Who Made the Breakthrough': How the British Press Represented Patrick Steptoe and Robert Edwards in 1978," *Reproductive Biomedicine & Society* 4 (June 2017): 59–67.
3 Josh Halliday, "Female Nurse Who Played Crucial Role in IVF Ignored on Plaque," *The Guardian*, June 9, 2019.
4 Halliday's reporting turned up letters in Robert Edwards's archive showing that he tried in vain to ensure that Jean Purdy's contributions would be recognized. In 1980 Edwards wrote to Oldham Area Health Authority requesting that plaques at the hospitals involved in the project "do justice to the participants involved" and suggesting that Purdy's name be included. An administrator replied that the plaque would read, "Human in vitro fertilization followed by the world's first successful pregnancy, was performed in this hospital by Mr Patrick Steptoe, Dr Robert Edwards and their supporting staff in November 1977." In 1981 Edwards wrote a letter to Oldham Area Health Authority stating, "I feel strongly about the inclusion of the names of the people who helped with the conception of Louise Brown. I feel this especially about Jean Purdy, who travelled to Oldham with me for 10 years, and contributed as much as I did to the project. Indeed, I regard her as an equal contributor to Patrick Steptoe and myself." See Halliday, "Female Nurse Who Played Crucial Role in IVF Ignored on Plaque."
5 The second IVF baby, named Durga, was conceived using a method developed independently by Dr. Subhash Mukhopadhyay, a physician and researcher in Kolkata, India.
6 "More than 8 Million Babies Born from IVF Since the World's First in 1978," *ScienceDaily*, July 3, 2018.
7 Although in 1978 the media fixated on Lesley Brown's blocked fallopian tube as a stand-in for female infertility, then as now, about 50 percent of fertility issues are due to poor sperm quality.
8 Megan Garber, "The IVF Panic: 'All Hell Will Break Loose, Politically and Morally, All Over the World,'" *The Atlantic*, June 25, 2012.
9 Jessica Grose, "When It Comes to Fertility, Access Is Everything," *New York Times*, November 8, 2019.
10 Rachel Donadio, "Why IVF Has Divided France," *The Atlantic*, October 6, 2019.
11 As Sophie Lewis writes in *Full Surrogacy Now* (New York: Verso, 2019), 26: "Let's bring about the conditions of possibility for open-source, fully collaborative gestation.... Let us build a care commune based on comradeship, a world sustained by kith and kind more than by kin. Where pregnancy is concerned, let every pregnancy be for everyone."
12 See Elaine Tyler May's *Barren in the Promised Land: Childless Americans and the Pursuit of Happiness* (Cambridge, MA: Harvard University Press, 1995). See also Grose, "When It Comes to Fertility, Access Is Everything."

STIRRUPS——The lithotomy position, in which a person lies on their back with legs raised and bent at the knees, is commonly used in gynecology to open the pelvic region for examinations and surgical procedures. In the West, this is also the posture typically employed in hospital births. Both rely on medical stirrups to support the feet. In her practice, midwife Stephanie Tillman works to dispel the (often severe) discomfort many patients associate with this cold, clinical design, often forgoing stirrups entirely during exams and births.

DESIGNING MOTHERHOOD——Stephanie, you're a Yale-trained midwife, and in your bio for your blog *Feminist Midwife* you describe your clinical practice as seeking "to engage providers and consumers in conversations about sex positivity, reproductive justice, queer care, empowerment and power-transfer, trauma-informed care, consent and values clarification." Can you tell us how you got into this work, and what keeps you going?

STEPHANIE TILLMAN——I started out doing public health work as a sex educator. Thinking holistically about how to take care of people and communities, and what impacts them broadly, really resonated with me. When I entered into midwifery, I felt that I was part of this newer generation of diverse people who are carrying the profession forward. I'm queer identified, and I very much align with the reproductive justice movement. I also believe this kind of care should be available for everyone, and that we should be reclaiming midwifery's African American and Indigenous roots and really bringing midwives of color to the forefront.

I work on the South Side of Chicago, which is a very difficult place for many people to live and raise families, and my patients are resilient and incredible. Their lives are so rich with love and community, and they have a right to be healthy. I wanted to bring the best model of care to people who otherwise might not receive it. Being part of a newer generation of midwives, I see that there is a stark difference between ourselves and midwives who have been in practice for a very long time, and who have maybe come from the White feminist wave of body reclamation. This definitely did a lot for women and did a lot for women's health care. Today, we're concerned with reproductive justice alignment. We see midwives as available to take care of everyone, queer people and trans people included, and also people from a range of economic backgrounds. I feel part of a new wave of people who want more for midwifery. That really keeps me going.

DM——That's really inspiring. Let's talk about care practices. Many of us take stirrups for granted as just one of the many uncomfortable things that come with having a pelvic exam. Can you tell us why using stirrups is helpful from a provider's perspective?

ST——Many providers see stirrups or foot pedals as making their day easier because they keep everyone in the same position and facilitate getting to the cervix easily. When someone's bottom is toward the end of the table, their knees are out to the side and their feet are stuck; it's an easy position for the clinician to do things. But we can get to the cervix easily from many different positions. And in my experience, having people find their most comfortable position and working around that ultimately takes less time. Also, we can use language that supports people in understanding what's happening to their bodies and allow them to move and be comfortable. Because being in stirrups is not comfortable for everyone. They restrict movement, and the position can also be activating for survivors of abuse.

——REPRODUCTION

DM—— **How did you start thinking about this?**

ST—— I started asking the people I was taking care of what position they would be most comfortable in. I'd say, "I could probably get to your cervix in that position." Because it's not just about taking away the stirrups. It's about saying, "What position are you going to be comfortable in while we do this exam?" Actually, midwives in the 1970s developed ways for differently bodied or disabled people not only to be in different positions to have babies, but also to be in different positions for any kind of a cervical check. There's a booklet called *Table Manners* [1982] that has pictures of people who are walking with crutches or are in wheelchairs.

DM—— **We both just immediately wrote down "Table Manners"! So how can one best accommodate those with disabilities and create the conditions for a positive experience during a pelvic exam?**

ST—— I have done pelvic exams for people in wheelchairs without issue, and they haven't needed to get up onto the table. Other people can't open their hip to the side. We can always find a modified position. And if those options are available for people whose bodies cannot get into what is considered the standard position, why are we not offering that for everyone? Why can't we say, "What position would be most comfortable for you? Let's try it out"? I also take care of enough people with a history of assault that I think we should use trauma-informed care across the board.

DM—— **Have you completely eliminated using stirrups in your practice?**

ST—— The hallmark of the midwifery model of care is meeting people where they are. If someone asks for them, I'll say, "Usually I don't use those because most find it more comfortable without. If you want stirrups, that's totally fine with me. If you're open to trying it without, we can do that too." But I've eliminated them for the most part because many people don't like them, and it's much harder for people in stirrups to have agency. They're metal and mechanical feeling, they make this horrible sound, and that's not the vibe I want. The patient is in a splayed position, there's nothing under their pelvis, they're kind of off the end [of the table] and feeling vulnerable. I really wanted to think through how we should be caring for people respectfully and communicating with them directly. And I also think about the way we should set patients up to be more comfortable in every aspect.

TABLE MANNERS

A Guide to the Pelvic Examination for Disabled Women and Health Care Providers

The Diamond-Shaped Position

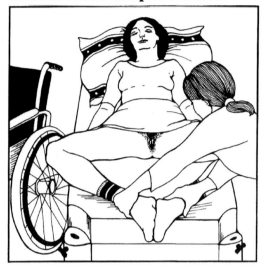

The Knee-Chest Position

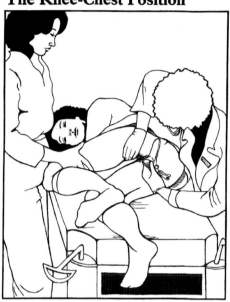

The OB Stirrups Position

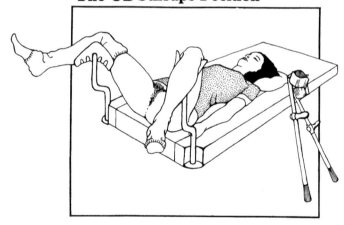

TABLE MANNERS *Table Manners: A Guide to the Pelvic Examination for Disabled Women and Health Care Providers*, written by Susan Ferreyra and Katrine Hughes and illustrated by Anne Waltzer, was first published in 1982 by Planned Parenthood in San Francisco. Ferreyra and Hughes, identifying as "two physically disabled women with experience in the fields of family planning, education and counseling," based their text "on the assumptions that disabled women are sexual, and that they deserve quality health care services which are accessible and sensitive to their needs," as they wrote in the introduction. Today, the designers of the Yona speculum (see p. 55) and midwives like Stephanie Tillman, who operates under the Instagram handle @feministmidwife, have expanded this language to include trans and trauma-informed care practices.

The Hearing-Impaired Woman

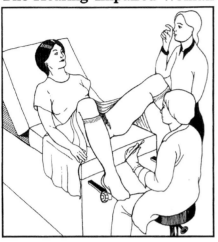

The Visually Impaired Woman

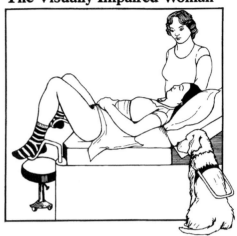

The V-Shaped Position

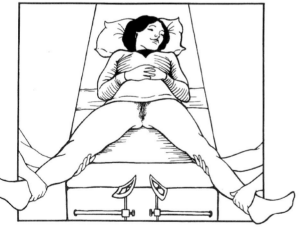

The M-Shaped Position

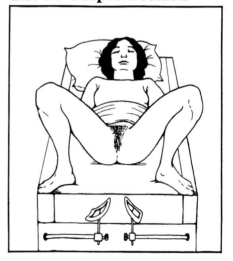

The Client's
Rights and Responsibilities

The Client Has The Right To:

1. Receive accessible family planning services;
2. Be treated with dignity and respect regardless of age, race, sexual preference, physical and mental abilities, etc.;
3. Specify how your belongings and/or adaptive devices are handled during the visit;
4. Have privacy and confidentiality of your records;
5. Receive explanations and answers to questions;
6. Receive education and counseling;
7. Be interviewed and examined in a private room;
8. Bring a friend to assist you during your visit;
9. Know the names of people serving you;
10. Consent to or refuse any care or treatment;
11. Review your medical records with a clinician;
12. Consent to or refuse the presence of an observer during the interview or the examination;
13. Decide whether or not to have children, and when;
14. Request a particular clinician when scheduling an appointment.

The Client Has The Responsibility To:

1. Tell appropriate staff about your disability;
2. Request reasonable accommodations during your visit;
3. Be honest about your medical records;
4. Ask questions when you don't understand;
5. Follow health advice and medical instructions;
6. Respect clinic policies;
7. Keep appointments or cancel at least 24 hours in advance.

When you want to know   — ASK

When you have questions   — SPEAK UP

When you have problems   — COMPLAIN

When you like what happens   — SMILE

ARTIFICIAL WOMB——When the twenty-five-year-old, Chicago-born, New York-based feminist and activist Shulamith Firestone published *The Dialectic of Sex: The Case for Feminist Revolution* in 1970, she introduced a new dimension to the Marxist understanding of the relationship between labor and production: that of biology.

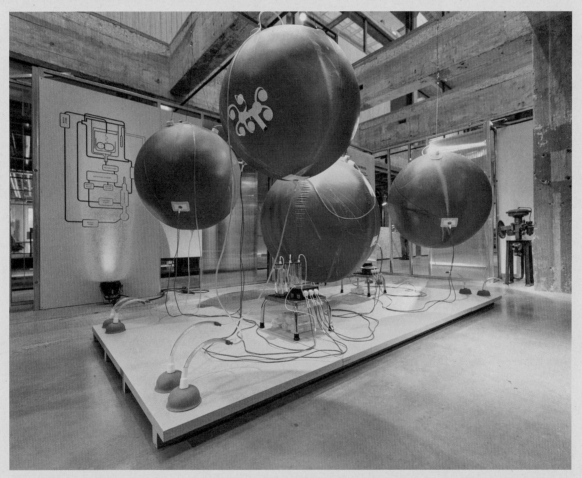

Next Nature Network's speculative design proposal for an artificial womb on display at Dutch Design Week in Eindhoven in 2018

Unforgettably describing childbirth as "barbaric" and—quoting a friend—"like shitting a pumpkin," Firestone noted that "the original division of labor was between man and woman for the purposes of child-breeding," the former and latter respectively occupying analogical roles as owner and the means of production.[1]

Liberation from this equation, and from heternormative familial structures entirely, Firestone implied, would occur only when human reproduction transcended biology. The Computer Age, she declared, called for outsourcing to artificial wombs the reproductive labor that women were unquestioningly expected to undertake on behalf of society. It would be the logical apogee of the increasing technological interventions of forceps and cesarean sections into the parturition process.

"Pregnancy," she wrote, "now freely acknowledged as clumsy, inefficient, and painful, would be indulged in, if at all, only as a tongue-in-cheek archaism," a custom as contradictory and bizarre, she imagined, as the women of her era, no longer virgins at marriage, wearing a white wedding dress. She hoped for not only a biological renunciation but also freedom from the "drudge jobs" meted out asymmetrically to her gender and a move toward communal raising of all children concomitant with the "disappearance of motherhood."[2] Edward Grossman took up the topic for a more popular readership in The Atlantic a year later in an essay titled "The Obsolescent Mother," where he fretted, "Is the artificial womb inevitable?"[3]

Yet the debate over extracorporeal human reproduction was, of course, much more complex. Human gestation is no mere mechanical process, and even if it were, did everyone want to transcend it? As the feminist scholar Alice Adams asked in the early 1990s, "Was women's ability to give birth a root cause of women's oppression or a peak emotional experience and—at least potentially—a means of achieving political power?"[4]

Subsequent generations of feminists who have grappled with this question have often concluded in favor of Firestone on the grounds of the unequal strain of the emotional and physical labor involved in childbirth and child-rearing. Evie Kendal, an Australian feminist bioethicist and critic who is among the most

powerful and exciting voices of the current generation of thinkers on this topic, points to these "unjust social burdens" as a rationale to argue for wider governmental and public support for research in pursuit of the artificial womb. She also highlights the health risks of pregnancy, suggesting that "under usual circumstances it would be considered only logical for someone to actively avoid developing a physical condition that is guaranteed to cause significant, prolonged discomfort...severe injury or even death. Any failure to do so could be interpreted as antithetical to self-preservation."[5]

Her argument for state-sponsored extracorporeal human gestation is echoed in the work of the Philadelphia-based writer Sophie Lewis. Lewis's radical Full Surrogacy Now (2019) builds on Firestone's work and on Donna Haraway's notion of expanded kinship—as Lewis notes, a theory founded on the longstanding survival strategies of Black, queer, and other marginalized communities—to encourage "human subjectivities beyond the dyadic template." She points out that "the common idiom about raising a child, 'it takes a village,' is an everyday way of acknowledging that the [biological] template is and always was a fantasy; a person is not the result of a mother and a father simply adding together their unique identities of 'flesh and blood' and genes."[6]

The expansive, imaginative boundaries of science fiction have long been fertile ground for envisioning the possibilities of independent gestation technologies. Over so much of this speculative fiction hangs the specter of J. B. S. Haldane, the British scientist who in 1924 coined the term ectogenesis (ecto from the Greek "outer") with a vision of artificial womb technologies in lockstep with discriminatory scientific strategies for population control. Haldane advocated suppressing the higher birth rate of "less desirable" (read, non-Anglo) demographics, imagining a student of the future using a fully developed technology to "take an ovary from a woman, and keep it growing in a suitable fluid for as long as twenty years, producing a fresh ovum each month, of which 90 percent can be fertilized, and the embryos grown successfully for nine months, and then brought out into the air"; by the year 2074 ectogenesis would become a popular technique, Haldane

foresaw, with "less than 30 percent of children...born of woman."[7]

Aldous Huxley satirized this eugenic horror in Brave New World (1932), which opens with the Director of Hatcheries and Conditioning overseeing a Fertilizing Room where incubators hold "racks upon racks of numbered test-tubes," the embryos grown according to sociobiological hierarchies, from Alphas, who assume leadership roles, to the slave caste of Epsilons. Through "Bokanovsky's Process," lower-caste eggs are forced to divide and multiply to maintain thepyramid, with "a bokanovskified egg...making ninety-six human beings grow where only one grew before. Progress."[8]

Marge Piercy interrogated this paradigm of new tools in the hands of the same old patriarchal, racist order in her 1976 novel Woman on the Edge of Time. Her narrative follows a Chicana protagonist, Connie Ramos, who is committed to a mental institution in New York City. There Connie communicates with a utopian future in which the spell of biological reproduction and bonding based on blood has been fully broken in order that "we all became mothers," making the work a social responsibility to be shared by all people.[9]

The triangulation of science, literature, and artist imaginaries laid the foundations for a strand of speculative design that in the current century includes the Par-tu-ri-ent Pod (2017) and Next Nature Network's (NNN) artificial womb (2018)—projects that give form, and some tangible reality, to an idea still just out of reach of medicine and social mores. The former, a project submitted to the annual Biodesign Challenge by students from ArtEZ University of the Arts in Arnhem, the Netherlands, imagines a womb as an internet-connected portable perspex container where expectant parents can watch their fetus grow while parked in their living room, or which they can wear against their bodies to feel kicks.

NNN's project, shared with public audiences at Dutch Design Week in 2018, employed make-believe balloon-like wombs as a stage upon which to explore the ethical limits of biotechnology through a series of public debates. These conversations between experts on the topic of human reproduction and its possible biological and technical forms included midwife Beatrijs Smulders and the philosopher Anna Smajdor, who asked whether pregnancy is overvalued by society, why negative experiences of birth are often ignored, and what new and liberating possibilities might emerge once the female body is removed from reproduction. Such speculative projects underscore the imaginative leaps still required in pursuit of artificial wombs, which are sometimes wrapped up in other forms of hope and belief, as with the atheistic and alien-focused Raëlian religion, founded in France in the 1970s and now with tens of thousands of followers worldwide. The Raëlians believe that aliens called Elohim created humans about 25,000 years ago using biotechnology. In 2003 they announced that they were attempting to build a "Babytron" as part of their Surrogaid program to clone human life.

Science is no longer far behind our imaginations. Reporting the news that an Italian physician, Dr. Daniele Petrucci, claimed in 1961 to have successfully artificially inseminated and kept a human embryo alive ex-uterus for twenty-nine days, the major newspaper of the Chinese Communist party responded favorably: "If children can be had without being borne, working mothers need not be affected by childbirth. This is happy news for women." (The Vatican, unsurprisingly, took the opposite view.)

In 1997, Dr. Yoshinori Kuwabara of Juntendo University in Japan removed a seventeen-week-old goat fetus from its mother's uterus and kept it alive for three weeks in an artificial womb by mimicking amniotic fluid and feeding it nutrients through a tube inserted in the umbilical cord.[10] Two decades later, in April 2017, researchers at the Children's Hospital of Philadelphia (CHOP) announced that they had successfully kept a lamb alive in an artificial womb to the equivalent gestational age of the minimum current viability of a human fetus, between twenty-three and twenty-four weeks.

CHOP's system involves a large, translucent, bag-like container filled with fluid that is attached to custom-designed machines providing support to allow the lamb fetus to continue normal growth in a temperature-controlled, near-sterile environment. The fetus breathes amniotic fluid as it normally does in the womb, its heart pumping blood through its umbilical cord into a gas exchange machine outside the bag. Electronic monitors measure vital signs, blood flow, and other crucial functions. CHOP's goal is to perfect the technique so that within three to five years extremely premature human fetuses can be transferred to an artificial womb—what they termed an "extra-uterine support device" in a press release—to complete gestation, avoiding the severe complications of early birth. "These infants have an urgent need for a bridge between the mother's womb and the outside world," said study leader Dr. Alan W. Flake, director of CHOP's Center for Fetal Research. "If we can develop an extra-uterine system to support growth and organ maturation for only a few weeks, we can dramatically improve outcomes for extremely premature babies."[11]

At the annual conference of the American Society for Reproductive Medicine in 2001, Dr. Helen Hung-Ching Liu of the Weill Medical College at Cornell University in Ithaca, New York, announced that she had engineered endometrial tissue to form on a uterus-shaped scaffold and successfully implanted a human embryo for six days. Such leaps are made on the shoulders of other designs that in some sense mimic the womb, such as the incubator (see p. 247) and early in vitro fertilization efforts (p. 69), in particular a genealogical arc of experiments conducted with rabbit eggs and sperm. The latter began with the work of the Viennese embryologist Samuel Leopold Schenk in 1878 and was concretized when two doctors, Gregory Pincus and John Rock (who would later partner in developing the oral contraceptive pill), published work on fertilizing mammalian eggs extracorporeally. Pincus wrote in 1934 on fertilizing rabbit eggs, and Rock (along with technician Miriam Menkin) introduced human sperm to human eggs in his lab in Boston in 1944, the fertilized egg dividing outside a human body.[12]

And yet, both CHOP and Cornell researchers are deeply reluctant to make their findings public, at pains to stay out of thorny debates about gestational viability, including those tied to abortion laws. As Christine Rosen, a writer on bioethics and the history of genetics for the *New Atlantis* points out, "studies of amniotic fluid and the possibilities of liquid ventilation; efforts to mimic the lining of the womb using human uterine cells and a cocktail of hormones; and [neonatolists] constantly pushing back the boundary of viability" for premature babies risk "giv[ing] birth to a technology we will live to regret."[13] Because artificial wombs are now designs within our reach, they, like other forms of biodesign, require ethical systems to be conceived in tandem with the new frontiers they augur.

While artificial wombs may one day serve as yet another tool in the arsenal of infertility treatments and benefit the thousands of preterm babies born each year, there are always dystopian flip sides, as a writer for *Fast Company* mused: power outages, psychological aftereffects, "super-strong mutated babies grown in secret military labs. Totalitarian governments using yield management…. Eugenically ideal, artisan-crafted babies that only the wealthiest among us can buy into existence…. Productizing pregnancy."[14]

In 1965, just a few years before Firestone's provocative call for liberation from biological labor, *Life* magazine ran a staggeringly beautiful series, "A Child Is Born," by the Swedish scientist Lennart Nilsson. It offered a window onto the fetus in utero in details never seen before. His camera framed fetuses as free-floating entities, their nascent veins, brains, and bones backlit to astonishing effect (see p. 85). They looked like independent organisms in a magical, liminal space. Except that they were all dead. His investigations were only possible using aborted fetuses as subjects, an irony, given that his images were subsequently used by pro-life campaigners. Therein lies the rub. Firestone recognized that the continuing struggle is not what a uterus, whether human or artificial, can produce but its legislative freedom from the heteropatriarchy.

This technology of the artificial womb goes beyond the commodification of pregnancy posed by surrogacy, foreshadowing the possible production of new human life for military or workforce purposes, for organ transplant harvesting or other types of medical research, or simply to be

—REPRODUCTION

designed and sold to the highest bidder. Descriptions and explorations of artificial wombs assume precisely controlled environments, but what happens if instead of worrying about existing pregnancy complications such as preeclampsia or harmful habits like smoking while pregnant, we instead must worry about power outages, price hikes on the necessary drugs, or the psychological weight of being "made" and not "born"? Dr. Flake is quoted in CHOP's 2017 press release as predicting that, only a decade from now, "extremely premature infants would continue to develop in chambers filled with amniotic fluid."[15] A brave new world is already on the horizon. Now, we must prepare to explore the ethical quandaries posed by such designs, and from the perspective of those who currently have the capacity to gestate and support this labor—for it is they who will be most impacted by the changes just ahead.

1 Shulamith Firestone, *The Dialectic of Sex: The Case for Feminist Revolution* (New York: Morrow, 1970), 199.
2 Firestone, *The Dialectic of Sex*, 216. She further explains (208), "A mother who undergoes a nine-month pregnancy is likely to feel that the product of all the pain and discomfort 'belongs' to her ('To think of what I went through to have you!'). But we want to destroy this possessiveness along with its cultural reinforcements so that no one child will be *a priori* favored over another, so that children will be loved for their own sake."
3 Edward Grossman, "The Obsolescent Mother," *The Atlantic* 227, no. 5 (May 1971): 39–50.
4 Alice Adams, "Out of the Womb: The Future of the Uterine Metaphor," in "Women's Bodies and the State," special issue, *Feminist Studies* 19, no. 2 (Summer 1993): 270.
5 Evie Kendal, *Equal Opportunity and the Case for State Sponsored Ectogenesis* (Basingstoke, UK: Palgrave Macmillan, 2015), Kindle edition, 4. Anyone interested in the subject of the artificial womb should seek out Kendal's work, which includes further articles on this topic.
6 Sophie Lewis, *Full Surrogacy Now* (London: Verso, 2019), 147.
7 Quoted in Christine Rosen, "Why Not Artificial Wombs?," *New Atlantis* 3 (Fall 2003): 67.
8 Aldous Huxley, *Brave New World* (New York: Harper Brothers, 1932), 1.
9 Adams, "Out of the Womb," 275.
10 Rosen, "Why Not Artificial Wombs?," 69.
11 Children's Hospital of Philadelphia, "A Unique Womb-Like Device Could Reduce Mortality and Disability for Extremely Premature Babies," *CHOP News*, April 25, 2017, chop. edu/publications/ chop-news.
12 Their collaborator, the reproductive biologist Chang Min-Chueh, managed to artificially inseminate a rabbit in 1959.
13 Rosen, "Why Not Artificial Wombs?," 69.
14 Noah Robischon, "This Crib Is Designed to Grow Babies Outside the Womb," *Fast Company*, June 26, 2017, fastcompany.com.
15 CHOP, "A Unique Womb-Like Device Could Reduce Mortality and Disability for Extremely Premature Babies."

HOME PREGNANCY TEST——The modern history of the home pregnancy test—the design that declared "my body, my choice"—and the many millions of people around the globe who have used one (or more) over the last five decades owe much to a New York–based graphic designer named Margaret "Meg" Crane.[1] Her revolutionary design has given the people who have used it (and its subsequent spin-offs) greater privacy over their reproductive status and more agency over decisions related to it.

In 1967, when Crane was working as a young graphic designer at the offices of the global pharmaceutical company Organon in West Orange, New Jersey, she wondered why the urine tests routinely performed in the company's labs to determine pregnancy status were not available for people's use at home. Observing long rows of test tubes suspended over mirrored surfaces, she learned from a bench technician that the process was relatively simple: urine was added to a chemical mixture and left to rest for two hours, during which time the tube could not be moved. The result could then be read in the mirrored reflection of the tube bottom: a red ring indicated pregnancy, and a milky substance the opposite. Familiar with medical equipment from childhood visits to the home of her physician grandfather, and keenly aware of the feminist conversations ablaze in that moment, she decided to put this relatively simple process directly into the hands of people who needed it.

Organon's (universally male) executives were initially reluctant to pursue the idea of an at-home test, aware that their customer base—doctors, mostly men—would fear having their authority undermined.[2] Crane continued to push until Organon's Dutch parent company, AKZO, gave her superiors start-up funds for a market test. Unbeknownst to her, Organon hired the Chicago-based advertising agency Foote, Cone & Belding to develop test prototypes. Having caught wind of this, she turned up at a meeting uninvited and placed her own prototype on the table next to their three. She had used her skills in packaging design to create a sleek, chic kit in a clear

The Predictor home pregnancy test kit, designed by Meg Crane in 1971

——PREGNANCY

perspex container that neatly and transparently housed the mirror, pipette, and liquids needed to carry out the diagnosis.[3] Foote, Cone & Belding's director, Ira Sturtevant, arrived late to the meeting, walked down the table and, bypassing the other prototypes bedecked with "feminine" bows and tassels, picked up Crane's. He declared it his preferred choice, and when Crane combed the Yellow Pages to find a plastics company that could make her product for one-third of what the agency design would cost to produce, the winner was clear.

The first home pregnancy test came to market in Canada and the UK in 1971 as the Predictor—in a campaign that Crane worked on with Sturtevant, who later became her studio partner and husband until his death in 2008. The product gradually became available in a number of other countries under various brand names. Members of the United States medical profession bitterly fought its rollout, suggesting women were incapable of monitoring their own health.[4] But it eventually passed US Food and Drug Administration (FDA) review, and in 1976 the American pharmaceutical company Warner Chilcott sought approval for a product they had developed based on Crane's design—e.p.t, or the Early Pregnancy Test, later known as the Error Proof Test. Debuting in 1977, e.p.t became the first

home pregnancy test kit on the market in the US, although several others were approved that same year, including Predictor, Accutest, and Answer. The test took the same two hours it had in the lab and was more accurate for positive results (97 percent) than for negative (80 percent).

Advertised in mainstream women's magazines, the design was a radical transferal of power from the doctor's office to the user at home. Advantages, noted *Mademoiselle* magazine (where the Predictor was advertised in 1978), included "privacy and not having to wait several more weeks for a doctor's confirmation, which gives you a chance, if pregnant, to start taking care of yourself ... or to consider the possibility of early abortion."[5] Meg Crane had created a product that, in her own words, allowed "women to look inside their own bodies and make their own decisions, without anyone else—husband, boyfriend, boss, or doctor—getting in the way."[6] The Predictor prototype was acquired by the Smithsonian's National Museum of American History in 2015.

Today, the Philadelphia-based start-up LIA is rethinking the pregnancy test as a plastic-free and über-discreet experience that flushes away shortly after use, reducing environmental

impact and increasing privacy. Classmates Bethany Edwards and Anna Couturier-Simpson cofounded LIA, along with their faculty advisor Sarah Rottenberg, in 2015 in the University of Pennsylvania's Integrated Product Design master's program, which combines design, engineering, and business education. The company name is a play on the scientific term *lateral immunoassay*, a type of rapidly readable strip test that debuted in 1988 with Unipath's Clearview product and has since become the prevalent design. This earlier form employed a latex-coated test created by compressing nonwoven fibers into a highly absorbent strip treated with different protein antibodies that change color upon contact with urine to signal pregnancy status.

LIA has developed a biodegradable paper that remains durable when in contact with urine—long enough for a test result to register—yet breaks down almost immediately when flushed. It is lighter than six sheets of two-ply toilet paper, and its unbranded packet reflects LIA's user research, which highlighted pregnancy discovery as a deeply private experience. Approved for commercial sale by the FDA in December 2017, the test is 99 percent accurate, cost-competitive with comparable plastic-based products, and won't end up in landfills.

1 Urine-based pregnancy tests are found in the historical record as early as Ancient Egypt, when urine from pregnant women was described as changing growth outcomes for wheat and barley seeds. In the late 1920s, scientists at the University of Pennsylvania discovered that when urine from a woman in early pregnancy is injected into immature female mice or rabbits, the animals' ovaries enlarge—hence the euphemism "the rabbit died" used for a positive pregnancy test.

2 As Meg recalled in 2018, "I brought the idea to the executives at Organon, thinking this could be a very successful product for them. But they were very negative. They would lose their 'doctor' business. Women should not be doing this test themselves. This was for the medical community to control. This would bring outrage by the religious community. On and on." Email from Meg Crane to the author, September 10, 2018.

3 While the container for Crane's prototype came from her desk (it had been used to hold paper clips) and was purchased from a Japanese handcraft store in New York called Azuma, it is a close copy of the American designer Gene Hurwitt's classic plastic containers sold by AMAC Plastic Products Corp. in Sausalito, California, from 1965 to 1966 and in the permanent collection of the Museum of Modern Art, New York.

4 As she noted, with five decades hindsight, "The test was controversial from the start.

At Organon, when it was decided to try a test market, there were people in the company that considered me to be a pariah, and the idea of women testing themselves to be something [just] short of immoral. Some people in the company refused to work on the project. But women had no problem buying the test. Doctors were concerned at the time about women not getting prenatal care, but my own hope was that the sooner a woman could know, the better the outcome would be.

In the package instructions, we hoped to convince women to see a doctor if she got a positive result. But I was really interested in the privacy of the test, and that a woman should be the first to know." Email from Meg Crane to the author, September 10, 2018.

5 *Mademoiselle*, April 1978, 86.

6 Pagan Kennedy, "Could Women Be Trusted with Their Own Pregnancy Tests?," *New York Times*, July 29, 2016, nytimes.com.

PRENATAL VITAMINS——The story of the prenatal vitamin began on a hunch, when Lucy Wills, a young British doctor and hematologist, fed a monkey Marmite. Wills could not have imagined how successful it would prove when she serendipitously stumbled on the salty British breakfast staple to treat the monkeys in her lab in Bombay (now Mumbai).

Wills had been recruited to India in 1928 to investigate why so many pregnant people, particularly poor textile workers, were suffering from severe and often fatal macrocytic anemia. Suspecting that pregnancy-related anemia was linked to nutrition, Wills asked a group of pregnant women to record their diets. She took her findings to the lab, where she fed rats and monkeys diets similar to those of the participants in her control group. When Wills added Marmite to a particularly undernourished monkey's diet, its red blood cell count improved dramatically. Marmite, a commercial yeast extract made as a byproduct of beer brewing, and a rich source of vitamins, was included in British soldiers' rations during World War I. Wills began giving Marmite to the other monkeys in her lab, and later offered it to the group of anemic pregnant participants in her study.[1] Their recoveries were remarkable. Clearly, whatever it was that Marmite had, pregnant people (and monkeys) needed it.

The unknown, so-called Wills' factor within yeasty Marmite (and crude liver, found to be similarly effective) was later identified as folate, or vitamin B9. Many people consume some natural folate on a daily basis; food sources include leafy green vegetables, citrus fruits, and legumes such as kidney beans and lentils. During and immediately after World War II, a heightened interest in food and nutrition gave rise to a new concern with prenatal health, as well as fetal growth and development, especially within the fields of biochemistry, physiology, and agriculture.[2] In 1941, biochemists in Texas were able to isolate and identify Wills'

The English hematologist and physician researcher Lucy Wills (1888–1964) at work in her lab in Bombay (now Mumbai)

factor in a lab by concentrating four tons of spinach.[3] (Spinach leaves are what give folic acid its name; *folium* is Latin for leaf.) In 1945, chemists at the American pharmaceutical company Lederle synthesized folic acid. Lederle's "new yellow vitamin" that "builds red blood cells" and "helps anemic expectant mothers" embodied the promises of biochemical blood manipulation.[4]

In the 1980s, a group of British researchers investigating birth defects discovered that folic acid was beneficial not only for pregnant people, but also for growing fetuses. Richard Smithells and his team led a study on folic acid's ability to prevent neural tube defects (NDTs), common congenital malformations that can lead to spina bifida or anencephaly.[5] Yet, they determined that, to effectively prevent NDTs, folic acid must be taken very early: a month before conception, to build up the body's store, and during the first weeks of pregnancy, a stage when many do not yet know they are pregnant. Public health organizations, mostly in the United States, Canada, and Britain, began running publicity campaigns urging doctors to prescribe folic acid and recommending that those who wished to become pregnant take daily folic acid supplements, just in case. In 1994, the United States added folic acid to the grain supply in an effort to ensure that those who became pregnant would not be folate deficient.[6]

Since the mid-1990s, governments and health organizations around the world have designed policies to increase dietary intake of folic acid before and during pregnancy in order to reduce the risk of birth defects in babies.[7] Yet, even as the globalization of biomedical knowledge has helped make folic acid a star in reducing this risk, experts have disagreed about not only mandatory folic acid fortification, but also whether synthetic folic acid is as beneficial as naturally occurring folate. Indeed, as many as 60 percent of Americans have genetic variations (known as methylenetetrahydrofolate reductase, or MTHFR) that reduce their ability to convert folic acid on their own, and so must take prenatal vitamins with food-based sources of folate.[8]

The fact that so many of us are encouraged, at an appropriate point, to swap our birth control pills for prenatal vitamins underscores many of the underlying issues in reproductive health care: the risks and benefits of highly medicalized and consumer-driven pregnancies, balancing individual and social responsibility, and the role of health education and body literacy. Perhaps the toughest pill to swallow is the fact that not everyone has access to the kind of food that supports healthy pregnancies and birth outcomes. Nutritional supplementation is seen as a magic bullet and is relied on heavily throughout the world, while many social and economic determinants of maternal and fetal health continue to be overlooked.

1 Lucy Wills, "The Nature of the Haemopoietic Factor in Marmite," *The Lancet* 221 (1933): 1283–86.
2 See the online exhibition *Making Visible Embryos*, by Tatjana Buklijas and Nick Hopwood, 2008–10, sites.hps.cam.ac.uk/visibleembryos.
3 Herschel K. Mitchell, Esmond E. Snell, and Roger J. Williams, "The Concentration of 'Folic Acid,'" *Journal of the American Chemical Society* 63, no. 8 (1941): 2284, doi.org/10.1021/ja01853a512.
4 Lederle Laboratories, *The Nutritional and Clinical Significance of Folic Acid* (New York: Lederle Laboratories, 1950); quoted in Salim Al-Gailani, "Making Birth Defects 'Preventable': Pre-Conceptional Vitamin Supplements and the Politics of Risk Reduction," Studies in *History and Philosophy of Biological and Biomedical Sciences* 47, pt. B (September 2014): 280, doi.org/10.1016/j.shpsc.2013.10.009.
5 Robert Smithells et al., "Possible Prevention of Neural Tube Defects by Periconceptional Vitamin Supplementation," *The Lancet* 315 (1980): 339–40, doi.org/10.1016/s0140-6736(80)90886-7.
6 Lara Freidenfelds, *The Myth of the Perfect Pregnancy: A History of Miscarriage in America* (Oxford: Oxford University Press, 2020), 106.
7 See Al-Gailani, "Making Birth Defects 'Preventable,'" 278–89.
8 James A. Greenberg et al., "Folic Acid Supplementation and Pregnancy: More than Just Neural Tube Defect Prevention," *Reviews in Obstetrics and Gynecology* 4, no. 2 (2011): 52–59.

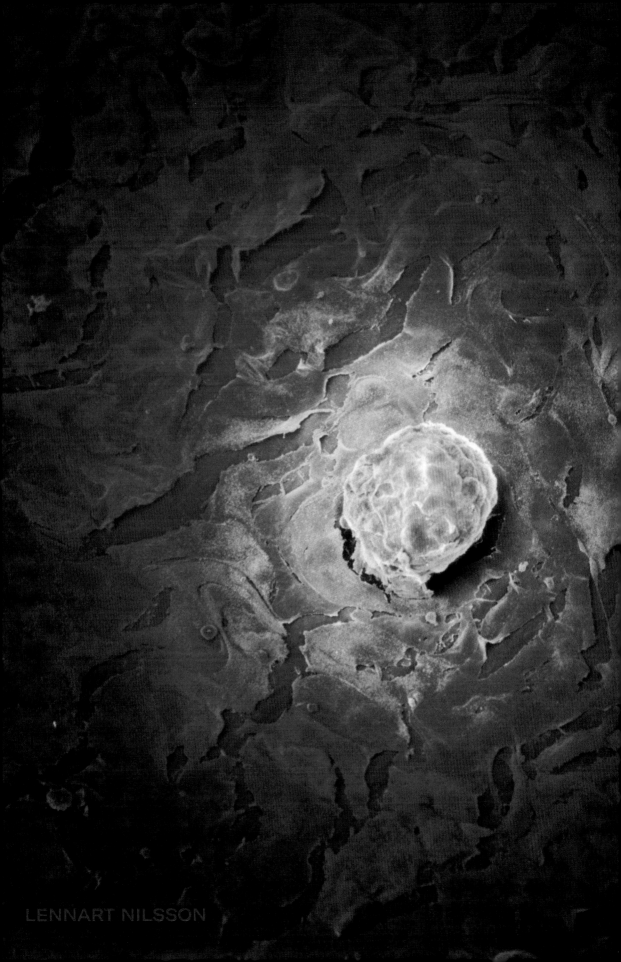

LENNART NILSSON On April 30, 1965, the Swedish photographer Lennart Nilsson published a suite of images of fetuses in utero in *Life* magazine. Taken with an endoscope, and spread over sixteen pages and the magazine cover, they represented more than a decade of experimentation with a photographic tool that allowed him to capture areas of the body formerly inaccessible to the human eye. Nilsson's work was published in book form as *A Child Is Born* in October 1965 and went through five updated editions in the following decades. While the endoscope technology improved so much that it could eventually be used to photograph living fetuses (often captured during procedures such as amniocentesis), some of Nilsson's subjects—especially during the early years of his project—were the result of fetal demise due to miscarriage or abortion.

1—— An eight-day-old human embryo implanted in the uterus imaged by a colored scanning electron micrograph (SEM)

2—— A human fetus in the amniotic sac, eleven weeks

3—— Human fetal legs at sixteen weeks. The fetus can now grab and pull the long umbilical cord. The skeleton consists mainly of flexible cartilage

4—— A human fetus in the amniotic sac, eighteen weeks. At this stage it measures approximately 14 cm. The fetus can now perceive sounds from the outside world

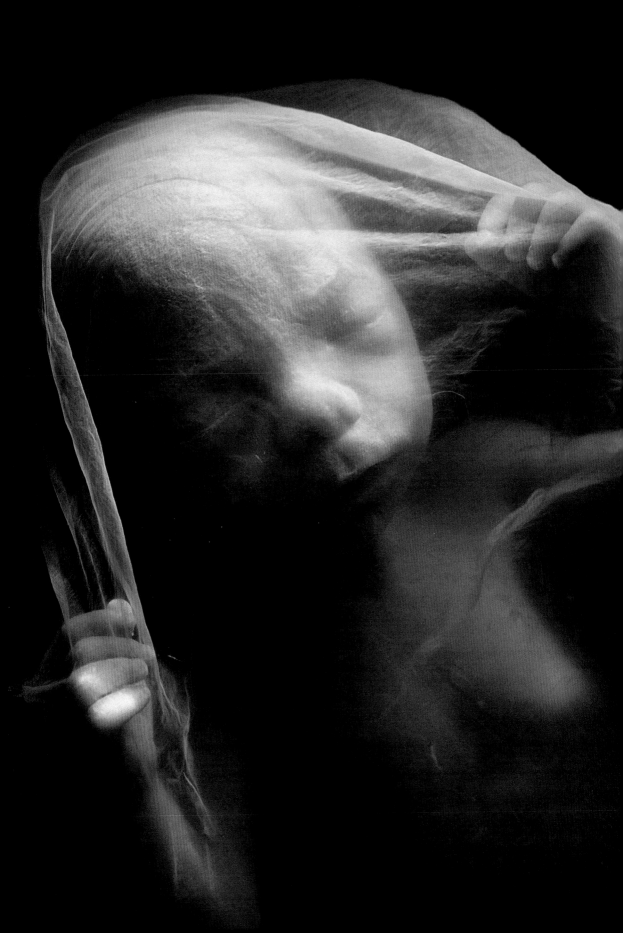

SONOGRAM——Scotland has given the world myriad designs that have irrevocably shaped modern life, including the telephone, the adhesive postage stamp, the bicycle, penicillin and insulin (Alexander Fleming's double whammy), and the television. In this very long list of inventions, one that is little known even by Scots themselves is obstetric ultrasound, developed in the 1950s in Glasgow and now one of the most common medical tools used during pregnancy across the globe.[1]

Ian Donald was the Regius Professor of Obstetrics and Gynaecology at the University of Glasgow in the 1950s, when he partnered with John MacVicar, an obstetrician at the city's Western Infirmary, and the industrial engineer Tom Brown to build various obstetric ultrasound scanner prototypes over nearly a decade of collaboration. In 1963, they produced the Diasonograph, the world's first commercial ultrasound scanner.

Utilizing sound waves with frequencies higher than the upper audible limit of the human ear, and measured in hertz (Hz), ultrasound technology had long been employed in Glasgow's industrial factories and shipyards.[2] A crucial moment in the design's development occurred in the spring of 1955, when the husband of one of Dr. Donald's patients who worked for a boiler fabrication outfit allowed the doctor to divert the company's industrial ultrasound technology from its usual deployment—checking for flaws in welds—to test whether it could differentiate between tissue samples (including an ovarian cyst and a juicy steak). It could.

Similarly applied to a pregnant human abdomen, the technology produced a dark oval with crackling shadows. The image offered a window into the uterus, with white lines indicating a placenta in formation and, at a nine-week scan, a fetal heartbeat pulsing away at about 140 beats a minute.

Donald, MacVicar, and Brown's article "Investigation of Abdominal Masses by Pulsed Ultrasound" was published by the esteemed medical journal *The Lancet* in 1958

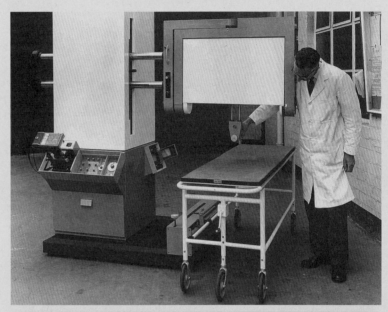

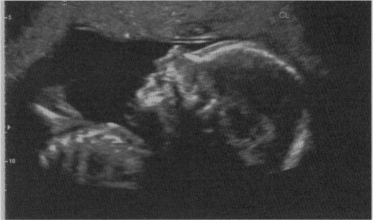

The first Diasonograph, built at Kelvin & Hughes at Hillington, Glasgow, c. 1964. Below, an example of a sonogram image in the twenty-first century

——PREGNANCY

following their years of research.[3] The transformation of the ultrasound echo into visual information allowed accurate dating of a pregnancy through correlation of fetal size with charts of normative growth trajectories, enabling more precise medical management of the patient and more accurate timing of biochemical tests, such as one made possible by another contemporaneously emerging technology, amniocentesis. Sonogram technology was taken up widely as machines dropped in price beginning in the 1970s. However, displacing embodied maternal knowledge in favor of scientific rationalization delivered by external machinery was resisted by some who saw it as part of a larger project of medicalization of pregnancy and birth that usurped a pregnant person's own intuition.

In 1961, a twenty-three-year-old industrial design graduate of the Glasgow School of Art, Dugald Cameron (who became its director in the 1990s), streamlined the apparatus in what was his first paid design commission after finishing his course of study.[4] Cameron had been recruited to figure out the problem of patient and physician comfort after the University Hospital in Lund, Sweden, placed an order based on an early version of the scanner developed by Donald and his colleagues. Cameron recalled needing to do some serious revision, given the menacing aspect of the prototype:

I thought it looked like a gun turret and that it was thoroughly inappropriate for pregnant ladies.... [W]hat we thought we ought to do was to separate out the patient, the doctor, and the machine and try and put these three things in a better

ergonomic relationship with one another. That was the first drawing which I had been commissioned to do, and for which I received an order for £21.[5]

Oral histories of the midwives and expectant mothers who experienced the first obstetric ultrasounds performed by Dr. Donald and his colleagues in Glasgow hospitals between 1963 and 1968 relay the wonder and delight of staff and patients alike. Pat Anusas, a young midwife who worked at the Queen Mother's Hospital between 1963 and 1965, recalls watching one of the early scans: "I still to this *day* can't believe what I saw... didn't know if it was going to work or not—but it did work. And both the mother and I were so excited—she couldn't believe she could see her baby."[6]

Right-to-life campaigners, in the United States in particular, have deployed ultrasound imagery as campaign propaganda and, recently, as an additional hurdle to be surmounted in some states before an abortion can be performed.[7] Lesser known is that Ian Donald held his own faith-based opposition to abortion. Dr. Deborah Nicholson, author of a comprehensive thesis on the medical history of obstetric ultrasound, notes that he "often performed ultrasound scans on women seeking terminations of pregnancy with the express intention of dissuading them from pursuing this action. In particular, the scan images would be shown to these women, while the implications of what was displayed on the image [were] carefully pointed out by the eminent professor using emotive language."[8]

While the black-and-white ultrasound image is immediately recognizable to many people, few meet the specialists—experts in anatomy, physics, and pattern recognition—who make these internal portraits. Dr. Tom Fitzgerald, formerly a general practitioner, began using ultrasound in 1982 at the Victoria Hospital in Glasgow before applying to train in radiology, a growing specialty at the time. As he notes, an ultrasound is more than a routine screening: "You're trying to get as much information about and for the patient as you can... even though most pregnancies don't need any intervention there's a small percentage that do. The earlier you find out that they do need some help, the better."[9]

Dr. Fitzgerald recalls the changes over the course of his career as relating not only to upgrades in technology but to improvements of the patient-radiographer relationship. Patients initially came in without their partners. Now three-dimensional scanning—which emerged from the work of Dr. Kazunori Baba at the University of Tokyo in the mid-1980s—offers the ability to visualize the unborn in increasingly lifelike ways, and whole families might turn up for the scan, viewing it as an event. In the early days the scan did not show movement, with the in-utero picture instead built up from many different still images, and the substrate between the transducer wand and the baby bump was olive oil, a messy medium since replaced by a clear, water-based gel.[10] Yet, as Dr. Fitzgerald outlines, breaking bad news when something atypical is detected or a heartbeat can't be found never gets easier. Ultrasound, he stresses, has always been and still is about empathy as much as technology.

1 For a comprehensive overview of the origin of obstetric ultrasound and the attendant public and medical debates over its use, see Malcolm Nicolson and John E. E. Fleming, *Imaging and Imagining the Fetus: The Development of Obstetric Ultrasound* (Baltimore: Johns Hopkins University Press, 2013).
2 "Although radar used electromagnetic waves rather than ultrasonic waves to determine obstacles and measure distances, it was a direct precursor of subsequent ultrasonic systems used in medicine in the later 1940s. In parallel, there had been the development, in the 1930's, of pulse-echo ultrasonic metal flaw detectors to check the integrity of armour plating in tanks, metal hulls in ships, and pressure vessels such as boilers and it was this industrial technology that was first adapted and used in the Glasgow experiments for the application of ultrasound for medical obstetrics purposes." Alastair S. Macdonald, "Ultrasound Scanning and Imaging, 1956–1972," in *Ultrasonic Glasgow: A Celebration of The Glasgow School of Art's Contribution to the History and Development of Medical Obstetrics Ultrasound* (report), The Glasgow School of Art, 2019, 6, radar.gsa.ac.uk/6988/1/Ultrasonic-report.pdf.
3 Ian Donald, John MacVicar, and Tom G. Brown, "Investigation of Abdominal Masses by Pulsed Ultrasound," *The Lancet* 272 (June 7, 1958): 1188–95, doi.org/10.1016/S0140-6736(58)91905-6.
4 *Ultrasonic Glasgow*, an exhibition held at the Glasgow School of Art in the fall of 2019, celebrated the creative design history of this landmark technology.
5 Alastair S. Macdonald, "From 'Gun Turret' to Diasonograph: The Dugald Cameron Archive," in *Ultrasonic Glasgow*, 10.
6 Susan Roan and Emma Keogh, "Human Echoes: An Oral Record of Women's Lived Experience of Ultrasound during Pregnancy in 1960s Glasgow," in *Ultrasonic Glasgow*, 35–36.
7 Usually in the form of a transvaginal ultrasound probe inserted into the vagina.
8 Deborah Nicholson, "Secrets of Success: The Development of Obstetric Ultrasound in Scotland, 1963–1990" (PhD thesis, University of Glasgow, 2003), 88, theses.gla.ac.uk/3400.
9 Tom Fitzgerald, interview with the author, September 2020.
10 "On the very first ever scans, it was actually olive oil that we used instead of gel. It was quite a messy business.... The water-based gels came later, and they were more expensive." Dr. Tom Fitzgerald, interview with the author, September 2020.

AMNIOCENTESIS——Pregnant with her first child at the ripe age of thirty-seven after several miscarriages, my mum voluntarily allowed a hypodermic needle to be inserted into her stomach a few months before she gave birth to me in the early 1980s. (I have always wondered if my significant fear of needles began in utero.) The procedure she underwent, known as amniocentesis, from the Greek *amnion* (the innermost membrane) and *kentein* (to prick), is a way to test for certain fetal abnormalities before birth.

The fluid that cushions a fetus during its gestational journey is a rich soup of genetic information that includes cells sloughed off by the fetus as it grows. About a decade before I was born, and following midcentury scientific experiments in several different labs, doctors began routinely to tap precious milliliters of this biological flotsam for use in genetic screening. Mum was one of many pregnant women over the age of thirty-five, categorized as "geriatric" mothers, whose fetuses had a statistically greater chance of chromosomal differences that might result in, among other things, Down's syndrome, cystic fibrosis, or spina bifida. So she agreed to have a needle plunged through her bulging abdomen, uterus, and into the amniotic sac that contained me.

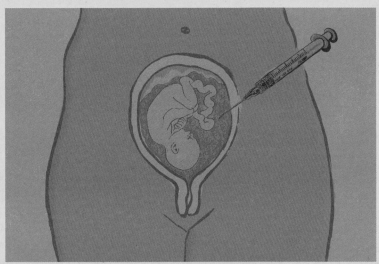

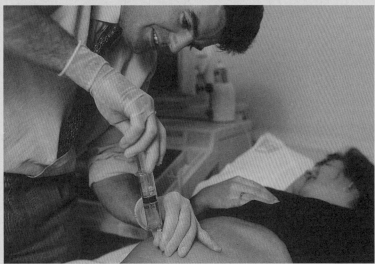

Illustration of amniocentesis and, below, the procedure being performed in a hospital, 1980s

Generally a short twenty- or thirty-minute outpatient procedure, amniocentesis is usually performed between fifteen and twenty weeks gestation, when the membrane around the fetus has consolidated. By that stage, too, the commitment to becoming a parent has become firm for many, and so when amniocentesis is refused it is often on religious or personal grounds. As one *New Yorker* writer reflected in 1980 after her own experience of waiting a month for the results, an amniocentesis test has the potential to "deeply violate the experience of a much wanted pregnancy," because in its shadow lies the prospect of termination—what has been called "the barely hidden interlocutor of all prenatal testing."[1]

Needle punctures to the amniotic sac were performed as early as the 1870s for the purpose of alleviating the problem of excessive amniotic fluid, and in 1930 in order to visualize the placenta. But the test as we know it today emerged from research into fetal well-being undertaken by Robert Lisle Gadd, a Manchester obstetrician who presented his results at the William Blair Bell Memorial Lecture at the Royal College of Obstetricians and Gynaecologists in London on May 28, 1965.[2] Gadd's codifying of the procedure was a capstone for other research trajectories. In 1949, for example, a research team led by the Canadian anatomist Murray Lewellyn Barr discovered that when two X chromosomes are present in embryonic cells, one is typically inactive and forms a chromatin mass—now termed a "Barr body" —observable under a microscope. This made it easier to detect instances of sex-linked diseases in amniotic fluid.[3]

In 1966 scientists successfully cultured fetal cells to allow karyotyping—the ability to determine the number and visual appearance of the chromosomes in the cell nuclei—thus tying the ability to access amniotic fluid to the possibility of predicting certain disabilities and hereditary diseases. Today, the world's first amniotic stem cell bank operates in Boston, where individuals can store personal reserves of this biological material with an eye to the cultivation of future cells that can be deployed in personalized medical remedies for as-yet-undiagnosed diseases.

Early amniocentesis was performed "blind," but once it was paired with ultrasound for guidance in the early 1970s (thanks to Danish doctors Jens Bang

and Allen Northeved), infection, fetal injury, and miscarriage were minimized, and the test became more widely available. By the mid-1970s, US public health officials declared that the procedure had "move[d] clearly from the realm of a research procedure to a part of clinical practice," and they urged its use—in terms that framed disability as an economic and social burden:

One of the main points of emphasis in the Department of Health, Education, and Welfare is prevention of disability. By focusing on prevention, we increase the resources available for other programs.... We can now assure the older woman who is pregnant that she need not fear birth of a child with Down's syndrome.... We can assure couples who are carriers of Tay-Sachs disease that they can have normal children without facing the agonizing process of helplessly watching an affected child slowly die.[4]

An international study has suggested that in diagnoses of Down's syndrome, abortion rates are over 90 percent (more recent, US-only statistics hover at around two-thirds of pregnant people opting for termination).[5] Thus the biomedical capture of *liquor amnii* has come to define not only personal pregnancy outcomes but wider cultural values around chromosomal differences, disability, and disease, positioning pregnant people as "'moral pioneers' ...recruited as judges of standards for entry into the human community."[6]

In a landmark study conducted between 1984 and 1993 in

New York City, and spurred in part by her own experiences, the cultural anthropologist Rayna Rapp investigated the decision-making processes and outcomes related to this new technology. Her approach was in the tradition of projects such as *Our Bodies, Ourselves* (see p. 31) that centered women and their voices in direct contrast to health officials who skewed overwhelmingly male, White, scientific, and ableist in approach. She nailed the test's knotty intersection: the technological transformation of pregnancy, the crossover between reproductive and disability rights, and, raising the specter of eugenics, the "idea that science and technology provide positive resources for improving or even perfecting life."[7] The latter ethos frames women as "Wise Shoppers" who view amniocentesis as another purchase through which to optimize pregnancy and motherhood.[8]

In the two decades since Rapp's landmark scholarship, disability justice advocates have brought language and attitudes around disability—including around prenatal testing—into a new millennium. Challenging narrow perceptions of what constitutes a life worth living, as well as ableist attitudes and contemporary eugenics, their work has moved genetic testing into the more complex and richer realm of lived experience.

My mum was never faced with a "positive" result, and she kept the pregnancy that resulted in me. She became disabled herself just a few years after my birth, an anecdotal confirmation of the general truth that personhood is not a statistical, static concept but something always becoming.

1 Suzannah Lessard, "The Talk of the Town, Notes and Comment," *New Yorker*, August 11, 1980.
2 The subsequent publication by Henry L. Nadler and Albert Gerbie, "Role of Amniocentesis in the Intrauterine Diagnosis of Genetic Defects," *New England Journal of Medicine* 282, no. 11 (1970), put the procedure on the map.
3 Given its potential to determine sex, amniocentesis is restricted in countries where it is used electively by parents who wish to

abort female fetuses. For example, in India, the Pre-Conception and Pre-Natal Diagnostic Techniques (PCPNDT) Act of 1994 prohibits the use of technologies for sex selection before or after conception and regulates their sale to registered bodies only; violations carry a stiff penalty of up to three years imprisonment and a 10,000 rupee fine.
4 Theodore Cooper, "Implications of Findings from the Amniocentesis Registry for Public Policy," *Public Health Reports* 91, no. 2 (March–April

1976), 116. Cooper, then Assistant Secretary for Health, US Department of Health, Education, and Welfare, continued: "Medicine is often criticized for the lag between development of an advance and the time it becomes generally available to the public. Let this not be the case with amniocentesis.... Few advances compare with amniocentesis in their capability for prevention of disability.... Physicians and women must know about amniocentesis, its indications and its potential benefits, so that

pregnant women who wish to do so can avail themselves of this procedure." His paper was based on an address he gave on October 20, 1975, to a symposium of the American Academy of Pediatrics in Washington, DC.
5 Rayna Rapp, "Refusing Prenatal Diagnosis: The Meanings of Bioscience in a Multicultural World," in "Anthropological Approaches in Science and Technology Studies," special issue, *Science, Technology, & Human Values* 23, no. 1 (Winter

1998): 60. See also Rayna Rapp, *Testing Women, Testing the Fetus: The Social Impact of Amniocentesis in America* (New York: Routledge, 1999).
6 Janelle S. Taylor, Linda L. Layne, and Danielle F. Wozniak, *Consuming Motherhood* (New Brunswick, NJ: Rutgers University Press, 2004), 68.
7 Rapp, *Testing Women, Testing the Fetus*, 3.
8 See Taylor, Layne, and Wozniak, *Consuming Motherhood*.

FETAL DOPPLER AND PINARD HORN——The volume on the Doppler fetal monitor was turned all the way up, and my lower abdomen was slathered in clear goo. My midwife maneuvered the sensor on my belly with her eyes fixed ahead, like a driver shifting from fourth to fifth gear. When she found her position through a forest of static a deep *whoosh, whoosh, whoosh* filled the room. The sound coursed through me like a revelation.

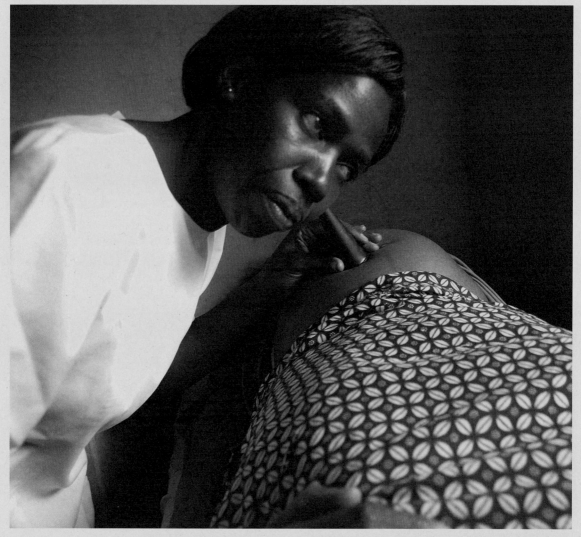

A Pinard fetoscope in use in Kenya, 2011

——PREGNANCY

Before I heard her heartbeat at around ten weeks gestation, connecting with my unborn baby was a bit like trying to remember a dream. She was real, but also completely theoretical. I felt her presence intensely and may even have spoken to her, though never out loud. But the Doppler filled the room with her—with her strong, steady, *loud* heartbeat.

I was listening to my midwife's handheld Doppler, a device that amplifies the fetal heartbeat, projecting it out through a speaker. The physician and inventor Dr. Edward H. Hon was at the forefront of developing fetal heart-rate monitors, using ultrasound in his design of the fetal Doppler in 1958. Long before this, practitioners had listened for fetal heart rates on Pinard horns, or fetoscopes. Part stethoscope, part ear trumpet, the Pinard is a simple horn-shaped object made of wood or metal. Both the Doppler and the Pinard are effective, but the glaring difference between them is *who* gets to hear the sound. Only the doctor or midwife employing the Pinard horn can detect the heartbeat, and must listen closely to hear anything at all. The Doppler's electronic audio output, on the other hand, enables practitioners, parents, and anyone in the room to hear the amplified sound.

When the French obstetrician Adolphe Pinard designed his fetal stethoscope in 1895 the device revolutionized medicine, but it was also just one step removed from pushing one's ear up against a pregnant belly. The Pinard horn is uncomplicated, inexpensive, and unquestionably safe. Unlike the Doppler, it doesn't require batteries or external power sources, and no special training is needed to use it.[1] Although the Pinard horn is all but obsolete in the United States, its simple design is an unofficial favorite of midwives, still used everywhere from Mali to Denmark. As one Mexican midwife explained the preference, "the Doppler often transmits a lot of noise: it gets confusing. So [it's] better with the Pinard."[2]

These days, Dopplers are sold online for use at home, and much of the marketing has to do with alleviating parental anxiety between prenatal appointments. The company Heartbeats at Home claims its fetal heart monitors are "simply the best way to gain the assurance and peace of mind every pregnant women desires," while UnbornHeart provides smartphone- and tablet-connected fetal Dopplers that "help reduce anxiety…and can offer reassurance for a pregnant mom."[3] Yet providers and advocacy groups have cried foul on the devices. They warn that users might be falsely reassured by the sound of the placenta or even their own heartbeats, and they emphasize that only trained professionals can properly interpret the sounds the devices pick up. Since ultrasounds of any kind can slightly heat body tissue, the US Food and Drug Administration calls for "prudent" use of the Doppler, recommending that they be employed only when there is a medical need, and only under expert supervision. "The number of sessions or the length of a session in scanning a fetus is uncontrolled [when Dopplers are used at home], and that increases the potential for harm to the fetus and eventually the mother,"[4] the FDA warns. By contrast, fetal movement counting, often called kick counting, is eminently safe for home use and requires no devices. You simply count the number of kicks in a given period, a first-line indicator of fetal health.

The similarly low-tech Pinard horn doesn't get much love from obstetricians and consumers in many industrialized countries, but in cultures where technology is less pervasive and pregnancy is treated less invasively, it is seen as a safe and effective tool for providers and parents. All the same, the Doppler was a true twentieth-century groundbreaker, and the design laid the foundation for another groundswell in maternal health care—consistent fetal monitoring during labor. But beyond being a game changer in fetal and obstetric medicine, the Doppler also gave parents the wonderfully novel opportunity to hear the sound of their unborn child's heartbeat.

As innovative as the Doppler is, many patients prefer the Pinard horn. "I felt at ease because I was surrounded by people who were calm and experienced and seemed to have everything under control, so the fact that I couldn't hear or experience the heartbeat myself, or see anything on a monitor, felt comfortable," Julie Cirelli, an American writer and editor who gave birth in Copenhagen, told me. "I had had plenty of 'high-tech' hospital visits where I felt cold, lost, and exposed, and this [appointments with midwives and use of the Pinard] by comparison was calm and comforting. Plus, the high-tech hospital equipment was really shitty! Half the time, I'd be at the larger hospital and they'd take inaccurate measurements or not be able to find the heartbeat for a moment, and it would be terrifying. The low-tech stuff was reliable and instant."[5]

1   Another reason why some favor the Pinard horn over the Doppler is that the device helps to determine fetal positioning. A Pinard horn must be pressed to a location very close to the fetal heart in order to detect a heartbeat, making it easy to determine fetal placement.
2   Robbie E. Davis-Floyd et al., eds., *Birth Models That Work* (Oakland: University of California Press, 2009), 9.
3   See the company websites at unbornheart.com. and heartbeatsathome.com
4   US Food and Drug Administration, "Avoid Fetal 'Keepsake' Images, Heartbeat Monitors," December 16, 2014, fda.gov.
5   Julie Cirelli, email conversation with the author conducted February 28, 2020."

ANTI-RADIATION CLOTHING—While many consumer groups are susceptible to fear-based product marketing, parents-to-be are particularly easy targets. Anti-radiation maternity clothing is a product sold to pregnant people as a precautionary measure, often in places where nuclear disaster lives in the collective memory and new radiation-emitting technologies abound. Yet the fear of radiation may be more real than the actual threat of significant exposure.

Health-related anxieties, both general and specific, are extremely common during and immediately after pregnancy, and radiation fears have a decades-long history. Amid a slew of articles addressing the nuclear fears common in the mid-twentieth century, *Life* magazine advertised radiation detectors to the readers of its March 18, 1957, issue—including a pocket dosimeter, a Geiger counter, and an ion chamber—priced between 25¢ and $167, "for the public or civil defense personnel" to "indicate the presence of radiation and…easily carried on the person."

For many today, especially in Asian countries, anti-radiation garments are seen as a valid precautionary measure for ensuring the health of pregnant people and their fetuses, equivalent to adopting other steps like abstaining from alcohol and unpasteurized food, taking prenatal vitamins, and exercising.[1] Historically, fears of radiation have been linked to nuclear arms, but contemporary parents now fret over radiation-emitting devices at home and in the workplace. While the side effects of wireless radiation have yet to be fully determined—claims include mobile-phone radiation causing cancer and interfering with sperm quality and count[2]—online retailers such as Taobao and companies like Belly Armor and Lambs produce blankets, maternity apparel, baby hats, and men's boxer briefs that they market with slogans like "keep the bad off your goods" and "advanced protection, everyday comfort, healthier you."

Most anti-radiation maternity garments act as a shield over the baby bump, either in the form of an apron-like dress or as an

A DUOYA brand antiradiation garment that retails on the popular Chinese website Taobao

elasticated wrap worn as a foundation garment or as a wide belt over clothing. Retailing for between fifty and a couple of hundred dollars apiece, they are usually lined with silver fibers that purportedly deflect electromagnetic waves. They often feature cutesy bows or childlike patterns, or are sold in bland colors, making clear that in this product category function usually wins out over aesthetics.

Product testers of anti-radiation clothing report, among other phenomena, wrapping their cell phone in it and seeing its signal disappear, suggesting that the products do their job. But in December 2011, a controversy arose in China on a popular news program of the state-owned China Central Television, when it investigated the anti-radiation clothing industry and concluded that although its maternity clothing was effective at blocking many electromagnetic waves, such designs might also deflect and intensify radiation on parts of the body not covered by the clothing. The subsequent public outcry was followed by a temporary dip in sales.[3]

Those who wear anti-radiation garments during pregnancy are often culturally predisposed to be concerned about radiation at all life stages, an anxiety born of historical calamity. Such fear of ionizing radiation has been termed by some *radiophobia* or (particularly in Japan) framed as an "atomic allergy."[4] Its genesis was the terrible fallout after atomic bombs were dropped on Hiroshima and Nagasaki at the end of World War

II, and it was further cemented by the subsequent testing of thermonuclear devices on Bikini Atoll in the Marshall Islands in the 1950s. In the latter experiment, the Japanese tuna trawler *Lucky Dragon No. 5* became collateral damage when post-blast nuclear dust, traveling much farther than anticipated, rained down on the members of its crew, who suffered acute radiation syndrome.

The world last saw anti-radiation protective gear on display en masse after a record earthquake and tsunami struck Japan, causing extensive damage, including to the Fukushima Daiichi Nuclear Power Station. A crew of tens of thousands of workers undertook remedial action after leakage occurred to bring radiation down to safe levels by scraping off topsoil, hosing down streets, and wiping down the exterior of buildings. The wipes and protective clothing were collected for separate incineration.[5]

These man-made atrocities and calamities translated into pervasive cultural anxieties, engendering psychological effects in the popular imagination that were as potent, if not more so, than the actual levels of radiation that populations were exposed to in later generations. One enduring image came from the 1954 Tōhō film *Gojira*, which depicted the original Godzilla as an enormous, terrifying prehistoric sea monster awakened from the depths and made powerful by nuclear radiation. But there have also been many tragically concrete aftereffects of nuclear fallout. Following

the 1986 disaster at the Chernobyl Nuclear Power Station in what was then the Ukrainian Soviet Socialist Republic, the radioactive iodine released was absorbed by, among other links in the ecosystem, cows and chickens that were then consumed by humans in milk and eggs, leading to an increase in thyroid cancer. During the mass displacement of people living in and near Chernobyl, pregnant women in those communities were advised to have abortions.[6] In Denmark, public fear of radiation traveling across European countries spurred some elective abortion even though there were negligibly low radiation levels in that country.[7]

Today, some of the most interesting designs for protective clothing can be found in Adam Harvey's Stealth Wear line of garments, which are made not to protect from radiation during pregnancy but for those worried about the pervasive CCTV, cellphone tracking, and facial-recognition technologies deployed worldwide (the garments block thermal radiation as a means of countering such surveillance). While those who are pregnant and new parents will always be receptive consumers of these types of products, the market for anti-radiation designs has multiplied exponentially with the advent of such surveillance methods. In future generations of maternity wear, it may well be not only possible but desirable to protect against radiation for reasons of privacy as much as health.

1 "Ask Uncle Wang," *Global Times*, Metro Shanghai section, August 6, 2013, globaltimes.cn.
2 See Igor Gorpinchenko, Oleg Nikitin, Oleg Banyra, and Alexander Shulyak, "The Influence of Direct Mobile Phone Radiation on Sperm Quality," *Central European Journal of Urology* 67, no. 1 (2014): 65–71, doi.org/10.5173/ceju.2014.01.art14.
3 Experiments conducted by the Chinese Academy of Sciences found that the clothing actually increased exposure by trapping radiation inside, much

like a greenhouse. "Experimental results show that under real life circumstances…the anti-radiation clothing intensifies the radiation…. When the electromagnetic waves get inside the garment from other directions, there are no outlets for them to be dispersed." Cited in translation in Mathilde Paquet, "Dress To Protect," *Unmapped Magazine* 6 (2014), unmappedmag.com/issue-6.
4 After the Chernobyl disaster, residents furiously rejected the term *radiophobia*. Adolph

Kharash, the science director at Moscow State University, wrote: "For those who were at the epicenter of the Chernobyl cataclysm this word is a grievous insult. It treats the normal impulse to self-protection, natural to everything living, your moral suffering and your anguish and your concern about the fate of your children, relatives and friends, and your own physical suffering and sickness as a result of delirium, of pathological perversion." Kharash, "A Voice from Dead Pripyat," on the website of Professor.

Paul Brians, Washington State University, translated from *The Chernobyl Poems*, December 5, 2016, brians.wsu.edu/2016/12/05/a-voice-from-dead-pripyat. See also Shi-Lin Loh, "The Origins of Japan's 'Nuclear Allergy,'" *Sources and Methods* (blog), History and Public Policy Program, Wilson Center, January 28, 2019, wilsoncenter.org
5 Fred Pearce, "In Fukushima, A Bitter Legacy Of Radiation, Trauma and Fear," *Yale Environment 360*, September 16, 2019, e360.yale.edu/features.

6 Evelyn J. Bromet et al., "Somatic Symptoms in Women 11 Years after the Chernobyl Accident: Prevalence and Risk Factors," *Environmental Health Perspectives* 110, suppl. 4 (August 2002): 625.
7 See L. B. Knudsen, "Legally-Induced Abortions in Denmark after Chernobyl," *Biomedicine & Pharmacotherapy* 45, no. 6 (1991): 229–31, doi.org/10.1016/0753-3322(91)90022-L.

SHOWING

SHOWING Showing can be bold, empowering, and beautiful; it can also be deeply gendered, uncomfortably idealized, and a sometimes impermissible sign of sexuality. But whether one hides a bump in capacious folds of fabrics or wears it proudly on a fashion runway, to show (or not show) a pregnancy is to engage in a dialectic in which social expectations burn as brightly as the truth of our bodily experiences.

1—— Frankie Smith shot by Arrows for the latter's 2017 documentary, *My Mama Wears Timbs*
2—— MCC lactation consultant Porsche Holland at her babyshower, 2017
3—— Sarah wading in Fish Eating Creek, 1980
4—— Artist Jamie Diamond pregnant with her daughter during the pandemic, 2020
5—— Showing, 1990s
6—— Popping a hip, 1980s
7—— Amber's mom pregnant with Amber, Miami, Florida, 1981

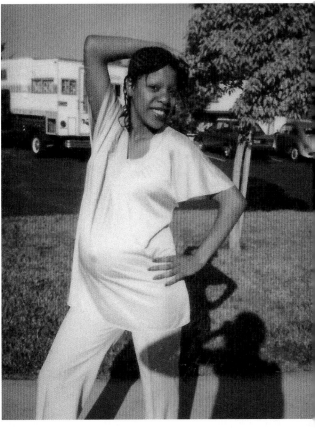

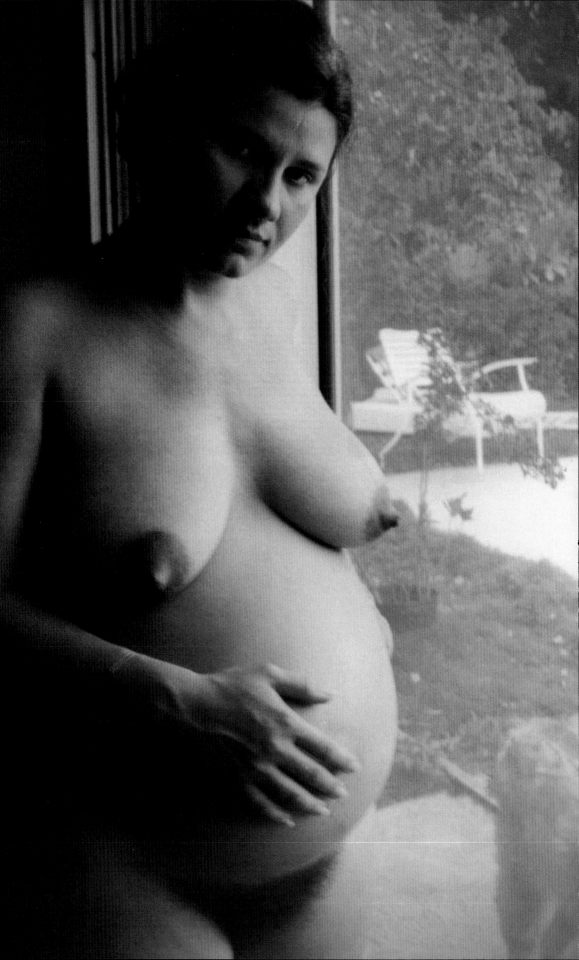

PREGNANCY CORSET——The corset is widely viewed today as an instrument of torture, oppression, and sexual exploitation, but for over four hundred years, from the Renaissance to the liberated 1960s, it was for many women in Europe and the United States "a lifetime companion, fitted in early childhood and worn until death."[1] Made from an armature of whalebone or metal stays encased in cotton, linen, silk, or satin and laced with ribbon or cord, the corset was used to reshape the figure in the image of each era's prevailing beauty ideal.

Its design thus reveals much about the complex and often contradictory expectations that have been brought to bear on pregnant bodies from the moment of conception through the postpartum period.

Although the idea of wearing a corset—an object designed to cinch, compress, and reshape the abdomen—during pregnancy may instinctually strike some as odd or even dangerous, the practice dates back to at least the fifteenth century and persisted well into the twentieth. As fashion scholar Catriona Fisk has documented, contrary to popular belief women were not "confined to invisible domestic worlds" during pregnancies in the past.[2] Life for all but the most wealthy went on as usual. Among working women, dress was used to negotiate the expectations of appropriate femininity within the physical realities of pregnancy. As a mainstay of fashionable dress and the "physical embodiment of solid virtue, decent self-control and respectability,"[3] the corset remained a woman's "companion" even through the gestation period, albeit with slight design modifications.

Maternity wear is typically understood as clothing designed specifically for pregnant people and is a relatively new category that emerged only with the advent of mass manufacturing in the late nineteenth century. An early pregnancy corset was therefore little more than a woman's everyday corset altered to fit her expanding form. From the fifteenth to the seventeenth century, the most common and economical adaption involved sewing ever-wider

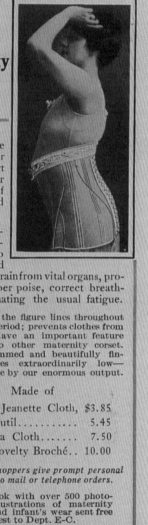

Lane Bryant

Maternity Corset

FOR the greater comfort and better health of mother and child.

Scientifically constructed to support and relieve all strain from vital organs, producing proper poise, correct breathing, eliminating the usual fatigue.

Harmonizes the figure lines throughout the entire period; prevents clothes from binding. Have an important feature found in no other maternity corset. Daintily trimmed and beautifully finished. Prices extraordinarily low—made possible by our enormous output.

Made of

Durable Jeanette Cloth, $3.85
Dijon-Coutil........... 5.45
Alexandra Cloth....... 7.50
Fancy Novelty Broché.. 10.00

Our expert shoppers give prompt personal attention to mail or telephone orders.

Season book with over 500 photographic illustrations of maternity apparel and infant's wear sent free upon request to Dept. E-C.

Lane Bryant
25 West 38th Street,   New York

Advertisement for Lane Bryant's maternity corset in an April 1915 issue of *Vogue* magazine

——PREGNANCY

stomachers to fill the gap in front-lacing corsets, while in the eighteenth century side laces were used to retain that era's fashionable long-waisted silhouette. It was only in the mid-nineteenth century that corsets designed to be worn exclusively during pregnancy emerged, identifiable by a profusion of "laces, press studs, flaps, buttons, [and] the directional use of boning."[4]

Pregnant women of the Victorian era were expected to hide their distended forms from public view, and a specially designed pregnancy corset "worked to contain and imprison the unruly, fecund body, giving it the appearance of taking up less space, of appearing less 'offensively' pregnant."[5] At the same time, moralists and some medical practitioners decried the potentially injurious side effects of corset wearing (specifically the marginal practice of tight-lacing) during pregnancy, which included miscarriage and stillbirth.[6] Taboos around discussing pregnancy and the Victorians' veneration of virginal femininity, however, prevented doctors from discussing their concerns openly, leaving women to resolve conflicting societal and medical expectations privately.

Patents and advertisements published in the late nineteenth and early twentieth centuries evidence a marked shift in the purported function and utility of pregnancy corsets. Breathable, elasticized "health" and "sport" corsets that promised freedom of movement

began to appear in the pages of fashion magazines. A 1913 advertisement for a maternity corset by H. W. Gossard Co. reflects this shift, making the claim that its model—"endorsed by physicians"—provided "perfect abdominal support" for "better babies."[7] However, like their predecessors, these manufacturers seemed willing to make concessions to fashion. Lane Bryant, while claiming in a 1915 advertisement that their "scientifically constructed" pregnancy corset was designed to "relieve all strain from vital organs, producing proper poise, correct breathing, [and] eliminating the usual fatigue," also noted that it "harmonizes the figure lines throughout the entire period" and "prevents clothes from binding."[8]

Articles published in the trade media at midcentury suggest that the practice of wearing pregnancy corsets was beginning to fall out of fashion. Despite growing consensus among doctors that abdominal support could help alleviate pelvic and back pain, *Women's Wear Daily* reported a sharp decline in the sale of pregnancy corsets and "surgical" girdles in 1953 owing to consumers' preference for light support or no support at all.[9] This shift in thinking was appropriately reflected in maternity fashions of the era. With the abandonment of any pretense that pregnant women should attempt the dangerously wasp-waisted midcentury silhouette, maternity fashions adopted a loose silhouette that

all but eliminated reshaping of the figure (see Tie-Waist Skirt, p. 103).

Demi Moore's infamous and oft-imitated 1991 *Vanity Fair* cover shoot encapsulates contemporary attitudes toward abdominal support during pregnancy (see Pregnancy Portraits, p. 129). In addition to challenging taboos surrounding the visibility and representation of the pregnant body in Western media, the image idealizes the notion (albeit glamorized) of an unbound, unburdened, physically fit, self-sufficient pregnancy. Heavily pregnant, Moore cradles her perfectly symmetrical bump in a gentle self-embrace that makes it appears weightless. Maternity fashions in the late twentieth century assumed a similar weightlessness, as body-skimming, lightweight stretch fabrics increasingly dominated the marketplace. Today, many women don't try to hide their pregnant bellies but rather brandish them proudly (but only as part of a body that is sufficiently slim and toned). In this context Moore's cradling gesture has become a visual shorthand for pregnancy—the only abdominal support a woman should need, perhaps—while elasticized support belts and girdles have become objects of last resort, discussed on mommy blogs and medical forums but used only when the weight of pregnancy has become too much to bear.

—**Lauren Downing Peters**

1 Leigh Summers, *Bound to Please: A History of the Victorian Corset* (London: Berg, 2001), 4–5. See also Valerie Steele, *The Corset: A Cultural History* (New Haven: Yale University Press, 2003), 1.
2 Catriona Fisk, "Looking for Maternity: Dress Collections and Embodied Knowledge," *Fashion Theory* 23, no. 3 (2019): 427, doi. org/10.1080/136270 4X.2019.1603871.
3 Harriet Waterhouse, "A Fashionable Confinement: Whaleboned Stays and Pregnant Women," *Costume* 41, no. 1 (2007): 56, doi.org/10.1179/174963007X182336.
4 Fisk, "Looking for Maternity," 426.
5 Summers, *Bound to Please*, 42.
6 Melis Mulazimoglu Erkal, "The Cultural History of the Corset and Gendered Body in Social and Literary Landscapes," *European Journal of Language and Literature Studies* 3, no. 3 (2017): 111, dx.doi. org/10.26417/ejls.v9i1. p109-118.
7 H. W. Gossard Co. advertisement, *Vogue*, October 15, 1913, 127.
8 Lane Bryant advertisement, *Vogue*, April 15, 1915, 113.
9 Sydney Stanton, "Medical Referrals a Key in Maternity Corset Selling," *Women's Wear Daily*, September 17, 1953, 15.

TIE-WAIST SKIRT——On December 8, 1952, less than a year after her television series debuted to audiences in the United States on the CBS network, the eponymous star of *I Love Lucy* opened the tenth episode of the show's second season complaining of feeling a little "blah." Standing by a mantelpiece in her TV home, Lucy (played by actress Lucille Ball) told her friend and neighbor Ethel that she was off to the doctor to figure out her unexplained fatigue, weight gain, and general malaise.

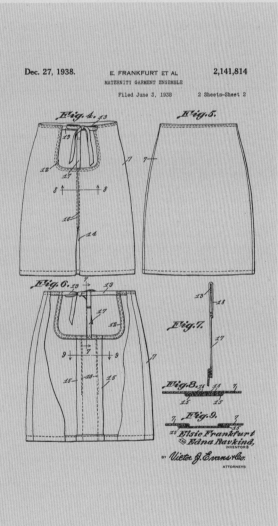

A pregnant Lucille Ball grapples with impending parenthood in a 1952 episode of *I Love Lucy* titled "Pregnant Women Are Unpredictable." On the right, the 1939 patent for Elsie Frankfurt's tie-waist skirt, the first design by the maternity clothing company Page Boy, which Frankfurt started with her sister

——**PREGNANCY**

Clever Ethel's expression shifted almost immediately from concern to elation, and after a beat she exclaimed, "Lucy, you're going to have a baby!"

In Lucy's midcentury cultural moment, the adjective that properly described her state was conspicuously missing, for both on-screen and off-screen the script for those "in the family way" was carefully calibrated. The word *pregnant* was considered so indecent that the episode was titled "Lucy Is Enceinte," purloining from the French to add a veneer of gentility. Had audiences reached immediately for their Merriam-Webster's, they would have found that Lucy's condition was being summed up *en français* by a word that denoted "the enclosing wall of a fortified place," a perfect connection to that other public mother figure, Mary, and her virgin conception so often signified in early Christian visual art by a verdant, fecund walled garden.

Cue the tie-waist skirt, the design that played a crucial role in normalizing public pregnancy. It was a midcentury maternity game changer. Hugely popular between 1939, just after it was patented, and 1959, the year that stretchy Lycra fabric was invented, the tie-waist skirt became a seminal garment for its ability to address the concerns of polite society, where maternity clothes were meant to function as—in the words of a 1928 *Vogue* editorial— "miracles of concealment."[1]

With a large U-shape cut out at its top where the skirt met the waistband, the design had a drawstring flexibly encircling the growing belly, while a vertical tab connected the skirt to one of a series of snaps on the waistband. As pregnancy progressed, the vertical tab could be let out and fastened to the next snap in the series, adjusting for fit while maintaining an even hemline. The tie around the waist, meanwhile, could be let out as the hips and rib circumference expanded. Combined with childlike accessories such as bows, tented tops (which hung down to hide the cutout at the top of the skirt), and Peter Pan collars, it was just subtle enough—a perfect panacea for the unutterable.

And this was the way Ball dressed, even as the *enceinte* storyline blossomed along with her bump. TV audiences were mesmerized by the drama playing out on their screens. Lucy embodied the tension between her character, circumscribed by domesticity, and her real-life role as an expectant mother working (as an actress, no less) outside the home. While the stereotype of a mother-to-be's home life was acted out, its public, popular aspect troubled traditional notions of propriety. After all, polite society still considered a burgeoning stomach a literal sign of sex, and an unflattering silhouette—something more safely kept behind closed doors.

The idea of having a pregnant actress portray a pregnant woman on television was considered so shocking that the show's major sponsor, Philip Morris, at first suggested that Lucy hide her changing body behind tables and chairs. But Ball, Desi Arnaz (Lucy's on-screen and off-screen husband), and the show's producers rejected that idea, transforming what could have been the end of the series into a new arena for television audiences. Under the very same lens employed in other episodes— the day-to-day happenings of an all-American middle-class family— Lucy's changing body, clothing, mood swings, cravings, and baby-name choices made a formerly private experience a completely public one in front of an audience of millions, reflecting the particulars and changing power dynamics of family life amid the emerging baby boom.[2]

Using clothing to hide pregnancy was an overwhelming social norm of the time, even if maternity and fashion have long been uneasy bedfellows. During "confinement," as the Victorians termed pregnancy—as opposed to "temporary disability," as the American working world terms it today—women were expected to conceal their growing abdomens within their homes and, if they left the house at all (as so many working-class women did), inside maternity corsets. In the United States, such corsets were advertised in newspapers and women's publications well into the 1930s. Fashion editorials that specifically addressed pregnant readers emerged slowly in mainstream publications from 1900 onward and highlighted darted, pleated, and laced dresses that played down a pregnant woman's changing shape. Invariably, the models who were featured, whether live or illustrated, showed little sign of being with child.

The young widow, mother, and New York dressmaker Lena Himmelstein Bryant Malsin was at the forefront of the gradual shift toward supplying pregnant people—and society at large— with less constraining maternity options. Her turn-of-the-century experiments laid the groundwork for the emergence of the tie-waist skirt a few decades later. Bryant's "No. 5" maternity gown—born from a client's request to create a garment that could accommodate her pregnancy—is an example of an early commercial ready-to-wear maternity dress. It helped launch a company that, by 1910, was turning over $50,000 in annual sales and advertising in a range of newspapers and magazines, including *Vogue*.[3] Cannily, Bryant recognized that, whether pregnant or not, women's bodies fluctuate in form, and thus she marketed garments with adjustable waistbands to women of all shapes and sizes, connecting the history of maternity wear with non-sample-size fashion.

The manufacture and retail of ready-to-wear clothing was becoming established in both factories and department stores in the early twentieth century, and maternity wear rode the wave. By the 1930s, high-end retailers like Neiman Marcus and Saks Fifth Avenue stocked maternity fashions, and Bonwit Teller had an "Anticipation Shop."[4] Women wanted something stylish, whether for work or leisure, and retailers responded, offering their own adjustable maternity garments that mimicked contemporary fashions, aped a non-pregnant silhouette, and tried (often unsuccessfully) to conceal the pregnant body. Most incorporated buttons, pleats, and ties or, worse, slits, hooks, grommets, and uncomfortable steel bands in an attempt to hide the bump beneath. Still, as the belly expanded the hem of the skirt would rise up—an annoyance that only got worse as skirt lengths shortened.

Then in 1937 a young engineer, Elsie Frankfurt, having decided that her pregnant sister looked like a "beach ball in an unmade bed," created a novel design. Using one of her sister's suits as a prototype, she cut out a window in the front of the skirt and, *voila!*— the tie-waist skirt was born. Elsie's simple yet innovative design enabled the skirt to stay in place around the hips and against the thighs even as the belly expanded through the window, hidden underneath a tented top. Working along with the growing figure, the design was comfortable yet fashionable and enabled the wearer to step out without any obligation to constrict, radically obscure, or disfigure her changing shape. Each tie-waist skirt would stay cylindrical, maintain a level hemline, and could be paired with an overhanging smock or suit jacket with narrowly and delicately cut shoulders, fine materials, and distracting details like collars, bows, cuffs, and buttons to complete the look.

The Frankfurt sisters went into business, marketing Elsie's design to the pregnant masses. They called their line Page Boy, the name driven home by the cute baby-as-birth-announcer holding a horn on their garment tag. In 1938 they opened their first boutique, next door to an obstetrician's office in Dallas. By the time *I Love Lucy*'s first episode aired, Page Boy had become the single most successful full-line maternity manufacturer in the US, outfitting everyone from housewives to Hollywood actresses. Although pregnancy remained a "condition" for midcentury Americans, the sheer number of pregnancies during the baby boom made women's reproductive capacities more visible than ever before. In 1954, just after Lucy introduced Ricky Ricardo Jr. to television audiences, there were well over four million births annually in the United States, and the demand for fashionable maternity wear was growing.

A front-page *New York Times* article of 1956 called maternity wear "big business," noting that prospective families were spending upward of $200 million a year in the sector. As the *Times* spun it, "the expectant mother, desirous of looking her best at a most important time of her life, is more liberal in spending money for her wardrobe."[5] Page Boy's advertisements seemed to suggest that pregnancy itself was a kind of metamorphosis that, if dressed properly for, could wall in the more out-of-control and future-oriented anxieties of pregnancy, trading all that was unruly and ugly for something more stylish. A woman's experience could be tasteful and modern with clothes made for a "pretty pregnancy" and "smart, young mothers to be."[6]

Pregnancy was sold as another event or life stage—cocktail-party guest, prom queen, bride, expert cook—for which women could buy a costume and play the part. According to the Australian writer Jessica Friedmann, commenting in the next century on the politics inherent to human reproduction, little has changed: "It is no wonder that motherhood is so pressingly marketed as feminine. It's the feminization of any work that allows us to pay lip service to its importance and then ignore its material conditions completely."[7]

With its popularity peaking right in the middle of the twentieth century, the tie-waist skirt—and the well-dressed pregnant woman it represented—was a midway marker between the hyper-concealed pregnant body, bound in a maternity corset, and the hyper-revealed pregnant body, exemplified by Annie Leibovitz's photograph of a seven-months-pregnant Demi Moore, taken for the August 1991 cover of *Vanity Fair*. In many ways, the tie-waist skirt transformed what it meant to be pregnant, shifting its perception from "trying" and shameful to public and empowered—although always through the lens of design consumerism, in this case by augmenting one's wardrobe choices. The skirt's scooped-out opening for the expanding abdomen remained unseen to all but the wearer, but it managed to reframe public pregnancy. For Lucille Ball and so many others of the time, dressing in this humble masterpiece of design changed the game. The tie-waist skirt helped to cement Ball's capital, cache, and celebrity and marked a decisive step in the evolution toward liberating generations of pregnant people to come.

In the new millennium, maternity wear has experienced mixed fortunes. Even as fashion choices have widened, dedicated maternity retailers like Destination Maternity have seen their profit margins tumble over the last decade, and fast-fashion brands like ASOS and H&M now dominate the market.[8] It is a garment sector that has struggled to monetize because—like so much design for reproduction, pregnancy, and postpartum—it has failed to attract venture capitalists or investors (see Breast Pump, p. 259).

It is also absent from fashion design education and other public stages, including perennially popular fashion exhibitions. Catering to bodies that fall outside of restrictive standard sizing—whether pregnant, fat, disabled, you name it—has rarely been the major focus of apparel design courses. Instead, cheap garments designed for deliberate obsolescence have allowed a cross section of pregnant women simply to buy a few sizes larger as their bodies change through the trimesters, and then to discard after use.[9]

This explains in part why no contemporary high-fashion houses produce maternity wear, even as they relish the inherent drama of the maternal form and send pregnant models down their catwalks.[10] In the realm of high fashion, designers of different genders, but often working at fashion houses still overwhelmingly helmed by men, created rarified garments to be worn by atypically-sized runway models. This big business public spectacle makes it into the permanent collections of storied museums, while fashion made for and by women with equal aesthetic merit for life stages like pregnancy is passed over because seasons trump trimesters. This is how culture is made.

Or perhaps, this is how culture was made—because the tides are changing, albeit slowly. When Hatch debuted in 2010, it was a rare outlier. Founded by former Wall Streeter Ariane Goldman, it is an upscale maternity-wear company that has grown every year since its founding. Hatch focuses not simply on clothing, but on a concept store and an Instagram lifestyle that creates community through interviews with doulas, lactation experts, and—Gasp!—pregnant people themselves. In the time of Beyoncé Knowles-Carter's internet-shattering 2017 twin pregnancy announcement becoming the most "liked" Instagram photo of all time, and of Kim Kardashian's globally known growing family, maternity fashion and the domestic preparations for baby and postpartum life have unquestionably become something to monetize. In the end, there's no Ivy Park (Beyoncé's sportswear line named in part after her daughter) or Skims waist trainer (Kardashian's shapewear often worn postpartum) without the tie-waist skirt. They—and we all—can thank Lucy for that.

1   *Vogue*, April 15, 1928, 108.
2   The episode "Lucy Goes to the Hospital" was broadcast to an unprecedented audience of forty-four million Americans.
3   Three years later annual revenue topped $1,000,000. See Tom Mahoney, *50 Years of Lane Bryant* (New York: Lane Bryant, 1950), 7; cited in Marianne Brown, "The Birth of Maternity Wear: Clothing for the Expectant Mother in America" (master's thesis, Fashion Institute of Technology, New York,

2009), 8.
4   The upper echelons of the fashion industry also got into the game: the feted Hollywood designer Gilbert Adrian created bespoke maternity two-pieces for his wife, Jane Gaynor, when she was expecting their child in 1940; couturier Charles James designed a maternity garment for Lane Bryant's fiftieth anniversary catwalk show, held at the Plaza Hotel in New York in 1954; and actress Lauren Bacall, a noted style icon, designed her own pregnancy wardrobe featuring

expressive, calligraphic peplum details and wrapped silhouettes (it was featured in the June 22, 1953, issue of *Life* magazine).
5   Glenn Fowler, "Baby Boom Helps Maternity Wear," *New York Times*, January 22, 1956.
6   From the front and back cover of Page Boy's fall/winter catalogue of 1952.
7   Jessica Friedmann, "Motherhood Is a Political Category," in "Human Parts", special issue, *Medium*, May 10, 2019, humanparts.medium.com

8   Ellie Silverman, "Maternity Clothes Overlooked Working Moms-to-Be: Retailers Are Looking to Change That," inquirer.com, updated February 9, 2019.
9   In the UK, the potency of Kate Middleton's royal pregnancies in 2011, 2015, and 2018 has shaped this taste. They occurred during intense austerity in the United Kingdom, and her fashion was scrutinized and praised by the British press, tabloid and broadsheets alike, who approved the wearing and rewearing of high

street brands like Jigsaw, ASOS, and Zara, as well as maternity-specific labels like Seraphine.
10   The pregnant model and actress Jourdan Dunn was an early pioneer in Jean Paul Gaultier's spring/summer 2010 show; Eckhaus Latta sent a pregnant model down the catwalk for their spring/summer 2018 show; and model Slick Woods even walked for Savage x Fenty while in labor in fall/winter 2018, going straight from the catwalk to the hospital to deliver.

SARI——Fluid by definition, the drape has evolved into broad categories of clothing, including shawls, sarongs, dhotis, and saris. Though rivaled in wear by the *salwar kameez*, a tunic and pant ensemble, it is the sari drape that has remained India's most iconic form of female dress. Eighty million women across the country—and farther afield, in Bangladesh, Sri Lanka, and beyond—don it on a daily basis, according to conservative estimates.[1]

Woman wearing a sari, Bangalore (now Bengaluru), India, 2006

——PREGNANCY

Worn by daily wage laborers building houses, maids cleaning homes, women working at office desks, and brides speaking their vows, the sari is an inherently adaptable garment, though it is perhaps through pregnancy and early motherhood that its versatility and range are experienced most fully.

Saris are worn across geographies, generations, milestones, and moments. As an unstitched garment—and thus built for a life of expanding and contracting—a sari may have been worn in pregnancy and postpartum many centuries ago and likely will be used this way for decades hence, traversing families and chronologies. Made of four to nine yards of cloth, a sari allows for minor adjustments in size throughout the day, whether loosened slightly after a meal or tied more securely for manual work.

Expanding waistlines as a result of pregnancy are thus easily accommodated. During pregnancy the sari is tied above the belly for additional comfort and coverage. The blouses worn with saris are traditionally stitched with a few seam lines and extra allowance, with the seams removed as the body changes or expands over time, including in the transitional period of pregnancy. Breastfeeding with modesty is easily managed through adjustments of the *pallu*—the loose, often decorative end of the sari—across the chest.

In rural areas it is not uncommon to see babies cradled in saris that have been suspended and tied as a hammock, providing a place of rest and safe containment. The inherent adaptability of the sari—its propensity to layer, cover, cradle, and comfort—makes it a garment uniquely responsive to the rapidly changing and growing pregnant body, as well as postpartum contours. Depending on the wearer's preference, folds may flatter or hide a growing belly. Prints and weave patterns can mask leaks, and the sari's edges can be used to wipe away tears or dab a mouth after feeding.

For many, the sari, imbued with these human traces, resonates deeply as an emotional garment, bringing to mind vivid memories of mothers and grandmothers.[2] In today's urban areas, where family life is increasingly atomized, these histories meet new and changing realities. Yet in 2017 an adaptation of a classic folklore poem, "Grandmother's Apron," was widely circulated and commented upon through informal text chains, revealing a lingering sentimentality for a garment many associate strongly with the arc of maternal care over a lifetime:

It was wonderful for drying children's tears and on occasion was even used for cleaning out dirty ears and as a hand towel

For sleeping kids her lap was the mattress and her *pallu* the warm cover

When company came, the ideal hiding place for shy kids were the saree *pallus*…

And when going out as little kids the *pallu* became an anchor, a guide to follow Ma in the big, bad world

And when the weather was cold, Ma wrapped it around our arms

Those glorious sari *pallus* wiped many a perspiring brow.[3]

Despite the marked richness of the topic, the sari's versatility and utility during pregnancy have not been studied in any depth (as is true of many maternity fashions). Its design seems to be accepted without any particular thought, its utility and importance disregarded as self-evident.

India's history with the drape can be traced back thousands of years, with documentation for its use extending back to the Vedic period of the Indus civilization (1500–1100 BCE). Although an unstitched cloth can be draped in an infinite number of ways, the sari has been documented in only about a hundred configurations across India.[4] The one most popularly adopted across South Asian communities is the *Nivi*— floor length, pleated in the front, and with its end piece, the *pallu*, draped over the left shoulder. This is the drape style worn by politicians, flight attendants, Bollywood, and popular media, and thus it is often the sari design that first comes to mind in many imaginations and stereotypes.

The *Nivi* also lends itself to the pregnant body—with no change of drape required—by simply being tied higher above the waist, a small but meaningful change that provides significant comfort. Popular YouTube videos share tips on how to flatter the waistline and belly bump using this same drape, highlighting the reality that diversity of drape in urban centers has diminished to a single narrative. Drapes found in rural areas can often be adapted with the same ease, highlighting the sari's most enduring paradox: singular in design, with infinite possibilities.

——**Malika Verma**

1 See Tiffany Ap, "Styling the Sari: New Anthology Broadens Sartorial Reach of Indian Garment," *Women's Wear Daily*, October 12, 2017, wwd.com.
2 Malika Verma et al., *The Sari Series*, 2016-ongoing, thesariseries.com.
3 Author unknown, adaptation of "Grandmother's Apron," shared with the author via a WhatsApp group in 2017.
4 See Chantal Boulanger, *Saris: An Illustrated Guide to the Indian Art of Draping* (New York: Shakti Press International, 1997), and Rta Kapur Chishti and Martand Singh, *Saris of India: Tradition and Beyond* (New Delhi: Lustre Press, 2010).

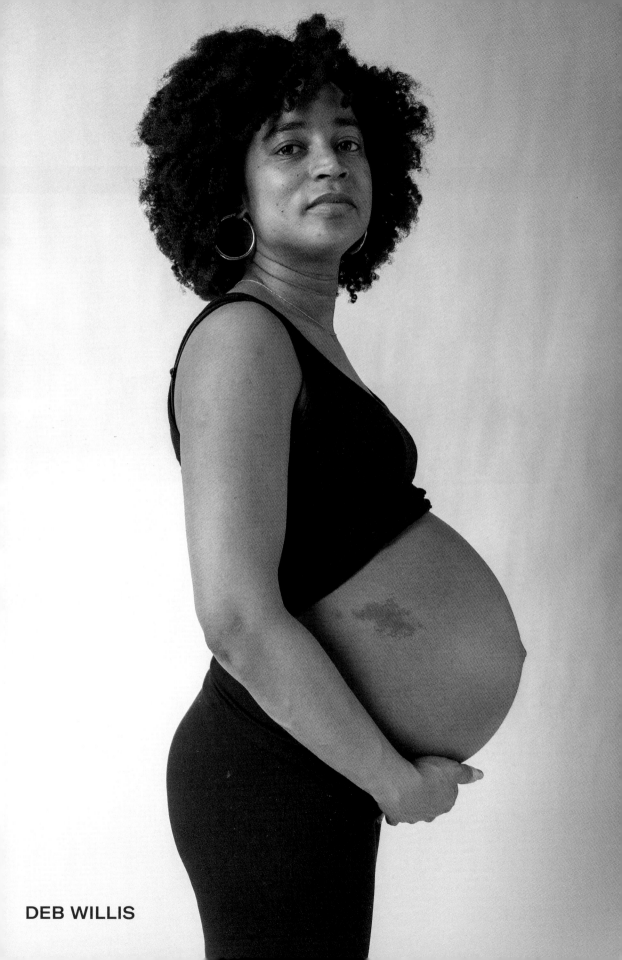

DEB WILLIS

DEB WILLIS This triptych by Deb Willis, a color lithograph printed at the Brandywine Workshop and Archives in Philadelphia, shows the artist pregnant with her son, reclining in a wicker chair in the winter of 1975–76. Above and below the images, a script in white cursive modulates from "A woman taking space from a good man" to "I made a space for a good man." In a 2010 interview with the *Huffington Post* about the piece, Dr. Willis recounted that, when she was an undergraduate, one of her professors told her, "All you're going to do is get married, get pregnant, have a baby and a good man could have been in your seat." Willis, a MacArthur fellow and now the chair of the Fine Arts program at New York University, said she never forgot the humiliation and embarrassment she felt in that moment. Her son, Hank Willis Thomas, is a celebrated artist in his own right. In the first and last images on these pages, Willis memorializes her son with his wife, museum curator Rujecko Hockley, pregnant with their first child in 2018.

1—— Deb Willis, *Zenzi Pending with Ru*, 2019
2—— Deb Willis, *I Made Space for a Good Man*, 2009. Lithograph, edition of 28
3—— Deb Willis, *Zenzi Pending with Ru*, 2019

2

GRACE JONES——Emerging triumphantly from an empire waist-line, the cardboard peplum of blue, gray, and yellow triangles cascades over a black columnar skirt. Dry ice fog gently laps at its edges. A black glove extends from the end of one ruched, white, leg-of-mutton sleeve to brandish a hot pink fan. The other arm is encased in a fierce, spiky, oversized blue epaulet.

Though we cannot see it, we can imagine that the hand below is balled into a righteous fist where it firmly meets the hip. Above oiled decolletage—with the perimeter of an areola just visible—and below a riotous PoMo tricorne hat topped with a flaming red exclamation mark, the subject looks straight at the photographer, caught mid-wink.

It is 1979, and Grace Jones—model, singer, actor, provocateur, and "a question mark followed by an exclamation point," to use *Ebony*'s description—is dressed and ready to take center stage.[1] She is also pregnant, due to deliver her baby in the winter and increasingly unable to hide that fact.

A Jamaican émigré who became well known as a model in fashion circles, Jones had also formed a reputation as an outrageous, incendiary, magnetic performer. The lyrics to her 1981 hit "Pull Up To My Bumper" made explicit how to get turned on enough to make a baby:

> Pull up to my bumper baby
> In your long black limousine
> Pull up to my bumper baby
> Drive it in between

But her bump was viewed as a potential turnoff for audiences. Designed by the initially reluctant father of her child, former *Esquire* magazine art director Jean-Paul Goude, and the Nuyorican fashion illustrator Antonio Lopez, her avant-garde attire was deliberately conceived so that her protruding belly would evade detection. As Goude recalled, "an event of that magnitude [pregnancy] didn't quite fit our business plans. Grace would find herself unable to promote her new record. We were stuck. What does one do in

Grace Jones in a constructivist maternity dress designed by Jean-Paul Goude in collaboration with Antonio Lopez, New York, 1979

——PREGNANCY

such a case?"[2] The solution was what he termed the "maternity mega-dress," designed to mask and reframe Jones's silhouette to ensure that she could still get booked to perform at clubs.[3] Like the rest of Jones's career, the costume was unabashedly bold in every way. Its big shoulders, voluminous sleeves, and towering ten-foot height provided a canny camouflage. It was simultaneously the dictionary definition of a fashion statement, worn to draw attention, and its antithesis, as it functioned to deflect and distract.

Lopez and Goude took their cues from the design vocabularies of the Bauhaus and the still-embryonic postmodern movement (Michael Graves's Portland Services Building was a year away, and the rebel Milan-based Memphis Group another three), using artifice and historical references to unapologetically refute many of the stereotypes of pregnancy. And yet, like so many fashion designs before it, maternity or otherwise, the ensemble was unwieldy and constricted movement even as it set its wearer free by enabling pregnancy to be performed in public (see Lucille Ball's tie-waist skirt precedent, p. 103). While Jones was already well able to transgress without the aid of a costume—her memoir provocatively notes that the first thing she did when she discovered she was pregnant was "give up quaaludes"—like many others before her, both in and out of the limelight, she hid her maternity in plain sight so as to continue to work as she wished despite societal expectations.

Jones also decimated tradition in the way she celebrated her impending motherhood. Her baby shower was held in the wee hours of the morning at the Paradise Garage (a.k.a. the Gay-rage), a legendary (now demolished) disco mecca on King Street in New York City's Soho neighborhood. The club was entered, as she recalled, "by walking along an extended ramp, like a fashion-show walkway, and that was such a thrill, your heart would be pounding like you were about to enter a fantasy. You were about to become surreal."[4] Blondie frontwoman Debbie Harry and Andy Warhol were the hosts. The October 1979 issue of *Jet* magazine described the woman of the hour arriving in a multicolored military ensemble, hoisted onstage onto a pedestal by "a compliment [sic] of 'macho' troops," while a standing-room-only crowd chanted, "Show us the stomach, honey!"[5] She treated them to a rendition of her song "Get Down On Your Knees."

The photograph of the singer, arms crossed, on the 1980 album cover of *Warm Leatherette*—a pose that she described later as channeling an "ominous, hard-eyed samurai filtered through something occult and African" —was taken around the same time, when she was in her third trimester.[6] It was also art directed by Goude, whose working relationship with Jones outlived their romantic partnership. Goude described his partner as "the manifestation of all of my fantasies" and focused on constructing a carefully perfected, idealized, outward-facing image of her artistic persona, which he characterized as "a completely modern creature, a slightly threatening alien, whose unique beauty transcended both sex and race."[7] The words of a lover and artistic collaborator, this description (versions of which were repeated in contemporary interviews) must also be viewed in hindsight within legacies of French colonialism and through the lens of gender.[8]

The few accounts of Jones's maternity costumes often neglect to emphasize her centrality to this design story. It was Grace Jones who brought the image, the costumes, and the attitude to life. Her performance in the mega-dress ensured that she, and those who came after her, could inhabit many identities as nascent mothers, including worker, performer, and reveler. Her donning of this dress refused gendered stereotypes of maternity, invented new paradigms of Black motherhood, and, through her immersion in the gay club culture of New York City and her own provocative androgny, challenged mainstream, heterosexual norms around human reproduction.

Over the last forty years such social taboos have sustained successive assaults through performance and fashion: Nenah Cherry performing on the UK's *Top of the Pops* while seven months pregnant in 1989, Demi Moore's 1991 *Vanity Fair* cover, MIA's 2009 onstage duet with Jay-Z at full term, and supermodel Slick Woods's exit from the Savage x Fenty runway directly into an ambulance waiting to take her to the labor ward in 2019 are but a few. These public pregnancies owe Grace Jones a nod. Outfitted in her costume in 1979, she stood on a narrow-wheeled platform and was pulled across the stage through dry ice fog, as if gliding across water. The show could go on.

1 Lynn Norment, "Dazzling Queen of Disco Flaunts Sex and Bald Head in Rise to Fame," *Ebony*, July 1979, 90.
2 Jean-Paul Goude, *So Far So Goude* (Paris: Assouline, 2006), 138.
3 It is worth noting that this was right around the time of the Pregnancy Discrimination Act, set in law a year earlier, in 1978, as an amendment to Title VII of the Civil Rights Act of 1964, which made discrimination on the basis of pregnancy, childbirth, or related medical conditions illegal. It mandated that pregnant women (it did not go so far as to say "pregnant people") should be "treated in the same manner as other applicants or employees who are similar in their ability or inability to work"; this included hiring practices and, because pregnancy was and still is classed as such, access to temporary disability benefits, as well as guarantees of holding the job until postpartum.
4 Grace Jones and Paul Morley, *I'll Never Write My Memoirs* (New York: Gallery Books, 2015), 207.
5 "Grace Jones Has Baby Shower in Gay Disco," *Jet*, October 18, 1979, 16.
6 Jones and Morley, *I'll Never Write My Memoirs*, 215–16.
7 Goude, *So Far So Goude*, 138.
8 See Miriam Kershaw, who, while she does not discuss the mega-dress or Jones's pregnancy, covers postcolonial referentiality and racism in her article "Postcolonialism and Androgyny: The Performance Art of Grace Jones," in "Performance Art: (Some) Theory and (Selected) Practice at the End of This Century," ed. Martha Wilson, special issue, *Art Journal* 56, no. 4 (Winter 1997): 19–25.

PATTERNS FOR PREGNANCY——Pregnant and postpartum bodies change rapidly, requiring clothing that adjusts correspondingly. Whether purchased off-the-rack, rented, borrowed, handed down, or bespoke, a maternity garment requires a special design that takes into account an expanding waistline and bust, and ease of breastfeeding postpartum. Erin Weisbart, an at-home sewer, has been taking on such challenges for years—and sharing the results with a wide online sewing community.

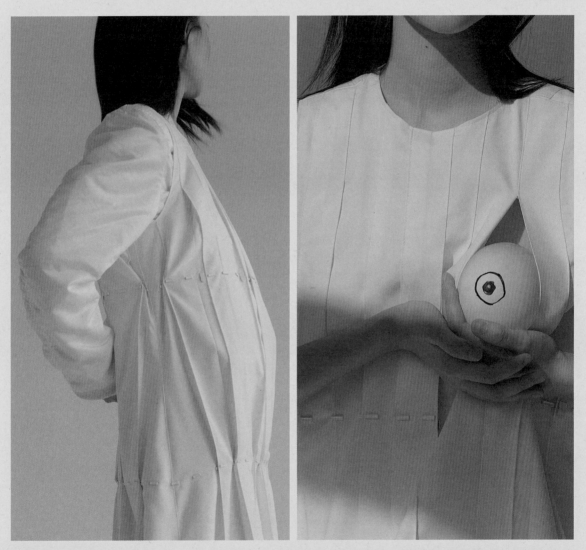

Wei Hung Chen, then a young graduate of the Parsons School of Design in New York, adapted his modular dress for pregnant and postpartum people as part of a commission for the MoMA exhibition *Items: Is Fashion Modern?* in 2017

DESIGNING MOTHERHOOD——Erin, you have an online sewing business, Tuesday Stitches. Along with your friend and business partner, Lisa Kievits, you also cofounded—and recently sold—MaternitySewing.com, an online platform dedicated to patterns for maternity clothing and to building community around maternity wear made on home sewing machines. Pregnancy is an interesting moment in someone's life because clothing has to adapt quickly, almost on a weekly if not daily basis to accommodate the changing circumference, shape, and feelings of your body.

While maternity wear can be purchased off-the-rack or online, there is a much longer history of people making or adapting their own clothing to wear during and after pregnancy.[1] How did you come to think closely about the design of maternity garments?

ERIN WEISBART——I've always sewn. I grew up helping my mom sew. And when I hit five foot ten as a young teenager, and nothing I wore was long enough, I took up sewing in earnest for myself. I started college as a costume design major, switched to a double major in biology and biochemistry, and then got a PhD in biochemistry, after which I was totally burned out and wanted to go back to sewing. I started blogging because that was a way to connect with people of the same interests and skills, and one of them happened to be Lisa. I started Tuesday Stitches and published my own sewing patterns, and Lisa had her own sewing-pattern company, too.

Then Lisa and I happened to get pregnant and have our first kids around the same time. We bonded over the challenges we were both experiencing as new mothers, from the practical to the personal, and of course how it related to our love of sewing. We'd say to each other, "I don't fit into my clothes, but I don't know what to sew because my body keeps changing!" Like me, Lisa lives rurally [in the Burgundy region of France; Erin lives on an island off the coast of Seattle]. She and I talked about wanting to build a community for pregnancy and postpartum in the online sewing space because we didn't have a local community.

DM—— What are the major differences between creating a pattern or choosing a fabric for any other sewing project and thinking very specifically about pattern design, textile choice, or other considerations for maternity clothes?

EW—— That's a good question. One answer is that they're completely the same. A body is a body. And if you know enough and are thinking, "How do I create something that fits all the angles and curves and lumps and bumps and shapes of any human body?" then it's not really that different if there's one extra bump. So if you know how to perform a full-bust adjustment on a pattern, then you can perform the same adjustment for a full belly. But the thing that I really had no concept of until I went through it myself—and that is not understood by people who haven't either experienced pregnancy and postpartum themselves or looked at it very carefully—was just how much the body changes. These changes are often quite unpredictable from one person to another and from one pregnancy to another. And in the postpartum period, some changes in the body are temporary, but others are permanent.

DM—— What are the major design considerations you begin with when creating a maternity garment?

EW—— The challenge of creating a pattern for a maternity-specific garment is identifying at what point in maternity we are designing for. Lisa and I tried to focus on early pregnancy and postpartum, when you don't have a huge belly but things are starting to change or are changing back. You probably want comfort. You don't want things to feel restricted, and, perhaps most importantly, you want things that feel like *you*. For anyone navigating any sense of body dysphoria, pregnancy and postpartum can just explode that. That was a major part of the conversation that Lisa and I wanted to have. What is maternity sewing? Yes, it's clothing, but it's also recognizing these experiences.

DM—— What pattern types did you market on MaternitySewing.com?

EW—— We wanted to expand the use of existing patterns instead of completely reinventing the wheel. We curated patterns from a lot of other designers and then carefully annotated these existing patterns, signaling what stage of pregnancy and postpartum they would be ideal for. We looked for designers who had released patterns that could reach people of all levels of confidence. They ranged from patterns that any beginner could tackle—a stable woven fabric that's going to be easy to work with, for example—to "Hey, this even involves some tailoring." We highlighted the skills required to sew each pattern, and optimal fabrics, like easy quilting cotton, or patterns that more advanced sewers would gravitate toward and that would need something like the drape of a rayon challis—really easy to find at any Jo-Ann's or Walmart—which, if you're not an experienced sewer, is not something that you're going to pull right off the shelf.

DM—— Is it a saturated market in terms of maternity patterns, or are you annotating both maternity and non-maternity patterns?

EW—— Initially, we found very few maternity-specific garments, so we did a lot of reaching out to designers who had designed garments that we thought were suitable for maternity—what we termed "maternity friendly." We encountered resistance; many didn't understand what we were trying to do and said, "Oh, I don't make *maternity* patterns."[2]

It was business; we needed to contribute financially to our families. But the community behind it was also really important to us. Getting people talking during and after pregnancy—about having a hard time, about being comfortable in their bodies, about their mental health—helped to normalize this experience. That's one of the reasons many people are drawn to sewing; it's a familiar experience.

I know women who say, "I have a large bust, and I can't buy anything off the rack that doesn't drown me in fabric or show off my cleavage, which is not my style." Or, "I'm petite, and I don't want to look like I'm wearing hand-me-downs or children's dress-up clothes." It's just so important that we talk about, represent, and create patterns for a full spectrum of bodies. For many people, the sewing community is such an important place for this. Sewing empowers anybody to be more comfortable in their body. When you go shopping, if you pull something off the rack and it doesn't fit you, the thought is, "Oh, there's something wrong with my body because it doesn't fit what's available." But when you make something, if it doesn't fit you it's because you made it wrong—and so you can just unpick it and make it right.

DM—— It sounds like sewing is also a way to shape your own identity, right? So often, pregnant people are told to consume things that other people have made for them.

EW—— For me it was everything. During my pregnancy I made very little because I was so sick, and then afterward I suffered from postpartum depression, and so sewing was incredibly empowering while my body was rapidly changing. Pregnancy and postpartum are times when one's identity changes drastically. To be able to hang on to some of my style was so crucial to feeling like myself. As it is for many people, style is a major part of who I am and how I present myself to the world.

DM—— In what ways do you think about sustainability when creating patterns? Do you think about the cradle-to-cradle life cycle of the fibers themselves, about garment workers being 80 percent female across the world, or about being able to carry on certain traditions of making over time? We ask this question because maternity clothing has for the most part been marketed as something temporary, for a specific moment in time—sometimes only days or weeks—because your body changes that rapidly.

EW—— Sustainability around maternity sewing is a really complicated question because your body does change so fast. You could very well have garments that will only fit you for a few weeks of your life. It takes a lot more work to produce a garment by your own hands than it does to plop down your credit card and have a whole wardrobe sent by mail.

We definitely sought out patterns that could be used at different stages, so during pregnancy but also for nursing, for example—perhaps with nursing clasps and a built-in shelf bra. Sometimes it was just looking at patterns and saying, "Hey, this has a scoop neck and it'll work for nursing." We emphasized that an early-maternity and postpartum body have very similar garment needs. Taking into account all those elements makes a maternity wardrobe more sustainable.

DM— This is very much the same line of thought explored by the young designer Wei Hung Chen with his modular dress [pictured], a prototype that allows pregnant and postpartum people to tailor the garment to their own wants and needs. It uses a system of hooks, eyes, and clips to allow its wearer to let it in and out, and it opens at the breasts for nursing. It acknowledges that the body is not a static, closed entity but something that is always metamorphizing—constantly blossoming and changing. You, Chen, and others have insisted upon your work representing different bodies, different sizes, different people, different genders. Can you talk about that?

EW— There have been a lot of women reclaiming sewing, once derided as "women's work." And that's wonderful. I think one consequence was a hyper-feminization of sewing, especially in the early days of the online sewing world. When I started as a sewing blogger, I saw a lot of very feminine dresses, and the patterns were all named feminine women's names. On the one hand, there's a sense of empowerment—the privilege of choice rather than the monotonous, difficult, and often dangerous factory work that sewing historically has been and still can be for others. But on the other hand, I see this approach leaving a lot of people out, most immediately anyone who doesn't want to present as feminine, who doesn't immediately connect with that identity. There's almost no visible discussion out there around nonbinary or gender-nonconforming pregnancy. It exists, but you have to seek it out. And we just wanted to do our part to include that in the everyday conversation, because sewing certainly empowers gender expression. Likewise, we wanted to be sure to amplify the voices of others often left out of images of pregnancy or postpartum, such as those with plus-size bodies or people of color. Lisa and I sold the business—not through a lack of passion for it, but because she was time-poor, having had her second child, and I was coming to the realization that I was probably only having one child. So we looked for someone else who was passionate about it to keep it going. It's the end for us, but I hope it's not the end for this discussion.

1 Catriona Fisk, "Looking for Maternity: Dress Collections and Embodied Knowledge," *Fashion Theory* 23, no. 3 (May 4, 2019), 401–39, doi.org/10.1080/136270 4X.2019.1603871.

2 Despite a universal need for pregnancy and postpartum clothing, *maternity* is still perceived by many fashion designers as a dirty word, one that they want to distance themselves from.

PREGNANCY PILLOW——A good night's sleep can be hard to come by in late pregnancy, disrupted by frequent night peeing, forced side sleeping, loose joints and ligaments, and a heavy and distended womb. There are also frequently backaches, heartburn, sciatica, hemorrhoids, and pregnancy rhinitis (a swollen, runny nose). This is why, perhaps, when it comes to pregnancy pillows—oversize cushions designed to fit around awkwardly shaped, expanding bodies—marketers conjure visions of marshmallow puffiness and cloudlike sensuality.

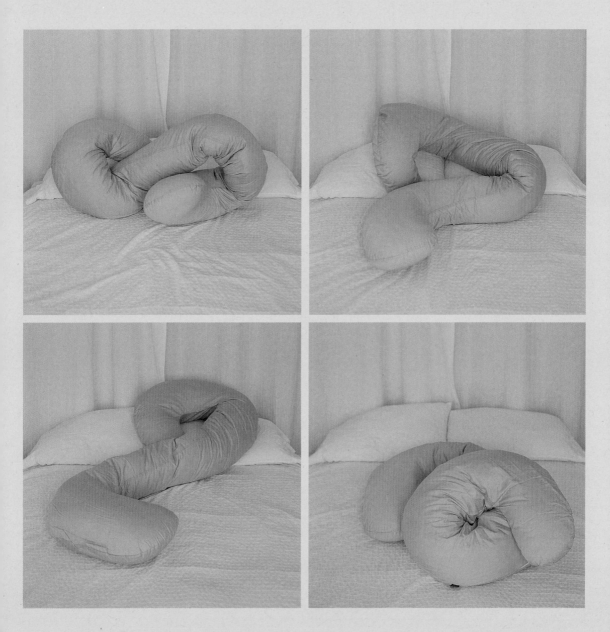

Today, pregnancy pillows named the Snoogle, Queen Rose, Moonlight Comfort-U, and Cozy Bump are shilled in advertisements full of lipsticked White women seductively intertwined with long tubular puffs snaked between their thighs and swooping around their heads and necks, like modern-day Ledas and Swans.

Not every pregnant person has a pregnancy pillow, and not everyone likes them. Some choose to improvise, placing as many standard rectangular pillows as they can against their body in different positions until they're feeling more comfortable. Many receive their pregnancy pillows as hand-me-downs. And some love theirs so much they write poetic online reviews:

> This pillow has to have been made by elves from Narnia, and it has to have been filled with downy fluff and the fibers of unicorn hide. The velvety smooth texture reminds me of a warm, safe place where as a child a lay [sic], to hide from the thunder and the rain to quietly pass me bye-eee-eye.[1]

Hugging a pillow to help oneself sleep is nothing new. Asian countries in particular have a strong culture of bolster-type sleeping pillows, from the Japanese 抱き (to embrace or cling) 枕 (pillow) to the Cambodian ខ្នើយអោបនោន (hug pillow). In 1923, a Western writer for the *Singapore Times* describes the pain of sleeping without his "Dutch Wife" (a euphemism for the bolster-type pillows adopted by Low Country colonies in Indonesia, where traders spent long periods away from their partners). "Never has a matrimonial separation been so cruel," he lamented, revealing at least one way that the practice of hugging a bolster as an aid to sleep has rippled across the globe.[2]

Pillows and various soft supports have long been advised to help bring pregnant and laboring women a little comfort. In 1947, Armetia Leto and Fanny Bartnik applied for a patent for their "Pregnancy Abdominal and Casing Pillow."[3] In 1968, Joan Gibson of the National Childbirth Trust designed the Hexam Air Bolster, an inflatable cushion to be placed below the knees and used in relaxation exercises during labor. But without a doubt the most prolific decade for inventors of pregnancy pillows was the 1990s, when reams of patents were filed for inflatable, fluff-filled, wraparound, S-shaped, and belly-hugging pillows and cushions to help prop up and comfort people during their nighttime hours of need.

The pregnancy pillow, particularly in the West, has from the beginning been a service to uncomfortable pregnant people everywhere. As a broad category, the pregnancy pillow is also deeply goofy—a bulgy house of fluff that promises comfort, a better night's sleep, and a good old-fashioned nocturnal embrace.

1 Review of the Queen Rose pillow on Amazon, amazon.com.

2 *The Singapore Free Press and Mercantile Advertiser*, September 3, 1923, 1, eresources.nlb.gov.

3 A. Leto et al., US Patent 2,562,725, filed July 24, 1947, issued July 31, 1951.

EXERCISE FOR PREGNANCY

EXERCISE FOR PREGNANCY As exercise has become more regulated, institutionalized, and commercial over the last century, since the birth of the modern Olympics in 1896, prenatal fitness has helped define expectations around what constitutes a healthy pregnant body. But such standards have rarely been based on research, making for wildly fluctuating ideas of what constitutes a pregnant person's optimal weight, heart rate, and body size.

1—— In May 2019, the American runner Alysia Montaño went public with the fact that her sponsor, Nike, had not supported her during her pregnancy and postpartum period. After broad public outcry and a congressional inquiry, Nike announced a new maternity policy for all sponsored athletes. Montaño now wears the New Zealand brand Cadenshae

2—— A prenatal fitness class at a YMCA, November 1986

3—— Tara-Brigitte Bhavnani of the Royal Ballet, London, danced throughout her pregnancy

4—— Pregnant and lifting weights in 1978.

5—— A group of pregnant women in an exercise class, 2008

6—— Mothers-to-be exercising during a "maternitybics" class at Tokyo's Tanaka Women's Clinic on March 6, 1987

7—— The film *Childbirth as an Athletic Feat*, recorded at Paddington LCC Hospital, London, in 1939, was informed by Dr. Kathleen Vaughan's belief that a pregnant woman "must regard herself as an athlete in need of training for her special job"

8—— Instructor Barbara Holstein shows her class a stretching exercise, September 1984

2   3   4
5
       6   7

Newborn Appearance
Newborn Behavior and Reflexes
Newborn Procedur
Newborn Appearance
Newborn Procedur

NATIONAL CHILDBIRTH TRUST——Prunella Briance did not have easy births. Her son was born by cesarean in a Cypriot hospital during a blackout, and it was unclear whether she'd survive his birth. Determined to have a better birth her second time around, Briance read books by Grantly Dick-Read, a London-based obstetrician famous for promoting "natural" (or unmedicated) birth (see p.216) and who believed that birth in general could be vastly improved if people felt confident and prepared rather than anxious and fearful.

But Briance's second child, a girl, was stillborn. Bereft and outraged by the disrespectful treatment she had experienced at her London-based hospital, Briance took out an advertisement in the personals column of the *Times* of London on May 4, 1956. "A Natural Childbirth Association is to be formed 'for the promotion and better understanding of the Dick-Read system,'" it read.[1]

Over the following days and weeks, Briance was flooded with letters and messages of support from mothers who, like her, felt that their voices were excluded from decision making around childbirth. They wanted to connect with others about their experiences. They wanted change. And so the Natural Childbirth Association (later, National Childbirth Trust [NCT]), an organization run by mothers for mothers, was born.

The NCT started in people's living rooms, and while its presence and influence across the United Kingdom has grown tremendously since the 1950s, the grassroots nature of the organization remains at the heart of its mission. Since the earliest days, NCT educators and volunteers have hosted gatherings and classes in homes, community centers, and neighborhood schools. They have produced guides, pamphlets, and books that empower people to better know their bodies and their babies. Over the years they have impacted national policies, about everything from the inclusion of partners in hospital delivery rooms and providing support for incarcerated mothers to the shifting medical standards around disability and birth. Beyond that, though, the NCT has normalized the

Change in Ante Natal Care was written by Sheila Kitzinger in 1981 as part of a working party set up by the National Childbirth Trust to investigate antenatal care in British hospitals

——PREGNANCY

experience of parenting and enabled generations of parents to find community and connection and forge deep friendships.

In its formative, doctor-knows-best years, the NCT was met with distrust from the medical establishment, and Briance and other early leaders were called to appear before the ethics committee of the British Medical Association (BMA). The BMA had received complaints from doctors concerned that the NCT was "challenging existing hospital rules and teaching midwifery."[2] The NCT responded by asserting that they were offering a completely different model of care: Mothers were teaching mothers, providing a network of peer support and access to information that was unlike anything they would receive elsewhere. Prenatal classes and parenting groups were offered in support of, and not instead of, medical care. Once the ethics committee was convinced that the group was not trying to topple the medical system, approval was given for the NCT to continue their work, though they were told to do so quietly.[3]

But the NCT didn't remain quiet for long. The women's rights movements of the 1960s and 1970s bolstered the NCT's mission. The cultural anthropologist Sheila Kitzinger, along with scores of other influential midwives, educators, and activists (including Joan Gibson, Caroline Flint, Nicky Leap, and Philippa Micklethwait, to name just a few), together created a chorus of powerful voices and developed a new lexicon around notions of choice, control, and cultural and individual rights. They empowered women across the UK to speak up and speak out against structural inequities, while arguing for parent-centered, evidence-based care.

Today, the NCT is globally recognized as an essential and pioneering organization dedicated to making birth and parenting better experiences, advocating for improvements in maternity care, and winning respect for the rights of parents and children. The NCT advocates at both the local and national level, providing access to well-researched information surrounding pregnancy, childbirth, and parenting. And their mission is also fundamentally practical: they create opportunities that help parents make choices—about where to have babies, who should be in the room, what kind of care to expect, and how to ask the right questions before and after birth.[4]

In a 1993 video titled "The National Childbirth Trust: Who We Are, What We Do, and Why We Do It," British national treasure Jenni Murray of BBC Radio 4 Woman's Hour explains, "the more parents know about birth, the less frightened and the more confident they'll be. Having more control helps them gain a sense of satisfaction and gives maximum benefit to the baby." The conviction behind the NCT's formation was simple, she continues: "If parents were better informed, they themselves would help to improve standards of care. And if they could make informed choices, it would help to create parent-centered care."[5]

Part of NCT's genius was and remains empowering people to make language out of the landscapes they already know—how to breathe through a contraction, how to feed a baby with one's own body, and how to ask in a multitude of ways for the respect we all deserve during the times we are most vulnerable. It's about channeling the rage at the inequities we experience and finding peace and connection through claiming the care that we warrant. This peer-to-peer model is not only very effective but can also be healing for everyone involved. "Having mourned deeply, I suddenly came to life," Briance said of those early NCT days.[6]

1   Elena Carter, "From Mother to Mother: The National Childbirth Trust Archive," *Wellcome Library Blog*, September 28, 2015, blog.wellcomelibrary.org.
2   Carter, "From Mother to Mother."
3   In an attempt to appease the medical profession, the organization changed its name from the Natural Childbirth Association to the National Childbirth Trust, dropping the word *natural* so as to appear more respectable to doctors; Carter, "From Mother to Mother."
4   Although countries like the United States lack a nationalized vision for high-quality maternity care and parental support, smaller organizations have pushed conversations forward. The Maternity Care Coalition, the YMCA, La Leche League, Zero to Three, and Respectful Infant Educators (RIE©), as well as many others, along with countless individuals who run birth and prenatal classes, parenting and support groups, have helped create community for families across the country and have advanced society in very real ways. Still, there's more work to do. We need policies that support midwives and doulas, culturally appropriate care, and systems that support breastfeeding, family leave, and accessible childcare, among many other things.
5   Caroline Flint et al., "The National Childbirth Trust: Who We Are, What We Do, and Why We Do It," Wellcome Library, London, circa 1993, wellcomelibrary.org.
6   Olivier Holmes, "Prunella Briance, Founder of the National Childbirth Trust," *Independent*, August 4, 2017, independent.co.uk.

ALGORITHMS FOR PREGNANCY——"Like many women I know," tweeted Talia Shadwell, a journalist at the *Daily Mirror*, "I use a period tracker app."[1] Opening it in early November 2019, Shadwell found she hadn't logged her last menstrual cycle, and the app flashed a warning that her period was "late" (it wasn't).

Recounting her experience in a subsequent Twitter thread, she noted the unusual barrage of baby-related digital advertisements in her feed over the preceding weeks. Because of her absentmindedness, "the app likely concluded I was pregnant and began communicating the information to third party apps and algorithms."

When she published a longer opinion piece a day later under an anodyne headline, she joked that the lede should instead have read, "Mark Zuckerberg, stay out of my uterus." Describing as "unsettling" the fact that technology might know her reproductive status before she did, she noted that the most provocative aspect of her experience was "how quickly the algorithms were eager to sell my mythical unborn baby things."[2] Until she corrected her cycle in the tracker app, Shadwell was bombarded online by retailers pushing products related to pregnancy and new motherhood. Once she input her correct dates, the ads quickly ceased (to be replaced, one imagines, by a different set of algorithmically and stereotype-driven ads).

Shadwell was, in fact, late to the party. Aware that new parents represent big business and that winning their customer loyalty early is key, companies have been exploring ways to target digital advertising to expectant customers for at least two decades. This practice exploded into public view in 2012 when a spate of articles—notably one in the *New York Times* titled "How Companies Learn Your Secrets"—breathlessly reported a story about a teenage pregnancy, a mailer containing Target

> **Talia Shadwell** ✔
> @TaliaShadwell
>
> Replying to @TaliaShadwell
>
> Like many women I know - I use a period tracker app. I opened it today and found I hadn't logged last month's cycle - it flashed a warning that I was very 'late'
>
> 7:12 PM · Nov 3, 2019 · Twitter for iPhone
>
> **149** Retweets   **19** Quote Tweets   **1.5K** Likes

> **Talia Shadwell** ✔
> @TaliaShadwell
>
> Replying to @TaliaShadwell
>
> Because I had forgotten to log a cycle, the app likely concluded I was pregnant and began communicating the information to third party apps and algorithms
>
> 7:13 PM · Nov 3, 2019 · Twitter for iPhone
>
> **437** Retweets   **76** Quote Tweets   **2.7K** Likes

Tweets from the journalist Talia Shadwell's timeline in 2019

coupons for maternity items, and an irate dad.

Now the stuff of urban legend, the tale centered on a Minneapolis father who strode into his local Target store to berate the manager because his daughter had received discount incentives on cribs and baby clothes. "She's still in high school," he protested. "Are you trying to encourage her to get pregnant?" When an apologetic store manager called to follow up days later, the father sheepishly admitted that he had since been made aware of "some activities in his house" that had previously escaped his parental radar, and he now knew that his daughter was "due in August."[3]

A tempting though possibly apocryphal tale (it was recounted in the article by the *New York Times* with an unsatisfying lack of detailed corroboration), it foreshadowed Shadwell's "creepy" recognition that personal data—whether about one's menstrual cycle or purchase history at big-box stores—could be monetized in service of the lucrative parent and baby market. In 2002, while working at Target, the statistician Andrew Pole was asked by colleagues in the marketing department whether there was a way to figure out if a customer was pregnant, "even if she didn't want us to know."[4] It turns out there was. Based on purchases of prenatal vitamins and maternity clothing, Pole could help his colleagues direct their ads toward what the *Times* writer called the "retailer's holy grail"—soon-to-be-exhausted new parents whose routines (and thus established purchase patterns and brand loyalties) are in a state of flux and therefore ripe for redirecting. Yet for those who lose their babies during pregnancy or shortly after birth, such carefully calibrated promotions can become devastating, repeated reminders of their loss. Tommy's, the UK charity that supports research into stillbirth, has an

online "how to" for turning off targeted ads on some social-media platforms that have harvested hashtags, viewing patterns, and posts from once-expectant parents.

While many people now recognize that data enables surveillance and targeted consumer communications, there is less understanding of how—contrary to the perception that they are objective and mechanistic—algorithms and the data sets that feed them are subject to significant biases in their design.[5] Indeed, understanding data sets and algorithms as deliberately designed, and thus subject to human biases, is important, as Catherine D'Ignazio, director of the Data + Feminism Lab at MIT, stresses:

An algorithm describes a process for moving from an input to an output. How you do that is the design. There are different values embedded, there are different decision points, and there are certain things you might choose to ignore and thresholds you have to set to determine what matters as an output. I think it'd be helpful for us to think of algorithms more explicitly as design than we sometimes do, because then we can invite more people to participate in the design process. Often [algorithms] are seen as purely technical work [and not] political decisions that may have impacts for many other groups.[6]

D'Ignazio points to a 2018 case study in the northern province of Salta in Argentina, where the local government health agencies announced, in collaboration with Microsoft and various NGOs, that they had developed an algorithm to predict teenage pregnancies and high school dropouts in order to prevent them. Such "predictive policing" was immediately criticized for undermining personal autonomy and discriminating against often poorer, younger, minority women and girls. As

D'Ignazio put it, "at least Target's just trying to sell you stuff you don't need. This case study in Argentina represents a whole other level of algorithmic invasion."[7]

Lauren F. Klein, a digital humanities professor and D'Ignazio's co-author of the landmark text *Data Feminism* (2019), also underscores the widespread misunderstanding of data and algorithms as factual, neutral, and objective. "Predictive models that are intended to help can just as easily harm," she notes, pointing to the high error rate of other predictive technologies used during pregnancy and birth, such as ultrasounds (see p. 89).[8] These errors can result in pregnant people being put in a risk category that sets up a cascade of interventions of sometimes questionable necessity, from genetic testing to induction of delivery to cesarean section.

The Target story highlights that, like most digital-marketing algorithms, those targeted toward pregnant people are usually designed without customer input or explicit permission. Responding to this reality, Kimberly Seals Allers, an award-winning journalist and birth advocate, is in the processing of creating the Irth app ("as in Birth but we dropped the 'B' for bias"), a way for people to rate maternal and birth health care provisions in the style of a Yelp review[9]. The app's particular focus is to counter racial inequity in maternal health outcomes. A Black woman and mother of two, Seals Allers personally experienced bias in the treatment she received during her first pregnancy. With Irth, users enter information such as their age, race, ethnicity, sexual orientation, city, state, and insurance type, and the app matches them with a range of user reviews that reflect their own identities so they can make informed provider choices. Irth's algorithm finally flips the data script in favor of pregnant and birthing people.

1   All tweet quotes in this essay are from Talia Shadwell's Twitter feed of November 3, 2019.
2   From Shadwell's Twitter feed of November 3, a sentiment she reiterated in "'Period Tracker App Spied on Me—and Told Advertisers It Thought I Was Pregnant,'" *Daily Mirror*, November 4, 2019.

3   Charles Duhigg, "How Companies Learn Your Secrets," *New York Times*, February 16, 2012.
4   Duhigg, "How Companies Learn Your Secrets."
5   Betsy Anne Williams, Catherine F. Brooks, and Yotam Shmargad, "How Algorithms Discriminate Based on Data They Lack:

Challenges, Solutions, and Policy Implications," *Journal of Information Policy* 8 (2018): 78–115.
6   Interview with the author, May 15, 2020. D'Ignazio and Lauren F. Klein examine the power dynamics inherent to data in its collection, use, and the designs that spring from its analysis.
7   Interview with the

author, May 15, 2020, referencing this case study: "Algorithms and Artificial Intelligence in Latin America: A Study of Implementation by Governments in Argentina and Uruguay," World Wide Web Foundation, Washington, DC, September 2018, webfoundation.org.
8   Interview with the

author, May 15, 2020. As Kate Crawford notes, even when data is processed completely by mechanical means, it will "always bear the marks of history…and it will always have the same kind of frailties and biases that humans have."
9   See the Irth homepage, birthwithoutbias.com.

PREGNANCY PORTRAITS——Between September 15, 2005, and October 5, 2007, the millions of people who walked through London's Trafalgar Square were greeted by a gleaming white, nearly twelve-foot-tall marble sculpture of a gloriously fecund, naked female form titled *Alison Lapper Pregnant*. I was one of them, just out of university with an art history degree. It stopped me in my tracks. There had been nothing like it in my course lectures and textbooks.

Alison Lapper Pregnant, by Marc Quinn, on the Fourth Plinth, Trafalgar Square, London

Sitting resplendent atop the Fourth Plinth, a perch originally intended for a nineteenth-century equestrian statue of King William IV, the figure, with its third-trimester belly, stood in unmistakable and stark contrast to the masculine, rigidly erect military and royal statues nearby. It remains one of the most compelling sculptures I have ever encountered.

The artist, Marc Quinn, first met his subject—another British artist, Alison Lapper—in 1999 as he was drawing connections between classical sculptures of centuries past and the bodies of physically disabled people of the present in his series *The Complete Marbles* (1999–2005). He noted that the former, often missing limbs due to the ravages of time, are celebrated as timeless, ideal human forms, while the latter, corporeally changed owing to accidents of genetics or illness, remain absent in much of visual culture. Lapper was born without arms and with abbreviated legs as a result of a condition called phocomelia.

In Quinn's portrait, Lapper's physical contours inhabit the same spare, elegant space occupied by surviving Greek and Roman marble statuary (the most notable comparison is the Venus de Milo, now in the Louvre in Paris). It was the first time the majority of the passing public—as well as those who saw the image in the mass media—had considered a physically disabled person's pregnancy, or identity as a mother, worthy of prolonged consideration, let alone muse-like elevation. Lapper's portrait depicted pregnancy as so many know it to be, as an experience on par with the heroism embodied by the decorated war veterans on nearby plinths.[1]

While portraits of pregnancy have long abounded in physical form, and now proliferate digitally, Quinn's sculpture is among the significant examples that lodge in our shared consciousness. Such images create new paradigms for how we metabolize and instrumentalize the knotty, powerful, irresistible drama of human gestation, and more importantly, how we regard—and subsequently treat, individually and collectively—humans who give birth. As *Alison Lapper Pregnant* proved, while portraits of pregnancy often reinforce and mediate motherhood as an identity constructed under the pressure of social mores, this fact

also lends the genre a potency to disrupt and reshape such constrictions. Indeed, writing in the *Guardian* when the sculpture was first unveiled, the critic Rachel Cooke seemed to suggest that a portrait that celebrated embodied states that are both uniquely and widely experienced had the power to "knock into a cocked hat the tired debate about what constitutes public art. This is public art, and let that be an end of it."[2] Quite.

Quinn himself suggested that his portrait of Lapper focused on someone who had "conquered their own inner world" rather than the one outside their body, and in so doing offered a signpost forward: "Most monuments are commemorating past events; because Alison is pregnant it's a sculpture about the future possibilities of humanity."[3]

Portraits in any medium and of any type are markers of cultural, political, and economic status, and the same is true for the majority of pregnancy portraits across cultures and chronologies.[4]

Distinct from birth portraiture (often in the form of photographs; see p. 225), pregnancy portraiture, immortalizing a temporary condition, usually engenders a strange mix of celebration, validation, veneration, and objectification of the subject. One of the very earliest pregnancy portraits—the so-called Woman (or Venus) of Willendorf, a hand-sized Paleolithic object discovered in Austria in 1908—is, some argue, a *self*-portrait. Like other figurines of its type, it was fashioned from limestone with fleshy, distended belly and pendulous breasts some twenty-five or thirty thousand years ago.

In whatever media, the curve of the swelling stomach and the implication of imminent blood, sweat, and tears counters the more typical focus of attention on the face. Such portraits are also almost uniformly ideal, which is why those that are not lodge so potently in the memory. Not a few are patterned on the enduring image of religious figures, including, in the Christian tradition, an expectant Madonna. It is rarer that they capture the messy grind of pregnancy—the sickness, exhaustion, anxiety, discrimination—and its aftermath.

The curator and historian Karen

Hearn has studied this genre for over two decades and in 2020 channeled the results of her exploration into a short-lived exhibition, *Portraying Pregnancy: From Holbein to Social Media*, at London's Foundling Museum, on view for six weeks before it was shuttered due to COVID-19. Her project captured the essential crux of picturing pregnancy: while these images auger new life, they are about the pregnant person and as such constitute a rich strand of history that documents the persistent presence of pregnancy in everyday life (how else would we all be here now?), even as such representations are often sidelined as visual and social curiosities. (Hearn also notes a subgenre of portraiture of pregnant people not yet "showing" but in retrospect confirmed by historical records to have been with child at the time of their sitting.)

My favorite of Hearn's examples is a pop icon from my own childhood in the UK, the Swedish-born, New York–raised musician Nenah Cherry, who began her career in London in the late 1980s. Her breakout and best-known song, "Buffalo Stance," was on the ascent when she was pregnant with her daughter, Tyson, in 1989 (another daughter, Mabel, has gone on to have her own successful pop career). That year, Cherry performed her hit on the extremely popular British television program *Top of the Pops* while seven months pregnant. Only weeks before, in December 1988—and almost three years before Demi Moore's iconic *Vanity Fair* cover— the photographer and filmmaker Andrew Catlin had captured her in sepia tones at age twenty-four, her light-colored leather jacket unzipped to expose her belly, hands laced over it. Some years later, Cherry said she had been asked by a journalist whether it was safe to be performing on stage while pregnant, to which she replied, "Yes of course! It's not an illness."

Her portrait packed a punch. While Grace Jones had camouflaged her condition onstage a decade earlier (see p. 113), Cherry set the scene for a slew of pregnant performers who came after her: Melanie Blatt, a member of the 1990s alt-pop group All Saints, performed onstage in London in 1998 wearing a crop top that fully exposed her second-trimester bump. She was in good company, with Victoria and Mel B of the rival band the Spice Girls expecting at the same time. Theirs was the era of Girl Power and Brit Pop, and they wanted a piece of it, pregnant or not.

For those living before the advent of modern medical innovations, an understandable motive for commissioning portraits of late pregnancy across most of human history was the ever-present specter of death in (or soon after) childbirth. (The concurrent fashion of writing a letter of advice to an unborn child is the textual equivalent.)[5] In the sixteenth century, a painting of Catherine of Austria, Queen of Portugal, by the sought-after court painter Anthonis Mor (now in the Prado Museum in Madrid), gestures more delicately to the sitter's "heavily gravid" state—the buttons on her richly brocaded garment open subtly where they pass over the waist.

A contemporaneous portrait by an unknown artist of Katherine Carey, Lady Knollys, at the Yale Center for British Art is an example of a paradoxical efflorescence of such paintings during Elizabeth I's childless reign. The illegitimate daughter of Henry VIII and a Lady of the Bedchamber to her cousin the queen, Katherine is shown holding a girdle bedecked with an image of the Roman god Mars, known for channeling virility and fertility as well as marshaling war. She was pregnant with her last child, which according to conflicting records was either her fifteenth or sixteenth. The child, a daughter, did not ultimately survive, but Katherine did, a not inconsiderable feat. As one contemporary writer analogized, using the language of maritime warfare and colonization that characterized this period in English history: "Going with child as it were a rough sea...: and labour, which is the only port, is full of dangerous rocks."[6]

More recent examples of pregnancy portraiture are as varied as the subjects. In little-known works scattered over several decades, the German Expressionist painter Otto Dix etched, sketched, and painted a variety of swollen bellies; a campaigner against the criminalization of abortion in the 1920s, his unflinching approach includes a 1922 depiction of a shriveled figure standing pregnant atop post-conflict rubble. Imogen

Cunningham's photographic portrait of a fellow artist, the mid-century jeweler merry renk (who preferred her name in lower case), is a magical meditation on the swollenness of this state. Alice Neel's series of pregnant nudes in the 1960s and 1970s were memorably described by the writer Julia Felsenthal as reflecting their subjects' "drawn, pensive faces, ungainly bellies, and angry nipples controverting any romantic notions of pregnancy glow. They gaze at Neel warily, as if to say, 'You better not turn me into some kind of fucking fertility goddess.' You can practically smell the hormones in the room."[7]

Neel's pregnancy paintings are often termed a tipping point, signaling a demand for motherhood to be accorded consideration as a valid subject in a male-dominated, male-oriented art world, though her paintings are in good company, not least in the work of her contemporary Helen Redman.[8] Redman's searingly personal portrayal in the 1960s of her pregnancy with her second daughter, Nicole, while mourning the loss of her first, Paula, who died as a toddler (see Helen Redman, p. 169), is an intimate, compulsive self-portrait of loss in the face of new life. Her *In Utero and New Beginnings* series, both from 1964, presage a lifelong exploration of pregnancy, birth, and matrilineage. Redman, now in her eighties, has painted many of her family members including Nicole when she was pregnant with her own child, Redman's granddaughter, Shira. As she wrote of her 1964 pregnancy series in *Frontiers* in 1978:

> I was trying to work through her [Paula's] death—these drawings were really a very deep kind of activity to keep me alive. I was in my ninth month of pregnancy when I started this series and I would work almost all day long at these every day. ...Most women in their ninth month are so lethargic, because of the weight that they can hardly move. I was just charged with a kind of insane energy to do these drawings. I must have done at least thirty in my ninth month —to show you how obsessive a series it was.[9]

Pregnancy portraits are now a fixture of popular culture in a much

broader range of media, with the objectification of expectant celebrities a staple of magazine covers. The attendant public consumption of deliberations over baby names, maternity cravings, weight gain, and pregnancy fashions is a means of constructing and dictating societal mores. In 1991 *Vanity Fair* ignited a firestorm when Annie Leibovitz's photograph of actress Demi Moore, naked and seven months pregnant, graced the cover of the August issue—posed in profile, cradling her stomach and covering her breasts, her gaze directed outward at newsstand browsers. In her footsteps followed Beyoncé Knowles-Carter, who in 2017 was photographed pregnant with twins by the artist Awol Erizku; the picture became the most popular Instagram photo that year, with 11.1 million "likes."

This playbook has a decades-long history: press photographs have captured public figures at various stages of their gestational journeys, including Lucille Ball, who broke boundaries by continuing to appear in her weekly television show, her real-life pregnancy written into the fictional portrayal of a mid-century mom (see Tie-Waist Skirt, p. 103). First lady Jackie Kennedy and Princess Diana were rendered mute fashion plates as they fulfilled dynastic expectations, while two-time Paskistani prime minister Benazir Bhutto enacted a more empowered public image of pregnancy when she became the first elected leader of a country to give birth while in office (her daughter, Bakhtawar, was born in 1990).

Reality television—from Discovery Channel's *A Baby Story*, an early entry in the genre beginning in 1998, through MTV's *16 and Pregnant* (2009–14), to *Keeping Up with the Kardashians*—has animated the pregnancy portrait.[10] The latter series, perhaps the genre's apogee, has demonstrated since its debut in 2007 that our fascination with human reproduction can, when skillfully framed and edited, also produce enormous economic capital.

These televised modes of self-presentation—carefully arranged and filtered for public consumption—have spilled over onto social-media platforms, none more so than the image-centered Instagram. There, an endless number of amateur "bump progress" pictures taken over weeks and months scroll alongside professional maternity shoots (packages can cost hundreds of dollars) in which expectant partners of all demographics, sometimes surrounded by family members, gaze adoringly at preg-nant bellies, at sunsets, or at one another. Found on that platform, too, are the 2.0 version of "mom-my bloggers," who channel their family dynamics into a sponsored slideshow of daily mantras for raising twenty-first-century broods across multiple intersections of race, class, religion, and parenting strategies. No matter the medium, such portraits of pregnancy tend to reproduce a circumscribed set of poses and tropes. This is why, when the format is even slightly shattered, the results are all the more powerful. The model Arrows (also known as

Ari Fitz) explored the intersection of masculinity and pregnancy in their short documentary portrait, *My Mama Wears Timbs* (see p. 97), of a fel-low masculine queer wom-an of color, Frankie Smith. Shot in 2017, the documentary honors Smith's identification as a tom-boy—the "Timbs" are Timberland boots—as a vibrant representation of motherhood. Smith talks about the ways in which clothing usually helps her define her identity, her jeans and a T-shirt from the men's rack allowing her to face the world "like how I want to present myself." Yet, as her pregnancy developed, she had to turn to ma-ternity clothing to cover her bump, especially at work, which entailed garments designed specifically for women. Their aesthetic compli-cates—and sometimes outright confounds—her preferred ways of presenting her identity:

They show off all my new curves.... I have to, like, prepare myself to go out into the world as someone that I wouldn't normally portray myself as. It's just uncomfortable.... I never want to do anything after work that is social without changing because I don't want any of my friends to see me in these wom-en's clothes. It's just...tough.[11]

Similarly thumbing her nose at clichéd expectations of a flower crown and flowing white dress for pregnancy, the comedian Amy Schumer bucked tradition in a 2019 *New York Times* profile, chasing ducks while running na-ked and pregnant through a New Orleans public park. In the words of social-media admirers from across the world, the result was hysterical, honest, and beautiful.

1 See Ann Millet, "Sculpting Body Ideals: Alison Lapper Pregnant and the Public Display of Disability," *Disability Studies Quarterly* 28, no. 3 (Summer 2008), dsq-sds.org.
2 Rachel Cooke, "Bold, Brave, Beautiful: Marc Quinn's Sculpture of Alison Lapper Has Completely Transformed Trafalgar Square," *Guardian* online, September 18, 2005.
3 Marc Quinn, quoted on the artist's website (under "Alison Lapper Pregnant: More about

This Artwork"), marc-quinn.com.
4 See Karen Hearn, *Portraying Pregnancy: From Holbein to Social Media* (London: Paul Horberton in associa-tion with the Foundling Museum, 2020).
5 Hearn, *Portraying Pregnancy*, 46.
6 Hearn, *Portraying Pregnancy*, 50; quot-ing Linda A. Pollock, "Embarking on a Rough Passage: The Experience of Pregnancy in Early Modern Society," in *Women as Mothers in Pre-Industrial England:*

Essays in Honor of Dorothy McLaren, ed. Valerie Fildes (London: Routledge, 1990), 48.
7 Julia Felsenthal, "Searching for Myself in Alice Neel's Radical Portraits," *Vogue*, February 26, 2019.
8 Denise Bauer, "Alice Neel's Portraits of Mother Work," *NWSA Journal* 14, no. 2 (Summer 2002): 102–20.
9 Helen Barchilon Redman and Kathi George, "Portraits of Nicole," in "Mothers and Daughters," special issue, *Frontiers: A Journal of*

Women Studies 3, no. 2 (Summer 1978): 34–39.
10 Interestingly, during the height of teen preg-nancy in the United States, in the 1980s—and decades before the phenomena of the selfie and reality television—photographic self-por-traiture ("phototherapy") was posited as a means of increasing self-esteem and thus decreasing ad-olescent parenthood (the hypothesis was based on the shaky assertion that "negative self-concept leads to poor contracep-tive behavior.... [and thus

perhaps] improving the adolescent self-concept improves contraceptive behavior"). Lynn M. Blinn, "Phototherapeutic Intervention to Improve Self-Concept and Pre-vent Repeat Pregnancies among Adolescents," *Family Relations* 36, no. 3 (July 1987): 256.
11 Ari Fitz aka Arrows, *My Mama Wears Timbs: A Short Documentary on Motherhood & Masculinity*, youtube.com, October 11, 2017.

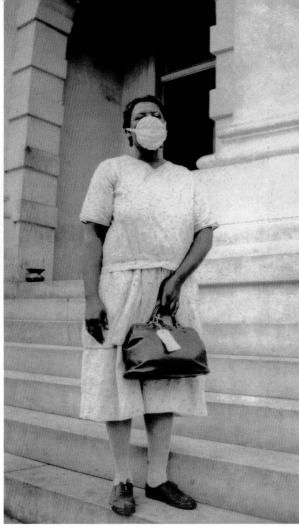

MIDWIFERY IN TRANSITION   Midwife-attended birth declined in the United States as the field of obstetrics grew in the early twentieth century. In 1931 the Florida legislature passed a law for "the control and licensing of midwifery for the protection of mothers at childbirth and authorizing the State Board of Health to make regulations therefore." *Control* was the operative word. These portraits and the page from this manual capture local Florida midwives—and by extension their peers across the US—during a time of great transition.

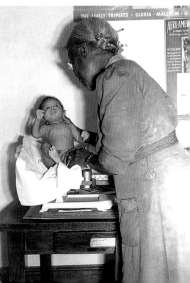

MISSISSIPPI STATE BOARD OF HEALTH
MIDWIFE PERMIT

County___HANCOCK_____   Number___1_____.

Issued to women who desire to practice midwifery, and who have been investigated and approved by the State Supervisor of Midwives and the County Health Officer.

THIS IS TO CERTIFY THAT_____FREDDIE SPEED_____

residing at _____BAY ST. LOUIS, MISSISSIPPI_____
is hereby given a permit to practice midwifery in Mississippi provided she obeys the laws governing this practice and observes the rules and regulations of the State Board of Health as pertains to the practice of midwifery   Permits not renewed yearly are invalid.

Felix J. Underwood M.D.
Executive Officer.

Lucy E. Massey
Director, Public Health Nursing

C. M. SHIPP, M. D.

*Date*___PERMIT FOR 1949___   County Health Officer.

Midwife Permit

A Good Midwife

Is clean in person, home and equipment

Has standard equipment kept in good order

Keeps her bag hung on the wall protected from dust and ready for use

Calls a physician in difficult or abnormal cases

Sends certificate of birth to the registrar within 5 days

Attends meetings and classes; is able and willing to learn

Has a medical examination as required by the local health department; takes treatment if needed

Sends in change of address when she moves

Writes the number of permit and postoffice address on all reports and letters

SENDS IN A LIST OF EXPECTANT MOTHERS TO THE COUNTY PUBLIC HEALTH NURSE EACH MONTH

Helps the public health nurse and physician in conference and clinic

Teaches her patients and all other women to go to a private physician or to the health center early in pregnancy for examination and to see the public health nurse each month

MIDWIVES——Maternity services and health policies predominantly reflect contemporary medical values of Europe and the United States, rather than Indigenous worldviews. Because of the systematic repression of culturally appropriate care practices, Indigenous women and adolescent girls have experienced significantly poorer maternal health outcomes than non-Indigenous people. The following conversation with Indigenous midwives makes clear the impacts of past and present maternal health service policies and health systems on Indigenous mothers and families.[1]

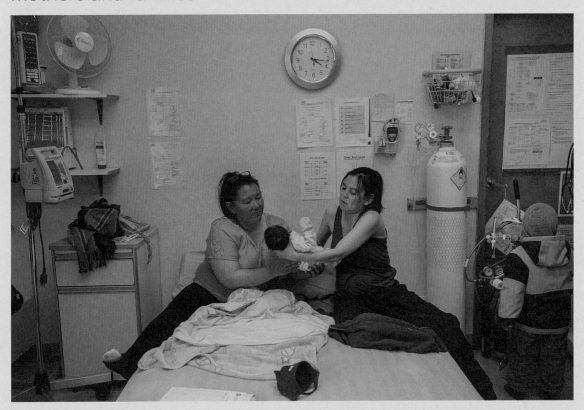

A clinic staffed by midwives in Inukjuak, population c. 1,800, in a remote region of Quebec. The clinic's presence means that women of the town can give birth in their own community

Culturally appropriate care providers and models of care can contribute to addressing the vast health disparities between Indigenous and non-Indigenous people. This excerpted conversation, introduced by Sarah Barnes, project director of the Wilson Center's Maternal Health Initiative, took place during a virtual symposium titled *Indigenous Midwives* on September 22, 2020.[2] The symposium was hosted by the Wilson Center's Maternal Health Initiative, in collaboration with UNFPA (the United Nations Population Fund) and the International Confederation of Midwives.

Moderator Sandra Oyarzo Torres, vice president of the International Confederation of Midwives, is the first Latin American woman to serve in this role.[3] The panelists, Indigenous midwives from Canada, Mexico, and New Zealand, reflect here on the histories of Indigenous midwifery practices and share specific strategies used to enhance and expand Indigenous midwifery care in the midwifery workforce, as well as examples of the successes and challenges of attempts to improve Indigenous maternity care.

SANDRA QYARZO TORRES (based in Chile)——Today we will highlight the importance of talking about Indigenous midwifery, learning from Indigenous midwives, and acknowledging the background of Indigenous midwifery. As a result of ongoing systematic racism within health care systems, Indigenous midwifery services have been drastically reduced and compromised. This has had a lasting impact on both maternal and newborn health outcomes and the preservation of culture in Indigenous communities.

First I want to introduce our panelists: Claire Dion Fletcher is an Indigenous Potawatomi-Lenape midwife practicing in Toronto, Ontario, the co-chair of the National Aboriginal Council of Midwives (NACM), and an assistant professor in the Midwifery Education Program at Ryerson University dedicated to the growth of Indigenous midwifery in Canada. Nicole Pihema is the first Māori president of the New Zealand College of Midwives, a member of the Ngā Manukura o Āpōpō Governance Leadership Group, and a representative for the Rural Health Alliance of New Zealand. And Ofelia Pérez Ruiz is an Indigenous midwife with three decades of experience and the spokesperson for the movement of the Regional Midwives of Chiapas in Mexico. Can you talk about what you think the meaning of Indigenous midwifery is in your regions? What are the main obstacles and challenges, and of course successes, that you've faced in your countries regarding Indigenous midwifery?

CLAIRE DION FLETCHER (based in Canada)——A really critical part of the history of Indigenous midwifery in Canada, which I'm sure is similar in the case of Nicole and Ofelia as well, is the role that colonization has played in the decline of Indigenous midwifery. This occurred through the outlawing and denigration of Indigenous midwifery as part of an attack on our Indigenous knowledge systems, our ways of being, our ceremonies, and our practices that really extended into all aspects of our communities. The knowledge and the power of women were attacked as a way to control us and to assimilate us and wipe us out. Control of our reproduction was and continues to be a tool of colonization. As recently as 2017 in Canada, we had official reports of Indigenous women being forcibly sterilized.

This is why the return of birth to our communities is so important to us, and why Indigenous control of our knowledge, our practices, and our health care and education—and specifically of our birth—is so crucial. In the nineteenth century, with the medicalization of birth, there was a decline of midwifery in Canada, almost to the point of nonexistence. And as the story is often told, the reemergence of midwifery started as a feminist consumer-driven movement in Ontario in the 1980s, with Ontario being the first province to re-regulate midwifery, in 1994. What this often-told story leaves out is the reemergence of Inuit midwifery with the opening of the midwifery program at the Inuulitsivik Health Centre starting in 1986. Because of our colonial history even our reemergence is often missed. The reemergence of midwifery in Nunavik, which is located in Northern Quebec, came from the demands and the activism of Inuit women themselves. Inuit women in Nunavik wanted Inuit midwives. They didn't want to leave their communities to be flown to the south to give birth alone in urban centers surrounded by people who didn't speak their language. They developed a community-driven sustainable Inuit midwifery program that was the first in this country and that to this day has some of the best health outcomes in the world.

NICOLE PIHEMA (based in New Zealand)——We share a lot of commonalities with our Indigenous sisters around the world. But Māori specifically don't say we're Indigenous. We say we're Māori. We say we're *tangata whenua*, meaning "people of the lands," because we have an affiliation to nature and we have affiliation to Papatūānuku, which is our Earth.

We know that having a Māori midwife for Māori women reduces the inequities that occur. As midwives, we're activists, and as Māori midwives, we have to be in [a constant state of] rebellion as well. We're rebellious activists to ensure that we advocate for these women. I know that we have lots of non-Māori colleagues who are actively supporting us and actively working toward [helping] us achieve self-determination. This is a huge obstacle for Māori in and of itself.

Claire touched on [the fact that] oppression has occurred through colonization. When you've been told from the beginning that you're nothing, it's really hard to pull yourself out of it and to think ahead. Part of our role in being rebellious activists is to support our *fano*, our family, into the midwifery profession to protect not just the profession but our families in a way that works for us.

We didn't necessarily have the term *midwifery*. We had *tohunga*, or practitioners of traditional healing who tread that line between the spiritual realm and the physical realm. There was a law enacted in 1907, the Tohunga Suppression Act, that sent traditional healing underground and placed Western medicine as superior. We now see a resurgence of midwifery in New Zealand, almost as if we're grasping to hold onto and rediscover these practices—from calling our babies into the world in our traditional language, to singing traditional songs, to encouraging them to grow and contribute to the people.

OFELIA PÉREZ RUIZ (based in Mexico)——I am part of a South Seas community in the State of Chiapas in Mexico and learned about midwifery as inherited from my mother and grandmother.[4] I'm the spokesperson of the new teaching movement in Chiapas that started in 2014. Currently, Indigenous midwives in Mexico number 600-strong. Midwifery existed before we were colonized by the Europeans. The native people had a care system for taking into account life, which includes the spirits, social life, and the body. And we midwives inherited this knowledge.

Through time the biomedical Western model was implemented within the Mexican population, devaluating other ways of taking care of health and life. As traditional midwives we face many obstacles. For example, in many areas of the country we are banned from attending births because the official healthcare institutions believe we endanger the lives of women. We are criminalized and made responsible for maternal deaths. Indigenous women prefer to receive all services at home, accompanied by family members and in their own languages, within their culture. For us, pregnancy and birth are not just an obstetric event but something that maintains the life and future of Indigenous people and native peoples in Chiapas. It is an option that cannot be linked only to poverty, but rather to a choice made by women.

SQT——**What has been the impact of the past and present health-service policies and models of maternity-service delivery on Indigenous mothers and their families?**

CDF——One of the things I wanted to talk about, specifically in Canada, is the evacuation policy. A lot of Indigenous women who live in Northern Canada have to leave their communities around thirty-six weeks [of pregnancy] to go [south] to urban centers to stay there for weeks, often by themselves. They then go to a hospital to have their babies, often alone, not always speaking the same language as the care providers there. And to have to do this at such an important time and not be surrounded by your family and your knowledge—like Nicole said, your language and your people—is so difficult.

NP— It's a form of violence. If we relate it to the amount of disharmony and upset that women around the world are experiencing during COVID-19 due to the inability to have their closest family members with them during birth—this is a normality for women in these communities. It's an accumulation of assault and violence over time that continues the thread of oppression, and it needs addressing and action.

SQT— **You need the support of governments, of organizations.**
OPR— There is a big gap between the policies and maternal health programs and the care that women actually receive in prenatal care. The policy doesn't get implemented because there are no health institutions, there are no labs, ultrasounds, or other things in communities that can help to improve care.

SQT— **What has worked to change policy and improve maternity services for Indigenous woman and their families?**
CDF— We need more Indigenous midwives because we need Indigenous people to take care of our Indigenous communities.
OPR— In Chiapas in 1994, we had the Zapatista movement that emerged to make racism evident and to show the problems that native peoples have been facing. They have helped to spread the discourse of the rights of Indigenous women and the rights of midwives—the relevance of women's health and the role of midwives. We must also promote horizontal teamwork among doctors, nurses, and traditional midwives. In this multicultural model we need to have health practitioners who speak local languages.
NP— I agree with all those things. Language is really important—language that is woman centered, language that is family centered, and also the language of the native peoples. The work we're doing is on the ground level; it's not high level. We're actually just getting on the street and working our way through as many families as we can to recruit them to midwifery.

SARAH BARNES (based in Switzerland)—**Are there concerns about appropriation of Indigenous care practices? And have there been sensitive and successful adaptations and adoptions of your practices?**
NP— That's a good question. I guess the simple answer would be, yes. Part of the resurgence means opportunities for business.
CDF— People can mistake cultural safety and cultural appropriation. Being a culturally safe health care provider doesn't mean you try to be an Indigenous midwife, because you can't do that. The best thing for us is to have Indigenous midwives from our own families and our own communities.
OPR— In our culture we have had changes, but that doesn't mean that we lose our culture.
CDF— There is this idea that being traditional means you don't change. Respecting our traditions and our knowledge doesn't mean that we don't also provide really excellent care and stay up-to-date with medical changes. It means we're trying to figure out a way to bring these two things together.

1 This interview was recorded with kind permission of the participants and moderator as part of a virtual discussion hosted by the Wilson Center's Maternal Health Initiative, in collaboration with UNFPA (the United Nations Population Fund) and the International Confederation of Midwives on Tuesday, September 22, 2020 3:30–5:00 p.m. EST. These introductory remarks were given by Sarah Barnes, project director of the Wilson Center's Maternal Health Initiative, as part of a panel on Indigenous Midwifery which she co-convened. **2** The Wilson Center is a nonpartisan foreign policy research and analysis organization "linking Washington to the world," and the Maternal Health Initiative—one of several thematic programs at the center—focuses on decreasing maternal deaths, as well as on issues related to global health and gender equity. In the United States, the risk of maternal death is twice as high for Indigenous women as it is for White women, and in Australia, the risk is four and a half times higher. **3** Sandra Qyarzo Torres has been a midwife for twenty-eight years and has dedicated herself to primary health care and universal health coverage in Latin America, where she is currently vice president of the Chilean Midwives Association. She is also an associate professor in the Faculty of Medicine within the Department of Education and Health Science at the University of Chile. **4** Ofelia Perez's contribution to the conversation was translated from Spanish by Irma Blanco.

MASCULINE BIRTH——The ability of humans to become pregnant and give birth is rarely imagined beyond women, and so medical and cultural descriptions and accommodations are almost exclusively designed for them. Yet there is a spectrum of experience, which includes masculine birth. Thomas Beatie is an advocate of transgender and sexuality issues, focusing particularly on transgender fertility and reproductive rights, who describes his own experiences becoming pregnant and giving birth to his children.

Thomas Beatie with his new son, Jensen James Beatie, on the day after giving birth to him at Saint Charles Medical Center, Bend, Oregon, July 26, 2010

DESIGNING MOTHERHOOD—You gave birth to your first child, your daughter, Susan, in 2008, and your son, Austin, in 2009. With Susan, you became the first man in modern history to carry and give birth to a baby. There are so many opinions and misunderstandings and such spectacle around reproduction and birth in general, but perhaps especially so around men who give birth. Instead of having others' opinions clouding the topic, what do you want to foreground about your reproductive experiences?

THOMAS BEATIE—Well, I have to be honest, I didn't expect my reproductive capabilities to have such an impact on public opinion. But I understand it; it's not something that's commonly seen. I want the understanding that people such as myself—I identify as male, I don't identify as trans, I live my life as a man—and people who have various gender identities, all have the right to have our own children biologically.

Masculine birth should be celebrated as much as anyone else giving birth. I was shocked by the extreme amount of negativity toward my story. Giving birth is a joyous time. It should be celebrated. I was just in shock that I had death threats and an extreme amount of negativity shown toward me. It is an inhumane reaction to saying, "Hey, look, we're growing our family. We're happy. I'm happy with my identity, and we're over the rainbow that we're finally having a baby." The response from certain sectors of the public was just so cruel. Obviously, things are getting better over time because transgender rights are in the media more regularly now. There's a little bit more support for people like me and families like mine. Not a whole lot, but it's getting better. When my story came out, it probably received a 99.9 percent negative backlash from the public. Now, for stories like mine, it's only about 95 percent negative. So it's getting better.

DM—It only gets better because of your extreme bravery in being willing to share your experience, even in the face of having such horrific responses. That's a double labor of giving birth to your children and also to a new consciousness and new perspectives on human reproduction.

TB—It's important for the discussion to happen. There's so much misunderstanding and so many misconceptions about transgender people.

DM—There's so little vocabulary for describing an expanded set of experiences around pregnancy and birth. So much of the language is gendered, as are so many of the expectations, socially and culturally. You used the phrase *masculine birth* just now. Is that your preferred descriptor for your experience?

TB—I've never thought about it. I just said it now.

DM—Do you want to coin the term?

LR—Might as well! I've never thought of a word to describe what I've done. Oftentimes I think of my experience without relying on gender. If you take away gender from the experience, I'm the birther. But there is a difference. I don't want to take away from the celebration of women giving birth, because traditionally that's what it's been. And I am by no means representative of all the other people out there giving birth who don't necessarily identify as being female.

DM—Do you embrace the term *fatherhood*?

TB—Oh, absolutely. I did this to become a father. I gave birth to experience fatherhood and be a dad, and my name is Daddy. I don't see it in any other way. This was the way my family was able to bring our children into this world. When I was married to my ex-wife [who experienced infertility] that was the only way that we could do it. Even though the process was different for our family, the result is the same as for many other families. We still have mother, father, husband, wife. I would never want to erase the term *motherhood* or the process of what women go through, because it's a different experience for women going through it than it is for me going through it.

DM— We really struggled with using *motherhood* in the title of our book. It's so obviously gendered, but it's also shorthand for acts that go beyond a gender binary and beyond people who have been pregnant and given birth. Is there a better term that we could be using, or is it that an expanded everyday parlance hasn't really been coined yet?

TB— I think it hasn't been coined yet. To expand the definition and include people such as myself—I think that's important. What I say now is, technically, I'm a birther. That's non-gendered and works for everyone who is giving birth. When I go to the grocery store to go shopping, they've got a parking space and a bathroom stall that says, "reserved for pregnant mothers." When I saw that when I was pregnant, I was like, "Well, what about me? Does that mean I can't park here?"

DM— The design of language—a really correct and generous and generative and thoughtful language with which to describe the experiences of pregnant people, birthing people, postpartum people, people who have uteruses—seems to be paramount here.

TB— Language is key to power dynamics, personal agency, and identity. When I was going through my pregnancy and birth the system was not at all set up for someone like me. I had to fight at the end to make sure that I was considered the father of my children and was listed as their father on the birth certificate. That recognition of birth fatherhood is still a work in progress across the world. In fact, I don't know anyone else, aside from myself, who has successfully switched the entry on the birth certificate to be both the father and the birther.

The nurses, the medical staff, the doctors—they all struggled with respecting me as the gender that I live. Even in the best situations, where they were supporters, they would slip constantly. They got the pronoun right about ten percent of the time, and they would profusely apologize after getting it wrong. But for the others, it was really a struggle. When I gave birth to Susan, the person who reports the live births said, "I'm sorry. We're going to have to list you as mother." And she refused to use my male pronoun. Many people refused to. Birthing aside, medical professionals must respect the identity of transgender individuals, period.

DM— I'm thinking of moments during your reproductive experiences that could have been designed better, and it seems like the basic respect that all birthing people want and need—particularly as expressed through language—is perhaps the main thing that needs to be better designed, whether through training medical professionals...

TB— Absolutely.

DM— ...or rethinking the design of the birth certificate, which is produced within systems that are not designed with inclusiveness and respect in mind.

TB— I don't even know how to get other people to try to understand who are not in this position. It'd be like a woman born with her last name who gets married and changes her name across all of her legal documentation to assume her husband's last name, and lives in that identity for years, suddenly going somewhere and having the people saying, "Hey, but this is not your last name," and calling her by her birth name. It's just completely dismissing her identity in the world.

The hardest phase of the whole having-children thing was getting pregnant to begin with. I know I'm in the minority as far as how I got pregnant. Ironically, many stories that you see of trans men getting pregnant and giving birth—they involve partners that have sperm. It's rare to see someone in my position having to deal with fertility doctors. I got the worst kind of discrimination from them. Several turned me away, saying I wasn't psychologically fit. The first fertility doctor I went to see, he said, "Why do you come looking like that? Shave your legs. Shave your face. You're scaring my staff." Ultimately, he said, "Our staff don't feel comfortable working with you. We can't help you."

DM— **Thomas, I'm so sorry. That's horrific.**
TB— I had to see the clinic's psychologist, and it went to an advisory board. In the end they said, "We haven't seen this situation before. We don't think that it's in the best interest for the child coming into this world." Who should have to go through that when they decide to have a family? Who has the right to say that I can't have my own biological children? This medical hostility forecloses discussion of transgender people's options. They don't realize—most people don't realize—that you don't have to become sterile in order to be the gender that you want to live. Transgender people do have the ability to live their lives successfully and be fulfilled, and also have their own biological children. That's my mission—to let other trans people know that this is an option. You should have your gender identity validated, even through the process, or especially through the process, of building a family. If people have access to knowledge about their own health and their own bodies, then they can make informed choices. That's not just a personal act—it's a political one, too.

Galway
PRO-CHOICE
CHOICE SOCIETY NUIG
TWO YEARS ON ...
GALWAY
REMEMBERS
MEMORIAL FOR SAVITA HALAPPANAVAR
OCTOBER 28TH, BROWNE DOORWAY, EYRE SQUARE
FROM NOON: LEAVE MESSAGES AND FLOWERS
6:00 PM: CANDLELIT VIGIL

1—— A flyer commemorating Savita Halappanavar, a thirty-one-year-old Irish dentist who died in 2012 from a septic miscarriage after having been denied an abortion

2—— Aletris Cordial was a popular over-the-counter remedy, described as a uterine tonic and taken as a preventative measure by women who had previously miscarried. It was made by Rio Chemical Company, St. Louis, in the 1890s

3—— Photographer Dianne Yudelson's *Lost* series reflects on her eleven miscarriages. Here, *Lost: Violet* documents some of the mementos she kept after one miscarriage, as she did after each

4—— "The peach tattoo is for our first born, Ellis Ford, lost at fourteen weeks at about the size of a peach. The other tattoo represents our three babies that came after him—a pea pod with two little peas lost around seven weeks, and a blackberry for Faith, lost around eleven weeks." —Kiersten Peterson

5—— A women's health talisman to "cure unstable embryo [threatened miscarriage]," from a manuscript copy of *Tian Yi fu lu* (Record of Spells of the Celestial Physician), first published in 1123

6—— "The day that I got my tattoo was very emotional, but it also provided me with some closure. I look at it every day and remember that I have been pregnant and hold onto the hope that it will happen again." —Jacqueline Neubauer

7—— Jizō statues at the Zōjō-ji, Tokyo, 2017

8—— "I lost a baby, who we named Ira, at twenty-one weeks. We had to have an abortion to save my life. Completely earth shattering. Thanks for asking for these stories and talking about these issues." —Anonymous

9—— "Tina's '3 Reds' tattoo represents her and her two sons—all redheads. Her youngest son died at age thirteen. My tattoo says, 'For you the snow will fall with flowers.' It's an American Indian proverb about how the world will change for your child. My three blue plumeria flowers represent my sons; the middle one was stillborn."
—Lisa M. Palmer

LOSS Pregnancy loss has a dictionary definition—it's called *miscarriage* before the twentieth week of gestation, and considered a stillbirth after that—and yet, every experience is unique. Loss of pregnancy can come with searing physical or emotional pain, disappointment, guilt, shame, or relief. Miscarriage can also occur in the earliest days and weeks of a missed period, and often goes unnoticed. Though pregnancy loss is incredibly common, it is nevertheless a cross-cultural taboo, and often remains unspoken. But such taboos are increasingly broken by those who wish to define such experiences on their own terms, in their own words.

2 3 4
5 6 7
8

匡胎動不安付

嚊婆帝南塗急搵

都毋吒婆利殷揢

右用鐵醋湯服

BABY ON BOARD BUTTON——When should you wear it? Where should you put it? Will anyone notice it? If they do notice it, will they do anything about it? If they don't, what should you do? And has anyone ever accused you of cheating by wearing it when you had no right to?

When questions like these appear on Mumsnet, a website started by a British mom eager to seek advice from other parents after a disastrous first family holiday with one-year-old twins, they invariably concern a small, white, circular button emblazoned with three words and the bullseye symbol of London's transportation system in bright blue. It is the Baby on Board button, designed to be worn by pregnant women traveling on London's crowded buses, overground trains, and Underground railway system to identify their condition as a jaunty hint that fellow passengers might want to offer them a seat.

Developed by the in-house design team of Transport for London (TfL), which manages the city's public transport network, the Baby on Board button, or badge to use the British term, was introduced in 2005. It has since proved so popular that more than a million have been distributed to pregnant women with the aim of making their journeys around London calmer, safer, and more comfortable.

From a social perspective, the button's introduction reflected the growing readiness of Britons in the early twenty-first century to recognize pregnancy as a natural condition that need not prevent people from continuing to lead active lives and fulfil their professional responsibilities. Previously, pregnancy had typically been regarded in a nineteenth-century light, as something so debilitating or embarrassing that those afflicted with it were expected to either disguise their bump or hide themselves away to protect themselves and their unborn offspring.

A Baby on Board button in use on the London Underground

Baby on board!

It was this attitudinal shift that encouraged TfL to devise a way of enabling the growing number of pregnant people traveling regularly on its buses and trains to clearly but silently signal to other passengers that they had a bona fide reason to sit down. Despite the flurries of uncertainty aired by Mumsnetters about the pros and cons of wearing the buttons and their occasional clashes with sceptical fellow passengers, the Baby on Board program is generally considered to be a success, as illustrated by the number of other UK cities that have adopted similar schemes.

From a political perspective, the project synced with the determination of London's then-mayor, Ken Livingstone, and the ambitious and energetic group of left-wing politicians with whom he had dominated the Greater London Authority (GLA) since its formation in 2000, to make their mark on the city. Because the GLA had—and continues to have—relatively limited powers, Livingstone and his colleagues focused their initiatives on the few areas that were under their control, the most prominent of which was public transportation. Taking a practical step to empower and support people during pregnancy slotted neatly into their strategy.

This political subtext was also reflected in the styling of the button, which explicitly referred to two of the most powerful elements of the London Underground's design heritage: the bespoke typeface and the bullseye symbol that were designed for the network by the calligrapher Edward Johnston in the late 1910s. Both projects were commissioned by the Underground's then commercial manager, Frank Pick, who was charged with persuading more people to use the subway. Pick did so by commissioning marketing campaigns that portrayed the Underground as a safe, efficient, affordable way for its passengers to make the most of London's city center and leafy suburbs. Johnston's trim, sans serif typeface was designed to be legible and instantly recognizable, as was his 1917 redesign of the original bullseye symbol, devised by Pick in 1908.

The positive response to Johnston's designs emboldened Pick to work with other gifted designers, artists, and architects, first on the Underground and then, following its takeover in 1933 by the newly created London Passenger Transport Board (LPTB), on all the city's public transport services. With Pick as its chief executive officer, the LPTB became a global role model of enlightened design management. Great artists, including László Moholy-Nagy, Paul Nash, and Man Ray, created its posters and brochures. The bus and subway stations were designed in a dashing Art Deco style by prominent architects such as Charles Holden. A young engineering draftsman employed in the London Underground Signals Office, Harry Beck, designed a diagrammatic map of the subway system in his spare time that remains the most influential map of its kind and one of the most memorable symbols of London. Pick himself devoted much of his spare time to traveling across the sprawling network, searching for flaws. Having noted details like peeling posters or broken door handles, he would dispatch a memo to whichever luckless station manager was deemed to be responsible, demanding immediate action.

As starry as his roster of artists, designers, and architects was, Pick's design strategy for London's public transportation was rooted in progressive values of empowerment, efficiency, and a determination to improve the quality of life for everyone living in or visiting the city, rich and poor alike. No wonder TfL's design team decided to evoke the Pick era by including digitized versions of Johnston's Standard Block Lettering and bullseye on the Baby on Board button. The implication was that the new TfL and other political initiatives of Ken Livingstone's mayoralty were reviving the optimism, empathy, and inclusivity of Frank Pick's early twentieth-century design coups.

—**Alice Rawsthorn**

BABY SHOWERS——I have four children, and I have never been to a baby shower. I am not personally opposed to them. In contrast to some aspects of our dominant Christian culture, such as Christmas trees and trick-or-treating, until now, I've never given baby showers much thought. Orthodox Jews just don't have them. Unlike almost every other moment of daily life, our pregnancies are almost completely devoid of communal input and ritual.

Many Jewish people say this is because of superstition—that we don't want to invite the *ayin hara*, or evil eye—but I think it's because of the inherent loneliness of pregnancy. I imagine that baby showers are analogous to bridal showers, a custom that's accepted in my community. Bridal showers drum up excitement for the bride. We rally around her and encourage her on the way to her next stage of life. We ply her with gifts to ease her way. We know that ambivalence and trepidation can be mixed with the excitement and anticipation of the wedding day.

So why don't we throw baby showers? Why don't we rally around the mother and give her advice and tell her about the wonders of motherhood?

We don't gather our girlfriends or buy pastel-colored balloons. We don't commission diaper cakes or chip in for the newest stroller. We don't buy cheeky onesies, and we don't serve petit fours. We don't even use that quintessential Jewish exclamation of *mazal tov* in response to an announcement of pregnancy, but instead the significantly more muted *b'shaa tova*, which means simply, "in good time." Many don't bother announcing their pregnancies at all. We don't infuse pregnancy with a sense of the communal because pregnancy in Judaism is intensely personal.

Pregnancy is traditionally a fraught and dangerous time for women. Our bodies are in danger, and so is the unborn child. Pregnancy is a liminal state. Its existence is that of two attached beings, one not yet born and one not yet a parent.

The game Pin the Sperm on the Egg™, designed by Claudette Dunn. Below, though her twin girls were born in winter, Shoshana Greenwald waited until spring to make the traditional Kiddush celebration in honor of their birth in her small synagogue on a Shabbat after services

Pregnancy, Judaism tells us, is a part of life. It is dangerous, and it is personal, and it is intense. And yet, in our large families, it is ordinary. I am reminded of the wedding ceremony, when the bride circles the groom seven times. She builds a fence around her small family and protects it from the outside world. Pregnancy is similar in that separation is actively created. Pregnant women are exempt from many Jewish laws. They may eat on fast days and are encouraged to eat whatever they crave. We support them, but we don't cheer for them. We help, but we don't celebrate.

When I was a newly married senior in college, pregnant with my eldest, my mother took me to Babies "R" Us. She sensed, perhaps, my ambivalence—that I was not comfortable with surrendering my autonomy, my very being, to the fetus that had taken up residency, and she thought that seeing all the cute products that come with contemporary motherhood would be a great way to increase my excitement, much as a baby shower with the gaggle of friends, the virgin cocktails, and the matching tablecloths does. But as soon as we walked into the store and I saw all the baby items, I felt overwhelmed and begged my mother to leave.

Rather than turning outward to my tight-knit community, I needed to turn inward. The single greatest moment of my pregnancy was when my husband's uncle, a doctor, reassured me that I probably didn't have a deadly blood clot while also alluding to the fetus as a parasite. Yes! I thought. It is taking nutrients, energy, and my figure. I relaxed into my ambivalence and finally started to bond with my unborn child.

Communal Jewish life kicks back in immediately after a live birth. We don't just focus on the newborn, we make the mother meals and offer to watch her other children. There is even a business, the *kimpeturin heim* (see *Kraamzorg* p. 271), in which the mother travels from the hospital to a high-end hotel or spa with her newborn and is waited on hand and foot for several days. There are nurses to care for the baby, lactation consultants on call, and delicious food to help with the transition. Infrastructure like this is made to support a veteran of many pregnancies, of many children.

The Jewish word *kimpeturin* describes the communal aspect and responsibility toward postpartum women. We focus on the baby, sure, but we also focus on the mother. This is reflected in the Jewish outlook on abortion as well. Judaism values life above all else, and so the question of when life begins is crucial, especially when the mother's life is in danger, mentally or physically.

According to one of the great Jewish authorities of the last century, Rabbi Moshe Feinstein, life begins only after the baby's head has emerged from the mother's birth canal. That is the beginning of personhood and also the beginning of the separation of the mother and the child, and that is when community reemerges as well.

The expectant mother retreats from communal life and reemerges when the pregnancy is finished. She attends synagogue when she can, and she recites a blessing that is recited when someone's life has been put in danger. The inherent danger of pregnancy is present in every stage of childbearing. Indeed, the very commandment of having children is not incumbent on women but on men, because the Torah will not command people to put their lives in danger.

Not proudly announcing our pregnancies is not covert sexual shame but instead an acknowledgement that one in four pregnancies end in miscarriage. We are quiet about it. We neither seek nor offer recognition. We do not gather for a party to perpetuate a myth—to tell the prospective mother that motherhood will be easy. Rather, we wait in uneasy anticipation until the live baby has been born, and then we support the mother and eagerly welcome the child into the Jewish faith.

—**Shoshana Greenwald**

GENDER REVEAL——Boots or bows? Touchdowns or tutus? Guns or glitter? Better judgment and common sense eventually catch up with many (though sadly not all) misguided ideas. As American as apple pie to some, while to many others a reinforcement of harmful binary stereotypes, the gender-reveal cake took less than a decade to emerge, explode in popularity, and then begin to disintegrate under closer scrutiny.

The design typology made its debut in 2008 when American parent-to-be Jenna Myers Karvunidis baked what is widely believed to be the inaugural entry in the genre in order to reveal the sex of her first child, and then posted about it on her blog. Shaped like a duckling, the cake had a pink buttercream filling that announced to gathered friends and family that she was going to birth a human with two X chromosomes. Her confection gained traction online, and a new ritual was born.

In the wake of Karvunidis's duckling cake, increasingly elaborate methods of revelation appeared, usually at parties staged in the later months of pregnancy. These included balloons that, when popped, spewed pink or blue confetti; themed pinatas; fireworks; and, in 2017, explosives that sparked an Arizona wildfire. Thoughtful observers pointed out early on in the trend that gender is a cultural construction, donned like clothing, and so ascribing restrictive expectations prior to birth is unhelpful at best. Yet, the practice began to be reconsidered more widely only once people started getting hurt, including an Iowa woman who died instantly after being hit by shrapnel when a homemade device misfired at a gender-reveal party in late 2019.

Gender-reveal cakes are underwritten by the prenatal technologies of ultrasound imaging and amniocentesis, which entered the realm of reproductive health in the 1950s. At the sonogram appointment where expectant parents can choose to learn the sex of their unborn child, some ask the technician to write "girl" or "boy"

Captain Gregory Veteto, of the 15th Marine Expeditionary Unit's Ground Combat Element, punts a football sent by his wife, revealing the gender of their baby during a weekly formation, November 1, 2017

——**PREGNANCY**

on a piece of paper and seal it in an envelope that is then passed on to a friend or relative who prepares a gender-reveal celebration. In addition to a plethora of cake designs, these events have spawned entire product lines and became profitable business opportunities for retailers.[1] While it is medical innovations that have enabled sex to be known prior to birth, it is arguably contemporary mass-media platforms that have ensured the hyper-dissemination—and thus trending popularity—of the gender-reveal-as-public-spectacle. It is little wonder that this ritual emerged, peaked, and jumped the shark in tandem with the widespread adoption of YouTube (2005), Twitter (2006), and Instagram (2010) as places to share, among other things, personal and family milestones.

Carly Gieseler, a media and communication scholar, describes the gender-reveal celebration as a "performative space at the threshold of life, a liminal moment that draws on the power of communitas while creating a sense of permanence and security in the categorization of sexual and gendered difference."[2] An outgrowth of the baby shower, which was traditionally for those identifying as women, the gender-reveal party is now (ironically) a place for extended kin of all identifications and ages to gather. Gieseler underscores that while "things like decorations and cake may seem lighthearted and frivolous, when they're driven by a consumer imperative they become a marker of appropriate parenthood

expected of expecting parents."[3] These events ground one of the most common (and problematically essentializing) questions that surround any pregnancy—"girl or boy?"—in a reductively binary coding of color that is itself rooted in Western dictates.[4] It is a palette and a problem that scholars have argued over. While pink is usually coded female and blue denotes male for most gender-reveal designs, confectionary or otherwise, the historian Jo B. Paoletti has posited that these color associations have not always been as rigidly adhered to as contemporary usage might suggest. Citing advertisements from the turn of the twentieth century, she frames the color-gender association as unstable, having evolved into current tropes in the years after World War II. In her 2012 book, *Pink and Blue: Telling the Boys from the Girls in America*, Paoletti cites a June 1918 issue of *Earnshaw's Infants' Department*, a trade magazine for manufacturers of baby clothes, which notes "a great diversity of opinion on this subject, but the generally accepted rule is pink for a boy and blue for a girl. The reason is that pink, being a more decided and stronger color, is more suitable for the boy, while blue, which is more delicate and dainty, is prettier for the girl."[5]

The sociologist Marco Del Giudice disputed Paoletti's claim, in a 2012 article and a 2017 letter to the editor of the academic journal *Archives of Sexual Behavior*, providing robust evidence to debunk what he terms a "scientific urban legend" of this "pink-blue reversal."[6]

Del Giudice combed electronic databases of books and newspapers of the last two centuries to postulate that deviation from the pink-blue gender-color association was limited, only showing some increase in its usage over the last half century.

A stronger argument for the impulse to color code lies in the history of communication design. Color helps market, sell, and create consumer traditions. Gender-reveal parties are the perfect illustration of this truth. A Google video search for "gender reveal" turns up more than 10.2 million results (and counting), from which viewers can watch couples, families, and celebrities across the world shriek as they become cognizant of one or the other color through designs they have made or purchased for that very purpose.

More recently, the tradition has morphed and grown, with purple frosting used to subvert the expectation that aspects of personhood can be described in binary colors or determined in advance of birth and life experience. Appropriation of a form for the purpose of critique or reclamation has precedents in design history and beyond—think of the iconic ACT UP "Silence=Death" posters that repurposed the pejorative pink triangle as part of AIDS activism in the 1980s. Yet in an era that rightly recognizes gender as fluid, not even alliterative cliches spelled out in frosting should save a cultural phenomenon that even its originator now says is well past its "best before" date.[7]

1 "Although particularly popular in the US, the parties are a growing trend in the UK. Online retailer Party Delights reports an 87% increase in gender reveal-related products over the past three years and attributes the craze to social media and viral videos." Rosie Blunt, "The Dangers—Physical and Psychological—of Gender Reveal Parties," BBC News, October 30, 2019, bbc.com.
2 "Carly Gieseler,

"Gender-Reveal Parties: Performing Community Identity in Pink and Blue," *Journal of Gender Studies* 27, no. 6 (2018): 661–71 (abstract), doi.org/10.1080/09589236.2017.1287066; see also Gieseler, *Gender-Reveal Parties as Mediated Events: Celebrating Identity in Pink and Blue* (Lanham, MD: Lexington Books, 2019).
3 Interview with the author, June 2, 2020.
4 This gender divide along color lines is

also reflected in nineteenth-century, middle-class domestic interiors, as scholars, including the design historian Juliet Kinchin, have noted. Dining rooms, a place for males to gather after dinner, were darker hued in decor, while the drawing room, decorated in lighter colors, was the domain of female groups. See Graeme Brooker and Lois Weinthal, eds., *The Handbook of Interior Architecture and Design* (London: Bloomsbury,

2017).
5 Jo B. Paoletti, *Pink and Blue: Telling the Boys from the Girls in America* (Bloomington: Indiana University Press, 2012), 85; see also Jeanne Maglaty, "When Did Girls Start Wearing Pink," *Smithsonian Magazine,* April 7, 2011, smithsonianmag.com.
6 See Marco Del Giudice, "Pink, Blue, and Gender: An Update," *Archives of Sexual Behavior* 46, no. 6 (June 29, 2017): 1555–63, doi.

org/10.1007/s10508-017-1024-3; and Del Giudice, "The Twentieth Century Reversal of Pink-Blue Gender Coding: A Scientific Urban Legend?," *Archives of Sexual Behavior* 41, no. 6 (July 21, 2012): 1321–23, doi.org/10.1007/s10508-012-0002-z.
7 Ian Burke, "The Woman Who 'Invented' Gender Reveal Parties Doesn't Think Gender Should Be Assigned at Birth," *Insider*, August 2, 2019, insider.com.

HOSPITAL BAG—In the early 1970s, Victor Papanek, the luminary designer-educator, offered an expansive, generous definition of design as "the conscious and intuitive effort to impose meaningful order." In addition to outwardly creative pursuits, he argued, "design is also cleaning and reorganizing a desk drawer, pulling an impacted tooth, baking an apple pie, choosing sides for a back-lot baseball game, and educating a child."[1] To this list one might add: packing a hospital bag.

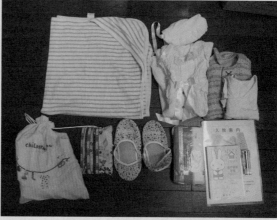

Hospital bag contents from around the world, from top left and clockwise: Tiff Rolf's (US), which included a birth plan and pajamas; Takako Ishikawa's (Japan), which included her insurance card and toiletries; Agnes Noti's (Tanzania), which included a basin and a flask; and Merina Milimo (Zambia), which contained a baby blanket, a peg for clipping the umbilical cord, and sanitary pads

In the final weeks of pregnancy, when it is generally recommended (to those planning a hospital birth) to prepare some sort of go-bag, "meaningful order" may seem like a pipe dream. Nevertheless, the task offers a sense of control, marking a singular moment between pregnancy and childbirth. Its execution closes out the months of discomfort, anxiety, discrimination, unsolicited advice, and unexpected complications that even the "easiest" and most welcome of pregnancies can entail, and anticipates the unknown.

Sharing DNA as it does with other portable vessels, the hospital bag is ripe for semiotic analysis. Its functional proximity to childbirth only intensifies its broader connections to historical ideas about women. At the close of the nineteenth century, Sigmund Freud's *The Interpretation of Dreams* (1899) associated luggage interchangeably with sin, female genitals, and the womb.[2] Advancing a feminist perspective in 1979, the anthropologist Elizabeth Fisher, in her Carrier Bag Theory of human evolution, posited that the first cultural device was probably a recipient—a pouch, net, or bag to free the hands and more efficiently collect and transport food in prehistoric societies where gathering was more important—though less "heroic"—than hunting. "Women, then," she continued, "would have been the first to devise containers: they themselves were containers of children."[3]

In the history of hospital births over the last century, hospital bags have proved to be intensely personal projects. Today, readymade bags are available for those preferring product over packing. But in general hospital bags stand out as one of the few designs *by* pregnant people rather than *for* them. As a result, online checklists and videos ("what to pack" but also "what NOT to pack") proliferate to guide the novice.

In countries like the United States, the hospital bag usually contains items that are not strictly necessary for giving birth. Depending on personal outlook and experience, these may be deemed either extras or essentials. One source for a wider perspective is the nonprofit WaterAid, which commissioned a series of photographs and interviews of expectant mothers around the world to illuminate the difficulties of childbirth where access to clean water is compromised.

Representing the United States in the WaterAid 2016 series, new parent Tiff Rolf described the car seat as the only mandatory thing needed to take a baby home. "The rest are things to make my hospital stay more comfortable: my birth plan, pajamas, flip-flops and slippers, snacks, mother's milk tea (to help with breast milk), and a cute outfit for the baby to wear home. And a present from him to his big sister—a lollipop and some Playdoh." In stark contrast is the packing list of Kemisa Hidaya in Uganda, who was obligated to bring much more:

1 Two nylon sheets which are spread on the bed during childbirth
2 Ten pairs of gloves, but I only bought two because I did not have money to buy 10
3 A pair of new razor blades for use during the childbirth process
4 Cotton wool roll for padding and cleaning blood in the process of delivery
5 Washing soap powder for cleaning the labor room after delivery
6 A bottle of Jik disinfectant
7 Bucket and basin for bathing and urination
8 Flask for hot drinking water and cups
9 A roll of toilet paper
10 Baby receiver to cover the baby
11 Nappies
12 Bedding for use while in the hospital
13 Emergency money[4]

In film and television history, dramatizations of pregnancy and delivery have rarely featured a hospital bag. But in some noteworthy circumstances it has proved a powerful prop. In the 1968 psychological thriller *Rosemary's Baby*, the bag significantly heightens the tension as Rosemary (Mia Farrow) begins unraveling the sinister circumstance of her impending delivery. Indeed, her packing of the bag marks the film's turn—a final moment of blissful normalcy before a concluding chapter of betrayal, panic, and darkness. Soon discovering the supernatural threats the viewer has long anticipated, she adds her new collection of witchcraft books to her suitcase and sets out alone to save her baby. But hope is clearly lost when she is found and led back home by her villainous doctor and complicit husband, now holding her hospital bag.

Moving from the supernatural to slapstick, perhaps the most memorable hospital bag in popular culture appeared in I Love Lucy. In the exceedingly popular season 2 finale, "Lucy Goes to the Hospital" (1953), the bag's representation of order—around childbirth as well as midcentury gender roles—is expertly subverted for comic effect. Due any moment, Lucy is cool and calm, but her husband Ricky is a nervous wreck. While she rests, he carefully rehearses with their neighbors Fred and Ethel to streamline the imminent trip to hospital.

Despite all their preparation, calm quickly turns to chaos when Lucy confidently declares, "It's time," and Ricky panics. He fumbles and spills her carefully placed bag, repacks it with their landline phone, and clambers out the door without it or Lucy. When they finally make it to the hospital, it is Ricky who needs a wheelchair. Lucy stands tall by his side, ready to go—bag in hand.

—Aidan C. O'Connor

1 Victor Papanek, *Design for the Real World: Human Ecology and Social Change*, 2nd ed., rev. (Chicago: Academy Chicago Publishers, 1984), 3.
2 Emily Ridge, "'A Purse of Her Own': Women and Carriage," in *Portable Modernisms: The Art of Travelling Light* (Edinburgh: Edinburgh University Press, 2017), 84.
3 Elizabeth Fisher, *Woman's Creation: Sexual Evolution and the Shaping of Society* (New York: McGraw Hill, 1979), 56; quoted in Ridge, "'A Purse of Her Own,'" 87.
4 Olga Khazan, "The Essentials for Giving Birth Around the World," *The Atlantic*, February 8, 2016.

LINDSEY BEAL

LINDSEY BEAL Based in Providence, Rhode Island, Lindsey Beal combines research about historical and contemporary women's lives with historical photographic processes, often including sculpture, papermaking, and artist books in her work. A focus on tools and technologies used by, designed for, or applied to women is a unifying thread throughout. As Beal reflected, "such designs directly affect our everyday lives through safety, health and medicine, sexual pleasure, appearance and fashion, and in providing for ourselves and others. They are a double-edged sword that can make our lives easier, freer and more enjoyable or can be used on or against us."

1— Glass Nipple Shield, The Dittrick Medical History Center at Case Western Reserve University, Cleveland
2— Glass Nipple Shield, Mütter Museum, Philadelphia
3— Gentle Expressions breast pump, Center for the History of Medicine, Countway Library, Harvard University, Cambridge, Massachusetts
4— Pewter Nipple Shield, Mütter Museum, Philadelphia
5— Breast Pump, Mütter Museum, Philadelphia

2 3

4

FORCEPS—Instrument-assisted delivery was recorded in sixth-century Hindu medicine and was mentioned in the writings of the Greek physician Hippocrates (460–370 BCE).[1] However, these procedures were to remove a dead fetus, thereby saving the mother's life. An instrument designed to deliver a living child safely first appeared in the late sixteenth or early seventeenth century. The four-hundred-year history of obstetrical forceps—never without controversy—speaks to the power of this medical instrument.

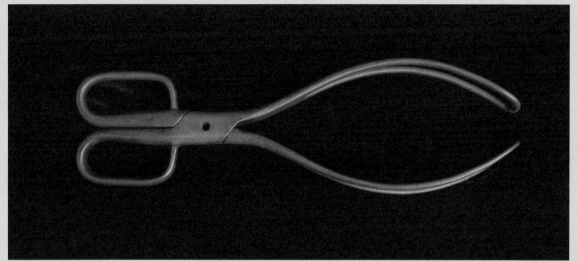

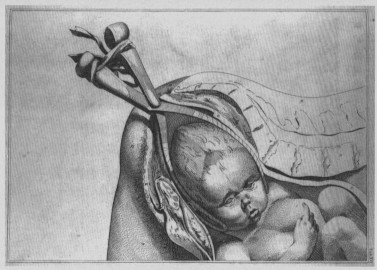

The Chamberlen forceps were named for Peter Chamberlen the Elder (d. 1631), who is thought to have invented the obstetrical forceps. The Chamberlens became famous for dealing with difficult births, but kept the forceps a family secret for more than a hundred years. Below, illustration from William Smellie's *A Set of Anatomical Tables, with Explanations, and an Abridgment, of the Practice of Midwifery, with a View to Illustrate a Treatise on That Subject, and Collection of Cases* (1754)

In 1569, William Chamberlen, a French Huguenot surgeon fleeing religious persecution, took his family to England. His sons, both named Peter, followed his career path. Scholars generally credit Peter the Elder (1560–1631) as the inventor of the forceps, the design of which was kept a closely guarded family secret for over a century.[2]

The family went to impressive and theatrical lengths to protect their design, arriving at the house of a laboring woman in a special carriage equipped with a large, cloth-covered, gilded box.[3] The forceps were protected and muffled by cloth veils in the interior. Once inside, the Chamberlens banished all but the laboring woman and then proceeded to blindfold her. During labor they used distracting noises, such as bells, to mask the sound of metal on metal.[4] While these techniques were extreme, they were highly successful in allowing the family to keep its design a secret for three generations.

Forceps brought prosperity and prestige to the Chamberlens. Peter the Elder became the obstetrician of members of royalty. His brother, Peter the Younger (1572–1626), was also a successful male midwife and surgeon. Peter the Younger's son, Peter the Third, or "Dr. Peter" (1601–1683), like his grandfather attended royalty and was the first of the family to obtain an actual medical license.[5]

Dr. Peter's son, Hugh the Elder, an accomplished midwife with a proclivity for get-rich-quick schemes (a trait passed down from his forefathers), traveled to France in 1670 in an attempt to sell the family secret.[6] The French physician François Mauriceau presented him with a test, a thirty-eight-year-old rachitic dwarf who had been in labor for six days. Despite Hugh's best attempts, both mother and baby died, and he was sent on his way. But he returned to England with

a copy of Mauriceau's book *Des Maladies des femmes grosses et accouchées* (1668), which he translated into English, publishing it in 1673 as *The Accomplisht Midwife*.[7] This very successful book contained a forward by Hugh in which he states:

My Father, Brothers, and my Self, (though none else in Europe that I know) have by Gods blessing, and our industry, attained to, and long practiced a way to deliver a Women [sic]...without any prejudice to her or her Infant.... By this manual operation we can also both shorten the time, and lessen the number of pains in a right Labour...without danger, and with advantage to both Woman and Child.[8]

Hugh the Elder never officially managed to sell the forceps. But he did contrive to swindle a Dutch obstetrician. There is scholarly debate as to just what instrument Hugh sold him; it was either a single blade of the forceps or a vectus, a singled-bladed instrument. An assistant of the Dutch obstetrician provided a sketch to a Belgian anatomist who refined the invention, adding a mirror-image blade. These forceps, dubbed the "Hands of Iron," were presented to the Royal Academy in Paris in 1720 or 1721. As for the Chamberlens' forceps, in the late 1720s Hugh's son, Hugh the Younger, toward the end of his career and lacking a male heir, released the secret of the tool.

Obstetrical forceps quickly gained favor within the medical community, and other physicians immediately began improving on the design. The Chamberlens' forceps had a cephalic curve to conform to the baby's head. By the 1750s, forceps had both cephalic and pelvic curves, increasing safety for both mother and child.

Regardless, obstetrical forceps had detractors from the moment they became known.

Throughout the eighteenth and early nineteenth centuries there were two factions within the obstetrical community: conservatists who were against their use, and interventionists who favored them. But lack of knowledge on proper placement and use of force, especially in the hands of untrained individuals, gave forceps the potential to end life as easily as save it.

As more physicians began using forceps, more attempts were made to improve on the basic design. In 1877, Etienne Stephane Tarnier invented axis-traction forceps, the first major innovation in a century. By the mid-nineteenth century, one in 167 deliveries used forceps.[9]

Forceps were also an instrument of transition. With their increased use came a societal change in the interpretation of women's bodies and pregnancy. Childbirth itself was defined as abnormal, and the pregnant woman seen as pathological and in need of medical intervention.[10] Obstetrical tools also allowed the physician increased control over the birthing process and the woman's body. They could shift the timeline of birth, intervening with invasive procedures if the birth was not progressing according to their satisfaction, and "fix" the situation.

The twentieth century saw an increase in hospital births. With more women under heavy sedation and unable to push effectively, the prophylactic use of forceps became standard practice. This era of increased anesthesia and invasive medical procedures continued well into the 1970s, gradually giving way to less invasive procedures like vacuum-assisted birth and to the even more invasive cesarean section, both of which effectively sidelined obstetrical forceps.[11]

—Anna Dhody

1 Sukhera Sheikh, Inithan Ganesaratnam, and Haider Jan, "The Birth of Forceps," *Journal of the Royal Society of Medicine Short Reports* 4 (2013): 1 2 J. H. Aveling, *The Chamberlens and the Midwifery Forceps: Memorials of the Family and an Essay on the Invention of the Instrument* (London: J. & A. Churchill, 1882),

224–26.
3 Peter M Dunn, "The Chamberlen Family (1560–1728) and Obstetric Forceps," *Archives of Disease in Childhood: Fetal and Neonatal Edition* 81 (1999): F232–34, fn.bmj.com/content/81/3/F232.
4 Ronald L. Young, "Obstetrical Forceps: History, Mystery, and Mortality" (2011), Digital Commons@The Texas Medical Center,

John P. McGovern Historical Collections and Research Center, *Houston History of Medicine Lectures*, Paper 13, digital-commons.library.tmc.edu/homl/13.
5 Young, "Obstetrical Forceps," 5.
6 Young, "Obstetrical Forceps," 7.
7 Dunn, "The Chamberlen Family," 233.
8 Hugh Chamberlen, "The Translator

to the Reader," in *The Accomplisht Midwife, Treating of the Diseases of Women...by* François Mauriceau (London, 1673), a 2.
9 Young, "Obstetrical Forceps," 14.
10 Hilary Marland and Anne Marie Rafferty, eds., *Midwives, Society, and Childbirth: Debates and Controversies in the Modern Period* (New York: Routledge,

1997).
11 John Elflein, "Percentage of Births Delivered by Forceps or Vacuum Extraction in the United States from 1990–2018," Statista, December 3, 2019, statista.com/statistics/276067/us-births-delivered-by-forceps-or-vacuum-extraction.

BIRTHING FURNITURE—The benefits of various birthing positions—kneeling, standing, sitting, squatting, or lying down—particularly with regard to pelvic posture, have been publicly debated at least since the 1880s.[1] Birthing positions can be chosen or mandated, intuited or inherited, self-directed or at the behest of other forces. Birthing furniture and other physical objects, structures, and accoutrements determine not only the physiology but also the emotional experience of birth.

In what follows, we mine medical manuals, period magazines, centuries-old etchings, and contemporary speculative designs to trace how birthing positions, furniture design, and social and cultural expectations have split and converged over time. Even in a single environment, birth furniture (and birthing positions) can vary dramatically, from the supine position a birthing bed facilitates to the more active, interchangeable, and spontaneous positions that equipment like yoga balls and peanuts, slings, bars, stools, pools, and chairs make possible. Some designs, such as birth shackles, may seem anachronistic but are still routinely used on incarcerated people, both while they give birth and postpartum. Even without any furnishings, birthing people find their way. In a bas-relief dating to about 60–30 BCE at the Temple of Esneh in Egypt, for example, Cleopatra is depicted giving birth in a kneeling position, her body surrounded and supported by other women.

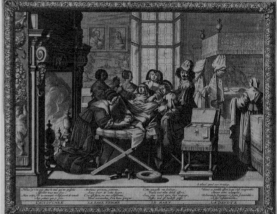

The May 1958 Issue of the *Ladies Home Journal*

In this issue of the popular women's magazine, among the usual representations of midcentury motherhood—gleaming appliances, cake recipes, and lipstick-wearing women in aprons—was a page with a letter penned by an anonymous labor and delivery nurse:

> When I first started in my profession, I thought it would be wonderful to help bring new life into this world. I was and am still shocked at the manner in which a mother-to-be is rushed into the delivery room and strapped down with cuffs around her arms and legs and steel clamps over her shoulders and chest.
> It is common practice to take the mother right into the delivery room as soon as she is "prepared." [This preparation would have meant shaved pubic hair and an enema.] Often she is strapped in the lithotomy position, legs in stirrups with knees pulled far apart, for as long as eight hours. On one occasion, an obstetrician informed the nurses on duty that he was going to a dinner and that they should slow up things. The young mother was taken into the delivery room and strapped down hand and foot with her legs tied together.[2]

The letter touched a nerve. Women across the country wrote in to share their own stories of abuse, including being strapped down and drugged in an effort to keep them still, quiet, and passive.[3]

Birthing Beds and Tables

The recommendation to give birth while lying down was, at least at first, well intentioned. It was formally introduced in 1598 by the French barber-surgeon Jacques Gillemeau, who claimed reclining was most comfortable and would help induce labor. The first birthing beds were actual beds, similar to furniture for sleeping. In the mid-1800s, medical designers added leg harnesses and stirrups to obstetric tables, which soon carried over to the design of birthing beds, as did leather straps and other restraints.[4] With the invention of plastics, birthing beds could be made lightweight, easily cleaned and assembled, and adjustable. Though there were no uniform obstetric practices until the first quarter of the twentieth century, the dorsal position (lying flat on one's back) and the lithotomy position (lying back with one's feet in stirrups) became biomedical birthing standards in hospitals.[5] Many types of birthing beds fold the birthing person into an upright position, inviting the power of gravity into the design.

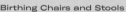

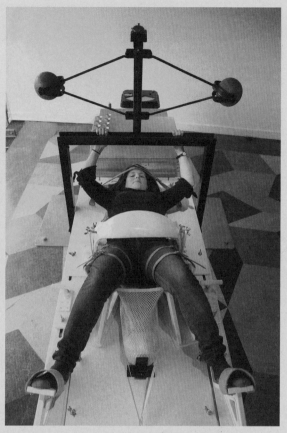

Birthing Chairs and Stools

Birth chairs and backless birthing stools help people feel balanced and supported in an upright position as they give birth. With three or four legs, they usually feature a semicircular cutout on the seat. The position of the body in the birthing chair not only makes use of gravity as the baby drops from the womb and emerges through the vagina, but also maximizes the ability of muscles (abdominal, back, stomach, legs, arms, and vaginal sphincter) to efficiently work in concert. Babylonian birthing chairs date back to 2000 BCE. An Egyptian wall relief dating to 1450 BCE in the birth room of the Luxor temple shows Queen Mutemwia giving birth to her son, Amenhotep III. A birthing chair is also depicted on a Greek votive from 200 BCE.[6] Some millennia-old birthing stools from Britain were designed to be carried while disassembled, suggesting that they belonged to midwives rather than individual households. Today, many birthing centers incorporate furniture and accoutrements made for sitting and squatting while in labor. The woodcut above shows a birthing stool from *Der schwanngeren Frawen und Hebammen Rosengarte*, by the German physician Eucharius Rösslin. First published in 1513, it became a standard midwives manual in Germany.

The Blonsky

In 1965, New Yorkers George and Charlotte Blonsky were granted a patent for an "Apparatus for Facilitating the Birth of a Child by Centrifugal Force." The circular table was meticulously engineered and incorporated safety features designed to protect both mother and child. When it was time to give birth, a mother would be instructed to lie on her back with her legs open; she would then be strapped into place and the table would be rotated at very high speed. To prevent the infant from flying out, a soft mesh net was there to catch it. The design would "assist the under-equipped woman by creating a gentle, evenly distributed, properly directed, precision-controlled force, that acts in unison with and supplements her own efforts."[7] Though lovingly and elaborately designed with only the best intentions, the Blonsky never made it to general use. This version was presented by the artist Marc Abrahams in the exhibition *Fail Better* at the Science Gallery at Trinity College Dublin in 2014.

Birthing Pools

While midwives from around the world have used water in one form or another to help ease pain and relax birthing people, birthing pools are a more recent phenomenon. Some trace their genesis to Moscow in the 1960s, when Igor Charkovsky, a former swimming instructor and self-described "father of sea births," encouraged birthing in the Crimean Sea. In the 1970s, Dr. Michel Odent designed a birthing room at the General Hospital in Pithiviers, in northern France. Dark, earthy colors and heavy curtains encouraged a feeling of seclusion and intimacy, enabling birthing people to labor in whatever positions they found most comfortable. In 1977 Odent installed a pool in the room. Though he envisioned water as a form of pain management, many of his patients birthed within the pools, and Odent is often credited with starting the trend of birthing in water.[8] The visual image of an uninterrupted flow of liquid can have a powerfully positive psychological effect, and the sense of weightlessness that comes with immersing oneself in water can be used to encourage intuitive movement and postures.

Stiliyana Minkovska's Ultima Thule

With greater numbers of birthing people and families exercising their right to actively participate in the birth experience, making it more physiologically and psychologically supportive as well as personal, positive, and even profound, designers are responding. In 2020, the Bulgaria-born, UK-based artist and designer Stiliyana Minkovska created Ultima Thule, a speculative design for an otherworldly, sanctuary-like birth environment made up of three flexible, sculptural pieces of birthing furniture. Using color, texture, and open-ended shapes to facilitate a variety of postures, the pieces work as "an aid that allows the pregnant body to adopt any desired position in order to prepare for parturition. The pieces are accommodating, which allows the expectant parent to sit, kneel, squat, rest, lean, and crawl until they find comfort. It is a gradual element, where the mother takes the journey on her own, or can be supported by a partner, doula, or a midwife."[9]

1 Horizontal birthing positions have been used in Western culture for only about two hundred years. Before this, any recorded history of birth shows an upright birthing position. See Lauren Dundes, "The Evolution of Maternal Birthing Position," *American Journal of Public Health* 77, no. 5 (May 1987): 636.
2 "Cruelty in Maternity Wards," *Ladies' Home Journal*, May 1958, 45; quoted in Tina Cassidy, *Birth: The Surprising History of How We Are Born* (New York: Atlantic Monthly Press, 2006), 65–66.
3 Tina Cassidy, *Birth: A History* (London: Chatto & Windus, 2006), 66–67.
4 Margaret Jowitt, "The Rise and Rise of the Obstetric Bed," *Midwifery Matters* 132 (Spring 2012): 16.
5 J. L. Reynolds, "Primitive Delivery Positions in Modern Obstetrics: Were the Wise Women Wiser Than We?," *Canadian Family Physician* (*Medecin de famille canadien*) 37 (1991): 356–61.
6 See Amanda Carson Banks, *Birth Chairs, Midwives, and Medicine* (Jackson: University Press of Mississippi, 1999), 3.
7 US patent 3,216,423, filed January 15, 1963, issued November 9, 1965.
8 In 1974 the French physician Frédérick Leboyer published *Birth Without Violence*, a book that scrutinized the birth environment from the perspective of the baby.
9 Stiliyana Minkovska, email to the author, July 15, 2020.

JANMA CLEAN BIRTH KIT / LIFEWRAP / SAFE DELIVERY APP

On a visit to a rural village in Rajasthan in northern India, Zubaida Bai noticed a midwife using a sickle—an implement normally reserved for harvesting grain or grass—to cut an umbilical cord. She calls this her "aha" moment. As she watched the midwife repurpose an agricultural tool as a medical one, she reflected on the infection she had contracted due to unsanitary conditions in one of the best facilities in India.[1]

"If I had everything and had to suffer an infection, what would women in these villages be facing?" she wondered.[2]

Born in Chennai, Bai trained as a mechanical engineer in India and the United States. She encountered the concept of a clean birth kit while attending a tech event in Denver. The kit, developed by the nonprofit public health organization PATH (Program for Appropriate Technology in Health), had a plastic sheet, a razor blade, a piece of thread, a small square of soap, and a plastic coin, all wrapped in a box with instructions.[3] Eager to learn more, Bai traveled to Nepal, where PATH had been working with local agencies to assemble and distribute the kits.[4] Unimpressed with the quality, she searched for more samples of such kits but found none that matched her expectations. She knew she was onto something, however, and started building her own improved version, assembled from off-the-shelf components.

In 2009, Bai founded ayzh (pronounced "eyes") and a year later launched her first product: Janma, the clean birth kit. Janma, meaning "birth" in Sanskrit, contains six tools to ensure safe and sterile childbirth conditions: an apron, a sheet, hand sanitizer, antiseptic soap, a cord clip, and a surgical blade. These essential tools were chosen to help health workers meet the World Health Organization (WHO) guidelines of "six cleans" during childbirth: the clean hands of the attendant, a clean surface, a clean blade, a clean cord tie, clean towels to dry and wrap the baby, and a clean cloth to wrap the mother.[5] Priced 50 percent lower than comparable kits and packaged in a jute

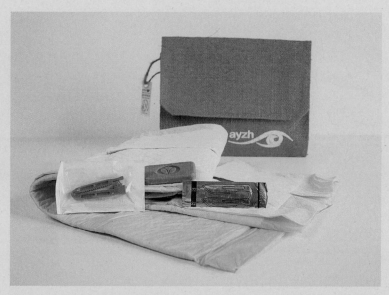

Launched in December 2010, JANMA is a $2 clean birth kit aimed at rural clinics, hospitals, primary health care centers, and midwives as an aid for safe delivery of babies and postnatal health

bag that mothers can reuse as a purse, Janma is becoming an integral part of delivery rooms around the world as a convenient, cost-effective solution to improving access to essential and sanitary commodities.

The effectiveness of kits like the Janma is irrefutable. According to the United Nations, India's maternal mortality rate per hundred thousand live births has been reduced by 65 percent, from 560 in 1990 to 190 in 2013. But that still means 50,000 people die every year in India while giving birth (17 percent from preventable infections), and more than 300,000 infants die the day they are born.[6] In addition to fighting these alarming statistics through its products, ayzh also incorporates community development into its business model. Bai hires local Indian women to assemble the packages, which helps them develop a stable income.

Though ayzh cultivates its ties to the local community, its reach extends well beyond the Indian subcontinent. According to the WHO, more than 800 people die every day in pregnancy and childbirth from preventable causes. And 99 percent of these deaths occur in developing countries. The complications that Janma addresses, such as sepsis and other severe infections, are the third largest cause of death, claiming nearly 11 percent of people who die during childbirth.[7] Since 2010 the company has distributed more than a quarter million kits in India,

Afghanistan, Gambia, Laos, Ghana, Malawi, Nigeria, Zambia, and Haiti, reaching half a million birthing people and babies, with demand from other countries continuing to grow.[8] This projected growth has the potential to prevent deadly or debilitating infections for six million birthing people over the next five years.

Janma is just one of many designs and products targeted at reducing maternal and infant mortality in resource-poor nations. The LifeWrap, made of neoprene and Velcro, is a wet-suit-like garment that acts as a first-aid device to stabilize people who don't have access to the resources to stop postpartum hemorrhaging. The LifeWrap interrupts the bleeding process and allows the body time to clot. During pregnancy the uterus is filled with blood vessels that supply blood to the baby; it then contracts after delivery to put pressure on the blood vessels to stop the bleeding, as with a cut. But sometimes the uterus doesn't contract down and bleeding continues, which can lead to organ system shutdown and death. Medication can help contract the muscles, but it's not always available in developing countries. Taking inspiration from NASA designs for female astronauts, Suellen Miller, an American nurse, created a low-tech solution to keep patients alive while they wait for treatment or during travel to a hospital or clinic. To date, LifeWraps have been used on more than ten thousand birthing people in

thirty-three countries, primarily on the African continent.[9]

Where Janma and LifeWrap rely on low-tech tools and techniques to reduce maternal and infant mortality, the Safe Delivery App leverages the growing ubiquity of smartphones to provide life-saving information and guidance.[10] Developed by the Danish organization Maternity Foundation, the smartphone application offers skilled birth attendants easy-to-understand animated instructional videos, action cards, and drug lists, equipping even those workers in the most remote areas with an on-the-job reference tool. Based on the premise that the key to fighting maternal mortality is training health workers and birth attendants, the app is a mobile health tool positioned to provide such instruction.

Each year, over 300,000 people worldwide die from complications in pregnancy and childbirth. While there are many efforts to combat such preventable deaths, the Janma clean birth kit from ayzh stands out. For founder Bai, the issues of reproductive health and safety are personal. As a mother, and a member of the local community her products serve, Bai breaks the dominant Western philanthropic and entrepreneurial paradigms that dominate design and innovation in countries around the world, impoverished or otherwise.

—Juliana Rowen Barton

1 Karen Frances Eng, "Women and Children First: Fellows Friday with Zubaida Bai, Who Creates Lifesaving Kits for Maternal Health," TED Blog, August 16, 2013, blog.ted.com.
2 Danielle Somers, "Empowering Women through a Simple Purse," USAID Impact Blog, June 25, 2016, blog.usaid.gov.
3 "Indian Muslim Woman among UN 'Champions and Pioneers,'" Matters India, June 25, 2016, mattersindia.com.
4 Since 1988, PATH has worked in Bangladesh and Nepal with the

Christian Commission for Development in Bangladesh, Save the Children, UNICEF, NGOs, and private agencies to design, develop, and distribute simple, clean delivery kits for use in the home. Beginning in 1993, PATH has worked on delivery kit development in Nepal with two key Nepali agencies, Save the Children-US and Maternal and Child Health Products Pvt. Ltd. (MCHP). For more on PATH's clean birth kit efforts in Nepal, see Vivien Tsu, "Nepal Clean Home Delivery Kit: Evaluation of the Health Impact,"

PATH: Program for Appropriate Technology in Health, May 2000.
5 "Safe and Effective Infection Prevention for Inpatient Newborn Care," Do No Harm Technical Brief, 2019, Every Preemie—SCALE, everypreemie.org/donoharmbriefs.
6 See the 2014 report "Ending Newborn Deaths: Ensuring Every Baby Survives," by the nonprofit Save the Children, with Alex Renton.
7 Khalid S. Khan et al., "WHO Analysis of Causes of Maternal Death: A Systematic Review," The Lancet 367, no. 9516 (2006):

1066–74, thelancet.com.
8 Somers, "Empowering Women through a Simple Purse."
9 See Ananya Bhattacharya, "A Garment Originally Made for Astronauts Is Saving the Lives of New Mothers in Developing Countries," Quartz, December 19, 2016, qz.com.
10 The garment typically costs around $55, but many low-income countries that are part of the United Nation's Life Saving Commodities group—established by the UN Population Fund to help scale

technologies to save sixteen million women and children by 2015—pay closer to $42. If washed and stored properly, each garment can be used more than a hundred times; this brings down the cost of its use per birth to well under a dollar. See "UN Commission on Life-Saving Commodities for Women and Children," Commissioners' Report, September 2012, United Nations Population Fund, unfpa.org/publications/un-commission-life-saving-commodities-women-and-children.

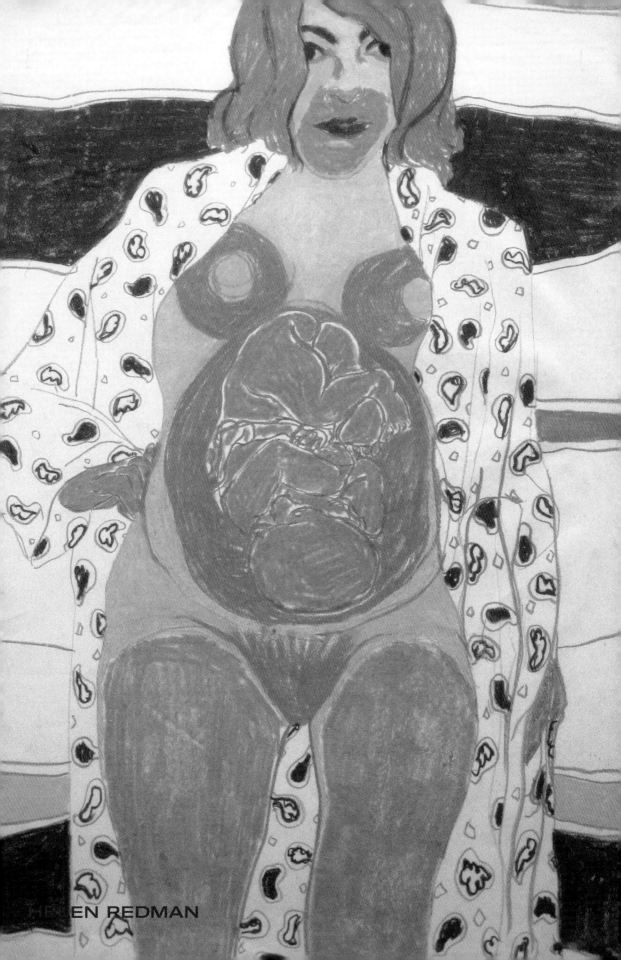

HELEN REDMAN

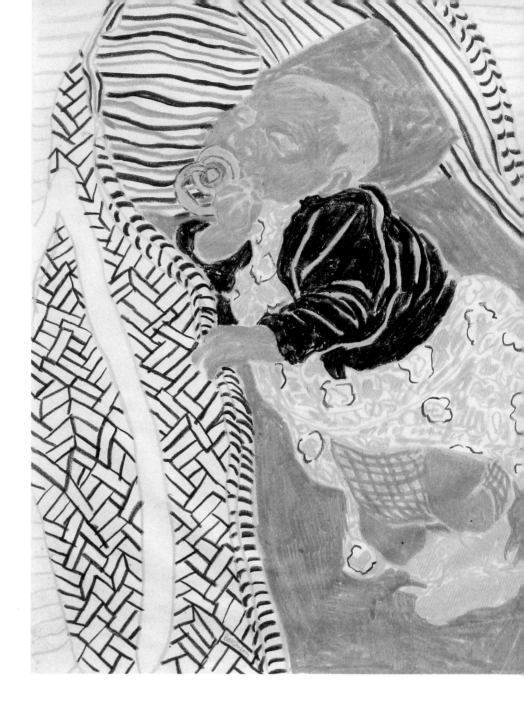

HELEN REDMAN In 1964, when Helen Barchilon Redman was five months pregnant with her second daughter, Nicole, her first daughter, twenty-month-old Paula, died suddenly of an unexplained infection. Redman recorded and reflected on her experiences in a powerful series of portraits of herself and, once she was born, of Nicole. She explained the work's genesis in the feminist journal *Frontiers* in 1978: "I was trying to work through her [Paula's] death—these drawings were really a very deep kind of activity to keep me alive." Now in her eighties, with a lifetime of feminist art engagement as part of her legacy, Redman has an expansive oeuvre centered on themes of matrilineage, generational ties, and human connection.

1— *Enrobed*, 1964. Oil pastel on paper
2— *Pink Faced Nicole en Panier*, 1964. Oil pastel on paper
3— *La Grossesse de Nicole* (age 20), 1984. Oil on canvas
4— *Centered Flux*, 1964. Oil pastel on paper

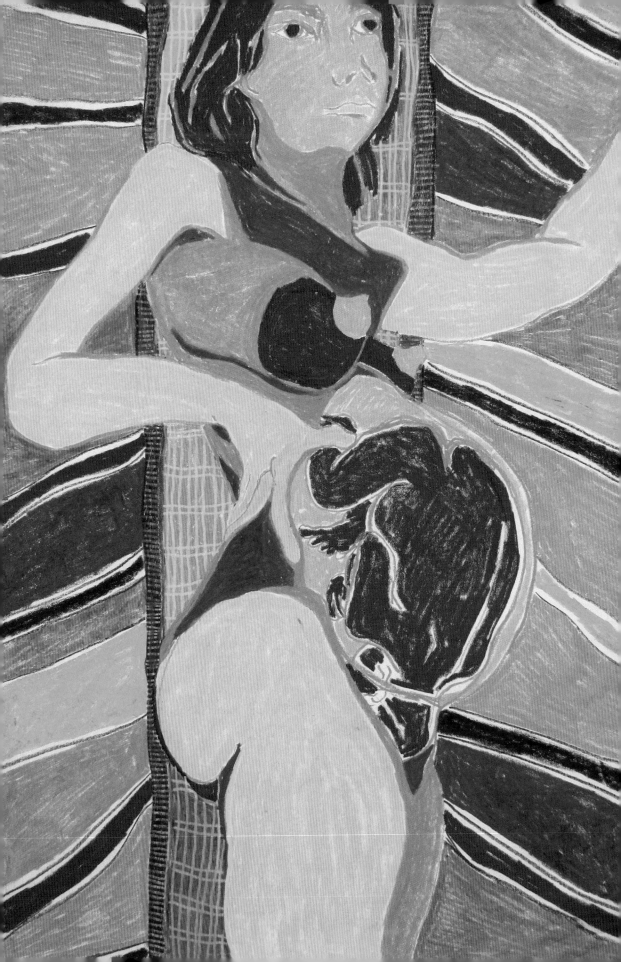

ELECTRONIC FETAL MONITORING——An electronic fetal monitor records a baby's heartbeat in utero along with the birthing person's contractions to ensure that fetal oxygen supply is adequate. While the type of monitor and its deployment varies, continuous electronic monitoring during labor is now one of the most widely experienced obstetric interventions.

Such designs produce what is known as a cardiotocograph, from the Greek words *kardia*, meaning heart, and *tokos*, meaning labor and childbirth. Continuous cardiotocography is often shortened to CTG and is also known (especially in the United States) as EFM, short for electronic fetal monitoring. Today, a Doppler transducer strapped to a laboring person's abdomen captures the fetal heart rate using ultrasound while a special monitor called a tocodynamometer picks up the pattern of uterine contractions by measuring the tension of the maternal abdominal wall (providing an indirect indication of intrauterine pressure). Both monitors transmit these signals to a console, where they are printed out on a continuously scrolling chart, one line tracing the baby's heartbeat and the other the waves of contractions.

If a higher quality signal is needed, a spiral electrode can be gently affixed to the baby's scalp in utero, though only after the waters have broken. Every time a contraction occurs, the flow of oxygen to the baby decreases slightly before picking up again as the muscle spasm passes. CTG enables medical staff to ensure that the baby has an adequate supply of oxygen—lack of which can lead to physical impairments, including cerebral palsy—at every stage of the birthing process, and to intervene if oxygen levels drop.

While written speculation on the presence of a fetal heartbeat can be found as early as the mid-seventeenth century in the Western world, it was the French physician René Théophile Hyacinthe Laënnec's invention of the stethoscope in 1816 that enabled his friend

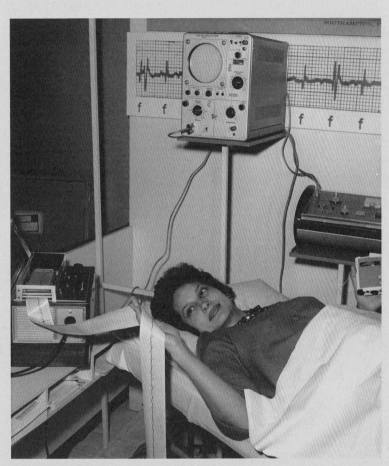

Mrs. Connie Fleischner, seven and a half months pregnant, holding the output from an EKG-500 "medical telemetering unit" in Chicago, 1962

and collaborator, a fellow Breton, Jacques Alexandre Le Jumeau de Kergaradec, to apply it to obstetrics.[1] In 1822, Kergaradec reported to colleagues:

Whilst examining a patient near term and trying to follow the movements of the foetus with the stethoscope I was suddenly aware of a sound that I had not noticed before; it was like the ticking of a watch. At first I thought I was mistaken, but I was able to repeat the observation over and over again. On counting the beats I found that these occurred 143–148 times per minute and the patient's pulse was only 72 per minute.[2]

Thus identified, the fetal heartbeat was another piece of information that could be used to monitor the progress of labor. But it was not immediately seized upon, and it was not until 1958 that specific tracking for fetal distress was developed by Dr. Edward H. Hon at Yale University. The Hewlett-Packard 8020A fetal monitor, released in 1968, was the first such device to be commercially available, and it gave rise to many competitors. These contemporary computers have a more analog precursor: Lorand's Tokograph. Named after the doctor who invented it in the early twentieth century for monitoring uterine contractions during labor, the tokograph is a compact instrument comprised of a bolt of graph paper coiled around a mechanized brass drum; a pen recorded surges transmitted from a wire held onto the patient with an elastic belt.

The practice of fetal monitoring was widely introduced to hospitals in the 1960s and 1970s without robust evidence of its efficacy from clinical trials. Yet the embrace of the technology was swift. According to the American College of Obstetricians and Gynaecologists, EFM was used for 45 percent of laboring women in 1980, 62 percent in 1988, 74 percent in 1992, and 85 percent in 2002. Today the use of EFM during labor is around 90 percent.[3] In the last decade, pilot tests of wireless monitors have been launched by the UK-based Monica Healthcare (the AN24), GE Healthcare (the Novii), and Philips (the Avalon model launched in 2020 as a single-use, 48-hour, disposable electrode patch). These devices allow ease of movement for laboring people. Manufacturers also tout fewer patient-provider interactions needed for repositioning (useful in a pandemic) and clearer monitoring of obese patients.

Regardless of typology, EFM machines have become the poster child for designs that overmedicalize birth. While modern medicine has undeniably improved many aspects of maternal health, technology is not a panacea. Changes in fetal heart rate often prompt a cascade of medical interventions, especially in pregnancies deemed high risk—already those most closely monitored. Such interventions range from limiting the ability of the birthing person to move freely during labor, which can be both emotionally and physiologically harmful, to an increase in the use of forceps and cesarean births.[4] Epidurals require continuous fetal monitoring and are common in labor induced with Pitocin. There is also the sound of the machine—a constant beeping punctuated by loud alarms when fetal distress is detected. It is little wonder that the New Republic in 2015 called EFM machines both "the most common childbirth practice in America" and "unnecessary and dangerous."[5] The World Health Organization explains clearly and powerfully what few birthing people are ever told—that "experience of care is as important as clinical care provision in achieving the desired person-centred outcomes," and that "continuous cardiotocography is not recommended for assessment of fetal well-being in healthy pregnant women undergoing spontaneous labour."[6] The view that EFM has no positive effect on infant or maternal outcomes in birth has been articulated in contemporary scientific and medical literature.[7] Yet these machines still crowd labor and delivery wards, especially in the United States, where overuse of medical intervention clouds many health care scenarios. This is perhaps unsurprising, given that a simple online search for "CTG" or "EFM" calls up a veritable treasure trove of personal injury lawyers ready to prosecute adverse birth outcomes. A printout of heart rate and contractions provides a literal paper trail for medical professionals who fear malpractice suits.

Designs for electronic fetal monitoring are so ubiquitous now that they will not disappear anytime soon. But the increasing awareness of their potential to lead to unnecessary interventions in some birth scenarios calls to mind the Hippocratic oath's caution that medical providers "first do no harm"—and reminds us that designers, especially in the medical field, should be guided by the same principle. This starts with the informed consent of birthing people, including advising them that in many cases strapping EFM sensors to their belly, rather than reducing complications, increases risk.[8]

1 See J. H. M. Pinkerton, "Kergaradec, Friend of Laennec and Pioneer of Foetal Auscultation," *Proceedings of the Royal Society of Medicine* 62, no. 5 (May 1969): 477–83, ncbi.nlm.nih.gov/pmc/articles/PMC1810975.
2 Quoted in Pinkerton, "Kergaradec," 482. The noted Dublin obstetrician Evory Kennedy remarked in 1843 that "it is a matter of regret to us that auscultation in pregnancy has not met with more opposition as the more it meets with the more it will attract the attention of the profession which is all that is required to establish its utility," 483.
3 "ACOG Practice Bulletin No. 106: Intrapartum Fetal Heart Rate Monitoring: Nomenclature, Interpretation, and General Management Principles," *Obstetrics and Gynecology* 114, no. 1 (July 2009): 192–202.
4 Between 1970 and 2016, the US cesarean rate increased from 5 percent to 32 percent. And "non-reassuring fetal heart tones" became the second most common reason for firsttime cesareans in the United States. See "ACOG Practice Bulletin No. 184: Vaginal Birth after Cesarean Delivery," *Obstetrics and Gynecology* 130, no. 5 (November 2017): 1167–1169."
5 Noah Berlatsky, "The Most Common Childbirth Practice in America Is Unnecessary and Dangerous," *New Republic*, August 13, 2015.
6 "WHO Recommendation on Continuous Cardiotocography during Labour," World Health Organization, February 15, 2018, extranet.who.int.
7 See Berlatsky, "The Most Common Childbirth Practice in America."
8 EFM is blindly accepted by most laboring people to whom it is applied. The authors cautioned that this flies in the face of both medical ethics and the "continually mounting evidence which proves the procedure is nothing more than myth, illusion and junk science." See Thomas P. Sartwelle, James C. Johnston, and Berna Arda, "A Half Century of Electronic Fetal Monitoring and Bioethics: Silence Speaks Louder than Words," *Maternal Health, Neonatology, and Perinatology* 3, no. 21 (2017), doi.org/10.1186/s40748-017-0060-2.

CESAREAN BIRTH CURTAINS—Cesarean births are rooted in the mythic. Some of the Greek gods were said to have arrived by cesarean, including Adonis (god of beauty and desire), Asclepius (god of healing), and Dionysus (god of fertility and wine). There are likewise references to cesarean births in ancient Hindu, Egyptian, Roman, and other European folklore. Some theorize that the Buddha was born through a slit in his mother's side, and even the character Lord Macduff in Shakespeare's *Macbeth* was supposedly a C-section baby.

The word *cesarean* comes from the name Caesar, itself derived from the Latin word *caedere*, meaning "to cut" (Caesar was said to have been cut from his mother's womb when she died before his birth).[1]

Cutting has always been crucial to the procedure, and these days, so are surgical coverings—drapes, curtains, and wearable personal protective equipment. Well into the nineteenth century, surgery was performed without anesthesia, let alone disinfectant or protective measures. Surgical gowns and hats were introduced in 1883 as a result of the British physician Dr. Joseph Lister's theories of microbial infection and wound disinfection in the operating room.[2] In the 1940s and 1950s, advances in antiseptic routines, the advent of fibrous synthetic materials such as nylon, polyethylene, polypropylene, and vinyl polymers, and the rise of medical supply companies led to surgical rooms, patients, and hospital staff being outfitted with protective fittings like drapes meant to safeguard the sterility of the environment.[3]

Today cesareans are the most commonly performed surgery in the world. The global cesarean rate has nearly doubled since the turn of the century, rising from 12 percent of all births in 2000 to 21 percent in 2015.[4] In the United States in particular, rates have skyrocketed since the 1970s. In just one generation the country's cesarean rate has increased 500 percent. One in three babies in the US is now born via cesarean, compared with one in twenty in the mid-1970s.[5]

There are many reasons why babies are birthed by

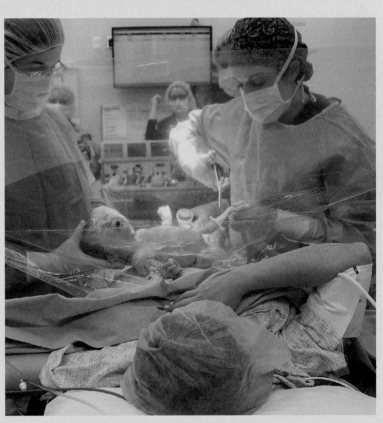

The clear drape in the operating room allows parents to see their newborn during the C-section surgery

cesarean, and the procedure can save lives. But it is also an overused and largely unwanted surgery. People's feelings about their cesarean births vary. But for many who undergo the procedure, the surgical and antiseptic measures meant to protect them can feel cold and frightening. What's more, these measures can delay parental contact and bonding, and may impair breastfeeding.[6] Numerous people report feeling cut off from their births (even the colloquialism C-section implies separation), and some say they feel cheated out of being able to see their babies emerge into the world.[7] But, increasingly, parents are now being invited to look behind the curtain, and it's changing the way they feel about their C-sections.

In a typical cesarean scenario, a birthing person lies flat with an opaque curtain pooled around their chest, shielding the operating field. The procedure is rapid and hidden from sight. Babies are whisked from womb to examining table, where they are cleaned, tagged, weighed, and swaddled before being introduced to parents, which can happen anywhere from five to thirty minutes after the birth.[8]

In 1991, the Baby-friendly Hospital Initiative was launched by the World Health Organization (WHO) and UNICEF. What began as a global effort to support breastfeeding inspired some hospitals to reexamine standard cesarean practices. In 2008, a group of practitioners characterized these practices as a throwback to the days when general anesthesia was required, when speediness

and postpartum measures were meant to prevent fetal anesthetic exposure and the need for resuscitation.[9]

As uncomplicated cesareans have become more common, and pain medication has become safer and more localized, a growing number of hospitals have modified the experience of cesarean birth. Baby-friendly hospitals around the world—but particularly in the United Kingdom, Australia, Germany, and the United States—now practice "gentle," "family centered," "natural" C-sections, and the surgical curtain itself has played a major role in facilitating more autonomy and agency in the birthing experience.

A version of the cesarean curtain designed in Japan in 2016 has two layers: once a uterine incision is made, the opaque layer is removed and the clear layer remains, allowing parents to see their baby emerge without compromising the sterile field. Another version, developed by three nurses in Virginia in 2015, is designed to allow the obstetrician to reach through a portal in the main drape and place the infant directly on the mother's chest, protecting the sterile environment while promoting immediate skin-to-skin contact. Simpler still, some obstetricians just move the curtain aside (though this seldom happens in the litigious United States, where breeches of sterility could lead to a medical malpractice lawsuit).

Cesarean curtains that are clear, have a window, or are simply dropped at the right time allow parents to watch their babies emerge and so

better experience their own births. A birthing person is able to see what is happening and actively take part. (The sightline ensures that only the baby, and never the incision itself, is visible.) By slowly "walking the baby out" of the incision, obstetricians guide the movement, pace, and tenor of the birth in a way that mimics vaginal delivery.[10] And instead of rushing the baby off afterward to be cleaned and cared for, the baby is handed directly to the birthing person for skin-to-skin contact and breastfeeding initiation.[11]

These changes are small but significant. Because a person's feelings about their birth can deeply impact their emotional state, the modified curtain not only greatly improves the birth experience but may even stave off postpartum depression. Jessica Warner, a mother of two children, one born with an opaque curtain and the other with a clear one, described her experiences:

The difference between the oppressive blue curtain in my face and the clear curtain letting me see that my baby was actually being born and not appearing out of nowhere meant the world to me. The clear curtain felt like a symbol or pact of trust, confidence, and collaboration between me and the OB. Being able to see her rising from my belly was just the most beautiful moment. C-section curtains like these are particularly revolutionary for those who wanted the autonomy and experience of vaginal birth but instead found themselves having a C-section.[12]

1 Until the sixteenth and seventeenth centuries, the procedure was known as a cesarean operation. This began to change following the publication in 1598 of Jacques Guillimeau's book on midwifery, in which he introduced the term section. Thereafter section increasingly replaced operation. See S. K. Majumdar, "Caesarean Section: An Historical Riddle," Bulletin of the Indian Institute of History of Medicine (Hyderabad) 31, no. 2 (2001): 139–53; and Tina Cassidy, Birth: A History (London: Chatto & Windus, 2006), 111.

2 Sara Gaines et al., "Optimum Operating Room Environment for the Prevention of Surgical Site Infections," Surgical Infections 18, no. 4 (2017): 503–7.
3 Jessica L. Buicko, Michael A. Lopez, and Miguel A. Lopez-Viego, "From Formalwear and Frocks to Scrubs and Gowns: A Brief History of the Evolution of Operating Room Attire," American College of Surgeons, History of Surgery Poster Competition, 2016, facs.org.
4 Ties Boerma et al., "Global Epidemiology of Use of and Disparities in

Caesarean Sections," The Lancet 392, no. 10155 (October 13, 2018), thelancet.com.
5 In 2018 the cesarean delivery rate decreased from 32 percent in 2017 to 31.9 percent. In 2017 the cesarean delivery rate had increased for the first time since 2009, when it peaked at 32.9 percent after increasing every year since 1996 (when it was 20.7 percent). See Joyce C. Martin et al., "Births: Final Data for 2018," National Vital Statistics Reports 68, no. 13 (November 27, 2019), cdc.gov/nchs/data/nvsr/nvsr68/nvsr68_13-508.pdf.
6 See Amy J. Hobbs

et al., "The Impact of Caesarean Section on Breastfeeding Initiation, Duration, and Difficulties in the First Four Months Postpartum," BMC Pregnancy and Childbirth 16, no. 90 (April 26, 2016), doi.org/10.1186/s12884-016-0876-1.
7 Anne Drapkin Lyerly, A Good Birth: Finding the Positive and Profound in Your Childbirth Experience (New York: Avery, 2013), 69.
8 J. Smith, F. Plaat, and N. Fisk, "The Natural Caesarean: A Woman-Centred Technique," BJOG: An International Journal of Obstetrics and

Gynaecology 115, no. 8 (July 2008): 1037–42, doi.org/10.1111/j.1471 0528.2008.01777.x.
9 Smith, Plaat, and Fisk, "The Natural Caesarean," 1037.
10 Smith, Plaat, and Fisk, "The Natural Caesarean," 1038.
11 EKG monitors are moved from their usual location on top of the mother's chest to her side, hands are left free, and the intravenous line is placed in the nondominant hand so that the baby can be greeted.
12 Jessica Warner, conversation with author, September 1, 2020.

BABY DRAWER—Almost every parent has at some stage dreamed about depositing their squalling infant into the waiting hands of an expert carer and settling back into a reclining bed for a restorative forty winks. For the postwar folks who gave birth in one of Kaiser Permanente's "dream hospitals," the first of which was built on Los Angeles's Sunset Boulevard in 1952, this fantasy became a reality with the help of a hyperefficient innovation: the sliding baby drawer.

At the Los Angeles hospital—and at others that followed as Kaiser Permanente expanded along the West Coast in the 1950s—the nursery of newborn infants was no longer relegated to one end of the maternity ward. Instead, it became a central command post from which the bedrooms of postpartum mothers radiated outward like the spokes of a wheel. Beside each mother's bed was a large, metal, filing-cabinet-like drawer that, when pulled open, transferred her baby's bassinet from its slot in the communal nursery to the privacy of her room, where she could bond with and—the medical staff hoped—breastfeed her infant, turning the tide against the prevailing trends of bottle-feeding and formula use. (Histories of the drawer make no mention of the uncomfortable twist and bend required to pick up the baby.)

The design was the brainchild of Dr. Sidney R. Garfield, a pediatrician and right-hand man of Henry J. Kaiser, the industrialist and multifaceted entrepreneur who founded Kaiser health care for his workers. Garfield and his colleagues had read of Yale professor Dr. Edith Jackson's recent project at Grace-New Haven Community Hospital, which encouraged maternal bonding and breastfeeding through "rooming-in."[1] Trialed between 1946 and 1952, the practice was welcomed by patients who rebelled against heavily sedated, intervention-laden deliveries and separated lying-in (see *Adventure to Motherhood*, p. 193). Jackson's protocols encouraged unmedicated birth when possible, and placing the bassinet in the new mother's room.

At the Los Angeles hospital, the "baby drawer" was one of many care contact points that

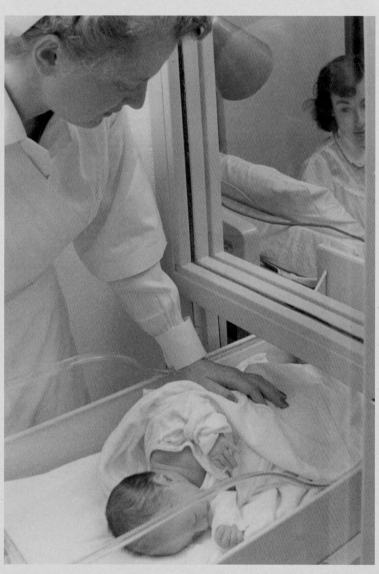

A nurse tending to a sleeping infant in a mobile bassinet in a room adjacent to the mother's at a Kaiser Permanente Hospital, California, 1950s

Garfield and his colleagues had set out to reconfigure in service of what they deemed a more humane and efficient medical environment. A light signaled when the baby was returned to watchful eyes on the other side of the wall, and a window above the drawer allowed both mama and nurse to oversee the transaction.[2] Decentralized nursing stations enabled more responsive care, and individual bathrooms, hot and cold water, and ice in each room offered dignity. It was a well-designed parturition calculated to reduce the steps each actor had to take in tending to their charges. In a promotional film, the drawer functioned as a mechanized midcentury stork that delivered a swaddled infant directly into the waiting arms of a lipsticked and impeccably coiffed mother radiant in a nightgown.

It was a watershed moment. No longer doggedly focused on combating postpartum infections, thanks to modern antibiotics, nurses could shift their attention toward supporting new parents learning to care for their baby and form a family unit. The mothers of this first generation for which hospital births were the primary experience "formed the small vanguard who adopted Grantly Dick-Read's natural childbirth techniques…and welcomed breastfeeding assistance when the La Leche League was formed in 1956."[3] In 1950, Faith E. Jensen, a student nurse, extolled these "new methods," which she witnessed during her time in Yale's maternity ward, receiving an indulgent pat on the arm from her grandmother whose deflating observation was that "most of the women in my generation had their children that way, only they had them at home."[4]

The standardization of the rooming-in experience at Kaiser Permanente was unsurprising given the extent of Henry J. Kaiser's industrial empire, which remade the western states in the early and mid-twentieth century in profound ways. His projects included construction of "thousands of miles of road, hundreds of bridges and tunnels," WPA dam projects during the Depression, and, from 1939, "an ever-widening circle of industries…cement, magnesium, shipbuilding, steel, aluminum, mining, home-building, aerospace and electronics, missiles, and nuclear power plants."[5]

The architectural plan of the dream hospitals was built around concentric "circles of service" that separated sterile staff spaces from patients, and both of these from visitor access. The model was used at least a decade earlier at another Kaiser facility, the Portland Child Service Centers, built in 1943 for Kaiser's shipyard workers. There, a centralized play area was ringed by a main corridor from which six classroom hubs emanated. The architect, George Wolff, credited Richard Neutra, an Austrian émigré to California, and his "ring school" concept as inspiration in a 1944 interview for Architectural Record. (Kaiser, a geodesic dome fan, favored circular plans.)

Before the plan or the drawer, however, came the design of the health care system itself. Garfield began his career as a doctor in the fee-for-service model, working in the California desert tending to laborers building the Metropolitan Water District aqueduct from the Colorado River to Los Angeles. Struggling to collect fees from patients and insurance companies, Garfield switched to a prepaid approach that provided him a more sustainable wage and placed no limits on the care of those who subscribed to his mutual-aid model. Kaiser and his son, Edgar, learned of Garfield's work and persuaded him to bring his skills to Washington State, where they were overseeing the construction of the Grand Coulee Dam. They eventually expanded the prepaid Kaiser Health model across their businesses in that state, as well as in California and Oregon, to provide health care to 200,000 of their shipyard and steel plant employees and their dependents.[6]

Local doctors in California, threatened by the popular and futuristic "dream hospitals" and "baby drawers," and supported by the American Medical Association (AMA), brought legal action against Garfield several times, charging unprofessional conduct, including placing "mass production ahead of the health needs of the patients." The AMA portrayed their private fee-for-service model as "a last bulwark of individualism against dehumanization by industrial society."[7] In reality, Garfield and Kaiser had created an amenity-laden experience that rivaled that of hotels. (To the deep chagrin of his medical staff, Kaiser once rented out rooms in the Honolulu hospital to capitalize on a seasonal tourist rush.)

Ironically, just as the hospital eclipsed the home as the site where birth happened, the baby drawer embodied aspects of aspirational midcentury domesticity. At home, the latest appliances sold the myth that they reduced housewives' work, making it easier to double down on the labor of housekeeping and childcare by supervising gadgets that did routine household chores, allowing parents (usually mom) to keep an eye on the family. In the hospital, at least, modern maternity meant that at the touch of a button such labor could be pushed through the wall, even if only for a brief moment of respite.

1   See Sara Lee Silberman, "Pioneering in Family-Centered Maternity and Infant Care: Edith B. Jackson and the Yale Rooming-In Project," Bulletin of the History of Medicine 64, no. 2 (Summer 1990).
2   "'When the mother wanted to take care of the baby,' Garfield explained, 'she'd pull the drawer out and there was the baby. If she wanted to put it back in the nursery, she could put it back in. That was a great hit.'" See "'Baby in the Drawer' Helped Turn the Tide for Breastfeeding," Our Story, Kaiser Permanente, July 31, 2019, about.kaiserpermanente.org.
3   Silberman, "Pioneering in Family-Centered Maternity and Infant Care," 264. See also Elizabeth Temkin, "Rooming-In: Redesigning Hospitals and Motherhood in Cold War America," Bulletin of the History of Medicine 76, no. 2 (Summer 2002): 271–98.
4   Faith E. Jensen, "Having a Baby Is a Family Matter," American Journal of Nursing 50, no. 10, 50th Anniversary Issue (October 1950): 674–75. See also Ingeborg Berlin, "A Student Looks at Rooming-In," American Journal of Nursing 50, no. 5 (May 1950): 316.
5   Mark S. Foster, "Giant of the West: Henry J. Kaiser and Regional Industrialization, 1930–1950," Business History Review 59, no. 1 (Spring 1985): 2.
6   It was "unique in its scale and consolidation of prepayment, group practice, and medical facilities"; Rickey Hendricks, "Medical Practice Embattled: Kaiser Permanente, the American Medical Association, and Henry J. Kaiser on the West Coast, 1945–1955," Pacific Historical Review 60, no. 4 (November 1991): 440.
7   Hendricks, "Medical Practice Embattled," 448.

ALL MY BABIES: A MIDWIFE'S OWN STORY (1953), DIRECTED BY GEORGE STONEY—In the United States, reproductive health care is in large part rooted in the expertise and generational knowledge of Indigenous and Black women.[1] The educational film *All My Babies: A Midwife's Own Story*, released in 1953 as a training aid for midwives and other health professionals, bears witness to this fact and foreshadows the systems that came to threaten it.

Filmed at a time when birth was moving from the home to the hospital, it stands out for the way it depicts and uplifts the role of the Black midwife in communities across the American South. It was written, directed, and produced by the filmmaker George C. Stoney in collaboration with the film's central figure, midwife Mary Francis Hill Coley, or "Miss Mary," as she was affectionately and respectfully known.

Stoney was introduced to Coley shortly after he was commissioned to make the film by the Georgia Department of Public Health and the Audio-Visual Division of the Association of American Medical Colleges, for whom he worked between 1950 and 1953. Before *All My Babies*, Stoney produced two other health-education films for the state, *Palmour Street*, on mental health and targeted to Black parents, in 1950, and *A Concept of Maternal and Neonatal Care*, which showed home and hospital births and addressed the individual needs of the postpartum period, in 1951. *All My Babies* was intended to help doctors, midwives, schools, and health departments within Black communities of the rural South understand best practices within midwifery.

The brief from state officials was to include 118 separate points within the film, from managing relationships between the midwife and public health specialists to breathing techniques during labor, and incorporating partners and siblings into the birthing process. The striking sensitivity and compassion Stoney showed toward the film's protagonists were partially inspired by the work of Italian

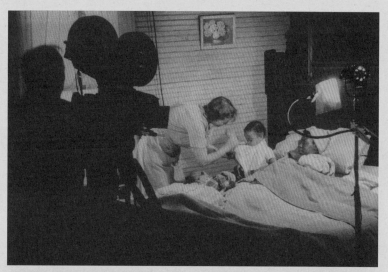

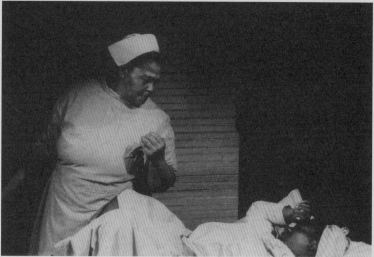

Stills from the film *All My Babies*, directed by George Stoney, 1953

neorealist directors, whose films of the 1940s and early 1950s were shot on location using nonprofessional actors and foregrounded the stories of the poor and working class. However, it was the evocative photographs of Walker Evans, Dorothea Lange, and others who—commissioned by the Farm Security Administration—documented the Great Depression, as well as a Canadian didactic film series on mental health, that he later cited as most influential.

Filming on location in Albany, Georgia, Stoney accompanied Coley over a four-month period, recording her careful preparations for and home delivery of babies among Black rural families experiencing various living conditions. Behind the scenes Dr. William Mason, a Black physician working for the Georgia Health Department, acted as a liaison for Stoney's all-White crew as they went about their work. Stoney himself spent several months with Mary Coley before shooting commenced, effectively becoming her pupil.[2]

The film not only presents a candid portrait of Coley and those she cared for, but also documents their surroundings and a community of health practitioners. While some acting was involved, actual homes, streetscapes, and medical offices were the backdrops for prenatal exams, and the film centers on—and shows in detail—the birth of a baby as Coley attends. Coley brought skill, traditions, ingenuity, and high standards of hygiene to her work. The strong,

positive influence she had on her patients and their families is unmistakable.

Yet for all its beauty and intimacy, *All My Babies* also foreshadows the demise of Black midwifery. Called "granny midwives," Black midwives once provided most of the care for poor and rural pregnant women of all races throughout the American South. Indispensable within their communities, they passed their knowledge down through generations during the institutionalized racism and violence of slavery in the antebellum period. Black midwives were also crucial during segregation; at a time when Black women were often denied admittance to hospitals, midwife-attended home birth was frequently the only viable option for Black families.[3]

Filmed during the Jim Crow era, *All My Babies* records the uncomfortable and enforced deference of Black midwives interacting with White doctors and nurses at the county clinic, and even shows Coley questioning her own excellent hygiene practices after a group lecture by the doctor. The film paints a rare portrait of how Coley's model of care coexisted alongside the growing medical-industrial complex, and of how Black midwives and their patients worked within an otherwise racist medical system. Distributed by the Center for Mass Communication at Columbia University in New York, the film traveled well beyond its original intended audience, along the way exposing dif-

fering interpretations of its message. In an interview in 1981, Stoney recounted a request from the Indian Minister for Health for copies to be shown to doctors and nurses in his home country. There, he stated, midwives were looked down upon. He wanted "'to show them that in the United States, where they have very fine medicine, the doctors are not ashamed to work with the midwives.' ... [Stoney] didn't have the heart to tell the Minister that here they are often held in contempt by the US medical establishment as well."[4]

Selected by the Library of Congress for the National Film Registry in 2002 as "a culturally, historically and artistically significant work," the film has transcended its didactic mission to become an enduring nonfiction classic.[5] Stoney's own conviction of the story's worth was evident from the get-go—he used his own funds to personally cover the cost of higher production standards even while the state retained all rights. Half a century later, his film still resonates. Providing free or low-cost training, education, and certification for pregnancy, birth, and postpartum health; empowering culturally appropriate care; and making sure access to these resources is universal remain some of the most effective and direct ways to collectively address maternal and infant health disparities. As one local state official remarked to Stoney in 1952, "Mary Coley knows her business."[6] Her design for maternal health has a lot to teach us today.

1 Other valuable resources for those interested in diving further into this area include a 1989 oral history, *Motherwit: An Alabama Midwife's Story*, a first-person testimony by the Black midwife Onnie Lee Logan recorded by Katherine Clark; and the photographs of the American photojournalist W. Eugene Smith, "Nurse Midwife," in the December 3, 1951 issue of *LIFE* magazine that document the work of Maude Callen, a Black nurse-midwife in rural South Carolina. **2** Lynne Jackson, "The Production of George Stoney's Film 'All My Babies: A Midwife's Own Story' (1952)," *Film History* 1, no. 4 (1987): 370. **3** Vann R. Newkirk II, "America's Health Segregation Problem: Has the Country Done Enough to Overcome Its Jim Crow Health Care History?," *The Atlantic*, May 18, 2016, theatlantic.com **4** Jackson, "The Production of George Stoney's Film 'All My Babies,'" 387. **5** "About This Collection," Selections from the National Film Registry, Library of Congress, loc.gov/collections/selections-from-the-national-film-registry. **6** George Stoney, interview by Lynne Jackson, November 4, 1981; quoted in Jackson, "The Production of George Stoney's Film 'All My Babies,'" 371.

can help you get:

med

hou

(215) 978-7040

MATERNITY CARE COALITION

MATERNITY CARE COALITION

Since 1980, Maternity Care Coalition
has served 140,000 families throughout
southeastern Pennsylvania, focusing
particularly on neighborhoods with high
rates of poverty, infant mortality, health
disparities, and changing immigration
patterns. MCC's activities, from their
signature MOMobile program, which
enables home visits to new parents,
to training community members to
become doulas and to provide lactation
support in a culturally responsive way,
support pregnant people and their
infants to give them the best possible
start to family life. Their vision is an
equitable future in which all families
are healthy and connected, all children
thriving and ready to learn. These
images show some of the earliest MCC
staff doing their pioneering work in the
1980s.

DOULAS AND BIRTH COMPANIONS—A doula is a person knowledgeable about pregnancy, childbirth, and motherhood who attends to another during labor and postpartum, a role that is as ancient as birth itself. Providing reassurance and techniques to manage pain, and acting as an advocate, a doula was often a member of the extended family in the days when the majority of people birthed at home. Today, doulas ensure that this legacy of culturally appropriate care continues.

A Maternity Care Coalition client in Philadelphia, 1980s

DESIGNING MOTHERHOOD—Tekara, we think doulas are magic makers. You're a doula and a community health worker with the Maternity Care Coalition, an organization that provides culturally appropriate support to pregnant people and families with young children throughout southeastern Pennsylvania, particularly in neighborhoods with high rates of poverty, infant mortality, health disparities, and changing immigration patterns. One of the amazing services MCC provides is making birth doulas available to people who might otherwise be unable to afford one. Can you tell us how you got involved with MCC?

TEKARA GAINEY—I had been doing full spectrum doula work for a while, supporting folks across the spectrum of possible pregnancy outcomes, including abortion, birth, and loss. I got into birth work when I came across the notion that doulas could address the maternal mortality crisis within communities of color. And when I started doing birth work, I absolutely fell in love with it. I intentionally sought out a doula community that could speak to birth as intersectional and community-based. And a doula friend of mine told me about Maternity Care Coalition's doula network and the work that they do in connecting birthing people to doulas at no cost to them, which increases accessibility for people who otherwise couldn't afford this service. And so I said, "Oh, sign me up, please. I need to be a part of this ASAP."

DM—We hear a lot about doulas these days. There are birth doulas, postpartum doulas, full-spectrum doulas, death doulas. A birth doula is a trained professional support person who is there to help educate a pregnant person and provide emotional and physical support during birth. Was there something about your particular path that led you to want to support birthing people in this way?

TG—The concept and function of doulas is not an innovative thing. Doulas have been around for centuries. But doulas as a public health intervention? That's fairly new. One really important reason I'm drawn to this work is that it's addressing something that's very pertinent in our society, not just here in the United States but globally. But I've always been obsessed with birth. Kids are always asked, "What do you want to be when you grow up?" And my answer was, "I want to be a baby doctor." I didn't know the name for it, but this pathway, it really chose me. And this fascination with birth developed into an appreciation of birth as a ritual and a rite of passage that involves not just the individual person giving birth but really the community, the whole family. It's also a way for people to connect with their ancestors, to connect with generational experiences. And it can also be a way for people to heal generational trauma, heal parenting styles that may not have been the most favorable for them—a way to change course. And witnessing that transition, witnessing that awakening in people, it's very humbling. I'm honored to be a part of that.

DM—Where is it that most of your work takes place?

TG—I support people in all birthing settings—so hospitals, homes, birth centers. The folks who need support through MCC's network primarily give birth in a hospital setting, but we do have a few folks who intentionally seek out alternative options such as birth centers or home births. Unfortunately, the options are limited and dictated by state legislation, availability of resources, whatever's offered in their area. Within the Philadelphia and Delaware Valley area, there's one birthing center, there aren't many home birth midwives, and insurance doesn't always cover that kind of birth. So even though there is interest [in other ways of giving birth], hospitals are by default where most people deliver.

DM—There's a misconception that doulas are only for those who plan an unmedicated, vaginal birth, but doulas are really there to support every kind of outcome, including cesarean births. Can you tell us about the different ways your role as a support person can play out within a birth setting?

TG—A lot of my work as a doula comes before the delivery itself, meeting with clients a few times just to go over what the expectations are, going over hospital policies. During labor, it plays out differently depending on the setting, the providers, and what the needs are. But ultimately our role is just to be a source of information, a source of reassurance, and a source of empowerment to say, "No, you've got this. You are the expert on your own health. You're the expert in knowing what you need to feel comfortable, and I am going to support you to make sure you can voice those needs."

There are so many things designed to take power away from birthing people in medical settings, especially for communities of color where discrimination and disempowerment in the health care system is prevalent. A doula's presence really has a way of shifting the power dynamics, but we are primarily there to serve our client and whatever their need is. We're not going in just rubbing backs and lighting candles, which is the common misconception, although we do have our special oils, and we bring out the rebozo [laughs]. But doulas are also a source of empowerment for folks to speak up for themselves, know their rights, identify moments when they're being mistreated, and advocate for the time and attention they need from their providers.

DM— Clinical studies show that continual support during labor produces all kinds of positive outcomes and no negative effects. There's also evidence that doulas can disrupt the pathways of adverse social determinants that lead to poor health and poor outcomes. And from a policy design perspective, doula services are a powerful way to dismantle the structural inequities that racism creates and that are lived out every day by Black and Indigenous women, whose families lose babies at disproportionately high rates. What is it like to be on the ground advocating for people we know that the system endangers?

TG— Our purpose and goal as doulas is really to walk alongside our clients to support them, uplift them, remind them of their power and choices. And oftentimes I kind of challenge the notion that it's the doula's role to decrease C-section rates or maternal mortality rates, and to improve communication between providers. Yes, our presence definitely does this, but we need to look at the greater systemic issue. The system itself needs to change. The way that we're training providers needs to change. The way that we view and value the lives of Black and Brown people needs to change. Putting the burden on the doulas to solve a health care crisis is extremely heavy.

DM— So true. That kind of systemic change can't come from doulas.

TG— Right. It's infuriating and frustrating to see providers continue to perform a cervical exam without the consent of the birthing person. It shouldn't be the doula's role to step in and intervene in something that shouldn't be happening in the first place. And don't get me wrong, there are some phenomenal providers—doctors and nurses who get it. However, that's not the case across the board. Implicit bias is strong in medical settings, and that needs to be addressed. It's a human rights issue, a reproductive justice issue, a women's issue, a queer issue. It's an issue for humanity, and it's a lot to take on. Doulas can't fix the problem alone.

DM— It's beautiful work, and you're on the front lines. So how do we attract new generations of doulas to the practice of culturally appropriate care that you follow?

TG— These days there are a lot of organizations that certify and train doulas, but the model in which they're training them may not be culturally appropriate. So investing in communities, investing in training, shifting training models to be more intersectional and culturally sensitive is important. And then bringing in community members and training them to do this work is essential, because they can speak to some of the needs of their communities more specifically than other people can. Because everyone births, right? Bringing in people who speak the language and know the lived experiences of the birthing communities— it'd go a long way. And then it goes further because there's the economic workforce component as well.

DM— Birthing a child is one of the most difficult tasks many of us will ever face. And to go through it and be well supported can be enormously powerful and even transformational for the birthing person. For those clients who have had a good birth, have you seen the experience lift them up?

TG— Absolutely. And I've seen how giving birth really impacts the way you show up for your child afterward. Feeling empowered, feeling listened to is everything—even if the experience is completely different than what you envisioned. Birth is one of the most unpredictable things in life. We can plan for it and do all this research, and you get there and something comes up that you never even thought about. But being treated with compassion makes all the difference. I've supported some folks who say, "Well, I expected a vaginal delivery and I ended up having a caesarian, but that's okay because I was part of the process the entire time. I was asked questions. I was able to speak to what my needs are. I was able to make my caesarian birth still just as beautiful as I envisioned my vaginal birth." And that's all we can ask for, right? Let people participate and have a voice. And there are many people whose birth experience went exactly as they planned, and that left them with even more power and strength to say, "I did that. That was the hardest thing I ever did, and there's nothing I cannot do after that." It's a beautiful thing.

DM— It is beautiful. It's also the ultimate source of connection because everyone has been through birth. Do you feel that this work gives you a greater sense of humanity and connectedness?

TG— Absolutely. I really do. Every individual was birthed by someone. We all went through this process. We all had this connection to the parent who birthed us. So approaching birth with compassion and love can be healing. It seems like such a simple and commonsense thing to do, but for some reason we've gotten away from that. We've gotten away from respecting birth as a physiological, normal process, a normal rite of passage, and made it so that it's dangerous. We need to get back to that sense of "we've all been there, we've all gone through it," and approach birthing folks with compassionate care. Because it is the hardest, the most challenging, the most transformational process anyone will ever go through.

#LISTENTOBLACKWOMEN—Language designs human experience. The hashtag #ListenToBlackWomen is an umbrella that encompasses a range of experiences and practices, including the exhortation to pay attention to Black women when they talk about their needs and intuitions around their own health. Khiara Bridges is a professor at UC Berkeley School of Law whose expertise lies at the intersection of race, class, and reproductive rights. She explains why words matter in the design of motherhood and reproductive health.

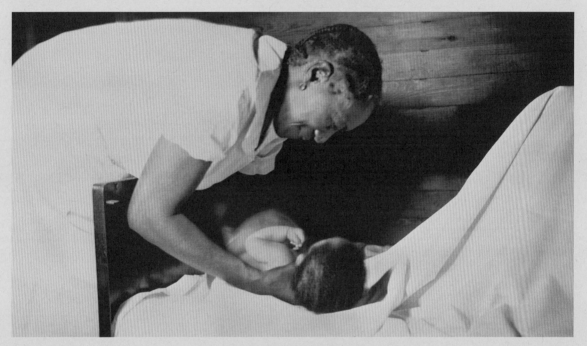

A midwife holding a just-delivered baby, c. 1920

DESIGNING MOTHERHOOD——You are a professor at UC Berkeley School of Law, and while you have a JD from Columbia Law School, your PhD from Columbia University is in anthropology. In your 2011 book *Reproducing Race: An Ethnography of Pregnancy as a Site of Racialization*, you persuasively make the case that, in the United States, Black women's personal or collective excellence, resilience, and achievement do not insulate them from adverse health care outcomes.

DR. KHIARA M. BRIDGES——People are increasingly familiar with the reality that there are racial disparities in maternal mortality—the reality that Black women are three to four times more likely than White women to die during pregnancy, childbirth, or shortly thereafter. What is interesting and important is that racial disparities in maternal mortality are not new. What's new about it is public awareness. Further, when folks hear that statistic, they tend to explain it in terms of class, to attribute it to Black women disproportionately bearing the burden of poverty in this country. People think that Black women are much more likely to die of a pregnancy-related cause just because they're poorer than their White counterparts. But that is not true. *Class-privileged* Black women are more likely than *class-privileged* White women to die from a pregnancy-related cause. There is a crucial racial component.

DM——Whether through words institutionalized as law and policy or through mass-media culture in the form of hashtags, language contributes both to the design of human reproduction and to the awareness of how design actually *works*. And we think this works in tandem with what you describe as a racialized medical system in the United States. The hashtag #listentoblackwomen was first tweeted by the social work scholar and activist Crystal M. Hayes [@MotherJustice] on February 26, 2012, as part of her ongoing investigation of birth and mass incarceration, and it has since surfaced a range of Black women's experiences in relation to reproductive health and beyond. Can you talk about how language intersects with design in this context?

KB——Two more hashtags that relate to Black women are particularly interesting to me. One is #blackgirlmagic, which I first noticed around 2016 [Twitter algorithms date it as early as 2011]. It celebrates Black excellence, Black women's resilience, Black women's talent. Around the same time, #sayhername was born as a movement, started by, among others, legal scholar Kimberlé Crenshaw, to mark the fact that Black women are killed by the police. The simultaneity of these hashtags—one asking people to recognize Black women's excellence, the other asking people to recognize that Black women are killed and policed and surveilled— was really remarkable to me. It demonstrated the complexity of Black women's existence.

DM——Although longstanding, the racially delineated health care system for pregnant people finally found a public language of debate with Serena Williams's birth story. She knew she might be suffering from a pulmonary embolism immediately postpartum, yet her intuition was discounted by medical staff.

KB——The reality is that racial disparity persists across income levels. So even when you are class-privileged, even when you are Serena Williams, even when you are Beyoncé, you're still more likely to die than a White counterpart. Now, I question whether Serena Williams and Beyoncé actually *have* White counterparts. But if there was a [White] tennis phenom or pop star of Serena's and Beyoncé's caliber, they would be much more likely to survive pregnancy than Beyoncé or Serena.

DM——You have degrees in sociology, law, and anthropology. Your research is wide ranging. How did you decide to write *Reproducing Race*?

KB——I've always been fascinated by pregnancy. One of my favorite uncles is an OB-GYN doctor in Miami. He is like a patriarch—my entire family has looked up to him. He's achieved so much as a professional, but also just as a Black man living in the South. I became fascinated by pregnancy because of him. But I knew I didn't want to be an obstetrician. I wrote papers in high school about abortion law and judicial bypass procedures for adolescent abortions. I worked at an abortion clinic in college, and I wrote my senior thesis about women's experiences in that clinic. I went to law school first, and I thought I was going to work with pregnancy as a lawyer—doing impact litigation and trying to influence policy. But I came to want to study how individuals experience the law. I understand my doctorate in anthropology as a means by which I investigate how law is lived, specifically how the laws around pregnancy are lived by pregnant people.

DM——**That makes us think again about the ways that the design of language—through law, through policy, through cultural expression—has had such an outsized effect on the experiences of people throughout their reproductive arcs, pregnant or not. How have Black women shaped these types of vocabularies in the United States?**

KB——We have Black women to thank for attention to the decision to become a mother and the decision to continue a pregnancy. Reproductive rights organizations have largely focused on the needs of affluent White women. The impediments to reproductive freedom that affluent White women have encountered have been laws that prevent them from terminating a pregnancy that's not wanted. So, reproductive rights organizations have spent most of their time and energy fighting for abortion rights. Not to naysay that fight at all—abortion rights are incredibly important—but while Black women have confronted the same restrictions on the ability to terminate a pregnancy that's not wanted, they have also confronted restrictions on the ability to become pregnant and to carry to term a pregnancy that is wanted.

Affluent White women have been encouraged to have many children. Their reproduction is supported and celebrated. Meanwhile, Black women's reproduction, poor women's reproduction, Indigenous women's reproduction, Latinx women's reproduction—nonwhite reproduction, non-affluent reproduction—is completely despised, problematized, and discouraged. And so Black women have fought for the right to become mothers, the right to become pregnant, the right to give birth, the right to parent the children that they give birth to with dignity and humanity. We have Black women to thank for conversations around the right to have a birth experience that accords with your values, your needs, and your health. I think that we are all much indebted to Black women's activism and their insistence on having their humanity recognized.

DM——**What you say chimes perfectly with the work of the reproductive-justice pioneer Loretta Ross (p. 43), and also with George Stoney's 1953 documentary *All My Babies* (p. 179), which celebrates midwifery practice in the United States through the work of Black women and the legacies of Indigenous birth workers.**

KB——Regarding midwifery—there has been a lot of skepticism of late about the medicalization of pregnancy and childbirth. Medicalization of pregnancy and childbirth is incredibly important when one has a risk for a poor outcome or when one has a pathology of some sort. But medicalization is wholly unnecessary when pregnancy and childbirth progress healthily. Midwives are the best stewards for pregnancy and childbirth when there are little to no risks apparent. The racial story there is that in the mid-nineteenth century, obstetricians began to try to wrest control over pregnancy from midwives by denigrating midwives as uneducated, superstitious, and unhygienic. Many of the midwives who were caring for both Black and White women in childbirth during this time were Black. The medicalization of childbirth is not only a story of gender, of male obstetricians wresting control over pregnancy from women, but a story of race—White people, White males wresting control over pregnancy and childbirth from Black women.

DM——**This book attests to this story time and again, from enslaved Black women providing the unwilling basis for the foundations of gynecology in this country, when they were tortured by J. Marion Sims as he developed the** speculum (p. 55), to nineteenth-century photographs of "hidden mothers," where scholars have suggested that some of the figures cloaked under blankets to hold the infants still enough for the exposure were women of color (p. 289), to the types of care work that, both historically and today, are done predominantly by Black and Brown women.

I want to come back to something you said about studying how law is lived. Are there specific laws, policies, or other linguistic tools that you think need redesigning in order to be able to improve reproductive health, birth outcomes, and maternal experiences for Black women in this country?

KB— In my work I delight in finding discrepancies between a law on the books and law on the ground—between how pregnancy is described in jurisprudence, specifically in Supreme Court cases, and how pregnancy is lived. For the most part, in jurisprudence pregnancy is celebrated as good for the person and good for the nation. But on the ground, when it's poor folks or undocumented folks or trans people who are reproducing—when there are non-normative people engaging in reproduction—all of that beautiful, lovely language around how pregnancy is good for the country and a person and a family goes out the window completely. My research often interrogates those moments of cognitive dissonance, when there is a disparity between how pregnancy is imagined and how pregnancy is lived.

DM— If you could wave a magic wand today to change one design in the United States, whether it's a system or a product or a law or something else, what would you change?

KB— I definitely think that single-payer health care systems do a much better job of diminishing the effects of racism. We do such a terrible job of providing health care to poor people in this country. It's hard to describe Medicaid as nefarious. It's hard to say that it was erected with bad intentions or designed to punish. But I think that there's no denying that Medicaid is punitive on the ground. It is dignity denying. If a person had some degree of class privilege and had a pregnancy while privately insured, and then that same person was stripped of private insurance and had to navigate a second pregnancy with Medicaid and the public health care system, I think they would be shocked. It's completely different in terms of privacy and the ability to make decisions about what your prenatal care will look like and what your childbirth will be like. We have the worst health outcomes in the industrialized world, yet we pay the most for our health care, and we still have millions who are uninsured. It's a terribly designed system. And I think this is due to race. In this country, when we think about a social safety net, we think about racial minorities because racial minorities have always disproportionately occupied the lower tiers of our social hierarchy and have had to overly rely on these safety-net programs. Our badly designed two-tiered health care system is informed by our dislike of Black and Brown people and our sense that the poor, who we have racialized as nonwhite, ought not to have decent health care. That is not to say that single-payer systems eradicate racism. But in a single-payer system racism has fewer opportunities to manifest in ways that are health denying and mortality increasing. That being said, I also think that there ought to be ways of designing one's prenatal care and birth experiences even within a single-payer system. So I would like to have two wands. In California there's a consortium of activists that I admire, Black Women Birthing Justice, that has coalesced around people's right to choose the way that their pregnancy, birth, and post-partum period will progress. Whether that means not giving birth in a hospital, or deciding to have a cesarean, or wanting a midwife or an obstetrician, so be it. That takes us right back to the hashtag #listentoblackwomen. Give them choice, give them agency, trust them to choose their reproductive experiences, period.

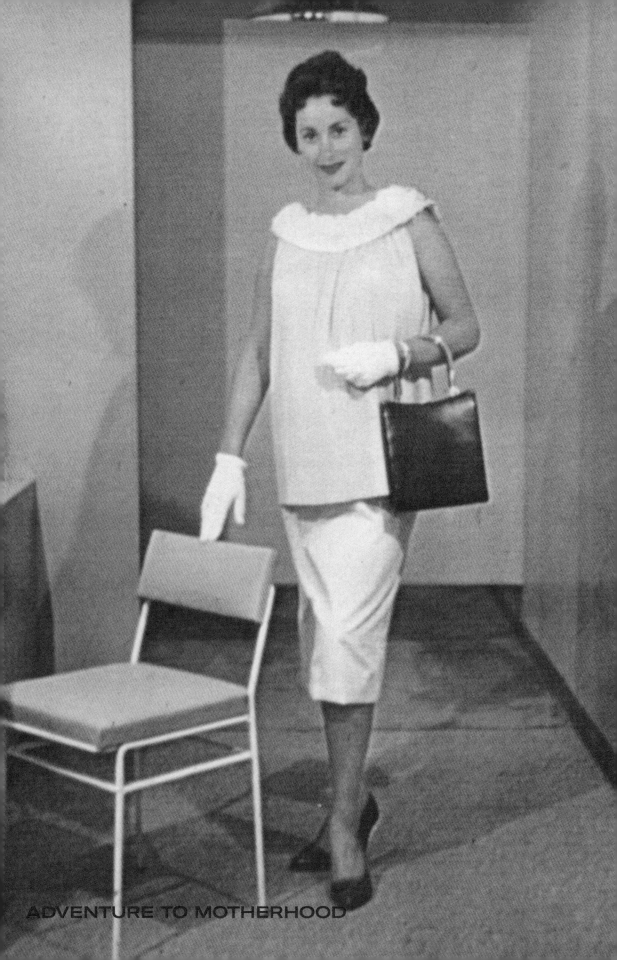

ADVENTURE TO MOTHERHOOD

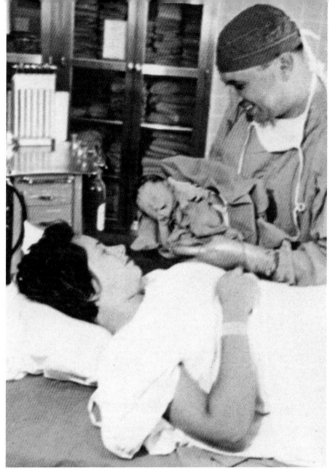

1— "Betsy, morale is one of the most important things during pregnancy and there is nothing like a nice appearance to give you a lift. Two or three stylish maternity dresses and an occasional trip to the beauty parlor will work wonders to keep your spirits high."

2— "Betsy gets a first good look at her baby and decides that every bit of the previous nine months of waiting has been worth it."

3— "A small incision is made in the perineum to prevent any serious tears or lacerations. Of course, this is not felt because of anesthesia.... With the entire area covered with sterile drapes and leggings, the doctor [uses] forceps to shorten labor and prevent damage to the mother and baby."

4— "'Well Betsy,' [the doctor] informs her, 'you're in excellent health and it certainly looks as though you're going to have a baby.'"

5— "During pregnancy there is a tendency to gain too much weight. You should not gain more than twenty pounds over the entire nine months. It is important to keep your monthly gain down to two pounds or less."

6— "If you gain too much weight, we may have to substitute skimmed milk or buttermilk for whole milk."

7— "A moderate amount of exercise each day is essential—walking is particularly good."

8— "Well Jim, congratulations! Betsy is fine and the baby is a beauty!"

ADVENTURE TO MOTHERHOOD
Adventure to Motherhood: The Picture-Story of Pregnancy and Childbirth was created by the obstetrician and gynecologist J. Allen Offen in Miami in 1960. In it, the real-life couple Betsy and Jim follow their doctor's advice to a T. Offen explains, "This book was written to tell a story, which is nearly as old as time itself." It is likely that the images within will provoke in contemporary readers both curiosity and terror in equal amounts.

2 3 4
5 6 7

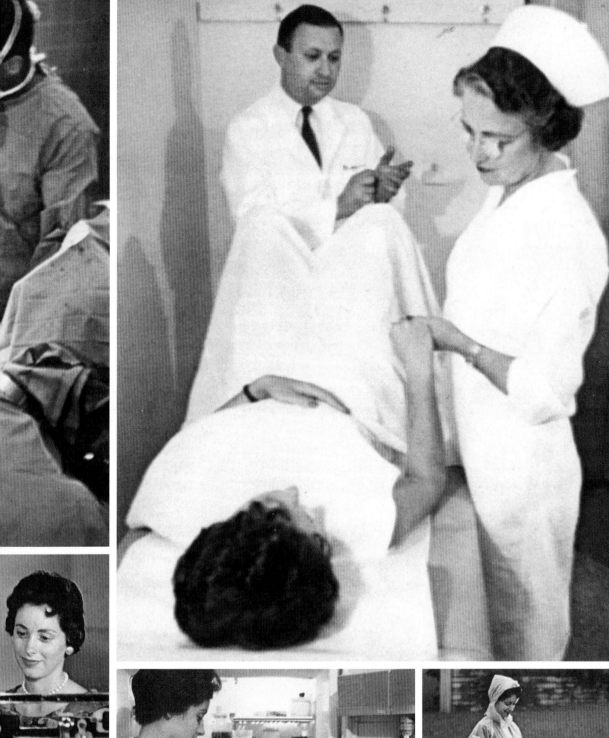

DESIGNS FOR GRIEF—*This world of dew*
is a world of dew,
and yet, and yet.
—Kobayashi Issa
(after the death of a child)[1]

When the Japanese Buddhist priest and poet Kobayashi Issa lost his daughter around two hundred years ago, he knew the laws of reality: nothing is permanent; everything passes. And yet, and yet.

When a baby dies, parents are thrust forcefully into a vicious tide where birth crashes and folds directly into death. Across time and cultures, seeing, holding, or simply honoring one's baby helps to ritualize the passage into parenthood. Birth and death, after all, belong to the in-betweens of our world. These are the liminal spaces of human experience. The deep waters.

Every era and culture handles death—and particularly the death of a baby—in its own way.[2] In our times of deepest need we turn to our communities, and often to the material world, to help begin the process of grieving.[3] Sometimes physical things facilitate our grief; these objects remind us of a loved one lost. Some are tied to our culture, religion, or traditions. Still others are designed to guide and assist us. A universal truth is that grief takes time. Tides will roll in, and tides will roll out. As with the ocean, there is a sense of the eternal in motherhood; ultimately, it's an experience that lives beyond life and death.

Día de los Muertos is a holiday celebrated throughout
Mexico and by people of Mexican heritage everywhere.
The Day of the Dead doesn't last just one day, as its name
implies, but rather three days. *Día de los Angelitos*, or Day
of the Little Angels, happens the day before the big events
of November 2—because, it is said, the spirits of children
are so eager to come back to the land of the living that
they run ahead of the adults, who arrive a night later. Each
year on November 1, parents who have lost children spend
the afternoon creating or decorating an altar, usually at
home or in a graveyard. In Catholic mythology, babies often
appear as spiritual beings, and paper angels and flowers
are frequently placed at grave sites. Family members leave
offerings to their lost one, many of which nod to care routines and domestic life. These altars, or ad hoc sculptures,
take many forms and may include special lighting, incense,
fresh and paper flowers, candles, balloons, toys, clothing,
and food. The playful, colorful, celebratory offerings cultivate a continuing relationship between families and their
lost children.

—Photos by **Dane Strom** in Jalisco, Mexico.

In Philippe Ariès's *The Hour of Our Death*, a history of death and dying in Western culture, first published in 1977, he observed that the belief that the dead are asleep is ancient and constant.[4] In the postmortem daguerreotypes of the late nineteenth century, stillborn babies were routinely laid on something soft and photographed from the side. This pose was described by the anthropologist Jay Ruby as the "Last Sleep" style, and it is a typically Western representation in its association of death with sleep.[5] Mothers, too, may appear in postmortem photography, as is the case in this American daguerreotype from 1855, titled "Lovely Light," in which a mother holds her deceased infant, a pose with many variations and that is still used today. Contemporary organizations such as Now I Lay Me Down to Sleep have a network of volunteer photographers who create "remembrance portraits" that help document the precious moments parents spend with their babies. In the era of social media, parents are emboldened by hashtags such as #stillbornbutstillborn, #babyloss, and #stillbornstillloved to raise awareness, share their grief, and make the loss of a baby more visible.

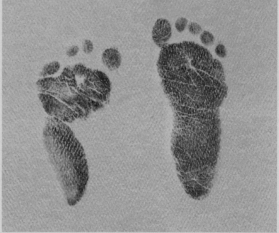

A 2016 study in Michigan of 377 bereaved mothers whose babies died soon after birth found that eighteen of the women did not get to see their babies, thirty-six did not get to hold them, and thirty-four were told that they were not allowed to hold them.[6] Although a major shift has been underway since about the 1980s, some hospital staff are still instructed to remove babies after they die. Although they might mean well, rushing and sweeping aside the realities of losing a child can make a deeply painful experience even sharper and more bewildering. Even in the best-intentioned hospitals, the amount of time parents are able to spend with their deceased babies is usually restricted because the body of the infant can quickly deteriorate. It was the positive psychological effects of taking time to bond with babies, even after death, that inspired the design of the CuddleCot. In 2009, the British company Flexmort began experimenting with a cooling cot that could prolong the amount of time parents could spend with their infant. Designers developed a modular cooling system that worked with a Moses basket and fan rather than refrigerant gas. They made the cot light and portable, empowering some families to bring their babies home to say goodbye in their own environment, and in their own time.

These footprints of Megan Brandow-Faller's firstborn daughter, Lotte, are a palpable reminder of her daughter's simultaneous absence and presence in their family. Within the tradition of printmaking, taking impressions of infants' feet has emerged as a relatively new, postwar development—first used for identification purposes but now tethered to family sentiment and emotional bonding. Lotte lived only twelve days outside the womb, undergoing three unsuccessful surgeries for a serious heart condition. Megan and her husband, Adam, had to endure the agony of seeing their newborn hooked up to a jungle of IVs, cords, tubes, and machines in an cold, sterile environment where the mother's strongest connection to her child was through a breast pump—a hospital-grade Medela Symphony—through which she produced milk for Lotte. Megan and Adam now have three boys, and they embrace Lotte's memory as part of their family and celebrate her birthday annually; her brothers remain living embodiments of their sister, of her absence and presence, and cherish her protective guiding spirit. Her absence is felt keenly at important family milestones—birthdays, "firsts," and graduations—and during routine tasks such as completing school forms that ask for information on siblings. Lotte's footprints testify to her very real though short time on earth and to her much beloved place in her family. Common memory objects for deceased children include locks of hair, plaster casts of limbs, and memento mori photographs, but the footprints were not originally intended as such. Lotte's attending nurses surprised Megan with the footprints around Mother's Day, while Lotte was on life support and it remained unclear whether she would live or die.

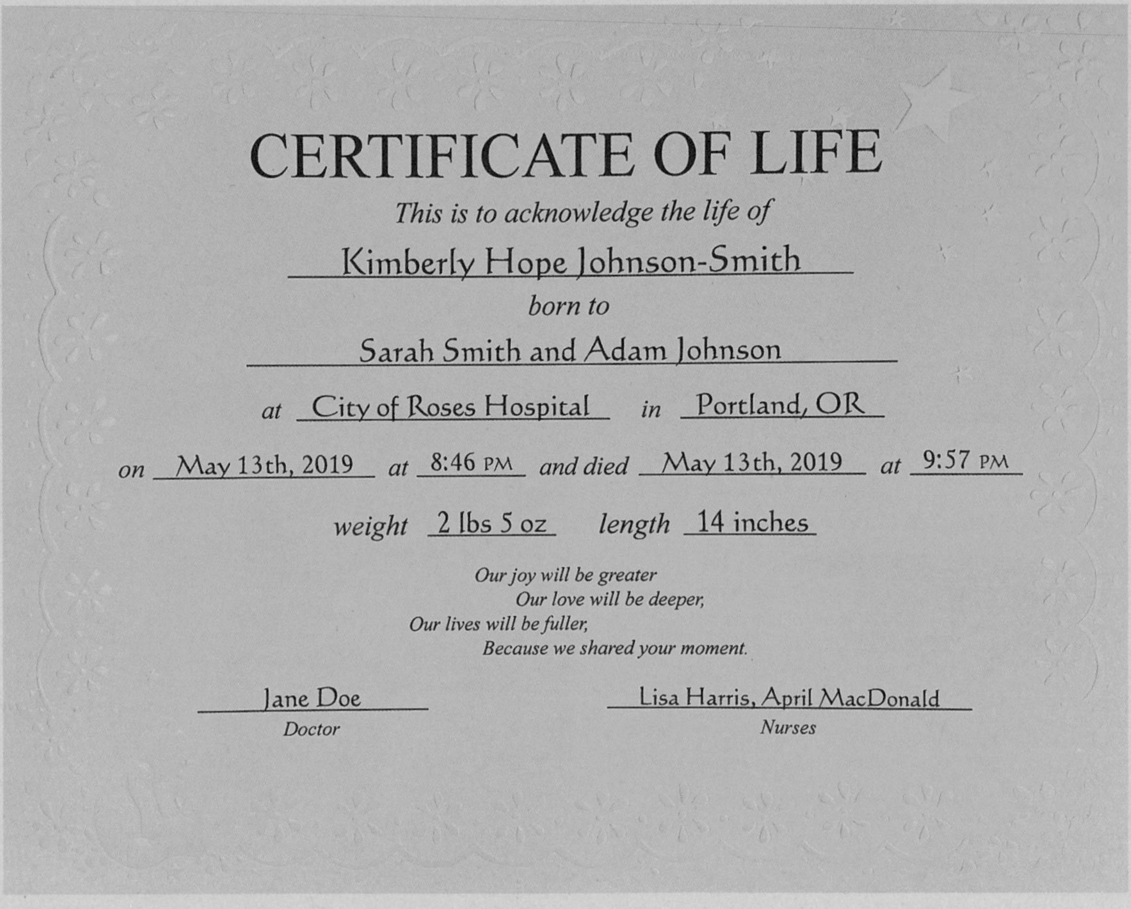

CERTIFICATE OF LIFE

This is to acknowledge the life of

Kimberly Hope Johnson-Smith

born to

Sarah Smith and Adam Johnson

at City of Roses Hospital   *in* Portland, OR

on May 13th, 2019   *at* 8:46 PM *and died* May 13th, 2019   *at* 9:57 PM

weight 2 lbs 5 oz   *length* 14 inches

Our joy will be greater
Our love will be deeper,
Our lives will be fuller,
Because we shared your moment.

Jane Doe
Doctor

Lisa Harris, April MacDonald
Nurses

The birth certificate is a small paper, but it is among the first legal documents an individual acquires. For the living, they establish who you are and give access to the rights, privileges, and obligations of citizenship. For those who have suffered a loss, whether and when a certificate is issued largely reflects the law and culture of a given place. The laws governing the issuing of birth and death certificates vary not only from country to country, but often also from state to state, owing to how various groups of people conceptualize life, death, and personhood. The group GriefWatch creates "Certificates of Life" for those who want them but may not otherwise be issued a certificate.

Heather DeWolf Bowser was planning a home birth, but her water broke unexpectedly at twenty weeks—too early for her baby to survive. "I wanted a wise woman by my side, or even just someone to just be with me, but it wasn't a choice." Because of the baby's gestational age, the laws designed to regulate licensed midwifery in her then home state of New Jersey meant Heather's midwife was not legally able to attend her birth. Knowing she wanted to avoid being induced in a hospital, Heather birthed on her own. "I had nothing to offer my daughter besides a warm, peaceful birth surrounded by her brother and her father. She only knew the warmth and safety of my own body. She only knew peace and spirit. I was able to do that for her. And it's one of the most powerful things I've ever done." In the days following, Heather created an altar to Luna, shaping a length of her umbilical cord into a heart. This photograph and the now sun-preserved umbilical heart are two of the objects that keep Luna close. "Every pregnancy holds the possibility of loss. Every woman on the planet has to contend with the fact that we hold both life and death in our bodies," Heather reflects. "What would it be like if our culture was less afraid of birth, and less afraid of death? What if these things weren't treated like emergencies? I suspect we'd be a lot better prepared to support women and help them move through their grief."

According to Celtic legend, the spirits of children who have died in or around birth scatter daisies on the earth to cheer their sorrowing parents. As the story goes, Malvina, a Celtic noblewoman, lost her infant son and became inconsolable. Shortly afterward her attendants arrived with the news that a wondrous new flower had come to earth, white in color, but tinged with pink the color of a baby's flesh at the edges. As Malvina looked into the eye of a single daisy, she understood that this humble flower was meant to console her. In Scottish and Celtic cultures, a bouquet of ox-eye daisies can be an offering to anyone who has lost a child somewhere along the path to parenthood.[7]

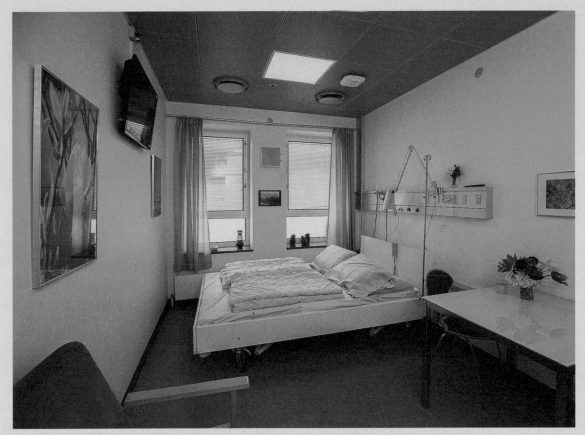

During the 1950s, birth policies in the Western world were influenced by prominent psychiatrists and biologists, especially John Bowlby, who developed the concept of "attachment" to describe the emotional relationship between mothers and their children. Historically, this parent-child bond has not been recognized in mourning, and many Western hospitals discharge patients just hours after losing a baby. Patients of Denmark's Aarhus University Hospital's perinatal-loss unit, however, are welcome to stay as many days as they like and are encouraged to take all the time they need with their babies. The specialist midwife Dorte Hvidtjørn and her team have taken particular care to make the unit comfortable, with warm lighting, double beds that sleep both parents, and fresh flowers cut from the unit's garden. This separate space and garden allow families to grieve away from the typically celebratory maternity ward. Specialist midwives also empower and guide families to bring their babies home to help with the grieving process. In the unit and at home, parents can hold their babies in their arms, care for them, and take photographs. This helps them ease their grief and process what has happened.

1   Makoto Ueda, *Dew on the Grass: The Life and Poetry of Kobayashi Issa* (Boston: Brill, 2004), 125.

2   In 2015 there were 2.6 million still-births globally; see "Maternal, Newborn, Child, and Adolescent Health: Stillbirths,"

World Health Organization, who.int/maternal_child_adolescent/epidemiology/stillbirth/en.

3   In her cross-cultural examination of death rites, Caitlin Doughty argues that the physical act of being with the dead helps mourners

everywhere, particularly when they can care for their loved one's body, altar, grave, or memorial. Doughty, *From Here To Eternity: Traveling the World to Find Good Death* (New York: W. W. Norton, 2017), 235.

4   Philippe Ariès, *The

Hour of Our Death* (New York: Oxford University Press, 1991), 89.

5   Jay Ruby, *Secure the Shadow: Death and Photography in America* (Cambridge, MA: MIT Press, 1995).

6   Katherine J. Gold et al., "Depression and Posttraumatic

Stress Symptoms after Perinatal Loss in a Population-Based Sample," *Journal of Women's Health* 25, no. 3 (2016): 263–69.

7   See Niall Mac Coitir, *Ireland's Wild Plants: Myths, Legends, and Folklore* (Cork: Collins Press, 2006).

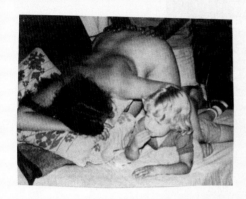

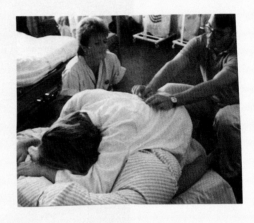

CARMEN WINANT

CARMEN WINANT In her 2018 book, *Carmen Winant: My Birth*, from which these images are drawn, the artist reflected that "very few people asked me about my birth. The delivery of another human being: weren't they curious about its effect?…I want to beg: *just ask me.*" Winant uses found photographs of people in various stages of childbirth, from sources as disparate as health manuals and yard sales, to expose details that are often too taboo for public consumption in either text or image. *My Birth*, which was also a landmark installation at the Museum of Modern Art in New York in the same year as the book's publication, meditates on the universal and unique aspects of birth. Winant asks whether, in picturing the process so many times over, we might understand childbirth and its representation to be political acts. Crucially, Winant understands the politics as extending to the bias expressed by the prevalence of representations of White women in much of the material published on birth.

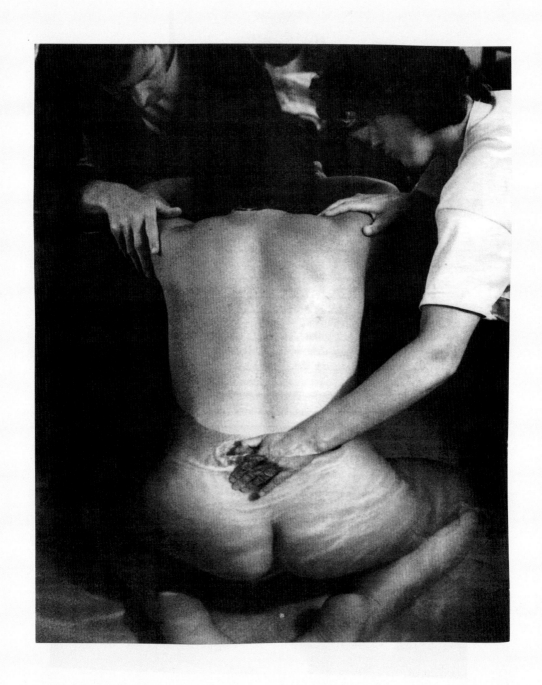

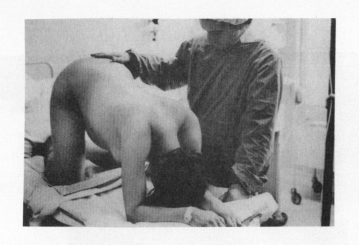

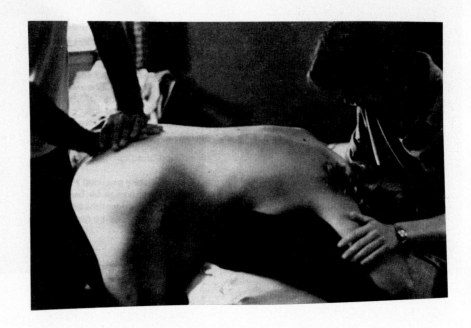

HOME BIRTH——I was born in a 1950s ranch house covered in a year-round tangle of vines and yellow trumpet flowers. At the time, home birth in Florida was largely attended by an underground network of unlicensed midwives. The pictures from the day I was born show midwives and my parents' dear friends scattered throughout the house and my mother playing piano in our sunroom.

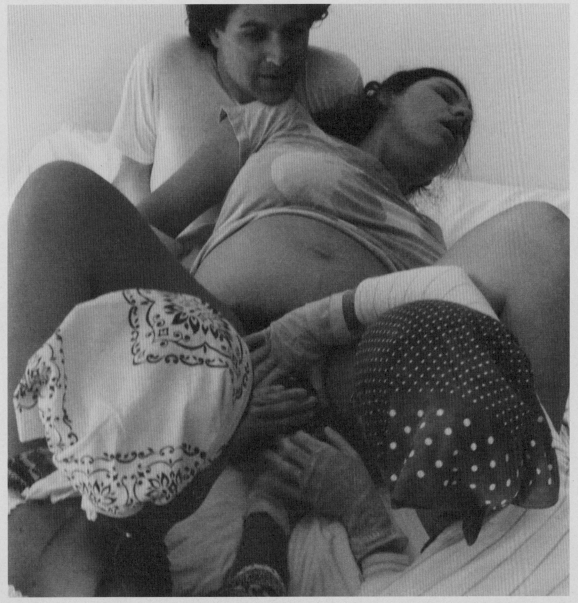

The author's mom laboring to bring her into the world, Florida, 1981

They show her taking deep, supported squats as she steadies herself on the kitchen counter. They show her encircled with support and community.

My parents fit all the home birth stereotypes of the time: they were ACLU lawyers, wore sandals, and ate vegetarian. They believed women had the right to choose whether and when to have a child, and where and how they would give birth. Working together, they initiated lawsuits in service of advancing the home-birth movement in Florida.[1] A few years later they would divorce and start new chapters of their lives and careers, but creating pathways for midwives was what they worked on when they were together and in love.

In the 1970s, second-wave feminists like my mom were reading about how women could reclaim their bodies, and how women healers had historically been marginalized and maligned. Thinkers and advocates such as Margaret Mead, Simone de Beauvoir, Betty Friedan, Sheila Kitzinger, and Ina May Gaskin were reimagining a mother's role and resisting patriarchal models of childbirth. They wanted the choice to have "natural" (or unmedicated) births attended by midwives. Some wanted to birth at home, far from the mechanized and anesthetized hospital system. In 1971, Barbara Ehrenreich and Deirdre English published Witches, Midwives, Nurses: A History of Women Healers, beginning it with a bold declaration:

Women have always been healers. They were the unlicensed doctors and anatomists of western history.... They were midwives, travelling from home to home and village to village. For centuries women were doctors without degrees, barred from books and lectures, learning from each other, and passing on experience from neighbor to neighbor and mother to daughter. They were called "wise women" by the people, witches or charlatans by the authorities. Medicine is part of our heritage as women, our history, our birthright.[2]

This birthright—especially when it came to actual birth—was part of my childhood. I remember turning the pages of books by Kitzinger, the social anthropologist and activist, that showed images of peaceful, respectful birth from around the world. I remember my mother giving birth to my brother in her bedroom and visiting my friends' homes when their siblings were born. Photographs of the obstetrician-cum-reformer Frédérick Leboyer's gentle births were propped up in my mother's office, and Gaskin's Spiritual Midwifery showed people on "The Farm," an intentional community and birthing center in rural Tennessee. These enlightened attitudes surrounding birth, mothers, and babies seemed to fulfill many of the promises of the women's movement: women gave birth freely—even joyously—at home, and babies took peaceful first breaths surrounded by their mothers' partners, friends, and midwives. Despite the radical social ideals that informed my parent's lifestyle, we lived in Miami, far from the rural idyll of the Farm. Still, to my child's mind, birth was normal. I had no illusions about its difficulties, but I knew it happened every day.[3]

For most of American history, the practice of midwifery was rooted in shared skill and wisdom passed on by Indigenous and later Black women. When early English settlers arrived, they brought their own traditional midwifery customs and practices.[4] Midwives did not receive any formal training; they learned their skills from attending births and sharing knowledge with more experienced midwives. Midwifery also tended to be an intergenerational occupation, passed matrilineally, and midwives were considered valuable and respected members of local communities.

Controversy over home birth began in the early part of the last century, provoking debate over the "midwife problem" in nearly every part of the United States.[5] In 1847, the American Medical Association professionalized medicine and standardized its practices, and the field of gynecology was growing. Dr. Joseph Bolivar DeLee, considered a founder of modern obstetrics, in 1915 declared childbirth a "pathologic process"; introduced forceps, episiotomies, and scopolamine injections as routine interventions; and denounced midwives as a "relic of barbarism."[6] By 1910 modern medicine had become the driver of care standards, and the hospital was promoted as a sort of hotel that provided practical services such as state-of-the-art tools, pain relief, and a place to recuperate. Though not everyone had access to a hospital (or a vehicle to get them there), this shift reflected a new American attitude: modern birth took place in a hospital, not at home. A highly publicized and national concern about the high infant and maternal death rates in the United States spurred many state health authorities to focus on improving obstetrical services.[7] Midwives, now far outside the sphere of "legitimate" medicine, became a focus of debate and were targeted for elimination in many states.

Although hospital birth brought new problems and dangers to mothers and babies, it quickly and efficiently eclipsed home birth while eroding the many foundations supporting culturally appropriate care by local midwives. In 1900, fewer than 5 percent of recorded births took place in hospitals, but by the 1920s hospital births had increased significantly. By 1930 the American Board of Obstetrics and Gynecology required a license to deliver a baby, leading to still more hospital births.[8] And by 1955 fully 99 percent of births took place in a hospital, a number that holds steady today.[9]

Still, home birth happened. For much of this time health care, like education and housing, was racially segregated as a result of explicitly racist Jim Crow laws. Many hospitals, clinics, and doctor's offices were completely segregated, and others had separate wings or staff for minority patients, who were not allowed to mingle under threat of law. A lack of trained Black medical professionals (a situation exacerbated by segregated education), coupled with the fact that midwives and other community-based caregivers were denied legal licenses, meant Black people had little choice when it came to hospital and clinic-based health care services, and often found such care to be insufficient and irrelevant to their lives and communities, particularly in the South.[10] In the 1930s, 80 percent of the fifty thousand midwives in the United States were located in the southern states. Black midwives delivered babies of all races south of the Mason Dixon Line well into the 1970s, despite many barriers.[11] In a triple bind, state laws restricted Black mothers from entering quality hospitals, mandated that midwives attending home births have a license, and then put racist barriers in midwives' way.

In Florida midwives were held responsible for the state's high infant and maternal death rates, despite health officials' admissions that, statistically, midwives experienced fewer incidents of maternal and infant death than physicians.[12] A 1931 Florida statute ordered that only someone who had attended fifteen births under the supervision of a licensed physician would be entitled to a midwifery license. The statute was created in response to the racist belief that so-called granny midwives were dangerous and unclean and so needed licensed physicians (read, White physicians) to educate and supervise them.

In the 1970s and 1980s, when the women's movement brought a renewed interest in home birth, midwives tried to obtain licenses under the statute and were denied by Florida's then Department of Health and Rehabilitative Services. The series of lawsuits and administrative actions brought by my mother ultimately forced the department to issue midwifery licenses. With guidance from a bill she drafted, the Florida legislature went on to update the standards of the 1931 statute, making licensure more comprehensive and so providing choice in childbirth and enabling a new generation to enter the field as direct-entry midwives.[13]

In the United States today, only 1 percent of births take place at home, and approximately 10 percent of births are attended by midwives (as compared to 50 to 75 percent in other high-resource countries).[14] This low number is a result not only of the low density of midwives per state, but also of the fact that midwives are not universally licensed to practice or integrated into regional health care systems. Especially in the case of home birth, there are numerous regulatory barriers, including the inability to secure third-party reimbursement.[15] Medicaid covers home birth in only half the states, and many insurance policies do not cover home birth at all. Subsequently, many pregnant people cannot access midwives because of legal or payor restrictions, a situation that disproportionately impacts low-income and rural communities.[16]

Yet in countries where midwives are integrated into the health care system the benefits are well documented.[17] Planned home births lead to substantially fewer unnecessary cesarean sections than do births in hospitals. And when a midwife attends to prenatal care and birth, pregnant people are much less likely to experience unnecessary intervention. Global health experts recommend that a simple way to improve maternal and newborn outcomes, reduce rates of unnecessary interventions, and realize cost savings is to scale up midwifery.[18]

In 2013, I gave birth in the kitchen of my apartment. It was on the top floor of a Roman revival–style brownstone, built in the late 1880s in the Prospect Heights neighborhood of Brooklyn (just down the road from the hospital where my grandmother gave birth in the 1940s). Over the years, this room of my own was where I grew up, nursed wounds, cooked countless meals, fell in love, and learned of my father's death. I knew and loved every corner and crevice of the place, and it was the only place I wanted to give birth.

Home birth is not for everyone, nor do I believe that it should be. What I do believe is that better access to home birth and midwifery is a public health and safety issue and that the US maternal health system is in drastic need of redesign. Birthing people everywhere deserve the best possible, most respectful care available, and they should receive it in the setting where they feel safest. For many people, this is a hospital. For those who are high risk, giving birth in a hospital is often the only option. But no matter where one gives birth, we all deserve to retain agency and autonomy and have unnecessary interventions minimized. And while place matters, even more crucial is access to compassionate, culturally appropriate, and respectful care that makes us feel safe, supported, and heard. Today, in large part because of doulas, it's possible (though not always easy) to have this kind of birth in a hospital.

The midwives who attended my births were both nurse-midwives. Prenatal

appointments were always enjoyed over tea in my living room, a dream come true for a homebody like me. During the births themselves, I faced enormous, transformative challenges, but I did so where I felt safest and among a caring birth team. Afterward I could eat breakfast in my bed with my partner and newborn. To be honest, these creature comforts were just as motivating as any of my political beliefs.

Though I thought I was simply following in my parents' radical footsteps, I realize now how many privileges are involved in choosing home birth today. This includes living in proximity to caring midwives and doulas, having a healthy body that society does not treat with suspicion, and being considered low risk enough to expect a good birth outcome. It's a privilege to have options in a country where the entire industrialized medical system funnels one toward the hospital. Most of all, though, there is privilege in having a straightforward birth and healthy baby. In a country where the maternal mortality rate is three to four times higher for Black and Indigenous women than it is for White women, and where Black infants are twice as likely to die in their first year as White infants and two to three times more likely to be born premature or underweight, these privileges are unconscionable.[19]

As COVID-19 has wreaked havoc around the world, there has been a resurgence of public conversations surrounding midwifery and home birth. Hospitals across the country are limiting the number of people allowed in labor and delivery rooms, and people are again turning to home birth as the safest, most viable option. They're also looking to midwives and realizing there simply aren't enough of them.

In June 2020, in my home state of Florida, the work of the midwife and reproductive justice activist Jennie Joseph culminated in a historic moment: the opening of the Commonsense Childbirth School of Midwifery.[20] The school is the first direct-entry training program for midwives, and the first and only Black-owned and nationally accredited private midwifery school in the country. CCSM is creating pathways for midwives of color to provide culturally appropriate care, enabling them to once again become autonomous providers—trusted and venerated birth workers at the heart of their communities.

Because my first child was born in the kitchen, and my second in the doorway of our bedroom (this time in a 1920s house in the Hudson Valley), I think of my births often. As happens with any intense experience, giving birth in a space alters one's receptivity of the architecture, and one must pay dividends in the form of remembering while doing mundane things like chopping vegetables or crossing a threshold. The walls and doorways are the same, but the psychological shift is tremendous. Given the age of these buildings, and the history of the land they're built on, I find myself thinking not only about my own births but about all those who have given birth there before me: in a place safe enough to be with our pain, lay it down, and find the embodied clarity and beauty of giving birth on our own terms. And I think about the midwives, the ones who guided us here through that place.

1   In the early 1980s my parents, Terry DeMeo and Bruce Winick, both attorneys, represented the Florida Association of Lay Midwives and various individual midwives. See Katherine Simmons Yagerman, "Legitimacy for the Florida Midwife : The Midwifery Practice Art," *University of Miami Law Review* 37, no. 123 (1982): 123–50.
2   Barbara Ehrenreich and Deirdre English, *Witches, Midwives, and Nurses: A History of Women Healers*, (Oyster Bay, NY: Glass Mountain Pamphlets, [1971/72]), 3; a second edition was published by the Feminist Press in 1973.
3   Many in my generation learned about home birth through the powerful and now iconic 2008 documentary *The Business of Being Born*, produced by Ricki Lake and directed by Abby Epstein.
4   Richard W. Wertz and Dorothy C. Wertz, *Lying In: A History of Childbirth in America* (New Haven: Yale University Press, 1989), 44–46.
5   Frances Kobrin, "The American Midwife Controversy: A Crisis of Professionalization," *Bulletin of the History of Medicine* 40, no. 4 (1966): 350–51. Kobrin describes the early 1900s as a "contest" between "the increasingly self-conscious obstetrical specialist" and the midwife.
6   Dr. Joseph DeLee, "Progress Towards Ideal Obstetrics," excerpts from a paper presented to the Committee on Midwifery in Chicago 1915, collegeofmidwives.org/college-ofmidwives.org/.
7   Judy Litoff, *American Midwives: 1860 to the Present* (Westport, CT: Greenwood Press, 1978), 48–50.
8   By 1938 nearly 50 percent of recorded US births took place in hospitals.
9   Tina Cassidy, *Birth: A History* (London: Chatto & Windus, 2007), 62–63.
10   Vann R. Newkirk II, "America's Health Segregation Problem: Has the Country Done Enough to Overcome Its Jim Crow Health Care History?," *The Atlantic*, May 18, 2016, theatlantic.com.
11   Cassidy, *Birth*, 41.
12   Kobrin, "The American Midwife Controversy," 353.
13   A direct-entry midwife is an independent practitioner educated in the discipline of midwifery through self-study, apprenticeship, a midwifery school, a college, or a university-based program distinct from the discipline of nursing. Representative Elaine Gordon sponsored the House version of the bill (FLA. H.B. 887, 1982 Reg. Sess.), which was written by Terry De Meo, attorney for the Florida Association of Lay Midwives; it was modeled after the Washington State lay midwife regulatory law. The bill focused on three key issues: (1) the need for a lay midwife licensing law; (2) the standard of education that should be required; and (3) whether supervisory authority should rest with the Department of Professional Regulation, as originally proposed, or with the Florida Board of Health (later changed to the Department of Health and Rehabilitative Services). See Yagerman, "Legitimacy for the Florida Midwife," 141.
14   Steffi Goodman, "Piercing the Veil: The Marginalization of Midwives in the United States," *Social Science and Medicine* 65, no. 3 (2007): 610–21. See also Saraswathi Vedam et al., "Mapping Integration of Midwives across the United States: Impact on Access, Equity, and Outcomes," *PLOS ONE* 13, no. 2 (2018): 1.
15   Deborah Walker, Barbara Lannen, and Debra Rossie, "Midwifery Practice and Education: Current Challenges and Opportunities," *Online Journal of Issues in Nursing* 19, no. 2 (2014): 4, ojin.nursingworld.org.
16   Melissa Cheyney et al., "Practitioner and Practice Characteristics of Certified Professional Midwives in the United States: Results of the 2011 North American Registry of Midwives Survey," *Journal of Midwifery and Women's Health* 60, no. 5 (2015): 534–45.
17   In 2014 *The Lancet*'s series on midwifery concluded that "national investment in midwives and in their work environment, education, regulation, and management … is crucial to the achievement of national and international goals and targets in reproductive, maternal, newborn, and child health." Petra ten Hoope-Bender et al., "Improvement of Maternal and Newborn Health through Midwifery," *The Lancet* 384, no. 9949 (2014): 1226–35.
18   Wim Van Lerberghe et al., "Country Experience with Strengthening of Health Systems and Deployment of Midwives in Countries with High Maternal Mortality," *The Lancet* 384, no. 9949 (2014): 1215–25.
19   Regardless of Black women's income or education level, childbirth is more dangerous for them than it is for White women. Even Serena Williams had a dangerously close call during her delivery, after doctors failed to heed her request for a CT scan and a blood thinner. Despite her history of blood clots, they posited that "Williams' pain medication must be making her confused." See Amy Roeder, "America Is Failing Its Black Mothers," *Harvard Public Health Magazine*, Winter 2019, hsph.harvard.edu/magazine.
20   CCSM is accredited by the Midwifery Education Accreditation Council (MEAC).

PAIN——The way we feel pain has everything to do with history, culture, and our own highly personal experiences. It would take an entire book to record the varied experiences people have with pain and pain relief. No one approach to pain during birth is best, and none are universally available to all laboring people.

Where medication is involved, cost is almost always a factor. Access to information also shapes how we encounter pain, as does the agency to make decisions about how it is handled.[1] Our research tells us how deeply and historically pain is felt. Anyone who has ever used an analgesic in labor should give thanks to the nineteenth-century British monarch Queen Victoria, whose experimentation with chloroform at the birth of her eighth child, Leopold, set a public example that suffering was optional. (Until that point, the Christian church had hewed to the admonition in Genesis 3:16 that the descendants of Eve would bring forth children "in sorrow.") Instead, modern medicine began spurning such misogyny: "It is wrong to withhold relief from pain from poor or rich," declared O'Donel Browne, an Irish obstetrician, to an audience at the Royal Academy of Medicine in his 1949 presidential address.[2] Yet stereotypes about pain thresholds still abound, which makes advocating for empowered choices, especially those that are self-administered or self-directed, exceptionally important.

Breathing Techniques
Labor is often compared to tumultuous waves, and following that metaphor, breath can be an anchor. A number of breathing practices have been designed and discussed in the twentieth and twenty-first centuries. The familiar "hee, hoo, hee, hoo!" seen in Hollywood portrayals of childbirth was popularized by Dr. Fernand Lamaze, who brought the technique to France in 1951 after observing it in Russia. The Lamaze method gained popularity in the United States after Marjorie Karmel wrote her book

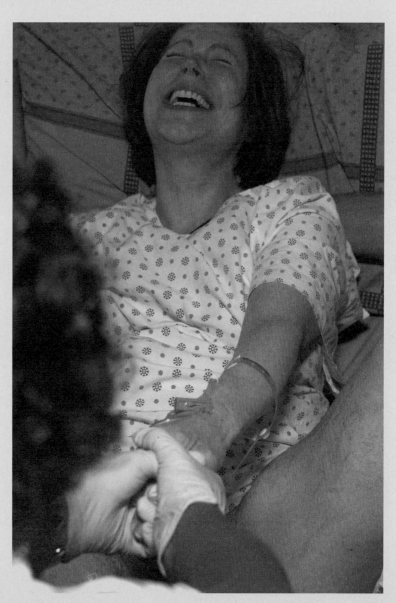

An image of a laboring person by Judith Elaine Halek from Debra Pascali-Bonaro's 2010 book *Orgasmic Birth*, which was also a 2008 documentary film

Thank You, Dr. Lamaze in 1959.[3] Other methods of purposeful, conscious breathing for birth include HypnoBirthing's 4:4 and 4:7 waves, abdominal breathing, alternative nostril and *ujjayi* breathing (both yogic pranayama practices), and Ina May Gaskin's "horse-lips" (or "raspberries").

These breathing techniques were designed to encourage relaxation during labor, enabling a birthing person to better cope with discomfort. "By synchronizing the breathing with the rhythm of the contractions it is possible for labour to be pleasurable, much like swimming in a stormy sea," the activist Sheila Kitzinger wrote in 1962. "If a woman tries to resist the uterine contractions, or merely to endure them, she will have severe pain; instead, she must go with them and cooperate with them in getting her baby born. As each one comes, therefore, she should *greet* it with her breathing."[4]

Epidural

"One of the greatest contrasts with most other methods of analgesia for obstetric labor is the marked quiet that prevails in the labor room," remarked a 1960 article on the epidural in the *American Journal of Nursing*. "Once the epidural is started the patients are quiet, cooperative, and usually happy."[5] Applied by an anesthetist who uses a needle to introduce an infinitesimally thin plastic catheter into the spine, an epidural works to block the nerves that send pain messages to the brain during birth. When it works, many recipients report their pain decreases exponentially, though numb legs means no walking around during labor and the need for a catheter for urination. Epidurals seem to spike some statistics, including a higher rate of forceps or vacuum delivery, but may decrease postpartum depression. The first epidurals were tested in the mid-nineteenth century; noteworthy was the American neurologist James Leonard Corning's proof of concept in 1885—injecting 111 mg of cocaine into the spine of a healthy male volunteer—which laid the groundwork for the deployment of epidurals during childbirth in the mid-twentieth century. Today, between 60 and 70 percent of US births involve an epidural.

Acupuncture and Acupressure

Acupuncture, a 2,000-year-old component of Traditional Chinese Medicine (TCM), is a process in which fine needles are inserted into the skin at particular points. It has been used to alleviate labor pain as well as to soften the cervix, stimulate the onset of labor, and promote postpartum healing. Acupressure is based on the same theories, but pressure is used without penetrating the skin.

In TCM, acupuncture and acupressure are believed to correct energy imbalances running along twelve energy meridians, or passageways, in the body. Stimulation is applied by needle, pressure, or heat at specific points along the meridians. Western researchers theorize that these techniques might relieve pain by changing pain perception or by stimulating the production of endorphins, natural pain-relieving hormones.

While further research is needed, acupuncture, and in particular electroacupuncture, in which a weak electrical current is pulsed through the needles, has been associated with greater maternal satisfaction as well as pain reduction in labor, though the effect is not as pronounced as with opioids or epidurals. Likewise, to the extent that acupressure has been studied, it has been associated with lower pain and reduced maternal anxiety. Both techniques are associated with shortened labor.

Acupuncture and acupressure provide promising alternatives for birthing people seeking pain relief. Acupressure is particularly cost-effective and can be provided by birth assistants with minimal training.

Water

Water has been used during labor—from birthing in proximity to sacred rivers and seas to employing hot compresses and baths—in cultures across the world. Using a pool as a form of pain management, however, is a relatively recent phenomenon. In 1977 Dr. Michel Odent installed a pool at the General Hospital in Pithiviers in northern France. Though he envisioned patients using the pool during labor, and not as a place to actually push, many ended up birthing within the pools anyway, and Odent is often credited with starting the trend of water birth. Part of what makes water birth so effective in countering pain is that it enables relaxation and intuitive movement. Sheila Kitzinger, an advocate for unmedicated childbirth, wrote, "Once floating in a pool, a woman in labour can move unencumbered. The water bears some of her weight and she has the sense of being in her own private world within the margins of her pool."[6]

In his best-selling book *Birth Without Violence* (1974), Frédérick Leboyer does not propose laboring in water, but he suggests immediately immersing the newborn baby in a warm bath as a means of easing the transition from womb to outside world. Researchers worldwide have found that laboring in water is safe, effective, and a highly satisfying strategy for managing pain, and that it poses no additional risk to either mother or baby.

Hypnosis

Hypnosis is a means of altering one's conscious awareness. It was the Scottish surgeon James Braid who first proposed the term in 1840, and soon after, hypnosis was used as an experimental form of pain relief, including for childbirth. In the 1950s several medical journals reported on how medical hypnotherapy had been used effectively in place of anesthesia, and research suggests that hypnosis can be an effective clinical tool for treating acute pain, including that caused by severe burns, dental procedures, surgeries, and birth. Researchers believe that hypnotherapy works by altering the higher centers of the central nervous system, changing how one perceives pain.

HypnoBirthing® was designed by Mickey Mongan in 1989 and is based on the work of Grantly Dick-Read, the British obstetrician who wrote *Childbirth Without Fear* in 1942. According to Dick-Read, use of hypnosis helps birthing people interrupt what he termed the "Fear-Tension-Pain syndrome," which he believed caused blood to flow away from nonessential organs such as the uterus to large muscle groups in the legs. Hypnobabies®, designed by Kerry Tuschhoff in 2001, builds on the work of hypnotist Gerald Kein's techniques, enabling birthing people to enter hypnosis, deepen it themselves, and remain mobile during labor. Both techniques teach birthing people to focus inward, reframe labor sensations as positive and productive, and feel safe, comfortable, and relaxed as they birth.

Twilight Sleep

Developed in Freiburg, Germany, in 1906 by obstetricians Bernhardt Kronig and Karl Gauss, the Twilight Sleep birthing method called for the laboring person to be injected with morphine at the start of birth pains and then given doses of scopolamine, an amnesiac with hallucinogenic effects. Scopolamine did not relieve pain, and so women were strapped to their beds in darkened rooms with gauze covering their eyes and cotton wool in their ears. Chloroform might be administered as the baby's head emerged. The drug combination and the environment were meant to erase the memory of pain entirely. Two editors of the US magazine *McClure's* traveled to Germany and reported favorably on the process, and readers at home campaigned for its availability in the United States. In 1914 Dr. Elizabeth Taylor Ransom, having gone through "hell" in two previous labors herself, obliged by establishing a maternity hospital in Boston's Back Bay that provided the treatment.[7] Ransom advertised the technique widely. Those who sought it out were usually wealthy and could afford to pay doctors to do their bidding. Subsequent babies born using Twilight Sleep were paraded as examples of its safety and appeal. The death during labor of a major advocate of the method, Frances Carmody, in 1915 lessened its popularity, though it continued in use until the late 1960s.

Orgasmic Birth

"All of the pathways that are involved in sexual pleasure are in fact stimulated by birthing a baby," Dr. Christiane Northrup narrates in the 2008 documentary *Orgasmic Birth: The Best-Kept Secret*, directed by Debra Pascali-Bonaro. "And when you can allow yourself to open in the same way that you open to orgasm, the exact same experience is possible."[8]

The idea that orgasm can be reached during childbirth has elicited everything from giggles and outright dismissals to fervent attempts to experience one's own "ecstatic birth," as Elizabeth Davis and Pascali-Bonaro phrased it in their 2010 book, *Orgasmic Birth*, which followed the documentary. It is a provocative idea that some see as a declaration of emancipation from the over-medicalization of childbirth. Others interpret it as yet another way to raise expectations and make birthing people feel inadequate if they feel pain instead of pleasure. Yet Pascali-Bonaro's message is that people can birth in all different ways, and if we shift from a culture of fear it is possible to have a positive and pleasurable experience. "I was at births and seeing people have great pleasure.... There was joy, there was ecstasy, there was bliss, there was relief. There was a huge gap in our vocabulary about birth."[9] Both the book and documentary *Orgasmic Birth* encourage people to think about what would make birth comfortable and enjoyable—even if orgasm is not reached.

Gas

First synthesized in 1772 by the British natural philosopher and chemist Joseph Priestley, and published three years later in his six-volume *Experiments and Observations on Different Kinds of Air*, nitrous oxide was a recreational drug before it was used for pain relief. Huffed at the turn of the nineteenth century by the British upper classes at "laughing gas parties"—so called because those who indulged were susceptible to fits of giggles—it later became a favorite analgesic for dental patients and those giving birth. The portable "Walton-Minnit" apparatus, first sold in 1936, was developed in England to mix nitrous oxide with air for self-administering. Studies have confirmed that medical providers can hold racial and gender stereotypes about pain thresholds, and so this and other self-administered methods are particularly important. They offer the birthing person control of their own medication, which is critical to agency during labor. Nitrous oxide is still available widely in the UK as part of the National Health Service provision for pain relief during birth, not least because it is cheap and effective. Less common in the US (in 2011, just two hospitals offered it), it is becoming more widely available (by 2019 in the US, an estimated 1,000 hospitals and 300 birthing centers provided it)—though the expensive hospital bills some users have accrued through its use (in one labor, almost $5,000) is no laughing matter.

Masturbation

Sexual pleasure can be part of the experience of childbirth, even leading to a "birthgasm" that occurs with or without external stimuli. Descriptions of this experience can be found in personal anecdotes, midwifery manuals (including the seminal work of Ina May Gaskin), and academic research that views giving birth "as a fundamental part of a birthing person's sexual cycle."[10] There is also direct orgasm initiated through soothing, kissing, touch—particularly of the nipples—and crescendoing via masturbation as contractions occur. Some birthing people use manual clitoral stimulation while others reach for a vibrator during contractions. Partners are optional but often integral. However deployed, masturbation and orgasm remain lesser known forms of pain relief compared to other nonmedical alternatives. Birth is rarely framed as a site of potential, and potent, sexual experience, and orgasm can require privacy and consent that is difficult to find in many birth settings. Yet birthing bodies are primed for pleasure, producing a cocktail of hormones—oxytocin, beta-endorphins, adrenaline, noradrenaline, and prolactin—that have the ability to initiate ecstasy.

Rebozo Sifting

Rebozo manteada, or gently "sifting" the body with a long piece of woven fabric, or rebozo, is used to help ease pain, slow breathing, relax tight uterine ligaments and muscles around the abdomen and pelvis, and optimize babies' positioning for labor and birth. Mexico has a long tradition of using a rebozo—whose color, texture, and pattern differ regionally—before, during, and after birth. Midwives, doulas, and other support people use sifting during pregnancy as well as in early and active labor. The technique is a true art form, though there are a few basics when it comes to its practice. As in most things birth related, consent is key: a support person first asks to enter a pregnant person's space. The rebozo is then wrapped around a pregnant person's abdomen, like a hammock around the baby, and moved back and forth rhythmically at varying speeds, depending on the desired outcome. This traditional technique was originally passed on by midwives orally, but today sifting has traveled to other parts of the globe via birth workers, books, and social media, and is growing in popularity. In 2018 researchers found that rebozos were used in 9 percent of all Danish births.[11]

Aromatherapy
Aromatherapy is a technique that uses plant and flower oils to stimulate the sense of smell to produce analgesic effects that promote relaxation and healing. It has been used extensively in labor to reduce pain and anxiety and to increase the laboring person's feelings of well-being.

Anxiety is associated with increased pain during labor by stimulating the release of stress hormones, which increase both the severity of the pain and the duration of labor. Reducing anxiety and increasing a sense of calm are therefore important goals in labor management. Aromatherapy has proven to be a safe, low-cost, and effective method for reducing both labor anxiety and the laboring person's perception of pain.

Aromatherapy can be administered a number of ways, including by direct application to the skin or by application to a pillow or clothing or placement in a footbath or birthing tub. A wide variety of oils have proved to be effective, among them lavender, Damascus rose, jasmine, geranium, chamomile, sweet orange, bitter orange, frankincense, and clove.

Laboring people consistently rate aromatherapy as a positive and valuable component of their experience.

Studies confirm that its use has resulted in reduced time in labor, lower rates of epidural and opioid usage, and postpartum physiological and psychological well-being.[12] Aromatherapy is generally free of negative side effects and, what's more, creates sense memories that can transport one back to more flowery memories of giving birth.

The Bradley Method
Designed in 1947 by the American obstetrician Robert A. Bradley and popularized by his 1965 book *Husband-Coached Birth*, the method encourages the view that birth is a normal, not-to-be-feared physiological process. During classes, mothers are taught to trust their body and focus on diet and exercise throughout pregnancy and are given relaxation exercises to help them through labor. The "coach" is the birthing person's main support, and his or her role is to help achieve an un-medicated birth and keep outside factors from interfering with the process. Teachers of the Bradley method believe that with preparation, education, and help from a loving, supportive coach, most pregnant people will be able to give birth without medication or surgery. Although criticized for its gendered, heteronormative assumptions, the method was revolutionary in mid-twentieth-century America, when birthing women were often strapped to tables and forced to accept forceps, episiotomies, and medication, while partners were relegated to "stork rooms." By contrast, Bradley taught couples to manage labor together and gave partners an active role in the birthing process. According to the Bradley method, when the birthing person inevitably

shouts "I can't do this!" the partner responds by affirming, "You *are* doing this."

From Natural to Unmedicated Birth
In his 1933 book, *Natural Childbirth*, the British obstetrician Grantly Dick-Read claimed that "healthy childbirth was never intended by the natural law to be painful." Birth, he insisted, "carried out by natural processes from beginning to end, influenced by natural emotions," enables one to "truly fulfill herself emotionally when she sees and welcomes the child emerging from her womb into the world."[13] The "natural birth" movement gained traction in the United States in the 1970s, when Ina May Gaskin's 1976 book, *Spiritual Midwifery*, described the transcendent experience of an unmedicated birth. At the time, the practice of and the phrase *natural childbirth* were intended to restore women's agency within the birthing process and push back against the paternalistic medicalized model. Yet the idea that only some births can be "natural" is imprecise and has shamed many who don't choose that path.

In May 2019, Jessica Grose, lead editor of the *New York Times* parenting section, declared that the paper would no longer use the phrase *natural birth* and would instead opt for *unmedicated birth*, and would even reframe the ideal as a "good birth." As Grose wrote, "I love the framing of a 'good birth,' because it removes the false dichotomy of 'natural' versus 'unnatural.' The outcome everyone wants for their delivery is a healthy baby and a healthy mother. Health includes emotional health, too."[14]

1 A 2006 study reminds us that lack of basic knowledge about pain options can cause mistrust as easily as it can offer a clear choice to decline intervention. See Heather Dillaway and Sarah Jane Brubaker, "Intersectionality and Childbirth: How Women from Different Social Locations Discuss Epidural Use," *Race, Gender & Class* 13, no. 3/4 (2006): 16–41.
2 See Ellie Slee, "Misogyny and the Epidural: A Primer," *Medium*, November 26, 2018, medium.com; also "The 1961 Roberts Fellowship in Journalism," *American Journal of Nursing* 60, no. 9 (September 1960): 1299.
3 Karmel, *Thank You, Dr. Lamaze: A Mother's Experiences in Painless Childbirth* (Philadelphia: Lippincott, 1959).
4 Sheila Kitzinger, *The Experience of Childbirth* (Middlesex, UK: Penguin Books, 1962), 132.
5 Clarissa Dasser and John J. O'Connor, "Continuous Epidural Block for Obstetric Anesthesia," *American Journal of Nursing* 60, no. 9 (September 1960): 1299.
6 Sheila Kitzinger, *Rediscovering Birth* (New York: Pocket Books, 2000), 195.

7 The method gained traction with the founding of the New England Twilight Sleep Association the following year and films supporting twilight sleep that circulated to women's groups throughout the United States.
8 Studies prove that, while rare, orgasmic birth does occur. See Thierry Postel, "Childbirth Climax: The Revealing of Obstetrical Orgasm," *Sexologies* 22, no. 4 (October–December 2013): 89–92.
9 From the 2008 documentary *Orgasmic Birth: The Best-Kept Secret*, produced by Pascali-Bonaro and Kris Liem.
10 Lorel Mayberry and Jacqueline Daniel, "'Birthgasm': A Literary Review of Orgasm as an Alternative Mode of Pain Relief in Childbirth," *Journal of Holistic Nursing* 43, no. 4 (December 2016): 331–42.
11 See Rebecca Dekker, "Rebozo during Labor for Pain Relief," *Evidence Based Birth*, July 24, 2018, evidencebasedbirth.com.
12 See Mahbubeh Tabatabaeichehr and Hamed Mortazavi, "The Effectiveness of Aromatherapy in the Management of Labor Pain and Anxiety: A Systematic Review," *Ethiopian Journal of Health Sciences* 30, no. 3 (2020): 449–58.
13 Quoted in Donald Caton, "Who Said Childbirth Is Natural?: The Medical Mission of Grantly Dick Read," *Anesthesiology* 84, no. 4 (April 1996): 955. Dick-Read laid out his theory in 1933 in his book, which was not published in the United States until 1944.
14 Jessica Grose, "Welcome to NYT Parenting: Here's Why We Won't Say 'Natural Birth,'" *New York Times*, May 7, 2019.

EMERGENCE

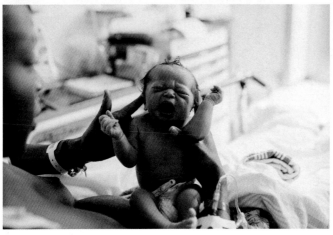

EMERGENCE Breath held, exhaled, inhaled, dissipated. A long hum of pain, a metamorphosis, shedding and growing, one becoming two or more. An initiation into a new environment. The baby emerges and so, too, does a new identity of the birthing person, emotionally and physically. From here on a continual process of becoming. A new self, and new kin.

1— A mother exhales while holding her child close, 2017
2— Hannah looks happily at Cinthia, who receives her second child, born at home in the company of her doula and her husband. This photograph is part of Greta Rico's documentary project *Urban Midwives*, which portrays the work of midwives in Mexico City and positions the midwifery care system as a political act of resistance.
3— A birthing person looks lovingly at their newborn child as the doctor finalizes the cesarean section, 2019
4— *Earth Day Birth* by photographer Stephanie Entin, 2018
5— A mother catches her child in her arms after giving birth upright, 2015
6— Lindsey Heddleston labors at home while supported by her beloved midwife, GB Khalsa.

2   3
4
    5

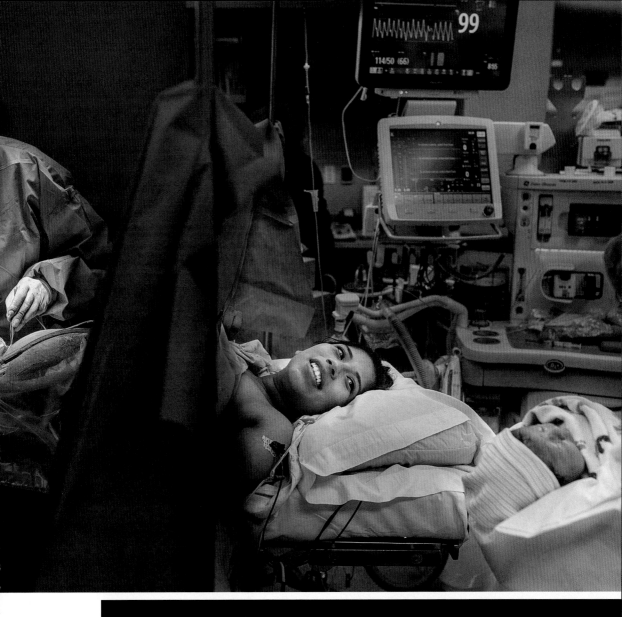

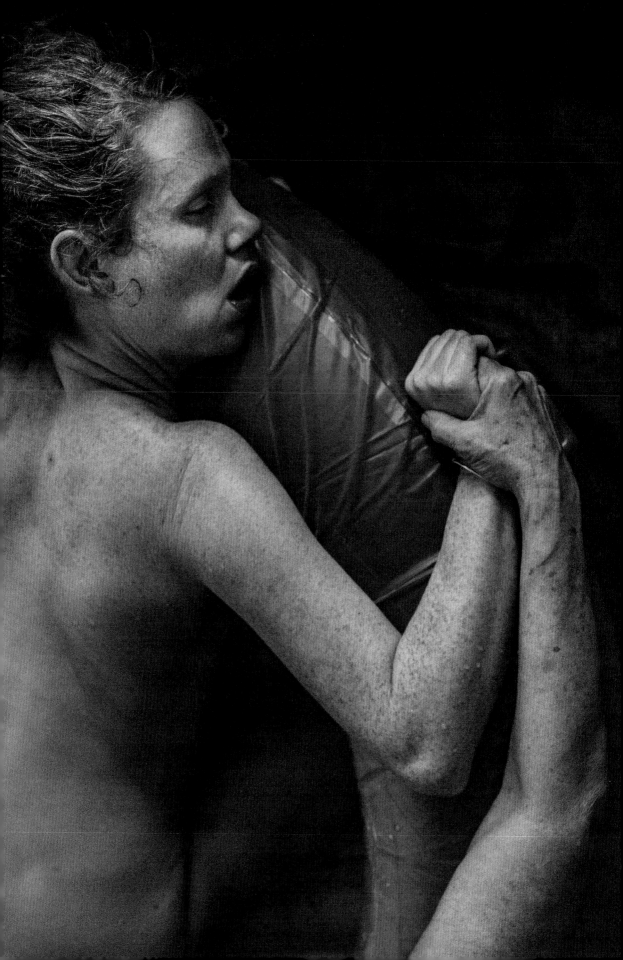

PERINEAL REPAIR SIMULATOR—The perineum, the area between the vulva and the anus, often tears during childbirth, and in some cases a deliberate cut, called an episiotomy, is made if the baby is in distress or to avoid a deeper tear. Such lacerations, whether intentional or not, vary in severity and subsequent recovery time, with around one-third of all postpartum people in the UK and US requiring stitches after childbirth.[1]

As with an obstetric fistula, a hole that develops in the birth canal after prolonged labor, perineal lacerations can cause grave discomfort and even incontinence, and thus skilled suture repair is key. Dr. Adam Dubrowski is a scientist on the faculty of Health Sciences at Ontario Tech University, where he is the Canada Research Chair in Health Care Simulation. He studies how medical workers acquire, maintain, and transfer skills and is part of a team that creates medical simulations, including a 3D-printed perineal repair simulator, for training purposes.[2]

DESIGNING MOTHERHOOD—Why do you design perineal repair simulator models, and how are they used?

ADAM DUBROWSKI—A simulation is a replication of a task or event for the purpose of training or assessment. It's been part of medical pedagogy for a long time. Our research lab serves the whole medical school. This particular project came about when the chair of the OB-GYN department came to us and said, "I'm responsible for organizing this part of the Royal College exams. We're using cow tongues [to teach perineal repairs]. Can we do better than that?" Our simulator is truer to life, but that isn't the only goal. The goal is also to standardize simulation so we can be sure that we teach and assess the right things. We also wanted to keep our simulators inexpensive so that they can be available anywhere in the world.

DM—Is it fairly standard for OB-GYN doctors who are training and taking their exams to have only practiced perineal repairs on a bovine tongue up to that point?

AD—Yes. Surgical clerks, or third-year surgical trainees, also learn how to suture on banana peels, for example. You'd be very surprised how good people have been at creating their own simulators. One of the models that we're working on right now is for surgeons to practice removing very small objects with minimally invasive instruments. The simulator before we got involved was a red pepper with some holes in it—you'd pick out the seeds. It's clever, but we can do better.

DM—While you're standardizing the learning process, bodies in the real world vary widely. Was it one particular person's vagina that you were mapping and using as a model, or was the model taken from multiple different anatomical measurements and synthesized?

AD—There's a website of free anatomical models that we use, though we do 3D scanning of body parts as well for the same purposes. So we took a free one and remodeled it, introducing certain anatomical markers like the anus and three different types of tears of increasing severity. We use a closed loop design cycle. Two of our designers build the first prototype digitally. Once we've moved it from the digital to a physical space, students, faculty, assessors—people in the field—tell us whether it looks and feels real, and whether it works well in an educational setting. We test with many experts within our institution to make sure that before it goes live it's robust. The first time [the perineal repair simulator] was used in a formal setting was at a conference in Newfoundland in 2018.[3]

DM— So the anatomical design was open source. Is the end result open source, too? If a university program or an OB-GYN resident wanted to, could they print it themselves?

AD— Yes, we follow open-source practices. It's on our website, and we have also put the files up on GitHub for open dissemination online. When we published it following the Rural and Remote Conference in St. John's [Newfoundland] in 2018, we essentially gave up the rights to commercialize it or to protect the IP. It's for educational purposes. We are a research and innovation center, so whatever we do, we put it out in the open so anybody can use it or modify it.

DM— Why did you choose to print it in bright pink?

AD— The first prototype was translucent. It had no color simply because that silicone was the easiest to obtain for us at that time. Then we dyed it hot pink just to give it some hue, and we chose that [color] because we didn't want to introduce any biases in terms of race or ethnicity.
We have had a few requests to make it different colors. It's just a case of putting some food coloring into the silicone to make it different hues. Christine Goudie, one of the designers, was working in Bangladesh on trainings with a volunteer medical corps called Team Broken Earth. She was there to deliver a three-day women's health care course in Dhaka, which included simulation-based training stations for the purpose of advancing clinical skills and ed-ucation so it could be applied to local labor and delivery.[4] The design enables the transfer of skills that can have a profound effect on patient outcomes—on patient lives. And if a small change in color makes it more accessible and contextualized, then all the better.

1 "Perineal Tears during Childbirth" (last updated May 2017), National Childbirth Trust, nct.org.uk.
2 Dr. Dubrowski's work generally takes place in rural, remote, and resource-poor or developing parts of the world, including in Newfoundland and Labrador, in the marine and offshore industries, and farther afield, in Ethiopia, Malawi, and Haiti, where he works with local health profes-sionals to implement simulation-based education to help surgeons and other clinicians build skills.
3 Christine Goudie et al., "Investigating the Efficacy of Anatomical Silicone Models Developed from a 3D Printed Mold for Perineal Repair Suturing Simulation," Cureus 10, no. 8 (August 22, 2018): e3181, doi.org/10.7759/cureus.3181.
4 The training sta-tions included the prevention of shoulder dystocia, helping babies breathe, the application of uterine compression sutures, and the repair of obstetric anal sphinc-ter injuries (OASIS). The OASIS manage-ment station provided an opportunity to practice anal sphinc-ter repair on anatomi-cally accurate silicone models.

PLACENTA—The placenta, that magical and mighty orb, is a gobsmackingly impressive organ. Formed in the first few weeks of pregnancy, along with the basic structures of a developing fetus, the placenta is connected to the uterine wall and to the fetus, providing it with nourishment, thermo-regulation, blood, and essential gasses by way of the umbilical cord.

The placenta also removes waste and fights off and eliminates pathogens. It builds immunity, allowing the antibodies in a pregnant person's body to pass through to the baby. It offers protective proteins to the fetal environment and moves fetal cells into the mother's body, where they can live on for decades. The placenta assists both the mother's and the baby's endocrine systems, creates hormones that support a pregnancy and fetal growth, and later sets the stage for labor itself.

The placenta is meaty and formidable. While in the uterus, it contains 20 percent of a pregnant person's blood, and once outside, it can weigh up to two pounds. Yet the placenta is far from the main event at birth. That honor belongs to the baby. Whether one has a cesarean or a vaginal birth, the placenta is always born after the baby. This aftereffect aspect has stuck: English speakers frequently refer to the placenta as "afterbirth," emphasizing how the organ is treated in much of the Western world—as an afterthought.[1]

Afterthought or not, the placenta must come out, and across time and cultures people have developed innovative ways of expelling it. In ancient Greece newborns who were still attached to the umbilical cord were placed on leather pillows filled with air, which were pricked and slowly deflated. As a newborn sunk lower, the umbilical cord gently tugged the placenta out.[2] Hippocrates advised giving sneezing powder to a mother while holding her mouth and nostrils closed.[3] Midwives in West and North Africa and the Middle East similarly encourage coughing or sneezing.[4]

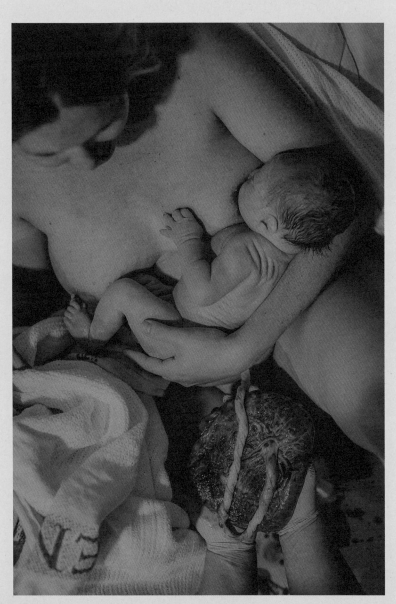

Placenta, baby, and mother immediately after birth

Cherokee tribes have used the herb blue cohosh to promote the birth of the placenta, and Navajo and Sioux tribes have used a self-administered belt, which can be tightened while standing to coax the placenta out.[5] In many cultures, including in Canada, South America, the Caribbean, Sierra Leone, and the Philippnes, the midwife helps the mother blow into a bottle or hollow gourd, encouraging her abdominal wall to press against the top of the uterus.[6] The nineteenth-century botanist and physician George Engelmann observed that many Indigenous American midwives coaxed the placenta out by having a mother straddle a hole dug into the earth, which was filled with heated stones, fir tree leaves, and steaming water. Engelmann noted that "this simple means seldom fails."[7]

Though many mammals, including mice, cats, and goats, eat the placenta (a practice known as placentophagy), relatively few human cultural groups have a tradition of consuming placentas. But even its name intimates its deliciousness: *placenta* is Latin for cake.[8] Culinary similes have spread culturally and temporally. In France, the placenta was for a time referred to as *pain*, *tarte*, or *biscuit*.[9] One of China's first and most celebrated pharmaceutical experts and practitioners of traditional Chinese medicine (TCM), Li Shizhen, included placenta—*ziheche*—as a medicine in the first draft of his *Compendium of Materia Medica*, completed in 1578. It wasn't until the mid-1980s, when Raven Lang, an American midwife who studied TCM, promoted placenta remedies during a conference of the Midwives Alliance of North America, that the idea

of placentophagy took hold in the United States.[10] Still, not everyone in the US knew the best way to consume it, though many ventured to guess. In 1983, *Mothering* magazine published the following recipe:

PLACENTA COCKTAIL
¼ raw placenta
½ carrot
8 oz V8 juice
2 ice cubes
Blend for 10 seconds
at high speed[11]

Today, placenta continues to be consumed as a balm for postpartum depression. After my first birth, a placental expert came to my house to prepare my placenta in a dehydrator; she then placed the dried placenta in capsules. After my second birth, my doula tossed raw bits of my placenta into a smoothie for me to drink after discovering me in tears. (The lion's share lived in the back of the freezer until recently, when we buried it with a dogwood sapling in our backyard.) My mother once grossed out a tough guy who boasted that he had eaten the still-beating heart of a fish he pulled out of the ocean. "Oh really?" she replied, "I ate my firstborn's placenta with onions."

Many cultures honor the placenta even as they dispose of it, creating practices and rituals that reflect deeply held beliefs. Traditionally, the Māori of New Zealand bury the placenta on ancestral land, emphasizing the relationship between people and the earth.[12] The Kwakiutl of British Columbia bury placentas to transmit clam-digging skills or expose them to ravens to encourage prophetic visions. In the Marshall Islands,

a placenta thrown into the sea will assure a baby's future as a successful fisher. In some West African cultures, a diviner is sometimes called in to tell the baby's future by reading the placenta.[13]

Many Western hospitals incinerate the placenta as medical waste, but some send placentas to researchers and even cosmetics designers. Between 1975 and 1992, around 360 tons of placenta were collected from 282 British hospitals. Many were used in the manufacturing of the protein albumin, used in emergencies, especially when people have suffered serious burns.[14] The company bioMérieux UK Ltd, a subsidiary of the French pharmaceutical company that collected the placentas, distributed a high-end face cream containing placenta, which supposedly revitalized and moisturized skin.[15] Human placenta is still a key ingredient in popular skin-care products around the world, most notably in Australia, India, Japan, and Vietnam.

Whether the placenta is venerated, smeared on the face, eaten, or simply tossed away, we know surprisingly little about it. As Angela Garbes has written, "We should be concerned with the placenta's role in pregnancy but also its role in drawing up the blueprints of adult health, as well as the health of mothers. And yet the placenta, though it is integral to the health of all human beings, is only regarded as a footnote in the study of women's reproductive health, which along with women's general health, is consistently undervalued in American society."[16] Innovators, medical researchers, and designers—take note.

1 See Angela Garbes's excellent chapter on the placenta, "An Organ as Two-Faced as Time," in her book *Like a Mother: A Feminist Journey Through the Science and Culture of Pregnancy* (New York: Harper Collins, 2018), 58–73.
2 William J. Carrington, *Safe Convoy: The Expectant Mother's Handbook* (Philadelphia: J. B. Lippincott, 1944), 135.
3 Tina Cassidy, *Birth: A History* (London: Chatto & Windus, 2006), 220.
4 Sheila Kitzinger, *Rediscovering Birth*

(New York: Pocket Books, 2000), 146.
5 See Sharon Muza, "Series: Welcoming All Families; Supporting the Native American Family," *Lamaze*, November 17, 2014, lamaze.org; and Alan G. Waxman "Navajo Childbirth in Transition," *Medical Anthropology* 12, no. 2 (1990): 191.
6 Kitzinger, *Rediscovering Birth*, 146.
7 George Engelmann, *Labor among Primitive Peoples: Showing the Development of the Obstetric Science of To-day, from the Natural and Instinctive Customs of All Races, Civilized and Savage,*

Past and Present (St. Louis: J. H. Chambers, 1883), 110.
8 Gabriele Falloppio, or Falliopius, who published anatomical drawings in mid-sixteenth-century Venice, named the placenta. He also named the vagina, but the fallopian tubes were named after him; he suggested calling them *uteri tuba*. See Cassidy, *Birth*, 223.
9 There is also "placenta cake," a dish from ancient Greece and Rome consisting of many dough layers interspersed with a mixture of cheese and honey

and flavored with bay leaves, baked, and then covered in more honey. The dessert is mentioned in classical texts, such as the poems of Archestratos and Antiphanes, as well as in Cato the Elder's *De Agricultura*.
10 Raven Lang, "The Midwifery Tradition: Roots and Renewal," Midwives Alliance of North America Conference, San Francisco, October 18–21, 1985.
11 "Placenta Recipes," *Mothering* 28 (September 1983): 76.
12 Joan Metge, "Working in/Playing with Three Languages: English, Te Reo Maori, and Maori Bod

Language," *Sites: A Journal of Social Anthropology and Cultural Studies* 2, no. 2 (2005): 83–90.
13 Kitzinger, *Rediscovering Birth*, 145.
14 Placentas are also used in the making of the enzyme glucocerebrosidase, which is prescribed for people suffering from a rare genetic disorder called Gaucher's disease that makes their digestive systems unable to break down fats.
15 Cassidy, *Birth*, 224.
16 Garbes, *Like a Mother*, 64.

BIRTH PHOTOGRAPHY——I recall that in the moments after the birth of our first child, the hospital staff encouraged us to document the experience by taking photographs.[1] There is an image of me, a tired mother, holding my newborn infant in my arms, gazing down at his face. In many ways the image is identical to those made in the moments after our two other children were born in the years since.

All three births took place at the same hospital; they share many of the same details, such as the hospital gown and the blue and pink striped blanket. Yet we have no other photographs of our first child after that day. He had died of an apparent cord entanglement in the womb before he was delivered. He was stillborn.

I have often reflected on why it felt so meaningful to make those pictures, and yet, at the same time, how the photographs themselves did or didn't speak to the differences of the experiences. In their composition, my pictures are similar to so many pictures that circulate, attached to emails, posted on social media, or (still today) printed on paper: so many mothers cradling new babies in their arms. These pictures are announcements of a life, and of motherhood. But images made around birth are also often private images, keepsakes to commemorate a momentous occasion that is also a very personal one.

In April 2018, I opened the Sunday *New York Times* and found, on the cover of the magazine, a photograph by LaToya Ruby Frazier of a newborn baby in the lap of his mother, his head fitting perfectly in her palm. A significant personal moment for one family, surely, but seeing it in a public setting like the *New York Times Magazine* imbued it with a different kind of power. At the top of the page were the words, "Why are black mothers and babies in the United States dying at more than double the rate of white mothers and babies?"[2] Only after my own stillbirth had I learned that one in 160 births in the United States ends in stillbirth,

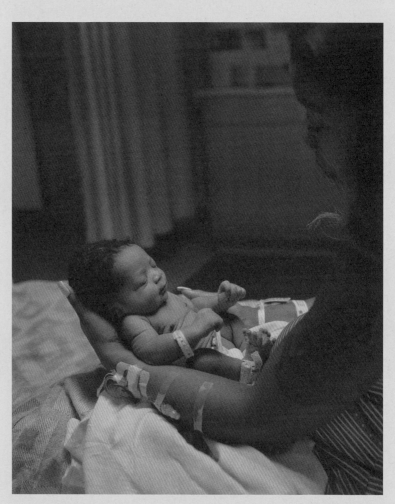

Simone Landrum Holding Her Newborn Son Kingston Blessed Landrum in Her Hands in Ochsner Hospital on December 20, 2017, New Orleans, LA. Photograph by LaToya Ruby Frazier for the series "Why America's Black Mothers and Babies Are in a Life-or-Death Crisis," New York Times Magazine, April 11, 2018

already a shockingly high number.[3] But the maternal, infant, and fetal mortality rates for Black women in this country are especially distressingly and unacceptably high, as reported in this feature story, by Linda Villarosa, which followed Simone Landrum, a woman who had experienced a stillbirth, through the subsequent birth of a healthy child. The article emphasized the benefits of informed and respectful care for mothers and babies, and Frazier's photographs accompanying the article included images of Landrum preparing for birth with her doula and introducing her new baby, Kingston, to his older brothers in the hospital room. Along with Frazier's, other photographs of the moments surrounding birth—like those by Caroline Catlin and Alice Proujansky, for example, which have also appeared in the New York Times—now remain seared in my mind's eye.[4] In the context of a major newspaper, photographs like these—mother- and care-centered images—bring forward the circumstances faced by women across the country every day that are otherwise overlooked.

On the day Frazier's photographs of Landrum were published in the Times, more than two thousand images of birth covered every surface, floor to ceiling, of two facing walls of a gallery in the Museum of Modern Art in New York, where I work. These images, cut from books, magazines, and pamphlets, and taped directly to the museum walls, comprised My Birth (see p.205), the artist Carmen Winant's contribution to an exhibition of recent photography that I had organized. Many of Winant's sources were connected to the feminist movements of the 1970s, and the representations of birth they included tended to share certain characteristics. Among the hundreds of images on the wall, there were hardly any of women of color, hardly any of

non-heteronormative couples, hardly any of caesarean births. Winant hadn't been able to find such images as she gathered printed materials on birth, through eBay or at garage sales. "How do you speak to a presence that isn't there?" she questioned herself. "I think about identity both in terms of who's being pictured and who's not being pictured."[5]

I was pregnant with my third child when the exhibition opened, and walking through the galleries was a daily ritual for me that was both fraught and poignant. When I would give tours of the show, participants encouraged me to pose with my baby bump in front of the installation, or asked if this was going to be my first birth, to which I would usually just answer "no" and smile. When I was by myself I would ponder questions about the work: There were so many photographs there, but did they picture my birth experience? And if it was hard for me to reconcile my experience with the images I found there, what about the museum's many visitors, with their diversity of birth experiences? How did they feel when they saw these pictures?

Many visitors were surprised to see images of birth in a museum at all. As one reviewer described, "On the day I visited, the space in front of it was filled with captivated viewers. They stood pointing, gasping, groaning; everyone seemed to be talking."[6] But Winant's installation was not the first time photographs of birth were exhibited at MoMA. One well known example is an image by Wayne Miller of the birth of his son, David, which appeared in Edward Steichen's landmark touring exhibition The Family of Man in 1955. The image depicts a masked doctor grasping the leg of a glistening baby, whose spiraling umbilical cord still stretches down to the sheet below. The delivering doctor was Miller's father, so there are three generations of men present in the picture (child, father/

photographer, and grandfather/doctor), and—unlike most of the images in Winant's installation—the mother herself is not visible.

Miller had been a member of Steichen's aviation photographic unit in the US Navy during World War II and, following the war, was featured in the 1947 MoMA exhibition Three Young Photographers. There he had presented a series of photographs, titled "The Beginning," also made at David's birth, though these images do feature the face (serene, then contorted) of his wife, Joan, as she experienced stages of labor. In the press release for the exhibition, Miller described his intentions: "I should like to think that through photographs of the emotions of everyday living, common to all men, it will be possible to explain man to man."[7] For this viewer, over seventy years later, the use of that phrase—man to man—is telling, but I am also struck by the acknowledged potential of a private photograph made public. Even intimate subjects, laden with the deepest personal emotions, are also socially embedded.

Photographs help us call out and confront the significant moments of our lives, whether those moments are traumatic or joyous. For me, the stillness of posing for a photograph in the moments after my first birth underscored the stillness of our child, but that pose also somehow marked the event: This really happened. Including such photographs within the wider projects of our lives and work, as I am doing here, also carries forward that reminder of life, however brief. Similarly, engaging with birth photographs—images that are usually personal and private—in a public setting like a museum or newspaper, or this book, challenges us to recognize and address women's lived experiences.

—Lucy Gallun

1   Though we had no special photographer and made pictures ourselves on the nurses' recommendation, there are photographers who specialize in images of stillbirth and organizations that coordinate the photography, such as Now I Lay Me Down to Sleep. For one such photographer, see Sarah Zhang, "A Photographer Has Spent 20 Years Documenting Stillbirths," The Atlantic, February 18, 2020, theatlantic.com. 2   Linda Villarosa, "Why America's Black Mothers and Babies Are in a Life-or-Death Crisis," New York Times Magazine, April 11, 2018. 3   See the Centers for Disease Control and Prevention (CDC), "What Is Stillbirth," cdc.gov/ncbddd/stillbirth/facts.html. 4   Caroline Catlin, "What I Learned Photographing Death," New York Times, July 18, 2019; Alice Proujansky, "Life's Unequal Beginnings," New York Times, March 9, 2013. 5   Carmen Winant, My Birth, 2018, transcript of audio, The Museum of Modern Art, New York, moma.org/audio/playlist/49/745. 6   Jen Schwarting, introduction to "Labor and Delivery: Carmen Winant Interviewed by Jen Schwarting," Bomb, August 7, 2018, bombmagazine.org. 7   Press release for the exhibition Three Young Photographers, MoMA press release archives, moma.org/research-and-learning/archives/press-archives.

BIRTH IN FILM—"I think my water broke!" The phrase conjures a familiar series of filmic images—suitcase handle, taxi door, hospital gown, furrowed brow, panting, baby's first cry—that have framed public, popular assumptions about birth.

Childbirth has been present in all corners of the cinematic art form nearly as long as the medium has existed.[1] In the last half-century, mass-market films have addressed contraception, working mothers, abortion, teen pregnancy, and infertility (*Baby Boom*, 1987; *Father of the Bride II*, 1995; *Knocked Up*, 2007; *Juno*, 2007; *Private Life*, 2018), while auteur-driven and genre pictures have exploited childbirth to represent extreme psychological states (*Three Women*, 1977; *mother!*, 2017) or fuel the subgenre of body horror by inflicting unspeakable pain and nonhuman progeny on women and a few men (*Rosemary's Baby*, 1968; *Alien*, 1979; *The Fly*, 1986). So too with documentary, whose considerations of the subject traverse Russian revolutionary cinema, ethnography, and decades of social-issue moviemaking (*Man with a Movie Camera*, 1929; *The Forgotten Village*, 1941; *Motherland*, 2017; *One Child Nation*, 2019).[2]

The ubiquity of childbirth as a narrative device in film does not, however, equal screen time: outside of medical training films, *actual* filmic images of birth are exceedingly rare, a lack stemming from the 1930 Motion Picture Production Code that considered child birth unfit for public consumption.[3] Amos Vogel, an early champion of alternative film, cited birth as one of the "Forbidden Subjects of the Cinema" in his influential book *Film as a Subversive Art* (1974), declaring that the medium "has treated birth as a guilty secret of mankind ... [to] be camouflaged by white sheets.... It remains for the underground to produce the classic films on the subject."[4] Indeed, an enduring and rich body of

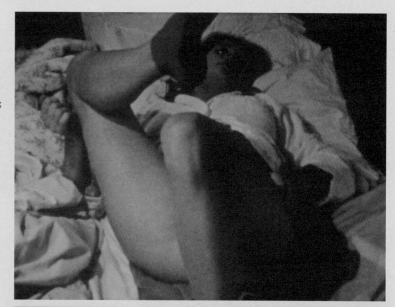

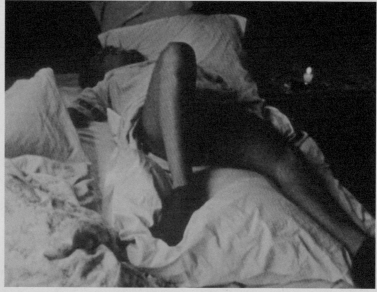

Stills from the film *Kirsa Nicholina* (16mm), directed by Gunvor Nelson, 1969

birth films exists, though to engage with it means looking beyond commercial filmmaking to an unregulated counter-canon shaped by artists and amateurs.

Home movies provide perhaps the richest trove of birth imagery. The use of portable small-format Super8 and 16mm handheld cameras, first introduced in the 1920s, flourished in the 1940s and 1950s thanks to a consumer class primed to record family events such as vacations, birthdays, or the arrival of a newborn. Low-cost and democratic, the home movie aesthetic was quickly seized upon outside the family unit—notably by home birth advocates and experimental filmmakers.[5] Stan Brakhage's avant-garde home movie *Window Water Baby Moving* (1959), a 13-minute film of his wife Jane giving birth to their first child, is undoubtedly the best known birth film. A staple of university film courses to this day, it originally screened in experimental film venues and was disseminated by alternative distributors—if always under the threat of obscenity laws. This silent film is highly lyrical, cross-editing frames of Jane's pregnant body glistening in the bathtub earlier in the pregnancy with extreme close-ups of the vagina, the baby's crowning head, the newborn girl's first breaths, and the afterbirth. Brakhage described the film as a collaboration with Jane, who took hold of the camera moments after giving birth to film the new father and who participated in the editing. Yet the work incited critical reactions in feminist circles for what was seen as its idealized objectification of the female body,[6] replicating gendered domestic dynamics in home movies.[7]

The influential Swedish-born, Bay-area based filmmaker and educator, Gunvor Nelson made the 16-minute film *Kirsa Nicholina* (1969) at the crossroad of the back-to-the-land and home birth movements, introducing a female perspective. Opening shots of a husband and wife walking nude on the beach segue to the birth of the titular Kirsa at a counterculture Marin County home. Wearing red socks and an embroidered terrycloth tunic, Nelson records her laboring body from various angles and distances, foregrounding her physicality and individuality. Even a subtle eroticism surfaces in the gripped sheets of the marital bed. As the baby emerges, the father's and physician's hands massage the crowning head, and the mother grasps its hand and cradles it to her chest, umbilical cord still attached. A friend lounges bedside. *Kirsa Nicholina* is an alternative birth film in every sense: a deeply expressive work that points to a world of possibilities outside the more common clinical setting, providing a glimpse of other positions, attendants, and methods. Two decades later, Vanessa Renwick's Pacific Northwest Olympia (1984) records a friend's home birth as she is cradled by midwives, prompting a new mother at a screening to remark, "I had no idea a birth could be like that. No one touched me at all while I was giving birth."[8]

Misconception, made by the filmmaker, scholar, and activist Marjorie Keller in 1973, is another powerful entry in this alternative filmic canon. Readings of the title have ping-ponged between seeing it as a "loving critique" of Brakhage, with whom she studied, and as a work of the women's movement. Regardless, it is a quiet masterpiece in its own right. In filming her brother and her sister-in-law Christina leading up to the arrival of their second child, Keller succeeds in presenting childbirth as a family life event, not a medical one. Christina is shown—through a multiplicity of angles—as mother, partner, caregiver to a toddler, individual, and woman. Throughout, sound plays a central role, with conversations—about the challenges of parenting, different birthing techniques, and pain control—captured but dislocated from any one speaker through the asynchronous treatment of image and sound. Keller juxtaposes audio of the doctor's examination with images of a home demolition next door in frank symbolism of both the feat of childbirth and gendered relations (a torn perineum for a bulldozer). Keller's camera is on the mother's face as the baby emerges—a cry, at the height of the pain, "I can't!" and later, on the phone, "It wasn't nothing, but right now it seems as if it was." Matter-of-fact but compassionate, full of awe but devoid of mythologizing, depicting tension without gender war, *Misconception* reveals the complexity and messiness of the start of life.

This film history foreshadows a moving-image revolution unleashed by consumer video and camera phones, and a digital visual culture around birth subject to its own politics of display and distribution. But many stories have yet to be fully recorded or addressed. Greta Snider's *Futility* (1989) and Nazlı Dinçel's *Solitary Acts #6* (2015), both narrating the ending of a pregnancy, are meaningful emblems of yet another counter-canon. We need abortion films, surrogacy films, miscarriage films, adoption films, stillbirth films, infertility films, and representations of women of color, Indigenous women, nonbinary people, and much more before Vogel's call will have been met.

—Sophie Cavoulacos

1 In Alice Guy-Blaché's 1896 *La feé aux choux* (*The Cabbage Fairy*), a very early narrative movie, a fairy delivers babies from cabbages.
2 Respectively, the films listed were directed by Charles Shyer (the first two), Judd Apatow, Jason Reitman, Tamara Jenkins, Robert Altman, Darren Aronofsky, Roman Polanski, Ridley Scott, David Cronenberg, Dziga Vertov, Herbert Kline and Alexandr Hackenschmied, Ramona Diaz, and Nanfu Wang and Lynn Zhang.
3 The code existed until 1968, when our current ratings system (G, PG, R, X) was put in place. It was a set of industry moral guidelines that films by major studios had to meet before they could be released. A few films produced around the time of the code's establishment—such as *Life Begins* (1932), set in a maternity ward—tested and set the terms for how pregnancy and birth could be depicted: only if absolutely required by the narrative, and as little as possible. Educational films, made to be shown in schools, lecture halls, and the like, were subject to more permissive rules.
4 Amos Vogel, *Film as a Subversive Art* (London: CT Editions, 2006), 258.
5 Some early examples of the home-birth genre are Elizabeth Grumette's *The Birth of Ludi* (1974), Margaret Lazarus and Renner Wunderlich's *Taking Our Bodies Back* (1974), and Suzanne Arms's *Five Women Five Births* (1978).
6 The spectrum of responses to Brakhage's film continued to contribute to rather than undermine its lasting influence, in my view. Lynne Sachs's "Thoughts on Birth and Brakhage," *Camera Obscura: Feminism, Culture, and Media Studies* 22, no. 1 (May 1, 2007) is revelatory in this regard, accessed at lynnesachs.com/tag/thoughts-on-birth-and-brakhage.
7 Patricia R. Zimmermann, *Reel Families: A Social History of Amateur Film* (Bloomington: Indiana University Press, 1995), xv. Since home movies were not distributed, it remains difficult to make definitive claims about them. Zimmerman's study and the recent exhibition, *Private Lives Public Spaces*, at the Museum of Modern Art in New York are among a critical history of this under-studied canon of modern motion pictures.
8 Vanessa Renwick, email to the author, February 19, 2020.

MOTHER'S GAZE

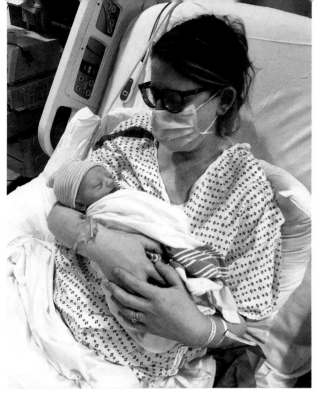

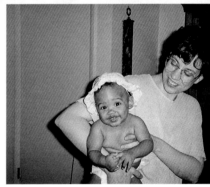

MOTHER'S GAZE The love pictured here is channeled through the look each mother gives her infant—an ocular intensity that reveals a flood of oxytocin. These images reflect on legacy, matrilineage, inheritance, and expectation. They capture deeply intimate connections through a look the camera can hardly contain.

1— Marty's first look at Nat, New York, 1992
2— A masked mother gazing at her newborn during the COVID-19 pandemic, April 2020
3— Alberta Richetelle and her daughter, Leigh, in their kitchen, c. 1974, Boston Women's Health Book Collective
4— Amber and Terry lock eyes, 1981
5— Zoë smiling in her beaming mother's arms, 1995
6— A mother embracing her children, c. 1975, Boston Women's Health Book Collective
7— A mother with neatly coiffed hair holding her newborn in a hospital bed, 1931
8— Terri-Lynn, Toronto, 2018, from the 4th Trimester Bodies Project

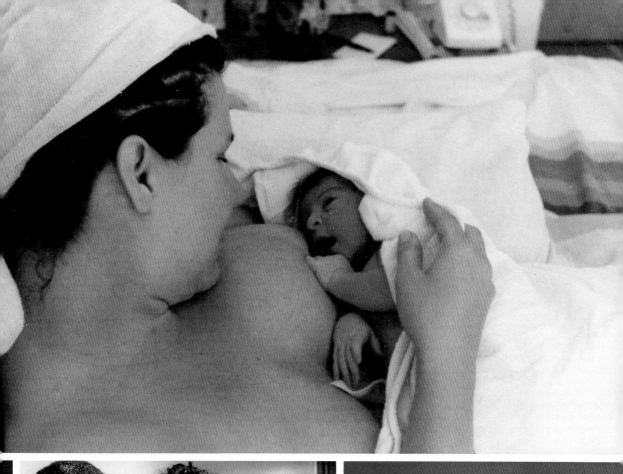

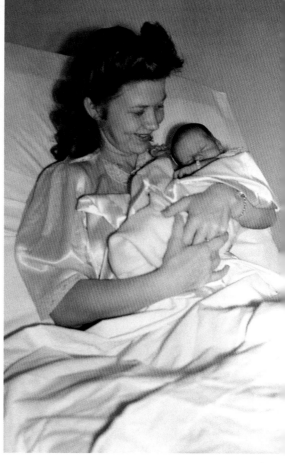

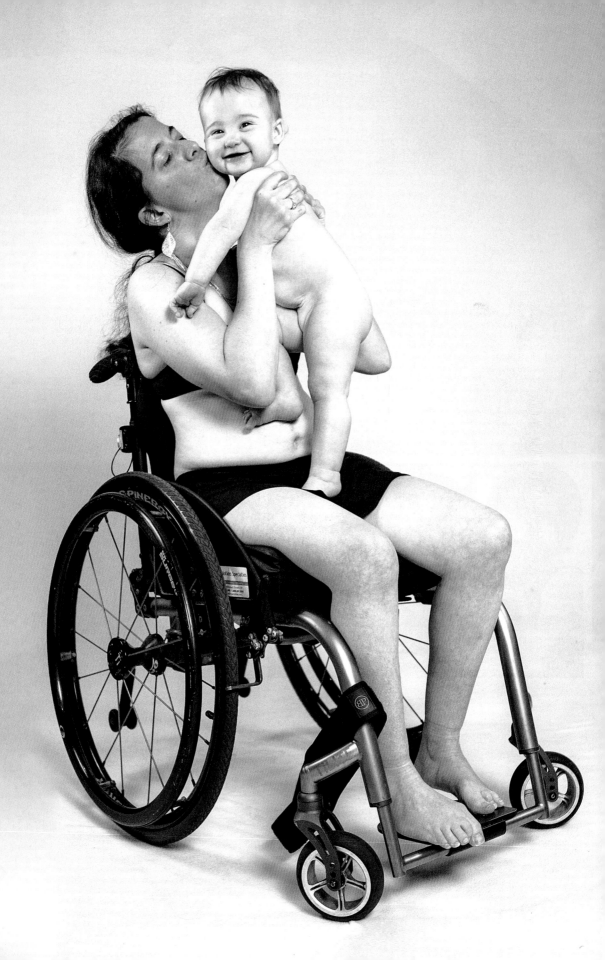

STEPS OF THE LINDO WING, ST. MARY'S HOSPITAL, LONDON—On November 15, 1977, outside the brick-walled Lindo Wing of St. Mary's Hospital in Paddington, North London, a new mum emerged wearing a woolen cape, a chic silk scarf over her hair, and a wide smile. She descended the five front steps with her husband and an entourage of nurses in tow. One of the nurses, Sister Delphine Stephens, carried her newborn son, and another held a parting gift, an instantly recognizable stuffed bear dressed in a duffle coat.

Thousands of parents had similarly left the Lindo with their new family member since its opening exactly forty years earlier, in November 1937. But this was no ordinary journey home. For the new mother was Princess Anne, the reigning monarch's only daughter, who had just produced Queen Elizabeth's first grandchild, Peter Phillips. As she reached the pavement, the princess turned to proffer a practiced handshake to the nursing staff and then stepped forward into the sunlight to greet the waiting press. Eager crowds jostled behind a line of London bobbys in black helmets. In that moment, framed upon a nondescript set of London steps, a new style of royal birth announcement was born.

Whether a birth is royal or not, the urge to announce news of it in a public forum is wide-spread and usually mani-fests through a newspaper announcement or a card sent through the mail. Both share news of a birth farther afield than medical and religious records or word of mouth. The very earliest newspapers carried birth announcements, offering public recognition of a family unit within a community, and from the mid-nineteenth century, announcement cards became commercially avail-able alongside other types of cards.[1] The stork is a constant on such designs; a postcard from 1917, for example, depicts a cherubic towheaded baby cushioned atop a weighing scale accompanied by a bird and the sing-song tagline "The stork has arrived with Cupid's donation to make us the hap-piest two in all creation." Today, online, the Emily Post Institute instructs, "One announcement per household is all you should send," replying to an inquirer

Princess Anne leaving the Lindo Wing of St Mary's Hospital, Paddington, with her two-day-old son, Peter Phillips, 1977

who wondered whether, in the digital age, an emailed notification of a new arrival should be followed by a hard copy.[2]

Princess Anne's offspring was not high enough in the chain of succession to warrant the closest scrutiny. But five years later royal birth announcements reached a fever pitch, and the steps of St. Mary's maternity wing were anointed a true architectural site of record, when Princess Diana, childlike herself at age twenty, stepped out of the doors on June 22, 1982, with the then thirty-three-year-old Prince Charles. They heralded the debut of the yet-to-be-named Prince William, second in line to the British throne. As she gave her trademark, shy, under-eyelash glance at the champagne-armed crowd, royal birth—and along with it formerly personal royal business of many kinds—was forever transposed from private chambers to public spectacle.

After Diana, the Lindo Wing became noteworthy (and remained so until recently) as the backdrop against which a very public form of motherhood was forged, and the site from which it fanned outward into public consciousness. The Lindo steps have been a contemporary ground zero for countless *People* magazine cover stories, gossip columns, and celebrity pregnancy shoots ever since. In the 1950s and 1960s, the press described Queen Elizabeth II's pregnancies as "an interesting condition" and otherwise left well alone. Other royal milestones had subsequently attracted polite press interest, but Diana's appeal was unprecedented.

The scene outside the Lindo Wing cemented an already

simmering and complex relationship between the young royal, her husband, and the British paparazzi. Diana's five-month bump, framed in a bikini on a beach in the Bahamas while on a babymoon, had been splashed across the front pages of the British tabloids, an extraordinary breach of press etiquette that had elicited a condemnatory response from the Queen. (The picture was obtained by two paparazzi equipped with jungle gear and binoculars.)[3] The royal birth announcement was another lucrative payday. Images of the princess sold newspapers like hotcakes, auguring contemporary marketability of maternity fashions, postpartum bodies, and celebrity pregnancy and birth.

Charles and Diana's public appearance broke with protocol in more ways than one. In 1946 King George VI dictated that royal birth could retain a modicum more privacy that it had traditionally been afforded. Until then, a senior politician—usually the Home Secretary—was present in the royal household to verify a birth of national importance. Her father's edict meant that the pregnancies of Elizabeth II, who birthed her four children at home at Buckingham Palace (as had so many of her forebears), were unbothered by prying eyes.[4] The public was made aware of a new twig on the royal family tree only when, like clockwork, a printed announcement was propped up on an ornate gold easel inside the palace gates shortly after a baby's arrival. Eager crowds of commoners viewed such decrees from a safe distance, through the bars.

Prince William was the first royal heir delivered in a

hospital, and his arrival also marked the first time a royal father was present throughout the labor and birth, a fact noted in the official comments released to the press—along with word that the new baby "cried lustily."[5] Two years later, a similar production delivered William's new baby brother, Harry, to a waiting public. A generation later, William and his wife, Kate, presented each of their three children on the same steps, Kate's attire in the first and last cases gesturing to her late mother-in-law's sartorial choices of polka dots and fire-engine red some thirty years earlier. Once again, the Lindo steps became the stage for countless reporters given the thankless on-the-scene job of reporting hours of newsless inertia as royal progeny took their time entering the world. In 2017, standing in front of the Lindo steps during the Duchess of Cambridge's third labor, the BBC reporter Simon McCoy handed back to his colleague in the studio with the frank admission that there would be "plenty more to come from here of course. None of it news."[6]

It took someone from outside "The Firm" to break the steps' spell (though not the rabidly invasive reporting of royal birth). In 2019, when Meghan Markle gave birth to the most recent Palace baby, Archie Harrison Mountbatten-Windsor, she and her husband, Prince Harry, eschewed precedent. After giving birth at the private Portland Hospital in London, they announced their new arrival on Instagram—forging their own distinct family brand even while following in the footsteps of myriad other millennial parents.

1   According to Debrett's, the British publisher of the authoritative tome on etiquette and behavior whose first issue was *The New Peerage* in 1769, it is the father's responsibility to spread the good news. Announcements can occur in broadsheets—"effectively *The Times* and *Daily Telegraph*"—and take on an abbreviated tone, listed alphabetically by surname: "Debrett—on 20th August to John and Charlotte

(née Berkeley), a daughter, Caroline Jane." John Morgan, *Debrett's New Guide to Etiquette and Modern Manners: The Indispensable Handbook* (London: Headline, 1996).
2   "Advice: Announcing a New Baby," The Emily Post Institute, emilypost.com. Today the stork has been replaced by online card-making services and Instagram and Facebook.
3   See Tina Brown, *The Diana Chronicles*

(New York: Anchor Books, 2008), 242.
4   "Ancient British Custom Scrapped for Royal Birth," *New York Times*, November 6, 1948, 9, timesmachine.nytimes.com.
5   As the *New York Times* reported in 1982, "Although the Queen is believed to have favored a birth at Buckingham Palace, the Princess chose instead the private Lindo Wing of St. Mary's, where rooms cost about $230 a day. Both she and Prince Charles

have modern ideas on birth and child-rearing, and they intend to keep the little Prince on their side of their apartment in Kensington Palace, rather than put him in the servants' quarters, as has been traditional." R. W. Apple Jr., "Princess of Wales Has Boy; Charles Is 'Over the Moon,'" *New York Times*, June 22, 1982, nytimes.com.
6   See Jaymi McCann, "Royal Baby? There's No News Here," *Daily Mail*, July 22, 2013, dailymail.com. The British

press had a field day with their American counterparts when the Duchess of Cambridge gave birth to her third child in 2018. Tony Appleton from Chelmsford, a town crier in no way associated with the royal household but bedecked in a red and gold brocade overcoat and three-pointed feathered hat, stood on the Lindo steps, rang his bell loudly, and shouted the news. US broadcasters lapped up this "official proclamation."

THALIDOMIDE——"I do know she carries the weight of the guilt today, still…. Apart from everything, that affects me the most…her guilt, because I do not hold her responsible whatsoever. She is as much a victim as I am, and she went through hell as well. As difficult as my life has been, she has gone through it every step of the way with me."[1]

Between 1957 and 1961, doctors in over forty countries prescribed to their pregnant patients a drug developed in West Germany and sold under various brand names to combat morning sickness and sleeplessness. As it turned out, the drug, thalidomide, when taken in the first six weeks of pregnancy, caused irreparable harm to the developing fetus, resulting in babies born with a range of disabilities, including radically shortened limbs, brain damage, and sensory impairment. In the UK alone, about 650 thalidomide-affected babies survived,[2] their experiences rippling outward through countless family members and their communities.[3]

Public understanding of the effects of thalidomide has often centered on an insensitive fascination with the physical effects of the drug on the roughly two-thirds of affected babies who lived past their first birthday. Histories of thalidomide, meanwhile, have focused on such tangibles as drug safety and approval of legislation in the wake of the drug's cessation as a prescription for pregnant people in 1961 (the drug continues to be on the World Health Organization's list of essential medications for treating cancer, HIV, and leprosy, among other uses) and survivor compensation. A key figure in the latter narrative is the Canadian-born, Chicago-trained Dr. Frances Oldham Kelsey, who in her first assignment in her first month at the US Food and Drug Administration withheld approval for thalidomide and was instrumental in unmasking its effects in pregnancy.[4]

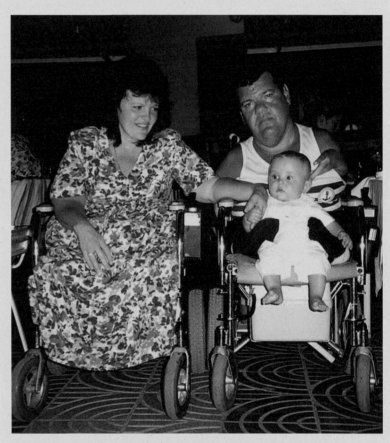

Geraldine Freeman with her husband and seven-month-old son, Charlie, in the 1980s

Many early histories of the drug's effects describe the panic, disorientation, and outright cruelty new parents, mothers in particular, faced immediately postpartum. Medical staff were often loath to acknowledge how thalidomide had physically impacted the newborn or, if they did, might suggest that the child be placed in care or left to die. These memories, handed down as family narratives, had a lasting effect. Leigh Gath of Northern Ireland, a thalidomide-affected child who grew up to have two sons, internalized her mother's experiences during her own pregnancies: "The only thing that I would take was folic acid and iron.... My doctor, who had been my doctor all my life, said he was giving me a prescription. 'What is it?' I asked. And he said, 'It's iron.' 'How long has it been on the market?' I asked."[5]

For thalidomide-affected children who had children of their own, developing identities as parents and in some cases grandparents allowed them to reclaim birth and parenthood as occasions of joy and mundanity. These personal stories are still being written by survivors now entering their sixties, forming compelling and emotional narratives around parenting and disability that are too often absent from accounts of motherhood and family life. One participant in an oral history of thalidomide survivors compiled by the Wellcome Library in London talked about the extra time it took to complete everyday parenting tasks for her small children: "I did discover that it didn't take everybody half an hour to change a nappy.... Whilst mothers were going off taking their children to classes... I couldn't get out the door."[6]

Gath recalled that after the birth of her first son, the maternity ward manager used the analogy of a dog picking up its puppies in its teeth by the neck scruff while helping her learn to maneuver her own newborn, including for diaper changes.[7] A father recorded by the Wellcome similarly talked about how—contrary to the advice often espoused by the medical profession, anxious social workers, and society at large—he chose to become a parent and, like most people, learned to manage his two children with the resources he had.

Katrina Gardner, a thalidomide survivor and mother of four, did the same when she became a grandmother, speaking with a sense of pride and family trust about changing the diapers of her five granddaughters. The Wellcome Library's oral history points to the instinctual ways in which the carer–baby dyad adapts quite naturally to physical challenges, with many thalidomider parents affirming that their babies' reflexes kicked in almost immediately, and they learned to cling on tight in the absence of a parent's arms.[8] Geraldine Freeman describes how she and her husband, also a thalidomide survivor, worked as a team to raise their two boys, adapting everyday objects to suit their needs, including a baby bouncer that she had attached to a frame so as to raise it to a level easier for interaction. Freeman also described practicing what she termed "voice control" with her boys when they were young to ensure that they would follow directions obediently when they traveled as a family outside the home: "If Charlie or Harry was sitting on the floor playing with their toys, I would deliberately ask them to get on my lap, even if they were busy doing something, because I needed to know that when I was out, that they would get on my lap when I told them to."[9]

Ruth Blue, an oral historian who has worked closely with survivors as a curator at London's Wellcome Collection and as an organizer at the UK's Thalidomide Society, helped conduct the oral histories with thalidomide-affected families in 2012. She notes that British-born survivors have only two things in common: their mothers took the same prescription, and their babies were born within a four-year period at midcentury. Apart from these confluences, thalidomide is one of the few experiences to bypass the still-rigid British class system, which it cut across indiscriminately.

Parent-child relationships in thalidomide's wake were shaped between the birth mother and the thalidomide-affected child, as well as in the latter generation's own experiences of parenthood. As Sarah Gaitley, the survivor quoted at the start of this essay, so eloquently articulates, part of thalidomide's aftermath was a deep, complex, and abiding guilt felt by mothers. And whether spoken or left implicit in these oral histories, there was an equally common desire on the part of the child to absolve their parent's suffering conscience, a tender and empathetic inversion of mothering. As affective relationships of care have deepened with the birth of successive generations in families touched by thalidomide, so too have stories of how they have (re)designed motherhood.

1 "Thalidomide Lives: Mothers' Guilt," in *Thalidomide: An Oral History*, Wellcome Library, London, 2015, at SoundCloud.com. All three thalidomide-affected adults I spoke with—Geraldine Freeman, Leigh Gath, and Katrina Gardner—echoed this theme. Leigh Gath says, "The mothers were put through hell at the time.... Until it came to light that it was a pill that had caused my disability, people used to cross the road to avoid her. They would blame the mum.... Rather than offer support, they turned their backs. I know that my mother was very, very lonely." Interview with author, September 19, 2020.
2 This number does not include so-called mercy killings or abortion.
3 Ruth Blue, "Thalidomide: An Oral History," Wellcome Library Blog, April 28, 2015, blog.wellcomelibrary.org.
4 There is much more to be said about Frances Oldham Kelsey's pioneering and brave work; a very accessible place to start is at Smithsonianmag.com.

5 Leigh Gath, interview with the author, September 19, 2020. Geraldine Freeman notes that her sister suffered severe morning sickness with her first child but refused medication. "When [the doctor] asked why, she said, "Because my sister's thalidomide." Interview with the author, September 21, 2020.
6 See "Thalidomide Lives: Parenthood," in *Thalidomide: An Oral History*, Wellcome Library, London, 2015, at SoundCloud.com.
7 "She put the bed up to a height... at about my chest and the chair. She put a nice soft pillow on the bed. She took Karl out of his little bassinet and she pulled a baby gro [one-piece pajamas] on him.... By the end of a half hour [of practice], I could just come along, bend down, flip him on my shoulder, and off we would go." Leigh Gath, interview with the author, September 19, 2020. For an excellent memoir of living as a thalidomide survivor, see Gath's *Don't Tell Me I Can't: The Triumphant Story of a Thalidomide Survivor* (New York: Book Republic, 2011).

8 "My first child, Dale, was probably far more mature for his years, realizing he had a mother that was different, and even from a tiny baby he would hold onto me; he would hold my clothes on my chest when I was holding him." See "Thalidomide Lives: Parenthood," in *Thalidomide: An Oral History*, Wellcome Library, London, 2015, at SoundCloud.com.
9 Geraldine Freeman, interview with the author, September 21, 2020.

DR. SPOCK'S *COMMON SENSE BOOK OF BABY AND CHILD CARE*—*Trust yourself. You know more than you think you do.* The opening words of Dr. Benjamin Spock's *The Common Sense Book of Baby and Child Care*, first published in 1946, are straightforward enough. But this simplicity belies the radical ideas Spock imparted to millions of parents raising the children now known as baby boomers, as well as the influence his work continues to have on generations of Americans.

In crafting his book, Spock strove for accessibility at every level. The writing was colloquial, his tone reassuring and approachable. Section headings in the first chapter include "Enjoy Your Baby" and "Parental Doubts Are Normal." He didn't mince words about the reality of parenting, though: "At best, there's lots of hard work and deprivation." He positioned himself as a benevolent expert with practical tips on feeding, sleep, discipline, common ailments, and developmental milestones from infancy to puberty. While dispensing advice, Spock also urged parents to feel confident following their intuition: "What good mothers and fathers instinctively feel like doing for their babies is usually best." And while emphasizing that affection was paramount, he insisted it needn't come at the cost of firmness: "Don't say, 'Do you want to … ?' Just do what's necessary."[1]

Spock structured the book in brief numbered sections rather than lengthy chapters, the first sentence in bold so that harried parents could get the gist right away. Though his editors wanted to assign a professional indexer to the project, Spock compiled it himself. Anticipating the urgency and desperation that often accompanies questions about mysterious rashes or violent tantrums, his index offered parents topics such as:

Biting humans
Bowel movement, beets in
One-year-old, developing a will
Vagina, objects in
Vomiting, projectile

Spock insisted that *Baby and Child Care* be published

DR. BENJAMIN SPOCK

New, extensively revised and enlarged

BABY AND CHILD CARE

The most widely recommended handbook for parents ever published—Authoritative, illustrated, indexed—Over 13,000,000 copies sold

A copy of Dr. Spock's *Baby and Child Care* of 1961, a new version of his bestselling *The Common Sense Book of Baby and Child Care*, which had already gone through fifty-eight printings. Spock's reissue was the highest selling title in the United States since bestseller lists began in 1895 simultaneously in hardcover (for reviewers and the medical community) and in an affordable 25-cent paperback (for everyone else). The books were published in May 1946. By the end of the year 750,000 copies—mostly paperback—had sold, thanks to fervent word of mouth.[2]

In the decades since, the book has sold over fifty million copies. "Throughout its 52-year history," a 1998 New York Times article that ran shortly after Spock's death noted, "'Baby and Child Care' has been the second-best-selling book, next to the Bible."[3] Nine revised editions have been published, two since his passing. Four generations of Americans have been raised under tenets put forth by Spock, and the franchise continues.

Spock embodied the American ideal of expertise: an Ivy League-educated, six-foot-four Olympic gold medalist, Connecticut Yankee physician with a penchant for Brooks Brothers suits. But his work, influenced deeply by Sigmund Freud and the belief that adult problems are rooted in childhood experiences, was subversive—a stark departure from the parenting manuals that came before it. Baby and Child Care's predecessors, including Dr. Luther Emmett Holt's The Care and Feeding of Children (1894) and Dr. John Watson's Psychological Care of Infant and Child (1928), emphasized discipline and rigidity, and didn't place much faith in parents. "Instinct and maternal love are too often assumed to be a sufficient guide for a mother," wrote Holt.[4]

Spock's advice was tender and revolutionary in comparison: "Every time you pick your baby up…even if you do it a little awkwardly at first, every time you change her, bathe her, feed her, smile at her, she's getting a feeling that she belongs to you and that you belong to her. Nobody else in the world, no matter how skillful, can give that to her."[5] Baby and Child Care pushed

notions of parenting forward, but Spock's ideas were not immune from criticism. In subsequent editions, in light of new evidence, he reversed his stances on compulsory circumcision and placing babies on their stomach to sleep. He paid attention to shifting cultural attitudes as well. "I always assumed that the parent taking the greater share of the care of young children (and of the home) would be the mother, whether or not she wanted an outside career," he wrote in the preface to the fourth edition, owning the sexism in his work. "Now I recognize that the father's responsibility is as great as the mother's."[6]

Through the 1980s the cover of Baby and Child Care featured a single cherubic light-skinned infant, while the latest edition, published in 2018, features two —one White and bald, the other Black with a head of curls. This edition also contains sections on screen time, same-sex parents, the Zika virus, and gender-nonconforming children.

Over the years Baby and Child Care's sustained popularity and financial success made space in the market for a deluge of parenting books from physicians, psychologists, journalists, parents, and self-proclaimed experts, each with their own brand of advice for new parents. Now we have books on attachment parenting, helicopter parenting, tiger moms, the superiority of French parenting, baby-led weaning, baby-food cookbooks, and an entire subgenre on sleeping (Ferberizing, Harvey Karp's 5 S's, and baby whispering).

Modern American capitalism perpetually requires another generation of consumers and workers, and runs on a gospel of efficiency and optimization. Parenting manuals promising quick and easy solutions to overwhelmed parents feed the system beautifully.

What would Spock have to say about all of this today? The same culture that propelled Spock to

fame in 1946 vilified him when he spoke out against the Vietnam War in the 1960s. In 1972, Spock ran for president as a candidate of the People's Party, on a platform that included free medical care, legal and accessible abortion, and guaranteed income for families. In this light, it seems impossible to separate his pediatrics from politics.

Parenting manuals often direct our attention away from the real problem: a systemic lack of support for parents and children (something Dr. Spock warned us about decades ago). The United States is the only developed country without paid family leave. The maternal mortality rate here has doubled since 1991—and Black women are four times more likely to die in childbirth than White women.

"Our race relations are barbaric—a disgrace to a nation that pretends to believe in freedom, equality, and God," Spock wrote. "We have areas of poverty and demoralization in our own country that could be well on the way to solution in a year if we had the tendency to face our responsibilities."[7]

There is no life hack or substitute for real care—the daily physical labor of tending to children, creating safe spaces where they can reveal themselves to us. The work of parenting is ceaseless and inefficient, as is love. Spock understood that. Throughout his life's work one constant was leveraging his own privilege.

Reading through the 1976 edition of Baby and Child Care, it is not Spock's words about diapers or weaning that resonate most, but his larger vision for raising our young: "Our only realistic hope as I see it is to bring up our children with a feeling that they are in this world not for their own satisfaction but primarily to serve others."[8]

—**Angela Garbes**

1 Benjamin Spock, The Common Sense Book of Baby and Child Care, 4th ed., rev. (New York: Pocket Books, 1976), 1, 24, 19, 2, 368.
2 Thomas Maier, Dr. Spock: An American Life (New York: Harcourt Brace, 1998), 154.
3 Jane E. Brody, "Final Advice from Dr. Spock: Eat Only All Your Vegetables," New York Times, June 20, 1998, nytimes.com.
4 Barbara Ehrenreich and Deirdre English, For Her Own Good: Two Centuries of the Experts' Advice to Women (New York: Anchor Books, 2005), 220.
5 Spock, The Common Sense Book of Baby and Child Care, 2.
6 Spock, The Common Sense Book of Baby and Child Care, xix.
7 Spock, The Common Sense Book of Baby and Child Care, 17.
8 Spock, The Common Sense Book of Baby and Child Care, 17.

DR. KEGEL'S PERINEOMETER AND PELVIC FLOOR
EXERCISE DEVICE——His name may be synonymous with pelvic floor contractions, but the American gynecologist Dr. Arnold H. Kegel was also a designer at the vanguard of postpartum health and well-being. Remember the strongman game of 1930s-era amusement parks, where the aim was to strike the base with enough force to ring the bell at the top? In 1946, Dr. Kegel similarly designed the "perineometer" to help measure and strengthen the pubococcygeus (PC) muscle.

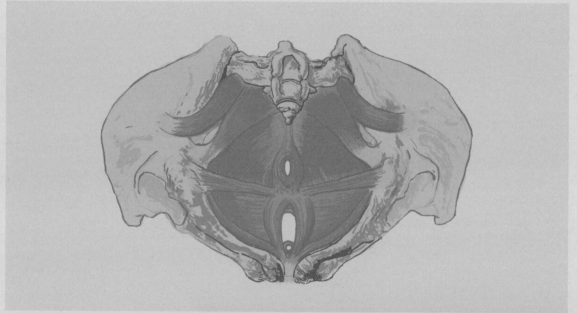

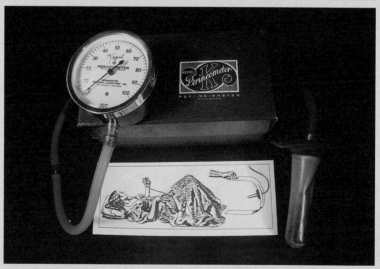

A perineometer and an illustration of its use from Arnold Kegel's *Stress Incontinence and Genital Relaxation* (1952). The instrument aided learning of "progressive resistance exercises of lax perineal musculature." The handheld pressure gauge provided information on the relative strength of muscle contractions. Above, an illustration of the muscle groups of the pelvic region

Named for the perineum (the area that extends between the vulva and anus) and the meter (for measure), the device had a rubbery end that was to be placed inside the vaginal opening; the user would then contract their pelvic floor muscles, sending a whoosh of air through the flexible pneumatic chamber, up through the hollow tubing, which was connected to a manometer calibrated from zero to one hundred millimeters. *Ding! Ding!*

Well into the late 1940s, the standard fix for a weak or prolapsed pelvic floor was surgery. But Dr. Kegel's focus on musculature shifted medical practice. As he wrote in 1948, "Everyone agrees that suitable exercises will improve the function and tone of weak, stretched, atrophic muscles.... Why then would it not be possible to restore through active exercise the normal anatomic relationships of pelvic structures?"[1] Kegel's research revolutionized gynecological and urogynecological practice, and his interest in postpartum pelvic musculature helped develop diagnostic procedures still used by pelvic floor therapists.

Today we think of Kegels as pelvic floor contractions that can be performed at any time and without the help of a device, but for Dr. Kegel, the perineometer was crucial to retraining weak or uncoordinated muscles. His rigorous program prescribed using the perineometer at home three times a day for twenty minutes at a time over a span of months. The rubbery chamber gave patients a sense of which muscles to engage and how forcefully they should contract them. The device's feedback element served as a visual aid, confirming that targeted muscles were being contracted.

Dr. Kegel's work was focused on the female pubococcygeus muscle. But while the PC muscle is vital for elimination control, sexual health, and postnatal recovery, it is just one in a complex network of pelvic floor muscles,

each with its own role and function. The musculature in a healthy pelvic floor has a full range of extensibility and contractility—not only can muscles tighten, but they also can relax and bear down efficiently. While weak pelvic floor musculature can occur for a number of reasons, including in men and children, pregnancy and childbirth can exacerbate these issues. When the pelvic floor muscles are weak or uncoordinated, sex can be painful, and for postpartum people, recovery can include anything from pelvic pain and backaches to urinary and fecal incontinence. Conversely, a hypertonic pelvic floor occurs when the muscles become too tense and are unable to relax. Many people with a clenched, tense, or non-relaxing pelvic floor experience symptoms such as constipation, painful sex, bladder urgency, and pelvic pain. Because Dr. Kegel's patients tended to have weak pelvic musculature, his research did not cover the full range of pelvic floor issues. Popular culture grabbed onto Dr. Kegel's undue emphasis on strengthening and toning the pubococcygeus, spawning numerous articles in *Cosmopolitan* and other women's magazines focusing on the same.

The perineometer may have helped illustrate the idea that retraining muscles could improve postpartum urinary-stress incontinence, but the device was a blunt instrument. Pelvic floor therapists working today use biofeedback and electronic stimulation devices that measure muscle activity, ensuring that the pelvic floor muscles are working together and firing and releasing as necessary. For this reason, a good pelvic floor therapist can be an incredible resource for all of us, not just those experiencing difficulties. In many Western and Northern European countries—France, Denmark, and Germany in particular—pelvic floor therapy is standard care for all postpartum people. And because *la rééducation périnéale*, as it is called in France, is seen as preventative medicine, it is viewed as a long-term cost-saving health

strategy. In the United States, conversely, postpartum pelvic floor health remains a mostly taboo topic, leaving many people feeling ashamed, isolated, and in pain. Though some insurance plans cover them, pelvic floor therapists are often not geographically accessible or affordable. Much like the perineometer, at-home devices are marketed as addressing pelvic floor issues without having to turn to surgery or incur unwanted expenses. While a number of these devices are high tech (many connect to smartphones via Bluetooth), others are decidedly unplugged (vaginal weights or Gwyneth Paltrow's "jade yoni eggs," for example). But a great many provide the same basic functionality as the perineometer: they can be inserted into the vagina and provide feedback and tracking. A single six-week postpartum appointment is all that is on offer in most of the United States, and so in the absence of better postpartum care, pelvic floor devices have become a Band-Aid solution to wider systemic issues.

Pelvic floor exercise is now widely considered to be the first-line treatment for urinary-stress incontinence and any type of vaginal prolapse, and at least in part, we have Dr. Kegel's pioneering mid-twentieth century research to thank. The perineometer in particular was a first step toward transforming pelvic floor issues from a shameful condition that one must endure to a normal occurrence over which we have agency. Beyond strengthening, releasing, relaxing, stretching, and practicing the coordination of our muscles, though, talking about these matters can go a long way in reducing shame and normalizing pelvic floor issues. As with most things related to our bodies, a combination of regular exercise, honest conversation, and expecting better access and service from our health care providers is essential for every single one of us.

1   A. H. Kegel, "The Nonsurgical Treatment of Genital Relaxation: Use of the Perineometer as an Aid in Restoring Anatomic and Functional Structure," *Annals of Western Medicine and Surgery* 2, no. 5 (May 1948): 213–16.

RAPHAELA ROSELLA

RAPHAELA ROSELLA Raphaela Rosella is an Australian artist from Nimbin, New South Wales, who works in the tradition of long-form photographic storytelling, collaborating intimately and sensitively with her subjects. The images here are from her 2011 collection *We met a little early, but I get to love you longer*, which documents women in her life—her twin, her stepsister, and new and old friends—as they grapple with the complexities of early motherhood and the turbulent and uncertain environments around them. Her lens does not shy away from unveiling the interlocking structural systems, institutions, biased media representations, relentless bureaucracies, and violent histories that feed intergenerational trauma, poverty, violence, addiction, the forced removal of children, incarceration, and what she terms "the burden of low expectations." Her intent is to challenge tropes of victimhood and social class bias with everyday stories of women's connectedness, belonging, and kinship.

1—— *Tammara and Tamika*, 2011
2—— *Mikah*, 2011
3—— *Mimi and Mikah*, 2011
4—— *34 weeks (Tammara)*, 2011
5—— *Watching TV (Mimi and Mikah)*, 2011

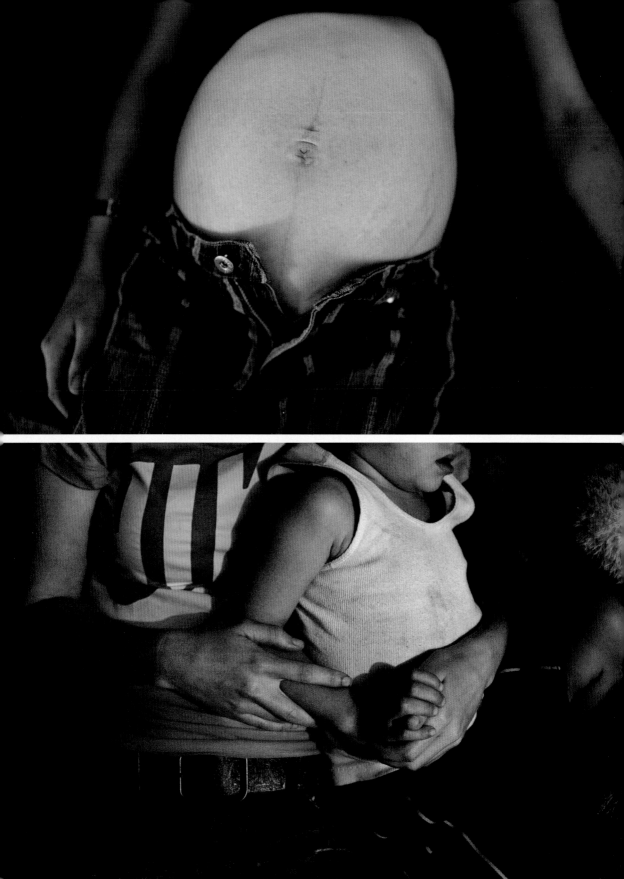

NEWBORN ID——"Switched at birth!" It's a familiar yet shocking plot device and tabloid headline and an undeniably gripping fear: a baby mistakenly or purposely swapped at birth, leaving parents to raise another child as their own. The idea has haunted the popular imagination for centuries. In folk stories from around the world, it is a meddling fairy or an evil force that mischievously or sinisterly exchanges someone's true baby for another child, usually one with inexplicable traits or afflictions.

The changeling theme has been embraced in European medieval literature, eighteenth-century melodramas, Gilbert and Sullivan's comic operas, fiction by Mark Twain, Bollywood cinema, Japanese anime, and television soap opera megahits, including *As the World Turns* and *One Life to Live*, to name a few. A human fascination and preoccupation, the idea of being switched at birth is made more compelling by the fact that it has actually happened—although very rarely.

When hospital birth began replacing home birth in the United States in the early twentieth century, the worry was suddenly more fathomable than ever before. In 1919, Dr. R. H. Pomeroy, an obstetrician at Brooklyn Hospital, wrote, "The matter of identification has certainly always been a major problem. I personally have worried over the subject for twenty years."[1]

At first, baby identification procedures were crude. As babies were shuttled between birthing beds and nurseries, hospitals often relied on mothers and nurses to remember which baby belonged to whom.[2] In the 1910s and 1920s a number of systems were tried: placing aluminum tags around babies' necks; pinning slips of paper or linen to clothing, or tying them to umbilical stumps; and even writing babies' names in wax pencil across their chests.[3]

Then Dr. Pomeroy and a colleague, Dr. H. J. W. Morgenthaler, approached a local glassmaker, and together they designed tiny beads of milk glass with little capital letters etched in black across their centers. Milk glass,

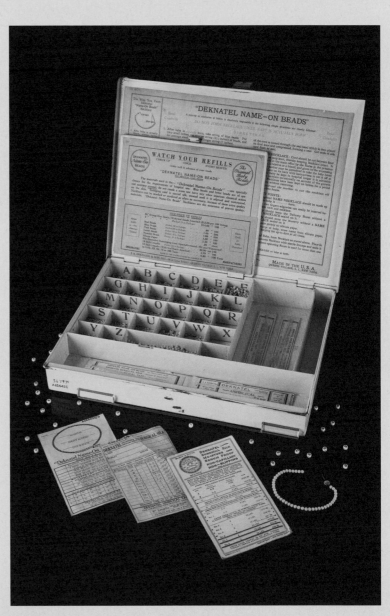

Designed by an obstetrician in Brooklyn in 1919, Name-On Beads were used in hospital maternity wards for fashioning bracelets and necklaces that spelled out an infant's name for identification purposes.

named for its white, milky, opaque appearance, came into fashion during the Victorian era because it offered a cheap alternative to porcelain. Milk glass manufacturers created mostly decorative pieces like vases, lamps, or serving ware, but because the material was inexpensive to produce, milk glass manufacturers often made custom architectural pieces and even jewelry.

Using milk glass beads strung together to spell the family name for identification purposes was completely novel, and the concept caught on quickly. As Dr. Morgenthaler explained, "The necklace is strung by the nurse before the baby is born, while the mother is in the delivery room, and after the baby is born it is simply put around the neck of the baby and fastened, taking about a half a minute to do it."[4]

The beads were simple, secure, inexpensive, easy to read, and, unlike other methods, didn't cause irritation to babies' sensitive skin.[5] The beads also were more like jewelry than a medical device and created an heirloom to be worn, treasured, and saved as a keepsake. "The patients think we have the finest nursery in the world because we put blue beads around the babies' necks," Dr. Morgenthaler wrote. "The mothers are immensely pleased with the necklaces and don't want us to take them off."[6]

In 1925 J. A. Deknatel & Sons, a novelty jewelry company best known for creating imitation pearls (or "Deknatel pearls") began

mass-producing the design. The kits came with A–Z enamel beads organized in trays. Accompanying instructions and advertisements spoke directly to maternity nurses, who were encouraged to string and fasten the diminutive identification jewelry before leaving the delivery room, preferably while the baby was being weighed and measured.[7] Deknatel Name-On Beads were sold directly to hospitals across the United States throughout the 1950s and were the gold standard in infant identification.

As technology in medicine advanced, so did infant identification, but the beads influenced the focus of future designs on wearability. In the late 1940s, it became standard for hospitals to give both babies and their birthing parent identifying bracelets so they could be matched to one another, and several designers experimented with adjustable bracelets that attached via studs let into holes. With the development of flexible plastics and vinyl in the 1960s, bracelets were not only matching, but made to be both adjustable and disposable. Policies shifted toward outfitting babies and parents with matching bracelets marked with corresponding identification numbers rather than names, but as the few baby-switching cases from the mid-century attest, they weren't foolproof. Variations of these bracelets are still worn by parents and infants today, not only as a security measure against babies being switched or stolen, but also as a health and safety precaution. (If misidentified,

babies could receive the wrong kind of milk or, worse, an unintended vaccine or procedure.)

As it always has, newborn identification still varies from hospital to hospital. Today, many labor and delivery wards use technology that is more commonly associated with department stores. Like a pair of jeans, identification bracelets are scanned when babies leave the room, and babies are protected from swapping or abduction by sensors that are designed to set off alarms. Such electronic security devices have long had drawbacks, including price tags that put them beyond the reach of some hospitals. The technology also sometimes fails or gives off false alarms that frighten parents and cause hospital staff to react unnecessarily. Other methods used by hospitals are scannable chips, radio frequencies, or simple plastic bracelets with openings into which paper tags are inserted. But the genesis for each of these designs was the simple glass alphabet-bead necklace of Pomeroy and Morgenthaler, created at a time when babies were being born and housed in hospitals at unprecedented rates.

Infant identification, in whatever form it has taken, and however it will evolve in the future, has a powerful, even Herculean role to fulfill—to connect a child to its biological parent after the umbilical cord has been cut. Such newborn IDs protect our most primal instincts and guard against parents' and hospital staffs' deepest fears, unfounded or not.

1 R. H. Pomeroy, "The Brooklyn Nursery Identification Necklace," *American Journal of Obstetrics and Diseases of Women and Children* 80, no. 6 (December 1919): 776.
2 In addition to name necklaces and bracelets, between the 1920s and 1950s some hospitals took X-rays of babies. "The X-ray is done, primarily, to ascertain if there is a deformity, a fracture, or an enlarged thymus, but it also serves as a means of identification." Other hospitals took a mother's fingerprint and baby's footprint in the delivery room, and the prints were placed on the back of a mother's chart. See "Identification of Newborn Infants," *American Journal of Nursing* 28, no. 1 (January 1928): 33.
3 Libby Copeland, *The Lost Family: How DNA Testing Is Upending Who We Are* (New York: Abrams, 2020), 255.
4 Pomeroy, "The Brooklyn Nursery Identification Necklace," 777.
5 As a nurse in Pasadena described, "When the baby is dismissed, the necklace is either cut and removed in the mother's presence, or it may be kept, on the receipt of one dollar. As the actual cost of the beads is about sixty-six cents, this makes the system pay for itself"; Identification of Newborn Infants," 36.
6 Pomeroy, "The Brooklyn Nursery Identification Necklace," 777.
7 "Identification of Newborn Infants," 33.

INCUBATOR—Describing the preterm birth of her daughter, Mira—one of some fifteen million babies born prematurely each year—the writer Sarah DiGregorio called it a harsh, early lesson on the limits of her power as a parent. Seeing Mira, weighing just one pound, inside a General Electric (GE) Giraffe OmniBed Carestation, the high tech plastic shell that kept her alive for her first fifty-nine days, "hurt me physically," she said. "I wanted to unzip my body and stuff her back in."[1]

While no man-made environment yet outperforms the safety and sustenance of the human womb, generations of incubators—both homemade and highly engineered—have been employed in its stead when that organ ejects its occupant earlier than expected. In 1880, the French obstetrician Étienne Stéphane Tarnier partnered with a Paris zookeeper to build one of the earliest incarnations, based on a poultry-hatching device. Oil lamps heated a lower chamber filled with water, and the warmed air rose to envelop the infant on an upper level.[2] But it was Martin Couney—a chimerical émigré from Prussia to New York by way of Paris, where he was influenced by the work of Tarnier and his contemporary Dr. Pierre-Constant Budin—who really brought this design to public attention.[3]

Tapping into an audience hungry for the technological marvels showcased at various World's Fairs since 1851, Couney set up "Infantoriums" in Europe and the United States, admitting tiny charges without a fee and a paying crowd to gawk. His shows, which spawned imitators, hit Berlin in 1896, London's Earl's Court in 1897, and the Trans-Mississippi Exposition in Omaha, Nebraska, in 1898. At the Pan-American Exhibition of 1901 in Buffalo, New York, the "weakly born" incubator occupants were reviewed in the August issue of *Scientific American* alongside new alcohol-fueled motors and high-speed trains.[4] Couney next moved the Infantorium to Coney Island's Luna Park, where it became the park's longest running attraction, operating from 1904 to 1943 and fascinating visitors to such an extent that they would

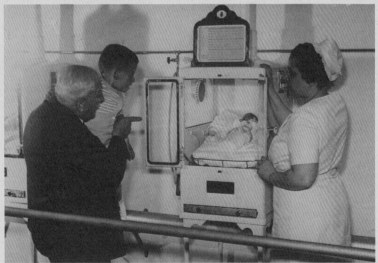

The midway at the 1933 Chicago World's Fair, with a building advertising incubators with living babies displayed within. Below, Dr. Martin Couney points to one of the premature babies in an Infant Incubator at the 1939 New York World's Fair. Dr. Couney is holding a young boy whose life was saved at birth by the incubator. Hildegarde Couney, the doctor's daughter and chief assistant, stands to the right

make repeat visits to check the progress of specific babies.

While Couney's work carried a coarse whiff of the sideshow, such august publications as the *British Medical Journal* and *The Lancet* were simultaneously reporting a precipitous rise in the number of deaths among preterm infants and thus "a pressing need" (nationalism and economic growth) to focus attention on premature babies, which only private business, it seemed, was willing to meet.[5] Incubators were expensive and inaccessible propositions otherwise. At the turn of the twentieth century most hospitals were for indigent people and were not geared toward preterm care or for serving the wealthy. Hardly stand-alone designs, incubators required a complex web of architecture and support, including a well-equipped site and nursing staff. At Luna Park, Couney provided room and board for the latter on-site, along with wet nurses, who adhered to a strict schedule of healthy meals and naps. A 1915 *Brooklyn Daily Eagle* advertisement for the position read, "$30 per month; no work; plenty to eat" (those caught with a hot dog were reportedly fired on the spot).[6]

While hospitals gradually formalized neonatal incubator facilities from the late 1930s onward, until 1971 health insurance in the United States (instituted in 1940) would only pay for such treatment if the infant survived more than fifteen days, making interventions a financial crapshoot.[7] In the special hell of the health care system in the United States today, where the majority of postpartum people

have no access to universal paid family leave, parents of preemies often return to work startlingly early to ensure that employer-provided health care continues for the days, weeks, and months when their new infant remains separated from them in an incubator. As DiGregorio succinctly observes, "the healthcare system we have now is only marginally less absurd than charging admission to a sideshow."[8]

One of the primary functions of incubators is to keep premature babies warm—"cold can kill" is a repeated mantra across the medical literature on preemies—and this does not always require a high tech solution.[9] In 1908 the *American Journal of Nursing* pointed out that while several incubator designs could be rented for at-home use, just as effective was "a large clothes basket, lined with hot water bottles and placed in a room which must be kept at an even temperature."[10] A century later, in 2011, the *British Medical Journal* reported that at MIMER Medical College in India, a team used the white expanded polystyrene foam boxes in which refrigerated vaccines arrived for warmth rather than cooling, cutting four breathing holes to form an incubator that allowed air or oxygen to circulate.[11] And in the late 1970s, faced with a shortage of incubators, the Colombian pediatrician Edgar Rey developed Kangaroo Mother Care (KMC), in which the birthing parent acts as a living incubator for low birth-weight infants through constant babywearing. Backed by the World Health Organization, KMC can be as effective as incubators in some cases, studies suggest,

increasing parental bonding and decreasing morbidity.[12] Today GE's Giraffe OmniBed Carestation, occupied by baby Mira, is one of the most common models worldwide. Its interior mattress, called a Baby Susan, rotates 360 degrees, has a built-in scale, and can double as an operating or X-ray table. Far from an antiseptic hunk of technology, it is the product of painstaking human-centered design—for example, the cot lowers to sitting level "because a mother in a focus group told [the lead designer] how she couldn't lay eyes on her baby for four days" because neither she nor the incubator could move.[13]

Working as part of the team on the Philips NICU of the Future is similarly personal for its lead designer, Colleen Newland, mother of a preemie (now a healthy toddler) who spent one hundred days in the NICU. From her lab in Boston, she and her colleagues designed individual family rooms where parents can spend long, undisturbed stretches enjoying skin-to-skin contact. Lighting is adjustable and soothing, simulating cycles of day and night rather than perpetual fluorescence, and a digital window offers a calming virtual view; beeps and blinking lights are minimized. Instead, a large touchscreen shares vital medical information between providers and parents in simple color-coded symbols. The design, also known as the Lotus Project, is currently in clinical trials at the Children's Hospital and Medical Center of Omaha, Nebraska—the city where Couney's modern incubator made its American debut just over a century ago.

1 Sarah DiGregorio, *Early: An Intimate History of Premature Birth and What It Teaches Us about Being Human* (New York: Harper Collins, 2020), 13.
2 Elizabeth A. Reedy, "Historical Perspectives: Infant Incubators Turned 'Weaklings' into 'Fighters,'" *American Journal of Nursing* 103, no. 9 (September 2003): 64AA.
3 Two benchmark books in this area are Jeffrey Baker's *The Machine in the Nursery: Incubator Technology and the Origins of Newborn Intensive*

Care (Baltimore: Johns Hopkins Studies in the History of Technology, 1996), and Dawn Raffel's *The Strange Case of Dr. Couney: How a Mysterious European Showman Saved Thousands of American Babies* (New York: Penguin, 2018).
4 "Baby Incubators at the Pan-American Exposition," *Scientific American* 85, no. 5 (August 3, 1901): 68.
5 See "The Use of Incubators for Infants," *The Lancet* 1 [149], no. 3848 (May 29, 1897): 1451–1524, accessed at neonatology.org/classics/

lancet.incubators. html; J. W. Ballantyne, "The Problem of the Premature Infant," *British Medical Journal* 1, no. 2159 (May 17, 1902): 1200.
6 A. J. Liebling, "Patron of the Preemies," *New Yorker*, June 3, 1939, newyorker.com. See also Mathilde Cohen and Hannah Ryan, "From Human Dairies to Milk Riders: A Visual History of Milk Banking in New York City, 1918–2018," *Frontiers: A Journal of Women Studies* 40, no. 3 (2019): 139–70, papers. ssrn.com.
7 See Mary Dabney Smith, "Incubator

Babies," *American Journal of Nursing* 11, no. 10 (July 1911): 791–95.
8 DiGregorio, *Early*, 73.
9 Preterm babies' bodies have a higher water content, higher ratio of skin to body mass, and lower energy reserves than babies born full term, making thermoregulation harder and thus requiring external support.
10 Jessie Forsythe Christie, "The Care of an Incubator Baby," *American Journal of Nursing* 8, no. 7 (April 1908): 526.
11 Luisa Dillner, "Innovation in Healthcare:

Finalists Reflect a Wealth of Potential," *BMJ: British Medical Journal* 342, no. 7801 (April 2011): 796.
12 See Juan Gabriel Ruiz-Peláez, Nathalie Charpak, and Luis Gabriel Cuervo, "Kangaroo Mother Care: An Example to Follow From Developing Countries," *BMJ: British Medical Journal* 329, no. 7475 (November 13, 2004): 1179–81, doi.org/10.1136/bmj.329.7475.1179
13 DiGregorio, *Early*, 82. DiGregorio notes the giraffe is one of "the quietest, most watchful animals in the world."

KUDDLE-UP——Even if you've never had a child, you've seen them before. If you were born in the United States after 1950, there's a good chance you were wrapped in one. The "Kuddle-Up," as it is called, is a white cotton blanket with alternating stripes of pink and blue along its edges. So ubiquitous it's nearly invisible, the blanket is used in hospital labor and delivery wards all over the world and is one of the first objects to touch the skin of countless newborns.

For better and for worse, the United States systematized and exported its management of hospital birth and postpartum care in the twentieth century, and no object tells the story of the standardized hospital birth experience quite so succinctly as the Kuddle-Up.

The first step toward the blanket's creation came in 1910, when a group of nuns approached A. L. Mills, an apron maker, with an idea. Instead of sewing aprons for Chicago's meat-packing industry, as he had been, Mills could make hospital garments such as surgeon's gowns and nursing uniforms, freeing the nuns to devote more time to caring for patients. The medical garment and textile supply business was born, and with it came many now iconic and universal hospital designs, including another of Mills's creations, the jade green surgical gown. Today Mills's company, Medline (initially called Mills Hospital Supply), is the largest privately held manufacturer of health care and surgical products, distributing more than 350,000 separate products. But the Kuddle-Up has been a company darling since Mills began selling it in the early 1950s.

Until then, receiving blankets were typically fashioned of beige-colored cotton. After some experimentation Mills designed the "Kuddle-Up in Candy Stripe." It was bright and clean feeling, and its pink and blue stripes made it suitable for babies of any sex. Medline creates other patterns —baby animals and tiny footprints, for example—but none are as popular as the classic Kuddle-Up. These blankets are not technically supposed to leave the hospital,

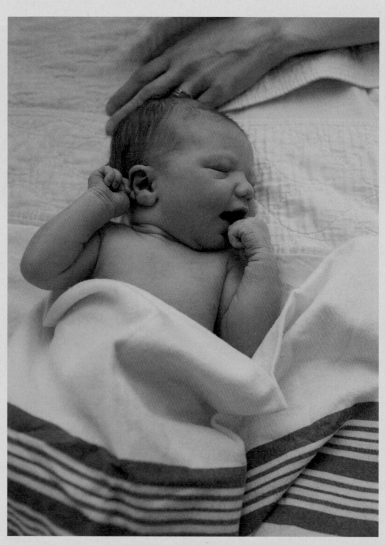

A newborn baby draped in a Kuddle-Up blanket, with its trademark blue and pink stripes

yet thousands go home each year and are often saved as keepsakes. At a wholesale cost of about $2.50 apiece, the blankets are inexpensive. They are also soft, durable, and washable and can be used again and again.

The Kuddle-Up's timing was impeccable. Before the mid-twentieth century most American women were under the care of midwives and gave birth at home.[1] Nineteenth-century hospitals were largely urban asylums for poor, homeless, or working-class married women who could not deliver at home but who doctors and philanthropists believed deserved medical treatment. With the failure to implement comprehensive health insurance in the 1910s, the advent of pain medication, and the shift from local-and state-trained midwives to the establishment of the American Board of Obstetrics and Gynecology in 1930 (which required that one be licensed to deliver a baby), American childbirth moved "from the bedroom to the hospital room," as the historians Richard and Dorothy Wertz put it.[2] In 1900, fewer than 5 percent of women delivered in hospitals, but by the 1920s the numbers were steadily increasing. By 1940, the number of hospital births had risen to 56 percent, and in 1950 that number soared to 88 percent. By 1969, 99 percent of births took place in hospitals, a percentage that remains steady today.[3]

Unfortunately, although the aim of standardized care was to make childbirth safer, hospital environments at the turn of the twentieth century exacerbated many birthing women's most pressing dangers. Hospitals began to standardize care well before infection was fully understood. Drawing on the advice of Civil War–era military hospitals, maternity wards established routines to prevent cases of puerperal (or childbed) fever, a widespread, painful, and potentially deadly uterine infection. A number of procedures were instated in hopes of halting the spread of disease. In 1900, each patient admitted to Sloane Maternity Hospital in New York was given an enema, a vaginal douche with bichloride of mercury, and had their head and nipples washed with kerosene, ether, and ammonia. To prevent lice, nurses shaved the pubic hair of charity patients, while private patients had theirs clipped. Unfortunately, this zeal against infection spread much of what was already there. In 1927, an epidemic of puerperal fever at Sloane killed 15 percent of its patients.[4] It only gradually became apparent to doctors and nurses that hospitals had to undertake more antiseptic routines as more and hardier strains of resistant bacteria developed. While the "safe" hospital was a result of extremely vigilant and ritualized interventions, the hospital environment itself had greatly contributed to defining birth as a dangerous and potentially deadly event. By the 1940s and '50s, a number of hygienic, standard-issue medical designs —rubber gloves, easily changeable rubberized bed sheets, and the Kuddle-Up—had become a routine part of hospitalized maternal and postpartum care.

Just as Henry Ford revolutionized the mass production of automobiles with the assembly line concept, the medical industry developed its own production protocols. Standard-issue medical supplies were implemented to assure safety and hygiene, but they also saved money and increased profit margins. And as the medical industry in twentieth-century America grew increasingly aligned with profit-seeking businesses rather than local makers and medical practices, companies like Medline flourished, becoming significant stakeholders in the American health care system.

While the Kuddle-Up blankets were once made in the United States, production has since moved overseas, and they are now made in Karachi, Pakistan.[5] The United States has succeeded in exporting its model of medicalized birth to developed and developing nations across the world, and it has also exported much of its stuff, too. But unlike rubber gloves and surgical masks, the Kuddle-Up is not a medical necessity so much as it is a byproduct of standardized care. In hospitals from Haiti to England to China, the blanket plays a bit part in birth stories in numerous cultures. And with the help of social media and newborn-related hashtags, the Kuddle-Up has become increasingly visible, so much so that an image of a newborn wrapped in a Kuddle-Up is an instant signifier of a hospital birth.

Seventy years after Mills designed it, the Kuddle-Up is Medline's best-selling blanket by a long shot. Medline is now one of the fastest-growing distributors of medical and surgical supplies in the United States, serving as the primary distributor to more than 450 major hospitals and health care systems there and abroad. But the company's baby is still, by a wide margin, the Kuddle-Up, America's most iconic baby blanket.

1   Richard W. Wertz and Dorothy C. Wertz, Lying In: A History of Childbirth in America (New Haven: Yale University Press, 1989), 137–38.
2   In 1915, progressive reformers proposed a system of compulsory health insurance to protect workers against medical costs and wage loss when one could not work. The American Association for Labor Legislation's (AALL) proposal, modeled on existing programs in Germany and England, was debated throughout the country and introduced as legislation in several states. Within the next ten years, many European nations would adopt some form of compulsory national health insurance, but similar proposals in the US were rejected due to resistance from physicians and commercial insurers. See Beatrix Hoffman, "Health Care Reform and Social Movements in the United States," American Journal of Public Health 93, no. 1 (2003): 75–85.
3   Wertz and Wertz, Lying-In, 133; and Debora Boucher et al., "Staying Home to Give Birth: Why Women in the United States Choose Home Birth," Journal of Midwifery and Women's Health 54, no. 2 (March–April 2009): 119–26, doi:10.1016/j.jmwh.2008.09.006.
4   Wertz and Wertz, Lying-In: 138.
5   Andrea Hsu, "Born in the USA? This Blanket Might Look Familiar," NPR's All Things Considered, in the series Pregnancy and Childbirth: Economics and Business, July 22, 2011, npr.org.

POSTPARTUM MESH UNDERWEAR——Long after babies are out in the world, and placentas and body fluids have been ejected in their wake, a postpartum person's uterus continues to bleed for days and weeks after giving birth. And every newly postpartum person can't pee without it stinging, can't sit without wincing, and—especially those who have given birth for the first time—can't glance downward without being struck anew with the sights, smells, and volume of postpartum bleeding.

Enter postpartum underwear. These stretchy panties that encircle a swollen abdomen and perineum are designed to contain uterine discharge and hold in place preparations that ice, heal, and offer localized pain relief to ravaged nether regions. Provided by hospitals, birthing centers, and home birth kits alike, or sold for a few dollars online, they are most commonly mass-manufactured in an expandable synthetic mesh that holds disposable mattress-like maxi pads. Often a mix of polyester and elastic configured in a brief or boxer style, the garment varies in gauge and itchiness. Usually worn pulled high up on the stomach to accommodate the still-swollen postpartum belly, the underwear have a loose waistband to avoid further irritating the stiches of those with sore C-section incisions. It's a design encountered by most postpartum people who pass through a developed world health care system, regardless of where the birth took place.

Disposable postpartum underwear, cousin to adult diapers, are an offshoot of research that began in the 1930s into commercial variants for babies.[1] These were combined with earlier technologies for sanitary napkins that emerged at the turn of the twentieth century. Like the candy-striped Kuddle-Up baby blanket (see p. 249) that became the ubiquitous wrap for newborns, disposable postpartum underwear were gradually enshrined from the 1950s onward as births became standardized and industrialized in hospitals in the United States and elsewhere.[2]

In online reviews of the underwear, users described their stinging

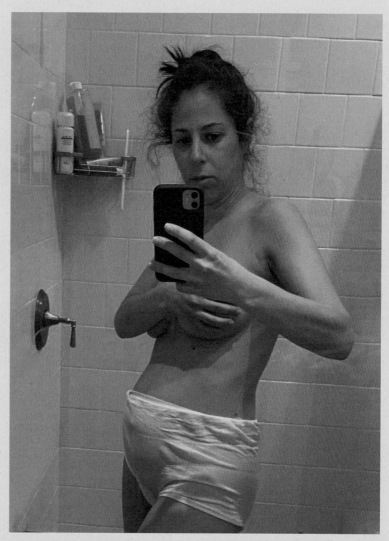

Jamie Diamond, a photographer and video artist, immediately after the birth of her daughter, Ella, in Philadelphia in 2020. Jamie is wearing the near-ubiquitous postpartum mesh underwear

postpartum vaginas—as well as the pain of bowel movements and the passing of various fluids from a torn perineal area—with terms like *raw* and *real*.[3] Little wonder, then, that a garment that alleviates the irritation would become a staple of the fourth trimester. While for some the underwear are hated reminders that trigger flashbacks to intense pain and indignity, for many others they are a badge of honor, despite their lack of sartorial flair. As the writer Edan Lepuki reflected in a 2016 essay for *The Cut*, "I felt safe wearing them. Eight months later, when my sister had her second child, I asked if she could get me a pair, just for old time's sake. I kept them in the back of my drawer like a talisman."[4]

Technically known as lochia, postpartum uterine discharge is comprised of tissue, mucus, and what one wearer memorably described on Instagram as "blood clots the size of jellyfish." The three phases of postpartum bleeding—bright red *lochia rubra* in the first few days that turns to pinkish-brown *lochia serosa* and then yellow-white mucus-like *lochia alba* at up to six weeks postpartum—are evidence of the body expelling the extra resources needed to nurture a pregnancy. Often described as the heaviest period a person will ever experience, lochia should be closely monitored by health care professionals caring for new parents, especially in the first twenty-four hours after giving birth, when particularly heavy flow can indicate hemorrhaging.

Postpartum mesh underwear are often used in tandem with a variety of other designs—including age-old and crosscultural herbal remedies like witch hazel and direct pain relief methods such as ice and sitz baths (*sitzen* is German for "to sit") of shallow warm water containing baking soda or salt, often mixed with aromatherapeutic additions such as lavender—in a multipronged attempt at relief. The more modern perineal irrigation bottle, a plastic container akin to a diner ketchup dispenser, completes the toolkit, giving those navigating the war zone left after a vaginal delivery a way to squirt pH-balancing water against their urine flow to temper the sting on stretched or stitched flesh. (The model Chrissy Teigen quipped that she got herself one as a "push present" in 2016.)

While advocacy groups such as the United Kingdom's National Childbirth Trust offer "an honest, clear account" of postpartum bleeding on their websites, NCT's statement that "it may be one of the few things you haven't discussed with friends" highlights that the bleeding—and postpartum perineal pain in general—is a jolting experience that catches many people by surprise, and for which they are underprepared both mentally and materially. This lack of clear information prior to birth, as well as the dearth of a dedicated range of consumer products, was a lacunae that two US companies, Nyssa Care and FridaMom, stepped into in 2019.

The genesis of the FridaMom line occurred in the aftermath of mother-of-three (and former Miami Marlins lawyer) Chelsea Hirschhorn's first and second births, when she—like many before her—repurposed pharmaceutical items, including a burn-relief spray meant for foot care, during her painful postpartum recoveries.[5] FridaMom's $99 "hospital bag" pack includes an ergonomic upside-down peri bottle, "instant ice" maxi pads, and disposable mesh underwear. In its launch year, FridaMom created a television advertisement showing the underwear being worn, the image described as "just a new mom, home with her baby and her new body for the first time." It was rejected by the broadcasting channel ABC and the Academy of Motion Picture Arts and Sciences, home of the Oscars, from airing during a break in the 2019 award show, a decision that caused an immediate outcry.[6]

Nyssa Care's reusable FourthWear postpartum underwear follows in the design footsteps of brands like Thinx and Knix, which have begun to raise public awareness—and reject social shame—around bodily fluid leakage and adult incontinence. Nyssa Care underwear are fashioned of flexible, breathable fabric made from post-consumer recyclables and contains a kangaroo-style pouch into which one can slip reusable heat or ice packs. Approaching design in terms of systems and not just products, the company employs on their packing team women past retirement age who have found it difficult to get jobs. Representing a rejection of the discardable design culture of the twentieth century, FourthWear undies can be washed and reused, and their packaging doubles as a diaper carrier. Both companies use social media to share firsthand accounts of perineal recovery, transforming it from something painful that nobody tells you about to an opportunity for real talk, design innovation, and—most importantly—healthy recovery.

1 David Dyer, "Seven Decades of Disposable Diapers: A Record of Continuous Innovation and Expanding Benefit," The Winthrop Group, Inc. on behalf of EDANA, August 2005, edana.org.
2 Disposable postpartum mesh underwear evolved from sanitary products marketed by companies such as Kendall Mills, Procter & Gamble, and Kimberly-Clarke.
3 Under FridaMom's Instagram posts regarding mesh underwear, commenters described their postpartum experiences in terms ranging from "pulsating pain" to "harder than a full time job and full time graduate school."
4 Edan Lepucki, "The Secret, Magical Underwear That Only Moms Know About," *The Cut*, February 17, 2016, thecut.com.
5 FridaMom operates under her already successful FridaBaby brand, which began with a cult favorite nasal aspirator, or snotsucker, the Frida Nose.
6 Guidelines from the Academy of Motion Picture Arts and Sciences prohibit commercials for a motley crew of reasons, including "political candidates/positions, religious or faith-based messages/positions, guns, gun shows, ammunition, feminine hygiene products, adult diapers, condoms or hemorrhoid remedies." See Brittany Shammas, "This Ad Is a Raw Look at Postpartum Life: The Oscars Rejected It for Being Too Graphic," *Washington Post*, February 10, 2020, washingtonpost.com.

FEEDING

W.H.Johnson

FEEDING For some, feeding babies is a deeply enjoyable, even sacred act, and for others it can be a fraught business. Debate over what is "best" often drowns out the truth that empowering people to make the decisions that feel right for them is what matters most. While the images here advocate for agency around feeding for parents with a wide range of lived experiences, what they don't show is the labor involved. Whether manifested in cracked nipples or the endless sterilization of bottles, this labor is still heavily gendered and often framed as an expression of "ultimate motherhood."

1—— Jazmyne Futrell (@mixedmombrownbabies on Instagram) on August 25, 2019
2——Catherine and Miles, from the 4th Trimester Bodies Project
3——Gabriella feeding August, 2020
4——William H. Johnson, *Maternal*, c. 1944. Oil on paperboard
5——Lourdes Grobet, *La Briosa*, from her series *La doble lucha (The double struggle)*, 1981
6——Amber and Alice, 2013
7——Vincent Ferrané, from his series *Milky Way*, c. 2017
8——A mother feeding twins, from Mabel Liddiard's *The Mothercraft Manual*, (1938)

2   3   4   5
6
7

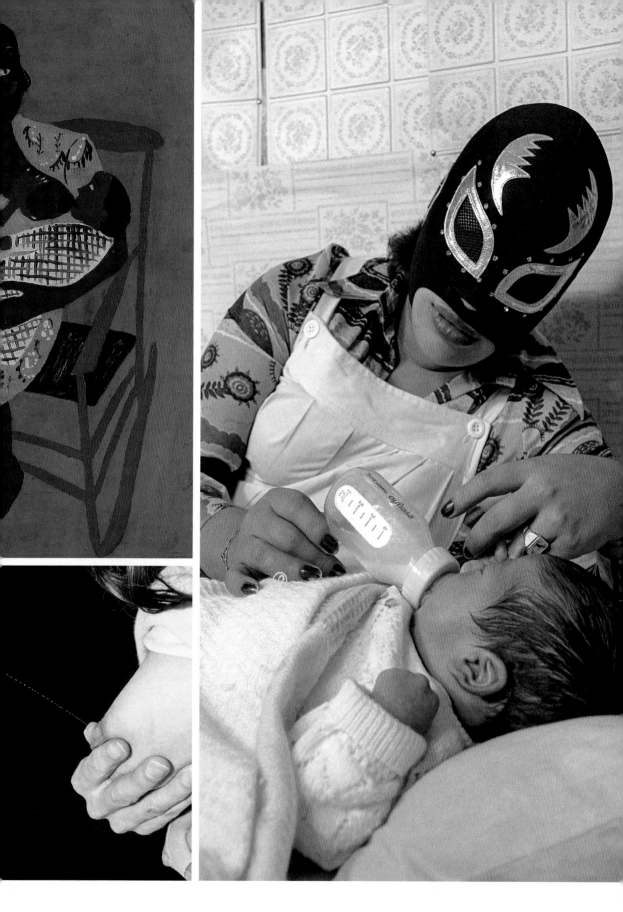

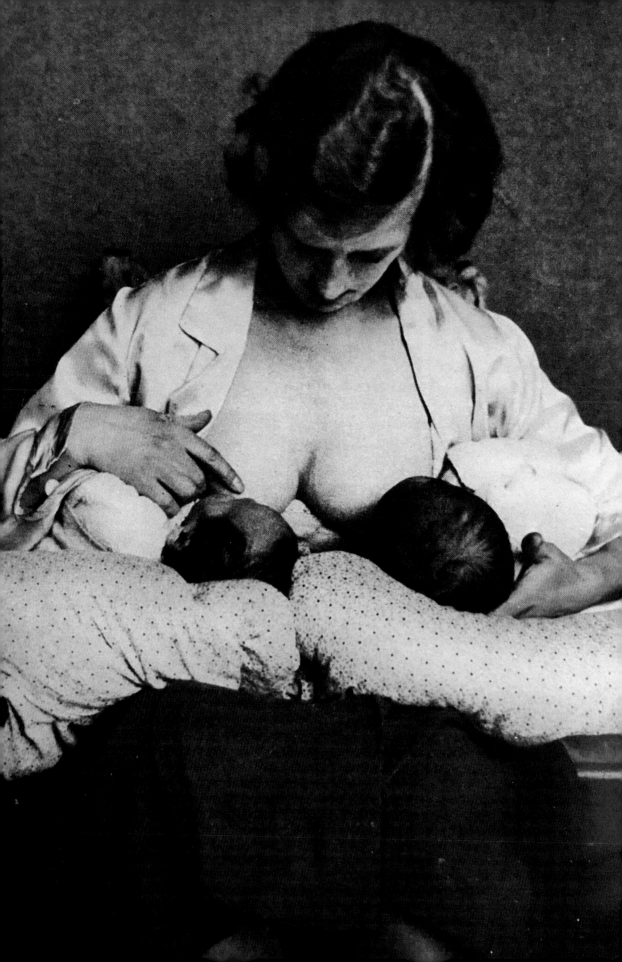

NURSING BRA—Since its invention in the early twentieth century, the modern bra has functioned in multiple, overlapping ways: as a technology of desire that, born from the lineage of the corset, reflects, enacts, and makes visible the power of the patriarchy over the female body; as a supportive accessory of pragmatic comfort; and as a platform for self-expression, identity, and politics.[1] In the case of the nursing bra, these complexities meet in tension with the changing demands, dreams, desires, realities, and assumptions of parenthood and breastfeeding over the past century.

In 1866, when the inventor Samuel M. Perry of Plainfield, New York, patented a novel design for a nursing corset with a hinged flap over the bust, motherhood—like womanhood in general—was a concept in flux. The Civil War had just been fought over the question of chattel slavery. Black women had often been forced to breastfeed the babies of their White masters. In non-slave states and after the war, Black and Irish women worked as wet nurses, their bodies nourishing the children of the White middle and upper classes.[2] For decades after emancipation, White mothers might dismiss nursing as feeling like "a slave" to their infant. A century later, the poet Maya Angelou spoke baldly about these power dynamics when she argued in a 1973 interview that "we have to thank black women not only for keeping the black family alive but the white family…. Black women have nursed a nation of strangers …who they knew when they grew up would rape their daughters and kill their sons."[3]

These constructions of motherhood, race, sexuality, and breastfeeding coexisted uneasily with powerful and sentimental ideas about the importance of a mother's nurturing breast. By the end of the nineteenth century, important changes in women's socioeconomic and political roles combined with an almost fanatical cultural embrace of scientific and technological progress to disrupt Victorian ideas about motherhood. The turn of the twentieth century opened space for new generations of women to make different choices about everything from clothing to employment. As more women worked as paid laborers in these

"My nursing bra… one of the nice ways of mothering."

Hickory

"NURSING BRA" Style 311. Soft and smooth as a fashion bra. Comfort lined in polyester/cotton, new one hand easy press clip opening. A10-16, B10-20, C10-22, D10-22, DD12-24. Honeybeige.

A 1970s advertisement for the Australian brand Hickory, owned by the underwear specialist Bendon Group and known for bras for breastfeeding, post-surgery, and post-mastectomy, as well as for bra fitting

years, demand for breastfeeding alternatives spilled beyond the boundaries of the middle class, sparking a surge in bottle-feeding among the working class. In the same period, a coalition of dress reformers made up of laywomen and physicians worked to free women from the restrictions of the corset as they advocated for more healthful and realistic options for women's bodies.

The US Patent Office began to issue the first patents for brassieres in the early twentieth century, many granted to women inventors and entrepreneurs. Early advertisements promoted brassieres as a way for women to smooth the "unsightly bulge" that the era's low-cut, less restrictive corsets created, highlighting not only the increasing ubiquity of bottle-feeding but the bra as an accentuation of a youthful, smooth, and distinctly non-maternal figure. Ready-made maternity and nursing designs remained a rarity in most wardrobes; fashion and textile archives attest that existing clothing was instead often recalibrated for nursing.

After World War II, as the birth rate exploded, the number of nursing people increased even though the overall breastfeeding rate remained low. Mainstream designers such as Maiden Form began to market improved nursing bras that offered supported, individual cups with leakage protection through the use of rubberized lining and space for absorbent pads, as well as hidden "pockets" that enabled discreet nursing.[4] Bra designers found themselves scrambling to provide nursing bras that delivered the era's sexualized, youthful breast shape without sacrificing any of the bra's more functional objectives: support but not constriction, breathability without leakage, and convenient access for the infant.

Breastfeeding mothers challenged the social and medical norms of the postwar nuclear family, which pitted the sexual interests of the husband against the interests of the mother and infant. When women chose to breastfeed, they subverted the rigid hierarchy of needs by privileging their identity as mothers over their role as wives—or, even more radically, by suggesting the two could coexist harmoniously. La Leche League, a revolutionary breastfeeding support organization that began in the suburbs of Chicago in the 1950s, was founded by women who adamantly rejected the period's iconic bullet-shaped bras and Playboy Bunny aesthetic. Instead, they embraced a maternal-centric identity that resonated widely. Their expansive membership shared tips, sewing patterns, and advice on nursing garments, including bras, when they couldn't find the options they wanted in stores or catalogues.[5]

By the 1990s the emergence of a personal-use, electric breast pump, marketed to lactators who worked outside the home, helped inspire nursing bra designs that allowed for hands-free pumping, perfect for "the mom on the go." The breast-pump bra offered to relieve the tension surrounding the breast by disciplining the breastfeeding experience to the fragmented rhythms of life as a postmodern cyborg. By the turn of the twenty-first century, definitions of family, motherhood, and infant feeding had evolved far beyond the postwar ideal of the nuclear family. More trans, non-gestational, and gender non-conforming parents pushed for the rights, access, language, support, and materials to feed their infants human milk. For these communities the concept of "chestfeeding" further subverts the historical tensions between the sexualized female breast, motherhood, and infant feeding by moving away from "the breast" altogether. While the experiences of parents who chestfeed remain under-documented, small studies have highlighted the lack of gender-neutral clothing options as an area of concern and distress. Bras, and especially nursing bras, have deep historical ties to constructions of womanhood and female sexuality, and these meanings often make them poor options for twenty-first century parents who choose to chestfeed.[6] As chestfeeders enter the fraught territory of human milk and the mammary, they challenge the gendered design history of the nursing bra, calling into question longstanding assumptions about breastfeeding and parenthood in new and powerful ways.

—Jessica Martucci

1   See Valerie Steele, The Corset: A Cultural History (New Haven: Yale University Press, 2001), and Jane Farrell-Beck and Colleen Gau, Uplift: The Bra in America (Philadelphia: University of Pennsylvania Press, 2002).
2   See Stephanie E. Jones-Rogers, They Were Her Property: White Women as Slave Owners in the American South (New Haven: Yale University Press, 2019), and Janet Golden, A Social History of Wet Nursing in America: From Breast to Bottle (New York: Cambridge University Press, 1996).
3   "A Conversation with Maya Angelou," Bill Moyers Journal: Original Series, November 21, 1973, billmoyers.com.
4   William Rosenthal, Maiden Form Brassiere Co. Inc., New York, Brassière, US Patent 1956250A, filed April 1, 1932; issued April 24, 1934; Brassière, US Patent 1979576A, filed April 1, 1932; issued November 6, 1934.
5   Jessica Martucci, Back to the Beast: Natural Motherhood and Breastfeeding in America (Chicago: University of Chicago Press, 2015).
6   Trevor MacDonald et al., "Transmasculine Individuals' Experiences with Lactation, Chest-feeding, and Gender Identity: A Qualitative Study," BMC Pregnancy Childbirth 16, no. 106 (May 16, 2016): 106, https://doi.org/10.1186/s12884-016-0907-y.

BREAST PUMP——In December 2018, the actor Rachel McAdams proverbially "broke the internet," when, as media headlines from *USA Today* to *Harper's Bazaar* breathlessly reported, she paired a breast pump with couture for a "badass" photo shoot. Six months postpartum, McAdams stared forward unflinchingly, scarlet-nailed hands perched atop her knees, sitting straight-backed in an opulent boudoir. The elasticized, nipple-baring nursing bra, plastic flanges, bottles, and tubes she sported commanded attention.

The pumping gear upstaged her tartan Versace jacket, Bulgari jewels, slicked-back hair, and bright red lipstick. The picture appeared in the niche high-fashion publication *Girls Girls Girls*. In a single image, the photographer (and magazine's founder) Claire Rothstein, in collaboration with her subject, turned the breast pump from a taboo, hidden, and quotidian product design into the accessory *du jour*. (Previously, breast pumps experienced their biggest public boost in 2010, when the newly passed Affordable Care Act covered their use.)

The breast pump is arguably the most ubiquitous design object governing parenthood in the United States today, if we look beyond designed systems such as racism and lack of family or universal health care. Until viral images like Rothstein's appeared, along with the concomitant echo of supportive posts that other pumpers shared on social media, most people had never seen a breast pump in action in public. Lauded as a product that helps lactating people move with freedom while still being able to breast- or chestfeed their offspring, it is also a design that follows neatly in the path of gadgets sold to the *I Love Lucy* generation for their home: washing machines, kitchen blenders, hair dryers, and other appliances. These "time-saving" devices maximized productivity behind the scenes so that women could do double (or triple) duty while making it all look effortless.

Little wonder the breast pump is operated out of sight, behind a locked door, hiding the labor involved—a work output historically

Named for Sister Maya Kindberg, the SMB (*B* for *Bröstpump*) was developed by the Swedish engineer Einar Egnell in the 1950s. It is shown here with a carrying handle, outer casing for the metal engine, and two extra glass bottles with rubber stoppers and knee tubes

not matched by the effort to design the machine itself. In 2017, Jessica Winter pointed out in the *New Yorker* the "surprising and incalculable" lack of investment in product designs for pregnant people, and the amount of money Silicon Valley "kingmakers are leaving on the table by shunning women and mothers and babies. Breast pumps make up a seven-hundred-million-dollar market, with ample room to grow."[1] Her piece drew attention to the secret society of those who haul their pumps back and forth between home and work, nodding as they notice each others' "On the Go" totes that house a popular device made by Medela, the Swiss giant in this field. Its members traverse race, class, and many other intersections, balancing jobs of myriad types outside the home with the multilayered and heavily gendered labor of child-rearing. In this regard, the breast pump is a design that epitomizes the struggles of people who continue to be told they can (and should) "have it all," a catchphrase the Princeton professor Anne-Marie Slaughter memorably called BS on almost a decade ago.[2] It is a contested object, for some representing freedom of choice and for others manifesting the unrelenting pressure to breastfeed at all costs.

Breast pumps were not the earliest relief mechanism for engorged breasts (human hands take those laurels). A mechanical pump was first used in the 1840s, when a Philadelphia navy officer discovered that the bloodletting apparatus he had developed could be adapted for hand-operated pumping of human milk to relieve pressure.[3] In the 1920s, the dairy engineer (and international

chess champion) Edward Lasker and pediatrician Isaac A. Abt pioneered a machine for capturing human milk for premature infants in the Chicago hospital where Abt worked. These early mechanical breast pumps were cumbersome, loud, and fairly painful for the lactating parent who employed them.

Einar Egnell, a Swedish civil engineer, was one of the first to design a breast pump by specifically observing human anatomy—rather than following Lasker's bovine template—after his friend, a gynecologist, challenged him to improve upon existing technologies in the mid-1950s. The resulting Egnell SMB breast pump of 1956 was named for Sister Maja Kindberg, the nurse who collaborated on its testing in concert with new mothers in Stockholm's major maternity hospital.

Pumps were confined to medical quarters—and thus available to relatively few new parents—until later in the twentieth century. The at-home electric pump was not developed and widely marketed until the early 1990s (Medela again hit early with the 1991 Mini Electric). Contemporary design updates include the 2018 prototype from Naya Health that used water suction (it turned out that H_2O contaminated the extracted milk, and the company folded), the second generation of the in-bra, cordless Willow, and the Haakaa manual pump, which seals to the breast and can work independently or be manually massaged. And now, of course, a plethora of apps are available to log milk production. Micro components such as flanges are also getting some love, with more flexible materials like silicone

adapting to the curve of different breast and nipple shapes.[4]

Although increasing attention is being paid to their design, pumps still require time-consuming sanitizing, and thus far no design replicates the hormones stimulated, the bonds forged, or the way in which a baby's mouth draws milk while breastfeeding, meaning that directly feeding an infant is often a far more pleasant (and often less arduous) experience. And while lactation breaks and spaces (see p. 261) are now required by federal law, many work spaces still lack adequate facilities.[5]

As MIT's "Make the Breast Pump Not Suck" hackathons in 2014 and 2018 highlighted, by its very existence the pump exposes the lack of a far more holistic design for family leave (see p. 293).[6] The pump itself is also markedly absent in recorded design histories. Egnell's design fits perfectly within the well-told stories of industrially inflected objects. This is demonstrated by the checklist for Alfred Barr and Philip Johnson's *Machine Art*, MoMA's inaugural exhibition of modern design in 1934, and the subsequent *Good Design* shows of the 1940s and 1950s, for example, as well as by later narratives of everyday "humble masterpieces" of design. Yet, the breast pump still awaits acquisition and display in many major museum collections.[7] This continued omission cements it as the everyday design used by millions and yet still too taboo to warrant closer scrutiny. The argument might be made that it is simply not yet aesthetically or ergonomically interesting enough to merit celebration. Either way, it's a design challenge ripe for the picking.

1   Jessica Winter, "Why Aren't Mothers Worth Anything to Venture Capitalists?," *New Yorker*, September 25, 2017. Two years later, in 2019, the global breast pump market size was valued at USD 1.9 billion; "Breast Pump Market Size, Share & Trends Analysis Report By Product (Open, Closed), By Technology (Manual, Battery Powered, Electric), By Application (Personal Use, Hospital Grade), By Region, And Segment Forecasts, 2020–2027," Market Analysis Report, Grand View Research, February 2020, grandviewresearch.com/industry-analysis/breast-pumps-market.

2   Anne-Marie Slaughter, "Why Women Still Can't Have It All," *The Atlantic*, July–August, 2012, theatlantic.com. In the United States—and in other countries—policy began to evolve in the wake of major civil rights legislation of the 1960s, including the Pregnancy Discrimination Act of 1978.
3   See Jessica Martucci's excellent *Back to the Breast: Natural Motherhood and Breastfeeding in America* (Chicago: University of Chicago Press, 2015), 180.
4   In a conversation with Diane Spatz, a doctor of nursing, lactation expert, and professor at the University of

Pennsylvania, she described witnessing one of these innovations in Dr. Peter Hartmann's lab at the University of Western Australia, along with fellow researcher Donna Geddes and doctoral student Danielle Prime: "All day long I got to measure nipples which led us to having different sizes of the shield…[and Prime made] a new shield design which is curved…[people] got out 11% more available milk when they pumped with it." "Designing for Body Fluids, Part I: Human Milk: Interview with Diane Spatz," *CONTEXT: The Journal of AIA Philadelphia*, fall

2019, 15, issuu.com/aia_philadelphia/docs/context_fall2019issue.
5   Today, federal law provides that employees are entitled to take breaks to express milk; US Department of Labor, Wage and Hour Division, dol.gov.
6   As a poignant *New York Times* op-ed in 2009 asked, "Why, as a society, have we privileged the magic elixir of maternal milk over actual maternal contact, denying the vast, vast majority of mothers the kind of extended maternity leave that would make them physically present for their babies?" Judith Warner, "Ban the Breast Pump, *New York

Times*, April 2, 2009, nytimes.com. See also the MIT Hackathon's excellent mini-publication *Speaking our Truths: 27 Stories of What It's Really Like to Breastfeed and Pump in the United States*, freely accessible at makethebreastpumpnotsuck2018.com/researchandstorycollection.
7   A notable exception are the breast pumps I sent to the Art Institute of Chicago for display, exhibition copies of which were eventually purchased by that institution.

MAMAVA POD——You may have seen one of the pods in an airport, a convention center, or a workplace. You may have used one to pump milk or feed your infant while traveling or going about your daily life. Sascha Mayer and Christine Dodson, the Vermont-based partners behind Mamava, teamed up to take the "lack" out of "lactation room," arguing that every lactating person deserves a clean and comfortable dedicated space in which to pump or breastfeed.

DESIGNING MOTHERHOOD——The Mamava is a flexible shelter design that offers choice to postpartum people who want to nurse or pump away from home in a clean, private, and comfortable space. How did you meet one another and co-found Mamava in 2013? How did you identify this as a niche that was not being served, and who were the designers and engineers you connected with to realize your idea?

SASCHA MAYER——We were moms ourselves, and we worked at the same design studio in Burlington, Vermont. There was an "aha" moment for me—an article in the *New York Times* by Jodi Kantor, which explored the idea that breastfeeding had become a privilege rather than a right, a kind of two-class system for workers. Women like me, with autonomy in their jobs, are in a private office; I could close the door and use my pump and continue to feed my child breast milk. But for women working in a grocery store or on an hourly wage, they just didn't have that control. We knew that the battle was also about breaking down the barriers around breastfeeding—why it's hidden, but why it's important. We worked with David Jaacks, a designer with an architecture degree who worked at a fabrication plant. His sweet spot was designing tradeshow booths and kiosks in malls, which we combined with our brief to make this [Mamava] user-centered, and a canvas for graphics. That latter idea came directly from our design experience working on things like snowboards—thinking of them not as a piece of equipment but as a canvas to express style and to communicate.

DM—— This makes sense for a design born in Vermont, where snow sports are well established. Taking elements from existing design typologies follows a rich tradition within architectural history, where a previously unknown function emerges—for example, an electricity plant or factory—but there's not an architectural language to describe the nascent technology, so designers creatively borrow to house it.

CHRISTINE DODSON——Yes! And David had the expertise in fire safety; he's actually a fireman. We were introduced by a manufacturing and engineering association that connects companies looking for production capacity in the state of Vermont. It was really the perfect match.

DM—— What's one design detail of the pod that you obsessed over and that you feel you got really right? And what's something that you still feel you're trying to crack?

SM—— The shape of the pod answers both of those questions. We give David credit for the shape. Within the process of prototyping and initial sketches, a lot of what came out was "eh." It looked like a Porta-Potty, or the dimensions weren't quite right, or it seemed confusing because it looked like a phone booth. The fact that it looks like a breast—I would say we obsessed over that. Some of the more regularly shaped initial sketches and prototypes just didn't quite hit it. We wanted it to look like nothing anybody had seen before.

The shape is still a challenge because it doesn't work everywhere. When we were initially designing, it was really meant for high-impact locations that were our personal pain points—airports, convention centers. What materialized was that everywhere lactating people work or go to, they need lactation spaces, so we're evolving and providing different, smaller, more discreet kinds of spaces.

CD— For the inside, the consideration was around designing a space that didn't make the person using it feel like they were being shut away. It's a choice, not a necessity, to hide human lactation. We designed the roundness and wider side of the footprint of the unit with that in mind. With others—partners or toddlers—using the space simultaneously two interior benches were key. Material wise, we understood that the units need to be really easily cleaned, so we looked to designs for food stations. We had to design a space that works beautifully for users, but also for facilities purchasing it, and that meets code and is easy to assemble and disassemble. We decided against plumbing, even though running water would be useful for cleaning the pumps, because that limits where Mamavas can go, adds cost, and makes them less universally usable.

SM— Part of the design of these units is the mobile app that helps someone not only find a Mamava, but also adjust the environmenby changing the lighting for themselves or their baby, or changing the air flow, or connecting with other users online for moral support. Breastfeeding can be hard. So is design! We're constantly revising and perfecting the app.

DM— **Can you tell me about the conversations you've had around inclusive design?**

CD— What's interesting about the ADA model [the Mamava model designed for maximum accessibility, including wheelchair use] was that the only other benchmark for that unit was a toilet stall. And in a toilet stall a disabled person has to get out of their wheelchair to get onto the seat, hence the grab bars. But a person in a wheelchair using a Mamava probably wouldn't want or need to get out of their seat. So we needed to rethink that paradigm. As far as the brand itself, our logo is not incredibly feminine. It's called the "happy breasts" logo, and it's a gesture of positivity. Our brand name has *mama* in it, but the non-gender-specific mammary glands are what make breast milk. I can imagine a person who identifies as male and is lactating might enjoy using the unit, too. Some of our clients who choose to do custom graphics use earth mother or mom and baby imagery. For us, it's been about a bigger idea.

SM— Just the idea of having a dedicated space to breastfeed or use a breast pump is an acknowledgement and a celebration of something that is a very natural and expected human behavior.

BABY FORMULA——Food historians consider manufactured baby food a byproduct of the labor struggles and scientific innovations of the Industrial Revolution.[1] Baby formula, too, has commonly been understood in the context of the many changes that accompanied that revolution. Through effective marketing touting its near equivalency to breast milk, and as a result of changing employment patterns that saw more women working outside the home, formula was transformed from an emergency supplement to a staple.

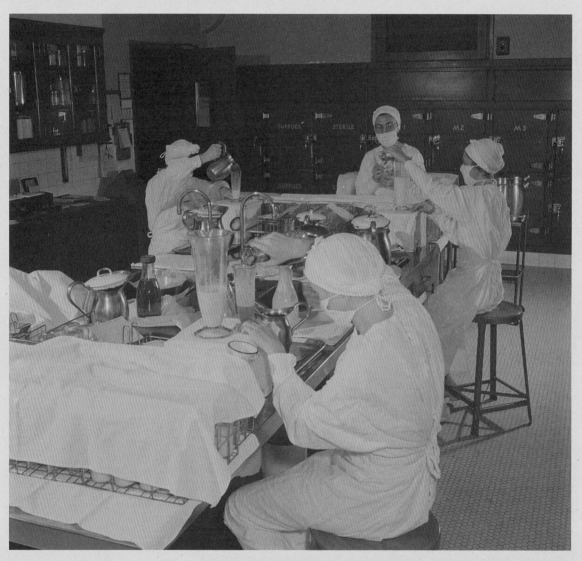

Student nurses prepare dozens of bottles for dozens of babies in a hospital's formula kitchen in 1942. Each set of bottles contains different amounts and is made up of various ingredients. Formula is made up once a day, and bottles are labeled and kept in the refrigerator until needed

Scientists spent decades trying to modify cow's milk to be more biologically similar to human milk and thus more digestible. Liebig's Soluble Food for Babies was the first commercial formula available in the United States, selling for a dollar a bottle in 1869.[2] Developed by the German chemist Justus von Liebig, the powdered formula—made of dried cow's milk, wheat flour, malt flour, and potassium bicarbonate—was designed to be mixed with heated cow's milk. Competitors quickly appeared: Mellin's Food for Infants and Invalids, Ridge's Food for Infants, and Nestlé's Milk. The latter required only water for dilution; priced at fifty cents a bottle beginning in the 1870s, it was the first completely artificial formula available in the US. With the drop in wet-nursing at the turn of the century, "percentage method" formulas, homemade mixtures of cow's milk, water, and cream (and later, evaporated milk), with honey or sugar added in ratios believed to approximate breast milk, were more common in Europe and the United States until the widespread acceptance of commercial formula in the 1950s. Advertisement-fueled anxiety prompted parents to turn to commercial formula out of fear that their own milk was inadequate either in quality or quantity.[3] By 1970 over 75 percent of American infants were either partially or fully formula fed.[4]

Since the passage of the Infant Formula Act in 1985, strict Food and Drug Administration regulations govern formula production in the US. Three companies dominate—Similac, Enfamil, and Gerber—with their products costing around fifteen dollars a can for the most basic.[5] With the rise of veganism and gluten-free dietary restrictions, many parents aren't satisfied with these American brands and, if armed with the means and resources, opt instead for two expensive and non-FDA approved European brands, HiPP and Holle. Social media groups, like the thirty-six thousand Facebook members of "UES Mommas," are abuzz with advice on how to access these black-market formulas (which, whether foreign or domestic, are sometimes stolen and sold illegally).[6]

As the composition and availability of commercial formula changed, so too did the feeding vessels. Before the invention of the modern nursing bottle, infants were fed milk of any kind with a spoon or drank from containers with a spout or narrowed end. In the 1840s, the American inventor Elijah Pratt patented his design for a rubber nipple, while the introduction of new materials like heat-resistant glass and plastic birthed new forms, such as the valved, double-ended Allenbury teat that allowed for easy cleaning and constant flow. By the 1940s, the US Patent Office had issued more than two hundred patents for bottle designs, including the iconic Pyrex bottle, made of heat-resistant glass and with a narrow neck, followed by a wide-neck version in the 1950s and plastic bottles in the 1970s.[7] Even as the forms have evolved, design goals such as milk flow and mimicking the breast's shape remain the same. Scientists and designers have also focused on addressing special feeding needs, for example, with the Haberman Feeder, developed for infants with impaired sucking ability due to a cleft lip and palate.

As with so many design histories, the story of formula is closely bound to foreign and domestic policy. When birth rates in industrial nations began to taper off in the 1960s, formula companies started marketing in non-industrialized countries, where poor sanitation led to increased mortality rates among infants fed formula prepared with contaminated water. Organized protests, including the famous 1977 Nestlé boycott in the US, called for an end to unethical marketing where products could not be safely used. In 2018, the "milk wars" reignited when the United States opposed a United Nations resolution asking governments to protect, promote, and support breastfeeding by restricting predatory promotion of infant formula.

Many factors contribute to how caregivers feed their children, but postpartum birthers' choices are frequently intensely scrutinized and emotionally charged. The ubiquitous "breast is best" adage encourages parents to breastfeed exclusively for six months, a guideline that researchers increasingly argue is flawed.[8] Breastfeeding advocates cite its contribution to the physical and emotional well-being of both mother and child, whereas formula proponents point to issues of body autonomy and the absence of the structural support necessary to reconcile work outside the home with breastfeeding. The Fed Is Best Foundation educates caregivers on the safest methods for breastfeeding, mixed feeding, and formula feeding. Its work reflects a postpartum birther's right to informed choice and body autonomy, and the right of infants to be fed irrespective of the parent's ability or choice to breastfeed.

Just as there is no "natural" or "best" birth, there is also no all-inclusive standard nutritional path for babies and families. Not all caregivers can make the "choice" to breastfeed, including adoptive, surrogate, and same-sex parents, and grandparents. There is one common denominator. All babies need to eat.

—**Juliana Rowen Barton**

1 See Harvey Levenstein, "'Best for Babies' or 'Preventable Infanticide'? The Controversy over Artificial Feeding of Infants in America, 1880–1920," *Journal of American History* 70, no. 1 (June 1983): 75–94, doi. org/10.2307/1890522.
2 Levenstein, *Revolution at the Table: The Transformation of the American Diet* (Berkeley: University of California Press, 1988), 122–23.
3 Jodi Vandenberg-Daves, *Modern Motherhood: An American History* (New Brunswick, NJ: Rutgers University Press, 2014), 83.
4 Stephanie J. Knaak, "Contextualizing Risk, Constructing Choice: Breastfeeding and Good Mothering in Risk Society," *Health, Risk & Society* 12 (2010): 198, doi.org/10.1080/13698571003789666.
5 Abbott Laboratories, maker of Similac, and Mead Johnson, maker of Enfamil, each control about 40 percent of the market. The Nestlé-owned brand Gerber holds a roughly 15-percent share.
6 Chris Pomorski, "The Baby-Formula Crime Ring," *New York Times* (The Money Issue), May 2, 2018, nytimes.com/.
7 Michael Schwab, "An Essay on the Social History of Infant Feeding," *Childhood* 3 (1996): 483.
8 A growing number of health care professionals, including the founders of the Fed Is Best Foundation, maintain that the "breast is best" doctrine ignores the real-world harm of promoting exclusive breastfeeding. For example, they point to the estimated 15 percent of birthing parents who don't produce enough milk, which can lead to dehydration, low blood pressure, hypoglycemia, and hypernatremia, possibly resulting in brain injury, or in rare cases, death. For more information, see fedisbest.org.

CARERS

CARERS Singing lullabies is care work. Changing diapers is care work. Being part of the so-called sandwich generation—simultaneously looking after both elders and infants—is care work. Care is taken for granted, undervalued, underpaid, unpaid. It is proclaimed as saintly, sung praises to, and shied away from all in the same breath. Care work is rooted in and yet often completely uproots blood and biology. It is the yearning for touch and the feeling of being touched beyond what is bearable. It is blissful. It is boring. Above all else, care is labor.

1—— Grandfather Tony and baby Cosima, 2017
2—— Amber Bracken's image of Nellie Nastapoka, age 85, with her four-month-old great-great-granddaughter Annie, who was born in the Inukjuak clinic, Inukjuak, Quebec, August 2020
3—— Jamel Shabazz's *Three Stages of Life*, taken in Hempstead, New York, 2002
4—— Deloris "Nunu" Hogan, founder of a daycare center, holding a young boy in Loira Limbal's documentary *Through the Night* (2020)
5—— Daniel and Alice, 2013
6—— A grandfather and his grandson in Pingyao, China, 2018. Photograph by Alex Huanfa Cheng
7—— A baby in loving hands, Costa Rica, 2000
8—— A found photograph of a woman of color watching over a young White child riding a tricycle, date unknown

**2   3
4
5   6   7**

NORLAND NANNY UNIFORM——Not all nannies wear uniforms. But not all nannies are Norland nannies. The fabled Norland College was founded in 1892 at Norland Place in London (it moved to the English city of Bath in 2003) to provide students with structured education and training in the care of infants and young children. The expertise of Norland's highly qualified and sought-after professionals is signaled through a distinctive and widely recognized uniform.

The institute was the brainchild of Emily Ward, a devotee of the early childhood education philosophies of the German kindergarten guru Friedrich Fröbel. Ward coined Norland's institutional motto, "love never faileth," and laid out a clear vision for the role of a nanny as one of empowerment and respect—for both herself and the families with whom she interacted:

> To the mother [it] means freedom from some of the most wearying anxiety that comes with the care of children, more leisure for her own recreation; pleasure in the company of an educated equal and the help which comes in working hand-in-hand with another bent on the same object.

> To the nurse it means a home where the ordinary domestic virtues of no special market value are appreciated—a position of confidence and trust, a healthful life, and above all, the sense that the character of a future generation is to a certain extent, in her hands.[1]

Ward instituted the Norland uniform to communicate the seriousness of her nannies' qualifications, which today include the professional degree BA (Hons) in Early Years Development and Learning and a prestigious Norland diploma. The uniform was a key aspect of professionalizing those taking on a role that then, as now, was often undervalued and easily dismissed.[2]

In its late nineteenth-century manifestation, the ensemble consisted of a dress in durable blue cotton appropriate for work, with an apron, detachable collar and cuffs, and a white cambric tie.

A contemporary Norland College nanny uniform featuring the iconic bowler hat

For formal occasions students wore a blue silk dress and a long cloak falling to six inches above the ground, as well as a bonnet (that protected them from the weather.[3]

The uniforms were initially supplied by the Debenham and Freebody store in Kensington, London, but in 1895 Norland established its own workrooms to produce them in-house, making alterations easier—and allowing for greater differentiation from the other uniform that had risen to public attention in the late nineteenth century, that of the nurse.[4] It is said that Emily Ward trimmed the bonnets herself in the early years of the institute, at her own house, until student numbers increased.

The original light gray color of the summer cloak and bonnet was found to fade too easily and was switched to brown in 1910. The bonnet was eventually replaced, with the headgear becoming in the 1960s the bowler hat still worn today. World War II put a stop to the use of blue dye (commandeered for the war effort), and the uniform transitioned to its current beige (topped off during the Blitz by a metal helmet bearing a capital N).

While the term nanny is used the world over to connote a dedicated carer based in a child's own home, Jonathan Gathorne-Hardy's The Rise and Fall of the British Nanny (1972) marks in the book's title what he believes to be its specific geographic origin (he calls it "the most remarkable and envied of all British institutions"). Though his claim is arguable, one of the most enduring depictions of the role is the magical London nanny portrayed in the

1964 Disney film Mary Poppins, adapted from Pamela Lyndon Travers's series of eight books.

Gathorne-Hardy's time-capsule text, based on almost three hundred correspondences with and recollections of British nannies, is a stark reminder of how intimately class was and still is bound to forms of domestic service. He cites a vivid description by a former nanny, Mrs. Wake, of the Victorian nanny working her way up from employment as a nursery maid at age twelve to become someone who managed a suite of servants and "wielded despotic power, to use benevolently or not according to her temperament," and goes on to describe the subsequent trend toward college-trained professionals in the twentieth century. Norland was at the forefront of this shift in more ways than one. Gathorne-Hardy notes the Norland insistence on zero tolerance for corporal punishment as entirely unique, an "enlightened view…amazing for the 1890s."[5]

Today, Norlanders are well-paid professionals, commanding an average starting salary of around £40,000, and are in demand immediately upon graduation by those who can afford them. Amelia, a class of 2021 Norland student (of Set 42, the "sets" being determined according to incoming year), speaks of "overwhelming pride" and a "sense of community and belonging" when she wears her uniform, along with a commitment to "uphold the prestigious standards of Norland."[6] This pride is unsurprising, given that the iconic shades-of-brown ensemble appears in public on Norlanders caring for, among others, the

offspring of British royals, making its wearers immediately recognizable as status symbols.[7]

The uniform's most recent redesign was in 2013. Students still wear formal attire for lectures and events, but now they also have a practical option (blue polo shirt, pullover, trousers, and white crested apron) for training and placements. Male-identifying students wear beige trousers, a white shirt, and a brown tie and blazer, both emblazoned with the Norland N. The college is developing unisex uniform options that will allow students to mix and match. Still, "socks should be dark and plain" and shoes "flat, brown lace up shoes (not light tan and not nubuck)." Name badges are required except when walking through Bath or traveling on public transport. Personal grooming is an extension of the uniform; hair must be worn above the shoulders, whether trimmed or in a bun. And—as with any other professionalized vocation—a code of conduct must be adhered to at all times when wearing Norland attire.

In a cultural landscape that fails to value care labor in all forms, the uniform fulfills many functions. Ultimately, though, it mediates what Katherine Holden describes, in her landmark study of singleness in England in the twentieth century (or nannies, whatever the truth to the contrary, are almost always idealized as single), as "the emotional costs of unmarried women's paid labor in bringing up other people's children…reconciling a relationship based…partly on financial gain and the workings of the labour market with its situation in the private sphere of the family."[8]

1   Holly Royce, "A Real-Life 'Mary Poppins' Manual Has Been Found," Metro (London), March 23, 2017, metro.co.uk.
2   This was also the moment that maternal care and maternal health in general were being professionalized, for example through the Midwives Act of 1902, which moved expertise from the purview of older married women who had experienced childbirth toward single, childless, college-trained women.
3   For further information on the history of the uniform, see Penelope Stokes, Norland: The Story of the First One Hundred Years, 1892–1992 (Bath, UK: Norland College, 1992).
4   For descriptions of the evolution of nanny attire in the later nine-teenth century, see Jonathon Gathorne-Hardy's The Rise and Fall of the British Nanny (London: Hodder and Stoughton, 1972), especially chapter 6, "The World of the Nanny," 170, 208.
5   Gathorne-Hardy, The Rise and Fall of the British Nanny, 178.
6   Norlanders share information on their daily activities on their blog, "Not Just Nanny Training," notjustnannytraining.blogspot.com.
7   Today, Norland graduates do not commonly wear their uniform while on the job (with the exception of royal nannies on public engagements, when extra security is always present) so as to avoid singling out their young charges as potential marks for kidnappers. Instead, the uniform is worn by approximately three hundred students while they complete their three years of study, and by around one hundred who graduate into their Newly Qualified Nanny twelvemonth practical placement each year. Tuition fees for Norland College in September 2020 were £14,990 a year.
8   Katherine Holden, The Shadow of Marriage: Singleness in England, 1914–60 (Manchester, UK: Manchester University Press, 2007), 209.

KRAAMZORG——Care practices for the immediate postpartum period—sometimes called the fourth trimester—may conjure thoughts of the Victorians, who employed a period of confinement after birth. Yet, such traditions predate the nineteenth century by a long stretch and are found across cultures. Most include aspects of physical and emotional care of the person who has just given birth, the newborn, and in some cases the family unit, too. Some are dependent on means and the privilege to take time to observe a postpartum period away from work or other duties, while other models are provided by the government or are part of the care work of an extended family. Sometimes this focus can be suffocating or overwhelming, as families adjust to their new identities and responsibilities, while for others this care is a lifeline.

European customs of "lying-in," Chinese practices of "sitting the month," and the Persian *chilla* (roughly translated as "quarantine") are all ways to focus on the health and well-being of new parent-baby dyads. Such periods vary in length, from a few days to several months. Universal to all is setting aside the time for a process of recovery postbirth that provides individualized support, care, love, time, and attention. Everyone should have this in abundance.[1]

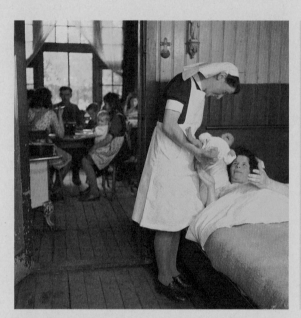

Created by Karen Kleiman and Molly McIntyre for The Postpartum Stress Center
postpartumstress.com

Kraamzorg *Kraamzorg* (postnatal maternity care) is the term given to the medical service provided to the postpartum person and their baby by a *kraamverzorgende* (maternity aide) in the Netherlands. Here, photographer Ad Windig captures a Dutch mother being attended to in the 1940s. Around 95 percent of birthing people there make use of this at-home service.[2] Every postpartum person is eligible for it, and insurance often covers some or all of the patient co-pay of €4.30 an hour. Between twenty-four and eighty hours of service is typically provided over a period of eight to ten days following delivery. Expectant parents register with a local *kraamzorg* service, and a *kraamverzorgende* meets with the family six to eight weeks before the baby is due. They discuss how they might offer a helping hand in a variety of ways during and after the birth, including guidance on feeding, bathing, recognizing the baby's needs, cleaning the home, and preparing food. The *kraamzorg* care model is available to all postpartum parents in the Netherlands, relieving some perinatal inequalities experienced as a result of socioeconomic and identity barriers.[3]

Postpartum Stress Center When asked how they are, postpartum people in distress often say, "fine." After all, we believe they feel joyful and content, and are delighted at all times. Our culture, which perpetuates the myth of the perfect mother, doesn't support disclosure of the deep inner turmoil that pierces the soul of a newly postpartum person trying to make sense of their strong and conflicting emotions.

At the Postpartum Stress Center, we define authentic suffering as that which is obscured by what they want us to know and what they will let us see. It's the pain they conceal. It's the terror that immobilizes them and keeps them up at night. It's what's in their suicide note when loved ones cry out that "there were no warning signs." Loved ones don't see it. Friends don't see it. As therapists, we might not see authentic suffering at first—especially if they don't want us to—but our clinical imperative is to find it and connect with it. When we sit with authentic suffering and hold their profound grief with expertise and intention, healing begins.

—**Karen Kleiman**, author of *The Art of Holding in Therapy* (2017) and cofounder of the Postpartum Stress Center in Philadelphia. Illustration by Molly McIntyre for Karen Kleiman's book *Good Moms Have Scary Thoughts* (2019).

I have felt happy:
- ☐ Yes, all the time
- ☒ Yes, most of the time
- ☐ No, not very often
- ☐ No, not at all

In the past 7 days:

1. I have been able to laugh and see the funny side of things
   - ☐ As much as I always could
   - ☐ Not quite so much now
   - ☐ Definitely not so much now
   - ☐ Not at all

2. I have looked forward with enjoyment to things
   - ☐ As much as I ever did
   - ☐ Rather less than I used to
   - ☐ Definitely less than I used to
   - ☐ Hardly at all

*3. I have blamed myself unnecessarily when things went wrong
   - ☐ Yes, most of the time
   - ☐ Yes, some of the time
   - ☐ Not very often
   - ☐ No, never

4. I have been anxious or worried for no good reason
   - ☐ No, not at all
   - ☐ Hardly ever
   - ☐ Yes, sometimes
   - ☐ Yes, very often

*5 I have felt scared or panicky for no very good reason
   - ☐ Yes, quite a lot
   - ☐ Yes, sometimes
   - ☐ No, not much
   - ☐ No, not at all

Postpartum Depression Diagnostic Tools   Ranging from "baby blues" to severe psychosis, postnatal mental distress is "the most common complication of childbearing" and often goes undiagnosed or is underdiagnosed due to the still-taboo nature of mental illness as well as stereotypical expectations of joyous maternity.[4] The Edinburgh Postnatal Depression Scale (EPDS), a standardized screening tool for postpartum depression, was designed by John L. Cox (a transcultural and social psychiatrist), Jenifer Holden (a psychologist and health visitor), and Ruth Sagovsky (a part-time psychiatry trainee) in Scotland in 1987.[5] Now used worldwide in over sixty languages, its ten straightforward questions set the threshold for clinical intervention, though its designers caution that the tool should never be used in isolation, without reflection on the patient's wider social support.[6]

La Cuarentena   My grandma gave birth to nineteen children. I asked her to share her pregnancy and postpartum wisdom; we talked about *La Cuarentena*. Traditionally in Mexico, a person has a forty-day recovery period after giving birth. Whenever one of my *tías* [aunts] had a baby, my grandma would visit her daily to make her food, clean her house, and hold the baby while mama took a nap. Dads are asked to sleep in a different room during these forty days. I still get judged because I didn't observe the *cuarentena* after I had my first child here in the United States. I also struggle with how sexist this tradition can be.

In my family the *cuarentena* diet consists of bland foods: plain oatmeal in the morning, chicken soup in the afternoon, and corn *atole* with a piece of bread at night. These foods are meant to nourish the mom, help heal her body, and boost her milk supply. All my *tías* complained about the food. Giving bland food to a Mexican might be the meanest thing you can do. My *abuelita*'s secret weapon was a *faja* [see p. 281]. That and taking care of her diet was her way of regaining control over her body.

—**Dr. Maricela Becerra**, professor of Mexican literature and culture

—POSTPARTUM

Postpartum Lactation Visit   Before offering services and support, I aim to build a rapport and help the client feel safe to share. Opening conversations can include asking about mom's day, her birth experience, and her motherhood journey so far. Recently, I met with a new mom who expressed challenges in being a recent immigrant and a need for help. After a little chat and some smiles, I explained my role and my availability for questions and future home visits. Mom was doing an amazing job breastfeeding, but had doubts about her ability to produce enough milk for her sweet baby girl. I explained the lactation as a supply-and-demand process and invited mom to latch the baby so I could observe and offer feedback. The home visit ended with encouragement to enjoy naps as she could and walks in the neighborhood to soak in the sun. Motherhood called me to this work. My own traumatic birth experience and interactions with obstetric care as a Black woman opened my eyes to systemic challenges in the United States concerning maternal health, which are often rooted in racism. I aim to educate families and be a voice for maternal and reproductive justice in society.

—**Porsche M. Holland**, M.S., doula and breastfeeding peer counselor, Maternity Care Coalition

Milk Bank   In my research, I continually see the ways in which groups of women convene to help each other during the post-partum period, especially when it comes to the myriad ways that humans feed infants. In the early twentieth century highly trained nurses facilitated the collection of human milk and administered it to ailing infants on a ship off Boston called the Floating Hospital for Children. Meanwhile, in New York, women in poverty could earn a living selling their milk, hand-expressing it inside the Mothers' Milk Bureau, known colloquially as a human dairy. Today, the Sirens Women's Motorcycle Club delivers donated milk to premature infants throughout the city, joyfully moving milk on bikes through the boroughs in partnership with the New York Milk Bank. In each of these case studies, I see systems of oppression that imperil birthing people and babies who are already vulnerable due to race, gender, immigration status, and socioeconomics. But I also see networks of people who collectively support each other and get milk where it needs to go. I see not just people's love for their own babies, but their dedication to one another, a dedication that is courageous, protective, adaptive, and persistent.

—**Hannah Ryan**, scholar of human milk and lactation in visual culture

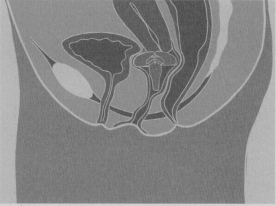

Nourishment   Food is always medicine, but this is especially true when people are healing. For postpartum people, diet is extremely important, and this is reflected in many models of postpartum care. The Los Angeles–based author Heng Ou used her own experience of *zuo yuezi*, the Chinese tradition of "sitting the month," to encourage other postpartum people to embrace the first forty days after giving birth as an essential period of rest and recovery.[7] The cookbook *From Mothers to Mothers*, published in 2017 by the Postpartum Nutrition Folklore Project at the University of California, Berkeley, includes recipes for slow-cooked pig's feet, seaweed soup with beef, and other postpartum specialties from Chinese, Vietnamese, Cambodian, Hmong, Filipino, and Korean traditions.[8] Recurrent is a concern for a balance between "hot" and "cold" food, a framework that springs from ancient sources, including various Indigneous and ayurvedic traditions.[9]

Pelvic Prolapse   Pelvic organ prolapse is a condition caused by a weakening of the pelvic floor muscles that allows the pelvic organs to descend into the vaginal canal. In extreme cases, the uterus may descend through the vagina and protrude outside the body. Prolapse affects a staggering 50 percent of people with vaginas over the age of fifty, and while it's not life threatening, it can be life altering. Despite its prevalence, most people don't hear about prolapse until their diagnosis. Today's nonsurgical treatment option is a pessary, a device inserted into the vaginal canal to support the descending organs. Historical pessaries have included pomegranates and balls of wool, but today's pessaries are made from silicone. Their fixed and rigid design can make them difficult and painful for people to insert and remove independently. When we first learned about pessaries, we had no doubt that they could and should be better, and we set out to design one that foregrounded comfort and addressed the lifestyle impacts of prolapse. By collapsing to half its diameter for insertion and removal, Reia's silicone pessary is easier to put in for exercise or take out for sex or sleeping. An approachable design gives its users confidence.

——**Meegan Daigler**, cofounder of Reia

Kimpaturin My mom uttered *kimpaturin*, a Yiddish word for a woman who has just given birth, with awe and respect. If someone in the community recently gave birth, I would find my mom arranging meals or cleaning help for the newest *kimpurtin*. And then there was the *kimpaturin* home where my mother would stay for a week after each baby to recover, for her a nonnegotiable part of giving birth.

With each of my births, my mom would gently suggest that I do the same. I live far away from family, and I experienced postpartum anxiety after some of my births, which left me emotionally and physically depleted. But as daughters often do, I dismissed Mom's suggestion. I thought it was ancient—after all, mom did it! I figured if everyone else managed, I could too. I was gravely mistaken. *Everyone else does not manage.* Postpartum depression is real and widely felt.

Mom was finally successful in convincing me to let go of my trepidations. I felt like a child going to overnight camp for the first time. A beautiful state-of-the-art building run by an Orthodox Jewish organization greeted us near Monsey, New York. Two staff members whisked my suitcases to my private room while a nurse came to take the baby to the nursery. Three nutritious five-star meals were served daily. The baby nursery was looked after by certified nurses around the clock. In this place of nurturing, acceptance, and recuperation, I felt human again. I finally understood my mother. My only regret was that I had waited so long.

—**Devorah Leah Marrus**, Chassidic feminist and mom of five

1 The American College of Obstetricians and Gynecologists highlight that "postpartum care should become an ongoing process, rather than a single encounter, with services and support tailored to each woman's individual needs" (a difficult prospect in a country without a universal family leave policy). See "Optimizing Postpartum Care," *ACOG Committee Opinion* 736 (May 2018), acog.org.
2 In 2015, 13.1 percent of all births in the Netherlands were home births.
3 J. Lagendijk et al., "Client-Tailored Maternity Care to Increase Maternal Empowerment: Cluster Randomized Controlled Trial Protocol; The Healthy Pregnancy 4 All-2 Program," *BMC Pregnancy and Childbirth* 19, no. 4 (January 3, 2019), doi.org/10.1186/s12884-018-2155-9.
4 Katherine L. Wisner, Barbara L. Parry, and Catherine M. Piontek, "Postpartum Depression," *New England Journal of Medicine* 347, no. 3 (July 18, 2002): 194–99, doi.org/10.1056/NEJMcp-011542.
5 John Cox, "Use and Misuse of the Edinburgh Postnatal Depression Scale (EPDS): A Ten Point 'Survival Analysis,'" *Archives of Women's Mental Health* 20 (2017): 789–90, doi.org/10.1007/s00737-017-0789-7.
6 Cox reports that clinicians should be careful using the tool, as "it has no items that tap directly the family relationships, is in no sense a check list of depressive symptoms, and converts a mood state into a numerical score"; Cox, "Use and Misuse of the Edinburgh Postnatal Depression Scale (EPDS)."
7 Written with Amely Greeven and Marisa Belger.
8 Published by the Asian American Pacific Islander Health Research Group at the University of California, Berkeley.
9 Cindy-Lee Dennis et al., "Traditional Postpartum Practices and Rituals: A Qualitative Systematic Review," *Women's Health* 3, no. 4 (2007): 487–502, doi.org/10.2217/1745505 7.3.4.487. Another common theme in postpartum food traditions is the concept of a "food train," in which extended kin bring nourishment to new parents, whether through a spreadsheet sign-up or word of mouth.

BABY CARRYING

BABY CARRYING Designs for baby carrying have precedents in every corner of the globe, including in the tied textiles of the African continent, Plains Indian cradleboards, and, in parts of Asia, special cold-weather carrier covers embroidered with motifs that are meant to assure a child's good fortune.

1—— A grandmother carrying her infant granddaughter in a back sling harness, Thailand, 2014

2—— A young street vendor with her baby in a *rebozo*, Oaxaca, Mexico, 2014

3——Ann Moore, inventor of the Snugli, carrying her daughter, Mandela, on her back during the Selma to Montgomery civil rights march, Alabama, March 1965

4——Members of the Mexican Zapatista Army of National Liberation (EZLN) in the community of La Garrucha, Chiapas, Mexico, 2005

5——A nineteen-month-old in a baby carrier, 2017

6——The reversible ring sling, 2012

7——A found photograph of a baby carried on a woman's back in a tied shawl, date unknown

2 3 4
5 6

FAJA——Luz Argueta-Vogel's practice is founded on a radically feminist reproductive health care model that is deeply rooted in her childhood experiences in El Salvador and her Indigenous heritage in Central America. After completing rigorous clinical training at Maternidad La Luz in El Paso, Texas, and attending home births in San Francisco, Luz went on to practice midwifery in Guatemala before returning to the Bay Area to serve home-birthing families there.

DESIGNING MOTHERHOOD——To begin, can you give us a sense of what *la Cerrada* is and where it comes from?

LUZ ARGUETA-VOGEL——*La Cerrada* means "closing." It originates in Spanish-speaking Latinx and Indigenous cultures of the Americas. But the ritual is syncretic, meaning it's a blend of different religions, cultures, and philosophies.

It's a ceremony that comes after *la Cuarentena*—a forty-day period when someone who has given birth goes into a state of rest, repose, and seclusion. The ceremony represents the symbolic closing after birth, and it prepares the postpartum person to reengage with the rest of the world. We time it for when the cervix is closed again after a birth. After the bleeding has stopped, there's no time limit to perform the ceremony. It can take place at the six-week mark, but if someone had a baby six months, six years, sixty years ago, and they still want closure and closing, the time is always right. It's never too late to have a closing ceremony.

DM—— Can you tell us a bit about how you perform *la Cerrada*?

LAV—— Just like everything I do as a midwife, there's form and structure, but the practice is also tailored to individuals and their families. And I like for *la Cerrada* to be a collaborative, co-creative process. After someone gives birth, they know what they're capable of, and it can be a really empowering time. Generally, the person feels pretty excited to make *la Cerrada* significant to them. They might choose that it be very intimate, or they can include their community and give a trusted circle an opportunity to speak, give affirmation, and acknowledge the mother.

Traditionally, a plant bath would be offered inside a Mesoamerican-style sweat lodge, or *temazcal*, which might be of adobe made from mud and wood or could be cement as well. In urban settings, we use a bathtub or shower. We also incorporate a lot of what's growing locally. The idea is to provide a physical and spiritual cleansing, and it's also about being tender to this person who has just performed a huge feat. It's about honoring them—mothering the mother. It's a way of saying, "Your body is sacred. And, here, allow me to care for you."

DM—— The warmth and cleansing aspect of water sounds so right.

LAV—— The idea is they're releasing and cleansing. It's the act of sweating things out. The use of steam—of fire and water together—is something we see around the world. It's used like prayer in action, a way of healing and cleansing the body.

DM—— Another aspect of the ceremony that we see across cultures is the act of binding one's abdomen after having a baby. There's the Malaysian *bengkung*, the Japanese *sarashi*, and in this case faja, which comes from the Spanish word for "wrap." So what is the faja, and how is it used?

LAV—— Traditionally, the faja is a rebozo, but it doesn't have to be. There are different versions of faja depending on things like weather patterns and weaving traditions, but in general the faja is a tightly woven fabric made from cotton. After the bath, I lay out the faja on the floor, and the postpartum person lays down on it. The top part is just above the iliac crest [or hip bones] and below the buttocks, and I stand above the person and hold the faja on either end and move back and forth to sift the person's pelvis. Afterward I'll do a uterine massage and make sure the uterus is centered with the fascia, and I give it a lot of love. And then I tie the faja. There's such a huge adjustment and rearrangement of internal organs that occurs immediately at birth, so the faja is worn while the postpartum person heals and regains strength and tone. It also provides a kind of psychic protection. It's an extension of support at a time when there's so much vulnerability. Also the faja just feels really good.

DM— **Can faja be used anytime the cervical opening is releasing blood? Like during your period or after a miscarriage?**

LAV— Absolutely. Faja can be used anytime the cervix is open and the uterus is bleeding. A design like faja enhances the body's own innate intelligence. It helps with cramps, and it creates subtle postural shifts, which can improve the way that we relate to bleeding. It affects how we sit, how we move, how we're aware of our bodies. And all of that can really improve the experience of menses or being postpartum. Because those are vulnerable times. And having a faja can really help engage our muscles and remind us to sit and move in ergonomic ways.

DM— **I think it's really interesting that what started as a traditional design for postpartum healing has transformed into a very extreme girdle in today's Latinx fashion market. This version of the faja is made from really unforgiving materials like vinyl and latex, and the idea is to squeeze it really tight around the hips and abdomen. It seems related to the conversation around "getting your body back" after having a baby.**

LAV— I think *faja* is a word that's used for a lot of things. What you're describing feels like an extension of all the other ways that postpartum bodies are pressured to look a certain way. It's a really extreme reappropriation of Indigenous traditions surrounding the postpartum period.

DM— **I think where faja differs from all the talk around "getting your body back" is that this kind of practice isn't really about going back to what existed before. I love that *la Cerrada* and faja are a way of helping people to move through new thresholds. The ceremony is about welcoming this new phase of life and honoring and caring for the new body that comes along with that. It's also a kind of induction into the community of motherhood.**

LAV— Hearing you say that brings a smile to my face. I really love seeing how these adults are able to receive care and feel relaxed at a time where they're really asked to care so intensely for someone else. Once we unwrap the faja, that's really the completion of *la Cerrada*. It's like the person is coming out of their cocoon. They're now ready to rejoin the rest of the world.

PETIT PLI——While the numbers on growth charts—both the median line and its major and minor curves—differ depending on the source and the historical moment, it is generally acknowledged that infants and children grow right before one's eyes. Little wonder that Dr. Spock (see p. 237) advised new parents to bypass the newborn sizes and purchase in the one-year-old range from the outset.

The Petit Pli two-piece, designed by UK-based Ryan Mario Yasin, which won the prestigious James Dyson Award in 2017

The Mothercraft Manual, first published in 1917, comes with a pull-out centerfold chart that suggests that the average weight gain in the first year of life more than triples (from 7.5 to 22 lbs.), while a general expectation is that babies grow in height by a half inch each month in their first year. Head circumference is also a standard measure of growth in the early years, expanding by up to three-quarters of an inch per month in a baby's first year.[1] The leaps and plateaus of infant and child growth are described as "pulsatile," with bigger growth spurts in height correlating to the spring and summer months.[2]

An aeronautical engineer by training, Ryan Mario Yasin founded his company, Petit Pli, in order that design might accommodate this reality. His odyssey began when the clothes he bought as a gift for his nephew were outgrown before they reached him. To his surprise, Yasin found that few children's garments are made to grow with their wearers, and so he resolved to design his own. Petit Pli is dedicated to styling the smallest among us, providing an outfitting solution that adapts to their rapid development.

During all this maturation, the clothing that babies and young children wear stretches, rubs, and pulls with their expanding repertoire of movements and acts as an absorbent canvas for myriad substances, including food, drink, and body fluids. Within the first three years of our lives we learn to crawl, stand, and walk; along the way our clothing helps to soften the impact of many an abrupt tumble. Yasin calls children "tiny athletes," and his apt description reflects an approach to outfitting that prioritizes the technical capabilities of garments—rather than, as is so often the case, color or surface decoration.

The results, which debuted in 2017, fall into the realm of the early twentieth-century designer Mario Fortuny's famous pleated silk gowns and echo the work of the contemporary Japanese fashion designer and iconoclast Issey Miyake, known for his 1990s Pleats Please collection. Petit Pli garments are expandable, accommodating growth from the early months of life through three years of age. The pleated tops and bottoms enlarge bidirectionally—stretching up to seven sizes—and spring back into their compacted shape when off the body.

Scooting, smearing, and stretching are baseline expectations. Tearing and staining are anticipated. The proprietary Petit Pli textile is thus formulated as a windproof and waterproof overlayer that resists the many tests it is subjected to. Yasin is also highly aware of the life cycle of the textile's base components, as well as its inevitable wear-and-tear cycle once out in the world. It is a mono-fiber, meaning that it doesn't have to be separated into component fibers for recycling, and it is also made from recycled fiber in the first place. No one (repeat, no one) needs extra things to do while supervising small humans, and so the clothing is machine washable, lightweight, requires no ironing, and takes up minimal space when folded.

In creating garments that grow along with their wearers, and that are made from a low-waste, technically robust textile, Yasin has established a model that encourages people to buy fewer, better-quality things and to think sustainably about clothing choices. A set retails for £130 (about $160 at the time of writing), which can be viewed either as a long-term investment, to be filed under the old adage about being "too poor to buy cheap shoes," or as a pretty penny to pay for clothing for those who are not yet, in many cases, able to speak for let alone dress themselves. You decide.

Adaptable clothing has historical precedents. Just as everyday garments were—and still are (see, for example, the Sari, p. 107)—adjusted to create maternity and nursing wear, children's clothing has often been modifiable, especially before fast fashion became the norm. Elasticized waistbands accommodate changing girth; belts and shoe straps can be buckled and velcroed in successive expansions; and adjustable straps on overalls elongate with the wearer's torso to increase the clothing's lifespan over several growth spurts. Ties on garments can be easily loosened and are found on historical infant clothing of various kinds.

The now-defunct garment company Vanta, based in Newton, Massachusetts, made many styles for children, including, in the 1930s, a well-advertised double-breasted vest that tied at the sides and could be let out as the child grew. (A similar feature was incorporated into the earliest Snugli baby carriers in the late 1960s, which came pre-stitched with instructions for parents to cut the threads as their little ones grew.) Historically, clothing for very young children has often lacked sex distinction, a trait that Petit Pli, with its color palette of warm beige, blues, greens, and black and its plain, utilitarian cut, also embraces (see Gender Reveal, p. 153, for more on "traditional" pink-blue color choices).

Petit Pli designs also upend the notion that there is any such thing as standard growth—and therefore standard sizes. Every child grows at their own pace. Yasin's approach discards outdated notions of the "right" patterns of growth and bypasses confusing sizing that diverges wildly between brands, clothing types, and geographic regions. Little wonder Petit Pli won the 2017 James Dyson Award, an international design honor that celebrates, encourages, and inspires designers of new problem-solving concepts. The first generation of its users are currently out in the world tugging, pulling, and stretching their clothes in the ultimate real-life test drive.

1   Data Table of Infant Head Circumference-for-Age Charts, National Center for Health Statistics, Centers for Disease Control and Prevention, cdc.gov.
2   Stine-Mathilde Dalskov et al., "Seasonal Variations in Growth and Body Composition of 8–11-y-old Danish Children," Pediatric Research 79 (February 2016): 358–63, doi.org/10.1038/pr.2015.206.

ÄITIYSPAKKAUS: THE FINNISH BABY BOX——In Finland between the two world wars, despite massive economic obstacles, modernist designers and social reformers committed themselves to building a new society, and they looked at designs made for children and their parents as a means for reform.[1] A new generation of community-minded government officials worked hand in hand with designers to address the urgent social and economic concerns of Finnish citizens. They created schools, health centers, clothing, books, and playthings ripe with possibility and the energy of social change.

While some design initiatives were large-scale or complex, others were simple, with a straightforward commitment to improving the health of children and those who birthed them. In 1938, the Finnish Social Welfare Committee introduced a novel public health intervention: the *äitiyspakkaus*, a box full of baby clothes and baby-care items designed to be distributed to low-income pregnant people in each of Finland's municipalities.[2] The concept grew out of a desperate situation. In the late 1930s, Finland's birth rate was in decline, and babies were dying at alarming rates: almost one in ten children died during their first year of life. Whereas initially about two-thirds of expectant people in Finland received the grant (which came in the form of cash or the box), by 1949 the benefit was available to all expectant families, including adoptive parents.

Äitiyspakkaus arrives about six weeks before a baby's due date, right around the time that a pregnant person might begin their parental leave. (Unsurprisingly, parental leave in Finland is also among the world's most generous, with nearly seven months granted to each parent, and extra allowances for single parents.) Understood as a rite of passage among Finnish parents, the box is, in a way, part of growing into parenthood.[3] The specific contents change every year, but the box always includes an assortment of useful, gender-neutral items. Because of the frigid climate there are things like snowsuits, insulated booties, wool caps and suits, and balaclavas. There are rompers, playsuits, onesies, leggings, mittens, socks, and tights, as well

A woman and two children unpacking an *Äitiyspakkaus* at home in Finland, 1949

as diapers, blankets, towels, a thermometer, picture books, and a hairbrush. There are also items for the parents: sanitary towels, nursing pads, nipple cream, condoms, and lubricant. With a set of sheets and a mattress at the bottom, the box itself even functions as baby's first bassinet and has been cited as a contributing factor in Finland's low rate of sudden infant death syndrome, or SIDS.[4] The changes in the box's contents also reflect shifts in history and culture. During World War II, paper replaced fabric for items such as swaddling wraps. In 2006, cloth diapers were reintroduced to reflect a commitment to environmental sustainability, and the baby bottle was left out to encourage breastfeeding.

The plan worked: the infant mortality rate in Finland is now among the world's lowest, having gone from 0.65 percent in 1935 to 0.025 percent today.[5] In 1944, a few years after *äitiyspakkaus* was introduced, Finland took the further step of creating neighborhood-based, free health care services for every pregnant person and all children under the age of seven.[6] The year the clinics began, only 31 percent of pregnant people were receiving prenatal care. The following year the figure jumped to 86 percent.[7] Today, over 99.5 percent of childbearing families in Finland use the clinics.[8] As a result of the high-quality care provided, Finland has one of the lowest infant mortality rates in the world, and its perinatal and maternity mortality rates are also among the lowest.[9]

Ulla Huopaniemi-Sirén, a Helsinki resident, book editor, and mother of three children, was placed in an *äitiyspakkaus* as her first bed when she was a baby in 1969. She recalls them as "something positively Finnish which promotes equality and safety among Finnish children.... I do feel that somehow it affects us mentally, too—[the box] is something that mothers-to-be talk about, compare their feelings about, even complain about. Mothers offer feedback on the box and are thus part of developing it. And the fact that it is available to every family, and not denied to people with higher income, is great. I think it can be compared to free lunches at schools from first to twelfth grade in Finland. These things are taken for granted in our society."[10]

The Finnish baby box is now internationally renowned, and the concept has been adopted and modified in culturally appropriate ways in places across the world, including in Japan, New Zealand, Scotland, Ukraine, Canada, Mexico, and disadvantaged areas in the United States. In many of these places the baby boxes are provided to specific populations or to those with lower incomes (such as New Zealand's Māori, or low-income pregnant people in certain Mexican states), while in others the box is given in exchange for completing safe-sleep workshops (as in Alabama, Ohio, and New Jersey). In other places, commerce has stepped in. There are now a number of companies that sell bespoke maternity boxes that can be shipped internationally, many of which signal Finnish culture by featuring Tove Jansson's classic Finnish Moomins characters on the box's exterior.

Finland has a strong tradition of family-centric policies, including government-issued health care, generous parental leave, free education for all, and an excellent general standard of living—perhaps not coincidentally, all factors that improve perinatal, postpartum, and infant health. Sanna Marin, the thirty-four-year-old, newly elected Finnish Prime Minister, is continuing this tradition, rethinking the hours within a workweek so families can spend more time together, and redefining paternity leave so it can better "promote 'well-being and gender equality.'"[11] Many of these conversations can be traced back to the simple cardboard box that has helped define Finnish parenthood. But it was never just about the box. *Äitiyspakkaus* is emblematic of a wider system that cares deeply about the health and well-being of its people, beginning with young children and their families.

1   Juliet Kinchin and Aidan O'Connor, *Century of the Child* (New York: Museum of Modern Art, 2012), 89.
2   In 1937 the Maternity Grants Act was passed in an effort to improve access to public health services for low-income mothers and their babies. Prior to the introduction of *äitiyspakkaus* in 1938, the grant came in the form of money: 450 Finnish markka for each newborn. Over the course of its existence the maternity grant has been funded through different parts of the government—first by the National Board of Social Welfare, and currently by Kela (the Finnish Social Insurance Institution).
3   The box is overwhelmingly popular, with 95 percent of mothers choosing the box over the cash grant offered by the government as an alternative.
4   Torleiv Ole Rognum et al., "A Scandinavian Perspective," in *SIDS Sudden Infant and Early Childhood Death: The Past, the Present, and the Future*, ed. Jhodie R. Duncan and Roger W. Byard (Adelaide, Australia: University of Adelaide Press, 2018), chap. 20, ncbi.nlm.nih. gov/books/NBK513379/.
5   See UNICEF Data: Monitoring the Situation of Children and Women, Finland, data.unicef.org/ country/fin.
6   To this day, pregnant people register for the *äitiyspakkaus* at the same place where they receive their prenatal care.
7   Elizabeth Cassin, "Do Baby Boxes Really Save Lives?," *BBC Magazine*, March 25, 2017, bbc.com.
8   Miia Tuominen et al., "A Comparison of Medical Birth Register Outcomes between Maternity Health Clinics and Integrated Maternity and Child Health Clinics in Southwest Finland," *International Journal of Integrated Care* 16, no. 3 (2016): 1, doi.org/10.5334/ ijic.2024.
9   See Finnish Institute for Health and Welfare, Helsinki: Perinatal Statistics: Parturients, Deliveries, and Newborns 2014, urn.fi; and UNICEF Data: Monitoring the Situation of Children and Women, Finland.
10   Ulla Huopaniemi-Sirén, Helsinki, interview with Amber Winick, New York, February 3, 2020.
11   The quote comes from a tweet reproduced in Kate Ng, "Finland to Give Fathers Same Parental Leave as Mothers," *Independent*, February 6, 2020, independent.co.uk.

BABY MONITOR——On February 27, 1932, Charles Lindbergh Jr., the twenty-month-old son of aviators Anne Morrow Lindbergh and Charles Lindbergh, was taken from his crib and carried out an upstairs window in his New Jersey home while his parents sat, unaware, by the living room fire. In the wake of this public tragedy, Eugene McDonald, president of the Zenith Radio Corporation, crafted a prototype that would help ease the anxieties of his own growing family.

Isamu Noguchi designed the *Radio Nurse* baby monitor, made of Bakelite, for Zenith Radio Co. in 1937. Courtesy of the Metropolitan Museum of Art, New York; Gift of John C. Waddell

—POSTPARTUM

Using a microphone, speaker, and radio, McDonald fashioned a device that transported the sounds of the room where his newborn daughter slept to a portable speaker, enabling caregivers to listen in from any room. In 1937, McDonald tasked the Japanese American designer Isamu Noguchi to design the device's casing. This was Noguchi's first major design commission, one he called "my only strictly industrial design" (he would later become known for bringing sculptural principals into daily life).[1] The resulting Zenith Radio Nurse was a streamlined, anthropomorphic form whose figurative curves and interlocking shapes combined inspiration from a Japanese kendo mask and a nurse's wimple.[2] In 1938, the Whitney Museum of American Art in New York exhibited the design, which *Time* magazine, in a review of the annual exhibition, named "Most exotic," with its "grilled bakelite face—prettier as a radio than as a nurse."[3]

The Radio Nurse was too expensive for most families (it sold for $29.95 in 1938, the equivalent of over $500 today), but later incarnations of baby monitors went on to become standard household items in many countries throughout the world. By bringing the sounds (and later sights) of a child's space into a separate adult setting, monitors profoundly impacted the way we conceptualize and occupy domestic space. In the United States, as early as 1890 it was advised that a baby should sleep separately; by 1950 many who could afford it arranged their homes to accommodate children sleeping on their own.[4] The baby monitor, though considered a luxury item well into the 1970s, was part of a major shift in the way many nuclear families live.

This sonic bridging of rooms did more than just change our homes; it revolutionized the way we care for babies.[5] Babies' sleep habits and how we interpret the sounds of their cries have long been hot button issues, constantly redefined in philosophical, historical, psychological, and cultural terms. A review of infant-care pamphlets published by the US Children's Bureau shows that, between 1920 and 1940, mothers were warned not to pick up a crying baby lest he learn "that crying will get him what he wants, sufficient to make a spoiled, fussy baby, and a household tyrant whose continual demands make a slave of the mother."[6] But in 1946 Dr. Spock's best-selling *The Common Sense Book of Baby and Child Care* encouraged parents to trust themselves when it came to sleep and crying (see p. 237). And in 1972 Dr. Mary Ainsworth, a developmental psychologist, argued on the basis of her research that responding to a crying baby did not spoil a child, but rather reduced crying in the future.[7] Designed specifically to amplify cries, baby monitors helped to further the notion that a cry was a signal that must be noticed immediately and responded to promptly.

Of course, the design also fueled the idea that babies *should* be closely monitored. In the 1990s several television news stations ran stories of caregiver misconduct caught on video monitors, paving the way for so-called nanny-cams.[8] Still, most video monitors are used in connection with a child's sleep routines. Infrared LEDs have made it possible to see ghostly nighttime visions of babies with glowing cat eyes. Sleeping babies are now also streamed via Wi-Fi onto smartphones and computers.

When the first patent for a breath-monitoring device was filed in 1979, it was indicative of a larger trend toward diagnostic monitoring that would gain momentum in the following decades.[9] In the 1980s and 1990s, some monitors were sold with the intention of reducing sudden infant death syndrome (SIDS); although epidemiological studies showed that these devices had no effect on the incidence of SIDS, this didn't stop marketers from making the suggestion.[10] Today's generation of wearable, connected devices gathers data on everything from sleeping patterns and the position of babies (on their stomachs or backs) to breathing rates, skin temperature, room temperature, and even, in some cases, blood-oxygen levels and heart rates. The "internet of toddlers" now also includes smart onesies, diapers that detect urinary tract infections, and pacifiers that warn of elevated temperatures.[11]

Certainly, many people live comfortably without monitors, while others see them as a necessary tool.[12] But whether they are considered reassuring, liberating, or just another thing to worry about, their history is telling. From audio to detect an intruder, to footage of our babies behind closed doors, to smart socks that sound an alarm at a fluctuating heartbeat, the baby monitor has revealed many caregivers' darkest fears and most intimate habits. While we keep watchful eyes (or ears) on our monitors, the strong presence of love, culture, and instinct is eternally just beyond the frame.

1   Joanna Banham, ed., *Encyclopedia of Interior Design* (New York: Routledge, 1997), 886.
2   Modern and cool looking, the Radio Nurse is one of the earliest examples of the power of alluring casing design for consumer electronics.
3   "Art: Whitney Annual," *Time*, February 6, 1939.
4   Peter N. Stearns, Perrin Rowland, and Lori Giarnella, "Children's Sleep: Sketching Historical Change," *Journal of Social History* 30, no. 2 (Winter 1996): 358, doi.org/10.1353/jsh/30.2.345.
5   Andrea Mihm, "The Baby Monitor: Parental Listening and the Organization of Domestic Space," in *Sound as Popular Culture: A Research Companion*, ed. Jens Gerrit Papenburg and Holger Schulze (Cambridge, MA: MIT Press, 2016), 215–23.
6   US Department of Labor, Children's Bureau, *Infant Care*, Bureau Publication No. 8, rev. (Washington: Government Printing Office, 1924), 44, viewable at HathiTrust.org.
7   Silvia M. Bell and Mary D. Salter Ainsworth, "Infant Crying and Maternal Responsiveness," *Child Development* 43, no. 4 (December 1972): 1171–90 (on p. 1188 the authors state, "A responsive mother, our data suggest, not only provides the conditions that terminate a cry...but also is likely to provide conditions that tend to prevent crying").
8   In 1987, Safety 1st released a video baby monitor; by 1993 it was the best-selling brand. Shaped like a miniature television, the tagline on the box reads, "Television and Baby Monitor all in one!"
9   Also in the 1970s, accessible monitors were developed for Deaf, deaf-blind, and hard of hearing communities by signaling cries with lights or vibrations.
10   In 2011 the American Academy of Pediatrics released a statement saying that home cardio-respiratory monitors were not effective in reducing the risk of SIDS. See Task Force on Sudden Infant Death Syndrome, Rachel Y. Moon, "SIDS and Other Sleep-Related Infant Deaths: Expansion of Recommendations for a Safe Infant Sleeping Environment," *Pediatrics* 128, no. 5 (November 2011): e1341–67, doi.org/10.1542/peds.2011-2285.
11   Artie Beavis, "13 Smart Products for the Internet of Toddlers," *Internet of Things* (blog), Arm Community, February 11, 2015, community.arm.com.
12   Through the decades since their creation, some baby monitor casings have been inconspicuous and simple; others have followed Noguchi's whimsical model, with biomorphic shapes or long orbs that clip onto crib rails.

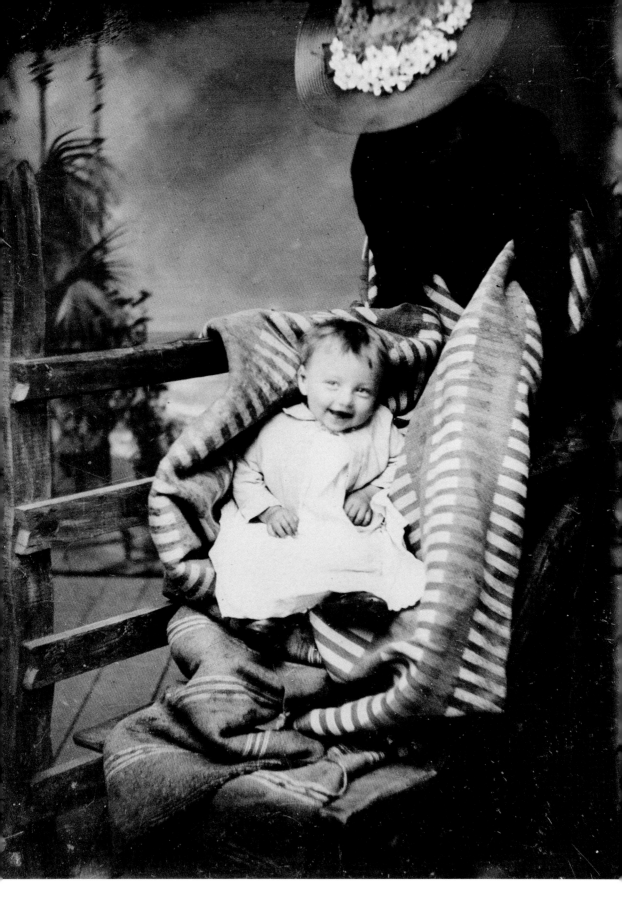

HIDDEN MOTHERS

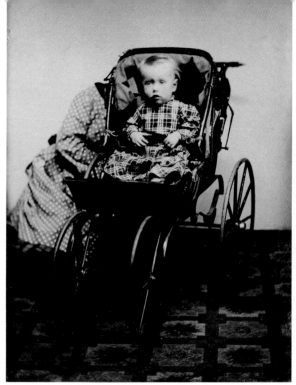

HIDDEN MOTHERS While nineteenth-century photographers had a range of apparatuses at their disposal to keep their sitters still, their tintype mementos of children required extra adult hands. These new-baby photographs, investigated in detail by the scholar Laura Larson, were made in the United States in the 1860s and 1870s, when exposure times were between ten and sixty seconds. A seated adult was typically draped in cloth before an infant was placed on their lap, or might be hidden behind the studio seat. Telltale shadows would eventually be concealed by the matting used to frame the resulting image. While some of these hidden figures were either studio assistants or family members, the colloquial description for them— "hidden mothers"— erases the fact that some were enslaved women denied the opportunity to mother their own children in the same way.

——In all cases, photographer unknown, tintypes, c. 1860s–70s

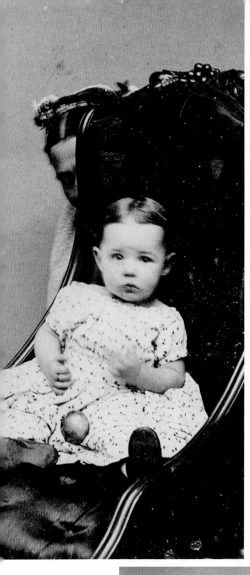

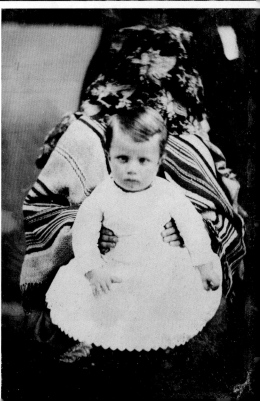

FAMILY LEAVE——This is a story about how my close friend and I set out to redesign a single object, the breast pump, and along the way realized it was a larger system—namely, lack of paid family leave in the United States—that needed our attention. In 2014 Catherine D'Ignazio, a graduate student in Media Arts and Sciences at the Massachusetts Institute of Technology (MIT), had just had her third child, a baby girl.

Back at work shortly afterward, Catherine made frequent stops—as many as four per day—to pump breast milk as she ran between classes and research meetings in our glass-walled technology design center. Sitting on the restroom floor to pump certainly wasn't the same tender experience she had while breastfeeding her daughter. And after leaving the pump parts out to dry beside the communal bathroom sink one day, she came back to find a hastily scrawled note placed nearby. "Too much information!" it read.

The more Catherine pumped, the more a great irony began to surface: here she was, at an elite engineering institute tasked with inventing the future, using a piece of technology that was painful and hadn't been redesigned in decades. Catherine shared her story with me, and together we began to ask, "Whose future are we inventing at MIT, exactly? Whose needs and whose bodies matter when we design technologies?"

Along with others in the building, Catherine and I vowed to create a new kind of pump that, well, *sucked* a lot less than what was currently on the market. In 2014 we brought our collective together for a daylong "hackathon" (a hands-on prototyping and problem-solving gathering common in technology communities), and then a larger event to which we invited 150 designers, engineers, and health care providers from the Boston community to explore ways of improving the pump. Shortly after the first gathering we wrote a blog post and crowdsourced public input. We expected a handful of responses, but instead we received thousands

Image from MIT Media Lab's second *Make The Breastpump Not Suck!* Hackathon, held in 2018

of ideas from parents across the country. People had many ideas for improving the pump itself, but one response stood out:

Ultimately, no pumping technology can overcome the fact that *our society pushes women back to work too early*, with loads of [milk-]supply-dropping stress about how costly childcare is, and *until we fix that on the policy front, no pump is going to meaningfully change the landscape of what nursing mothers are up against.*[1]

If we truly wanted to support breastfeeding in the United States, improving the design of the pump was not enough, we soon realized. Policy had to change. We needed to shift our thinking from designing *objects* to designing *systems*.

We became inspired by the reproductive justice movement, founded in 1997 by the SisterSong Women of Color Reproductive Justice Collective. The reproductive justice framework moves beyond the pro-choice/pro-life narrative of the 1970s and recognizes interconnected issues, including that parenting in a safe and sustainable community requires a healthy environment and that *economic* justice is key to making parenting decisions into actual choices, not theoretical ones. In the United States today, 25 percent of postpartum people go back to work within ten days of giving birth.[2] Framing breastfeeding as an individual choice, without reflecting on the circumstances that guide people's ability to make a choice (for example, going back to work may be the only economically feasible choice; many don't have the time or a place to pump at work; and so on), is misguided.

Paid family leave is associated with a variety of positive outcomes for parents, children, families, and employers. Among the domino effects are better health outcomes for babies and parents, making it easier for businesses to retain skilled workers, which in turn helps close the gender pay gap. But leave policies vary dramatically across the globe. For example, in Germany—one of several industrialized countries with plummeting birth rates—the birthing parent is offered six weeks of paid leave before giving birth, and eight weeks after, both at full salary. In Finland, not only is family leave quite generous, but all birthing parents are supplied with a baby box, a baby "starter kit" filled with necessities and that also serves as a bassinet (see p. 285).

The United States is the only industrialized nation in the world without *paid* family leave. The Family and Medical Leave Act (FMLA), signed into law by President Bill Clinton in 1993, provides up to twelve weeks of job-protected time off for people to care for a new child or a seriously ill family member, or to recover from a serious illness. Just 60 percent of the US workforce is eligible to take FMLA leave, as it omits part-time workers and people working for companies with fewer than fifty employees. And, critically, this time off is unpaid by default, employees it up to employers to decide whether or not to pay employees while they are caring for others or for themselves. In 2016, only 14 percent of private-sector workers in the United States reported having been granted paid family leave through an employer.[4]

At our second, larger hackathon in 2018 we recognized that technology alone can't help solve the range of issues families face. This "Make Family Leave Not Suck" Policy Summit reimagined and strategized about equitable paid family leave in the United States. During breaks between sessions, at meals, and at the culminating "science fair," participants from the hackathon (designers, engineers, and community activists, parents and non-parents alike) mingled with participants from the policy summit (activists and policy thought leaders) in a space encompassing both objects and systems. People discussed how different types of design solutions—addressing both technology and policy—could improve life for all parents, families, and babies.

After the event, we joined several hackathon participants in Washington, DC, as they presented their innovations to their state representatives and discussed the importance of implementing paid family leave in their communities. Following California's lead, several other states have implemented paid family leave, acting as policy laboratories for testing ideas that activists will push for at the federal level in the coming years. As designers committed to supporting birth and breastfeeding, it is critical for us to be literate about the systemic forces that shape these aspects of human reproduction and the policy interventions that connect them to other forms of human labor and experience. Our job as designers must include participating in the continued community organizing that lies ahead.

—**Alexis Hope,** for the "Make the Breast Pump Not Suck" project

1 Mother 2783, "Make the Breast Pump Not Suck" hackathon, September 20–21, 2014, MIT Media Lab, Cambridge, MA (author's emphasis).
2 See Sharon Lerner, "The Real War on Families: Why the US Needs Paid Family Leave Now," *In These Times*, August 18, 2015, inthesetimes.com.
3 "The Economic Benefits of Paid Leave: Fact Sheet," Joint Economic Committee, US Congress, August 1, 2019, jec-fact-sheet-economic-benefits-of-paid-leave.pdf.
4 Employee Benefits Survey, "Leave Benefits: Access," US Bureau of Labor Statistics (using wage data for March 2016).

DIAPERS——One night in 1946, a Connecticut housewife, Marion Donovan, was faced with a wet, crying baby yet again. As she changed her daughter's soaked cloth diaper, Donovan thought there had to be a better way to keep babies dry. On her quest for a dampless diaper, the shower curtain in the bathroom caught her eye. Before you could say "waterproof material," Donovan had torn down the curtain, cut out a section, and pulled out her sewing machine.

Three years and many shower curtains later, Donovan had designed the Boater, a reusable diaper cover made of surplus nylon parachute cloth that paved the way for the disposable diaper we know today.[1] Yet, most histories of the diaper gloss over Donovan's contributions, focusing instead on Victor Mills, the chemical engineer at Proctor & Gamble who created Pampers in 1961, more than a decade after Donovan designed the Boater.[2] Restoring Donovan to this narrative provides yet another example of women innovating and inventing products for themselves in areas dominated by men.

Until the mid-twentieth century, diapering babies in the United States meant folding and pinning cloth toweling in place, and then tugging a pair of rubber pants overtop to minimize leaks. What Donovan created was a new kind of diaper: an envelope-like plastic cover that she would refine to include an absorbent insert. Although rubber baby pants were available at the time, many mothers found that they caused diaper rash.[3] The Boater had a pouch for the diaper insert, keeping the wetness away from the baby's skin. The nylon fabric also allowed the baby's skin to breathe. "We couldn't say it, but it did cure diaper rash, and many doctors recommended it," Donovan explained.[4]

In 1949, Donovan began selling her Boaters at Saks Fifth Avenue in New York. They were an instant hit. "It is not often that a new innovation in the Infants' Wear field goes over with the immediate success of your Boaters," wrote Adam Gimbel, the president of Saks, in a letter to Donovan.[5]

More affection for and from baby
with revolutionary

Boater

new, NYLON diaper cover

*N*ow you can be sure of ABSOLUTELY DRY bundling clothes and bedding with this amazing BOATER. Brilliantly fashioned to give comfort to baby—bind-proof, leak-proof, it has plenty of freedom for action. Fold disposable or regular diapers into its waterproofed NYLON pocket and snap on. Takes a few minutes to launder. Designed with *four* protection flaps that keep all baby's clothes *as dry as hospital cotton.*

Three adjustable snaps on all sizes—small, medium, large, extra large. In pink, blue, white, yellow; at $1.95*

Advertisement for Marion Donovan's Boater diaper cover, c. 1949

But manufacturers were not interested. As Donovan would tell Barbara Walters in 1975, "I went to all the big names that you can think of, and they said 'We don't want it. No woman has asked us for that. They're very happy, and they buy all our baby pants.' So, I went into manufacturing myself."[6]

By the time Donovan's patents came through in 1951, she had sold the rights for her invention for a million dollars (almost $10 million in today's money) and had moved on to her next idea: replacing cloth diapers altogether with disposable absorbent paper versions.[7] When Donovan proposed making a disposable diaper, manufacturers again declined. It was a decade before Mills, then a grandfather, would draw on Donovan's vision to create Pampers, the first mass-produced disposable diaper.[8]

In the decades after Pampers hit the market, sales of disposable diapers grew exponentially. Today, disposables account for more than 90 percent of all diaper changes in the United States, with about eighteen million disposable diapers ending up in American landfills each year. The environmental impact has prompted some parents to look for alternatives from a pre-disposable world. Many have turned back to washable and reusable cloth diapers. Yet studies have shown that cloth diapers, despite producing less waste upfront, are not uncomplicated—the simple fact is that any diaper uses planetary resources, and introducing any waste to landfill or sewers has an impact.[9] Other families practice elimination communication (EC), relying on auditory and other kinds of cues to help parents and very young children communicate about the "need to go potty" long before the children can speak. Supporters of EC argue that it helps babies to tune in and come to know their bodily functions at a young age.

While many sanitary methods are visited upon babies' bottoms the world over, the diaper in its many forms is a design staple. Marion Donovan's Boater, however, deserves the status of a design classic.

—**Juliana Rowen Barton**

1 Explaining why she called her invention the Boater, Donovan said, "at the time I thought it looked like a boat." See Emily Matchar, "Meet Marion Donovan, the Mother Who Invented a Precursor to the Disposable Diaper," *Smithsonian Magazine*, May 10, 2019, smithsonianmag.com.
2 For example, Malcolm Gladwell focused almost entirely on Mills in a 1996 article he wrote for the *New Yorker*. Like Donovan, Mills had a long list of innovations and product improvements to his name, which made him a bit of a legend at Proctor & Gamble. For example, he figured out a simpler, continuous process for making Ivory soap, introducing machines for milling that ground the ingredients much more finely than before. He then found different applications for this process, including using it for Duncan Hines cake mixes, whose mixture of flour, sugar, and shortening had previously had trouble with its consistency. Pringles, too, are made using this method: the potato is ground into a slurry, then pressed, baked, and wrapped. Malcolm Gladwell, "Smaller," *New Yorker*, November 19, 2001, newyorker.com.
3 The Boater, on the other hand, was fastened with snaps instead of diaper pins or elastic and thus did not constrict the baby. Notably, the Pampers website claims that it was the first diaper that did not require safety pins; see pampers.com/en-us/pampers-heritage.
4 Heather Satrom, "Papers Illustrate Woman Inventor's Life and Work," Lemelson Center for the Study of Invention and Innovation, National Museum of American History, Smithsonian Institution, July 1, 2000, invention.si.edu.
5 Satrom, "Papers Illustrate Woman Inventor's Life and Work."
6 Matchar, "Meet Marion Donovan."
7 The Boater wasn't fully disposable; you could wash and reuse the nylon part. After selling the diaper patents, Donovan continued inventing products that solved household problems, including the Big Hangup, a hanger that could accommodate thirty skirts or slacks in a compact space, and a wire soap holder that attached to the overflow opening and drained directly into the basin to avoid the semi-congealed soap that forms in the bottom of a soap dish. See Robert Mcg. Thomas Jr., "Marion Donovan, 81, Solver Of the Damp-Diaper Problem," *New York Times*, November 18, 1998, nytimes.com.
8 Like Donovan, Mills was tired of changing and washing cloth diapers. In 1957, he was charged with developing new paper products after Proctor & Gamble bought the Charmin paper company. "One of the early researchers told me that among the first things they did was go out to a toy store and buy one of those Betsy Wetsy-type dolls, where you put water in the mouth and it comes out the other end," Ed Rider, the head of the archives department at Procter & Gamble, said. "They brought it back to the lab, hooked up its legs on a treadmill to make it walk, and tested diapers on it." In 1961, with his grandchildren's soggy diapers in mind, Mills developed an absorbent, leak-proof diaper that could simply be thrown away after use. See Gladwell, "Smaller."
9 No diaper choice is uncomplicated. Disposables bring absorbent materials, urine, and feces into landfills. Cotton, the material most commonly used for cloth diapers, requires immense amounts of water and chemicals to produce. Then there's the laundry issue, since cloth diapers require energy-expending hot-water cycles for proper cleaning. One study by the British government considered such factors and concluded that, environmentally, disposables beat cloth diapers by a hair. See "An Updated Lifecycle Assessment Study for Disposable and Reusable Nappies," Environment Agency, Science Report, August 1, 2008, gov.uk.

EMMI PIKLER'S ELEVATED DIAPERING TABLE——Somewhere along the way, we pick up the idea that changing diapers is a real drag. Films, television, magazines, and the Euro-American popular culture machine tell us over and over again that diapers are foul and irritating. Perhaps it's the poop, but diapering has also become the ultimate metaphor for caregiving as an unsavory act. When my first child was born, I enjoyed the closeness diapering brought, but like most new parents, I struggled.

I wanted to do the job well, but I had no clue what that even meant. How *does* one diaper well? Is it efficiency that counts? Gentleness? Cleanliness? I established my diapering routine quickly and without much thought. I placed my child on a changing pad, distracted her with toys and mobiles, and speedily juggled wipes and little legs. I sang phrases like "we're almost done, we're almost done" like a deranged mantra.

In those days it never dawned on me that changing a diaper could be a pleasurable time of learning and connection, or that it could help me better appreciate my job as a caregiver. Yet these are exactly the kinds of experiences that Emmi Pikler had in mind when she designed her Elevated Diapering Table. Visually and structurally, the design is simple: a high wooden table with a crib-like lattice surrounding three sides of the table's surface. The height eliminates the need to bend over, making the table ergonomic and comfortable for the adult to use. The table's surface is wide enough that a child can easily and safely roll from belly to back, but not so wide as to allow her to crawl. A thin pad makes the surface comfortable, but is not so soft as to yield under the child's weight. The protective lattice also engages a growing child, who might want to use its bars to grab or lean against, or pull themselves up to stand. (Babies are active during a Pikler-style diaper change, and their movement and participation are encouraged.) Because the table is open on the fourth side, it enables face-to-face connection. This cultivates focus on the activity of diapering and creates a sensitivity to the unfolding

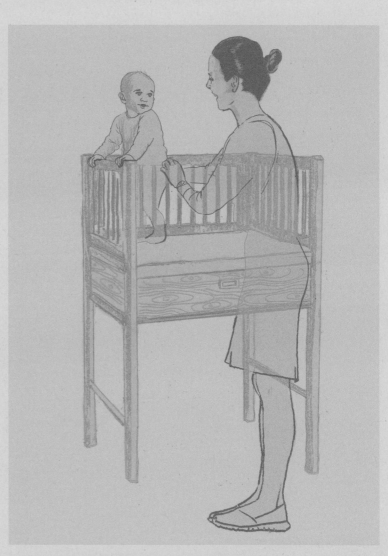

Emmi Pikler's Elevated Changing Table ensured that changing a baby was never "just a diaper change" but instead a moment for respectful, reciprocal interaction between carer and infant

relationship between caregiver and child.

Dr. Emmi Pikler was an unlikely designer. Born in Vienna in 1902 and raised in Budapest, she was a pediatrician as well as mother of three. Pikler framed caregiving as a noble endeavor and developed a vision counter to the prevailing authoritarian child-rearing beliefs. She advocated for a mutually respectful style of communication between children and adults, and believed children should be able to progress according to their own developmental timelines. She promoted movement, uninterrupted play, and deep, caring relationships, which to her way of thinking were as crucial to a child as oxygen. Pikler encouraged caregivers to use rituals such as feeding, bathing, and diapering as opportunities for deep and respectful connection.[1]

Pikler refined her theories at Lóczy, a Budapest-based orphanage that she founded in 1946 and directed until 1984.[2] Most of the children at Lóczy were casualties of World War II, and Pikler endeav-ored to provide conditions that would enable them to thrive. As much research laboratory as childcare facility, Lóczy was where Pikler developed her theories about children and their environments and determined how best to support babies' inborn capacity for emotional connection, learning, movement, and play. At the heart of Pikler's philosophy was the idea that a carefully prepared environment not only makes the caregiver's role easier and more rewarding, but also bolsters a child's cognitive, emotional, and physical well-being from the very earliest days of life. Pikler designed several toys, climbing structures, tools, articles of furniture, and even clothing, all meant to support independence, freedom of movement, play, respectful boundaries, and connectedness. Today, professionals from all over travel to the Pikler Institute in Budapest to immerse themselves in Dr. Pikler's theories and practices, and her style of care has rippled across the world.[3]

I discovered Emmi Pikler first as a design scholar, and then as parent. By the time my second daughter was born, diaper changes sounded a little like this:

It's time to change your diaper. I'm going to pick you up now. There. In this position I can see your eyes. Can you lift up your hips? Let's take this suit down and have a look. Yes, I see your diaper looks wet. Let's take it off. Can you lift your hips again? There, you used your feet to lift your bum! Thank you for your help.

At Lóczy, Pikler taught caregivers not only how to use her Elevated Diapering Table, but also how to connect and ask for participation from the child. The pace of the diaper change is slow and relaxed, with ongoing communication between the caregiver and child. This helps the child anticipate each step in the process. She makes decisions and helps to undress herself. While participating in the diaper-changing routine, the child learns language and how to care for herself. She moves freely. She develops autonomy, self-regulation, and a chance to feel close to the person supporting her.[4] The caregiver, meanwhile, moves at an almost ceremonial pace, displaying the kind of meditative awareness found in a Japanese tea ceremony. Using gentle "asking hands," instead of busy, fast-moving ones, and initiating eye contact transform the task from something onerous to a collaborative ritual—a time of connection and mutual appreciation. As a design, the Pikler Elevated Diapering Table creates a surprising shift in awareness, framing diapering as a mutually gratifying experience and creating a close and loving partnership between caregiver and child. Throughout her life, Pikler venerated children and those who care for them, and her designs literally and figuratively elevate the caregiver's role. Attaching value (and compensation) to such care is the more abstract, yet no less vital, piece of the puzzle that remains in dire need of redesign.

1 Magda Gerber, "The Lóczy Model of Infant Care," in The RIE Manual for Parents and Professionals, ed. Magda Gerber, Deborah Greenwald, and Joan Weaver (Los Angeles: Resources for Infant Educarers [RIE], 2007), 53.
2 Gerber, "The Lóczy Model of Infant Care," 52.
3 Magda Gerber popularized Pikler's methods of caring for infants and young children in the United States.
4 Deborah E. Laurin and Carla B. Goble, "Enhancing the Diapering Routine: Caring, Communication, and Development," Young Children 73, no. 3 (July 2018): 18–19.

CRIB——For most of human history, sleep has come to us much the way it did, or how we imagine it did, while in the womb. Around the world and through the centuries, the movement and intimacy of the body in the womb has been replicated with hammocks, cradles, beds for cuddling, and various soft and warm materials for snuggling and swaddling. Many of these designs, and the practice of keeping infants close, have existed for millennia.[1]

In the United States, sleep habits changed radically between the nineteenth and twentieth centuries, and the crib was part of this change, crystalizing many modern attitudes toward sleep and creating new dynamics and realities.[2] Surprisingly, infant sleep was not publicly discussed much in the mid-nineteenth century. Manuals for parents, though produced in great abundance, did not dispense advice on babies' sleep.[3] This doesn't mean that sleep came easier to American babies in those years; it simply indicates it wasn't an area of life that attracted much debate or attention.

Signs of change began to appear by the 1880s and 1890s. Neurologists of the era described a condition called neurasthenia, thought to have been brought on by the accelerating pace of modern life. A new wave of sleep advice swept the nation, and the hows, whys, and wheres of babies' day and nighttime sleep increasingly became a new focal point. A number of authorities began to criticize the practice of lulling children to sleep by nursing or rocking them in cradles, lest they become dependent on attention.[4]

Safety was also a concern. The Italian *arcuccio* (meaning "little arch") was an "apparatus to prevent the overlying of infants," designed to be placed on the mother's bed and over a sleeping baby, allowing the mother to sleep and breastfeed throughout the night without having to worry about rolling onto her infant, or having her infant roll out of bed.[5] In the years around the turn of the twentieth century, numerous design patents were issued for sidecar-style sleep surfaces that attached to the

A mother looking on as her twin babies explore their iron crib, early 20th century

bed, much like today's bedside cribs and co-sleepers.

Throughout the nineteenth century, middle- and upper-middle-class children slept near their parents or nurses during their infancy. When they outgrew this arrangement, they were moved to a shared bed with a sibling. But by the 1890s it was increasingly fashionable to isolate infants from adults during sleep, and by the 1940s families who could afford it gave their babies a designated bedroom. The danger of suffocation from adults rolling over was perhaps the most compelling argument for having babies sleep alone, but many twentieth-century parenting manuals also advised that co-sleeping could derail a mother's ability to prioritize sex. "Avoid taking the child into your own bed for company," one so-called expert advised, "jealousy could easily arise."[6]

By around 1930, about 70 percent of American households had electricity. People could stay up longer, and children increasingly had designated sleep times and spaces of their own. To make separating babies possible and safe, the use of traditional cradles waned in favor of cribs.[7] With their high wooden lattices, cribs enclosed babies for sleeping, making it possible to leave infants and toddlers alone for long stretches of time.[8] Aside from purportedly building self-reliance in children, the design had the added benefit of freeing caregivers for other activities; some cribs were even

advertised as a way to help mothers with their chores. Unlike cradles, cribs could not be moved to follow the caregiver's movements but rather separated babies from adult goings-on. And because they were relatively immobile, cribs delineated separate spaces for children and adults as never before, all while preventing young children from falling, suffocation, or wandering around.

By the 1920s and 1930s, cradles were considered outright antiques. Crib designs, meanwhile, improved steadily. Numerous patents were taken out on cribs of various materials and in different shapes and sizes, and the most innovative or useful models were often discussed in family magazines.[9] As crib design advanced, children's mattresses followed suit. In contrast to the homemade bedding that lined the bottoms of many cradles, firm children's mattresses promised to improve baby's posture and spinal health. Special crib sheets were sold to help ease frequent bedmaking and were available in different colors and patterns to complement the nursery decor. This fenced-in bed, not conducive to rocking, nursing, or other sleep-inducing comforts, required new ways of coaxing babies to sleep, and so the crib quickly inspired a new genre of sleep advice that has soared in popularity and will continue into the foreseeable future.

This significant change in children's furniture dramatically altered sleeping arrangements

and habits but above all made it possible for children to sleep alone. As a furniture typology, the crib has been wildly successful, providing a safe and separate sleeping space for babies in households and caregiving facilities throughout the world for well over a century. Contemporary crib designs trend toward convertibility: one can raise and lower the platform to different positions and adjust or remove the side rails depending on a child's age and developmental stage. Not only does convertible crib design extend the life of a crib, making it more environmentally sustainable, but it also has been a game changer for parents with disabilities. Accessible cribs are often designed with side rail doors, making it easier for those with mobility issues to care for and respond to babies.

Many brilliant designs affect only their time or place, while others become a larger cultural force. The crib helped change the way people think about sleep, not just in the United States but around the world. For over a century the design has held out the promise of health and safety, self-reliance, better sleep, and a little alone time for both parent and child. The crib—and much of the advice that has come with it—has thus cut a new path through the landscape of sleep, altering our relationships with our children and with ourselves, promising to jettison our fears and discomforts and bring us back to that place where we will all, as the old saying goes, sleep like babies.

1   Images of rocking cradles exist from the thirteenth century, and remnant of cradles have survived from the seventeenth century. There are earlier literary references to the cradle, such as in William Langland's 1362 narrative poem *Piers Plowman* 9, lines 78–79, which references a mother "wakynge on nyhtes … to rokke the cradel." See Ivan George Sparkes, *An Illustrated History of English Domestic Furniture, 1100–1837: The Age of the Craftsman* (Bourne End, Buckinghamshire: Francis Lincoln, 1980), 102–12; William Langland, *Piers Plowman: A New Annotated Edition of the C-Text*, ed. Derek Pearsall (Exeter, UK: University

of Exeter Press, 2008); Leanne MacDonald, "Walking at Night: Scribal Variants, Poverty, and Prostitution in a Piers Plowman Manuscript," *Medieval Studies Research Blog*, University of Notre Dame, July 16, 2015, sites.nd.edu/manuscript-studies.
2   John Locke (1632–1734) and Jean-Jacques Rousseau (1712–1778) both took positions on children's sleep. Locke advised that children should have "freedom of will" and should not be allowed to get used to routine. This included having children sleep on various surfaces so that they would learn to sleep anywhere easily. Rousseau advised against cradles because

over-zealous rocking could be harmful to babies. See Christina Hardyment, *Dream Babies: Child Care from Locke to Spock* (London: Jonathan Cape, 1983).
3   Peter N. Stearns, Perrin Rowland, and Lori Giarnella, "Children's Sleep: Sketching Historical Change," *Journal of Social History* 30, no. 2 (Winter 1996): 345.
4   Stearns, Rowland, and Giarnella, "Children's Sleep," 348.
5   The *arcuccio* was originally a seventeenth-century design, mentioned in the 1733 manual *The Art of Nursing*. While it didn't catch on worldwide, in 1895 it was suggested that parents use the *arcuccio* as a means

for curbing infant suffocation during sleep. See "The Arcuccio: An Apparatus to Prevent the Overlying of Infants," *British Medical Journal*, August 1895, bmj.com/content/2/1806/380.
6   Charis Ursula Frankenburg, *Common Sense in the Nursery* (London: Cape, 1922 [later editions, 1934, 1954]), 56, quoted in Hardyment, *Dream Babies*, 187; F. W. Goodrich, *Infant Care: The United States Government Guide* (Englewood Cliffs, NJ: Prentice-Hall, 1968); Benjamin Spock, *Baby and Child Care* (New York: Meredith Press, 1968).
7   Writers for the magazine *Scientific American* covered a number of

new crib designs just before the turn of the twentieth century, and many of these won patents and went on to become popular household furnishings. See "A Folding Cradle," *Scientific American*, September 10, 1898, 164.
8   The word *crib* originally referred to a long open box that horses and cows ate from, not unlike the manger where the infant Jesus was laid.
9   "Soft and Easy Is Thy Cradle': Nest for the World's Babies," *The Craftsman* 29, no. 3 (December 1915): 241; Dolly Carr, "Bed for the Baby," *Parents' Magazine* 14 (October 1939): 26, 107.

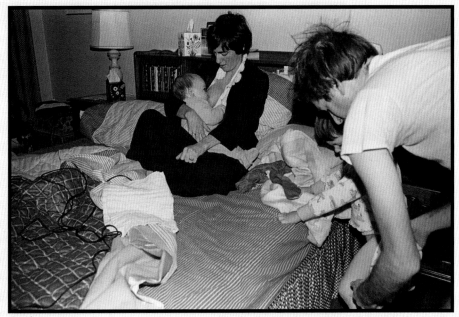

Oct 5, 1977

We were up all night again. David had an ear infection, and Jason kept waking up complaining that his foot hurt. It's been 3½ years now since we've had a full nights sleep without interruptions.

Sept 12, 1978

When Richard and I were first married, he told me I was to polish the bottoms of the pots and pans. I told him he was crazy, and if he wanted shiny bottoms, he could do it himself. So he did.

JUDY GELLES

March 3, 1979

On Tuesday, Thursday, and Friday afternoon Jason is at nursery school and David naps, and I have one and one half hours of free time to be creative and do important things.

JUDY GELLES "Documenting the struggles of a woman and a young mother were important to me. I did it in my own home, five small rooms, two small children; I wanted to keep a record as I lived it. Here it is, as it was." So wrote the late artist Judy Gelles about her photographic series *Family Portrait: 1977–1982*, in which she documented her life. To each image she added handwritten commentary from the contemporaneous journals she kept, exposing the mundanities, irritations, and doubts of her experience of motherhood. As Gelles reflected, "My intent is to show that reality is not hard and simple but multi-leveled and fragile."

1—— *Bedroom*, October 5, 1977
2—— *Dishwasher*, September 12, 1972
3—— *Self-Portrait Watching Soaps*, March 3, 1979
4—— *Bathroom*, May 23, 1978
5—— *Living Room*, June 10, 1979
6—— *Soccer Ball*, November 15, 1981

3 4
5

May 23, 1978

I would love to be able to go to the bathroom alone.

June 10, 1979

Living Room

Nov. 15, 1981
Jason is beginning to identify with Richard.
In fact he thinks his Dad knows everything.
In fact he truly idolizes Richard. I find
this all very strange since Richard is Never Home.

CAR SEAT——Most hospitals in the United States require a properly installed car seat before allowing caregivers to leave with a newborn, yet few of us know anything about the designers, the testing processes, and the public health policies behind one of the most ubiquitous designs new parents encounter. Flaura Koplin Winston, MD, PhD, of the Children's Hospital of Philadelphia and the University of Pennsylvania talks about her decades-long design efforts to ensure that infants and children survive car rides.

Ford Motor Company's Tot-Guard, 1973

DESIGNING MOTHERHOOD—Dr. Winston, you're the founder and scientific director of the Center for Injury Research and Prevention and director of the Center for Child Injury Prevention Studies at Children's Hospital of Philadelphia. You also hold the Distinguished Chair in the Department of Pediatrics. You know a lot about this subject! But how did you end up designing for infant and child safety, and especially child safety seats?

DR. FLAURA WINSTON—When I first looked at the data in the 1980s, I saw that a leading cause of death for children was motor vehicle crashes.[1] Then, soon after I completed my training in both engineering and pediatrics, I discovered the first case of a child dying from an air bag. This was a pivotal moment for me. I realized that while these early air bags saved adult lives, devices designed for adults could kill children. Children are not small adults; safety product designs need to take into account their particular needs. I saw that I could make a unique contribution to public health by focusing on *child* traffic safety. That's how I ended up working on infant and child car seat safety, which in turn gave rise to policies that shaped their design.

DM— It's something that you've done now for a really long time; you're an expert in this area. What keeps you motivated?

FW— I am not alone in wanting to protect children. Our success gives us hope, and the continued toll of traffic injuries gives us motivation and purpose. I am humbled by the stakeholders who realize the value and importance of the data that I generate by effecting change in product designs, regulations, education, and policy. We keep each other going. They look at the analysis and inferences from the research produced by me and my colleagues—mechanisms of injury, testing protocols, evaluation of product design, and the use of these products by real families—to guide them in their quest for continuous safety improvements, thereby achieving the greatest impact.

I always have the families and children in mind whose lives have been altered by having an injury or death, and I never want this tragedy to befall another family. That drives me to this day. Through data we can translate the biomechanical, human factors, and other needs that are unique to protecting children to those who can affect change to ensure optimal protection. It's not anything I could ever have done by myself. It is a partnership across multiple sectors that continues to work because no one wants a child to be hurt.

DM— Can you talk about how child safety seats evolved?

FW— Sure. If you look at very early designs [such as the one pictured on the previous page], they were not safety devices but were designed for child comfort or for having somewhere to put the child if they weren't going to be on your lap. It took thirty years for people to realize that child safety seats were safety devices. In these early years, adults were not in seat belts either. Then, in the 1940s and 1950s, John Paul Stapp, a US Air Force colonel and doctor, and an early safety pioneer, strapped himself into sleds and decelerated quickly [to mimic a crash] in order to show the benefits of and to optimize seat belts. In the 1970s, with the creation of the National Highway Traffic Safety Administration (NHTSA), auto safety research and regulations emerged, and the first car seat safety standard came out in 1971. Now, child safety has become a highly technical industry with many standards. We have robust testing, child test dummies, computational models, and more that allow the industry to produce car seats that save lives.

There are so many considerations: how to balance safety standards with designers' and consumers' aesthetic preferences; making the seat compatible with different cars; keeping it light enough to be portable; making it easy to use; making it compatible with a stroller. There are also designs for special-needs infants and children, adding other layers of consideration. And what's an acceptable price point? It's actually an incredibly interesting design challenge.

DM— What about usability? Buckling children into their car seats can sometimes feel like a wrestling match. Did you have to think about how to get people to adopt them?

FW— Yes, absolutely. It was understood early on that there were several barriers to surmount. The first was lack of awareness. The NHTSA, as well as organizations like SafeKids Worldwide, and subsequent laws helped with that. The second was lack of access, making sure that families could buy them. Another consideration was usability and compatibility with the car. To this day, a lot of child safety seats are misused because they're hard to use. But our research shows that a misused child safety seat is better than no car seat, in most cases.

Over the last decade in particular I've seen much more of an emphasis on making child safety seats more intuitive to install and use, using color coding and bigger buttons, though some still find installation hard. Two examples of advances in design that really helped—lower anchors and top tethers—were required by NHTSA for all cars manufactured after 2002. This federal standard provides an alternative to installing child safety seats using the vehicle's seat belts, making it easier to get a correct and tight installation.

DM— **There is constant innovation, which enhances safety, but this becomes quite a confusing thing for new parents picking through the plethora of different car seat options. Can you talk a little bit about where innovation runs up against obsolescence and user choice?**

FW— There's choice paralysis, for sure. There are so many child safety seats on the market in the United States. The good news: they all meet the same regulations, so they're all pretty good options. Parents may not also realize that a less expensive or an older model of a car seat might be a fine choice. There's this incredible pressure, particularly on mothers, to buy the "right" thing for their child at the "right" developmental phase. If you are buying new, don't succumb to peer pressure or marketing for a specific seat. Rather, pick the one that best fits your car and that you can figure out how to use.

I strongly recommend against getting a used child safety seat unless you can confirm the following three things: you're completely sure that it has not been in crash, you know it's not past its expiration date, and you've checked NHSTA's website to confirm that the seat has not been recalled. Child safety seat materials can degrade over time, and those that have been in motor vehicle crashes might have damage that is not visible, reducing their protection. Just like with any other technology, buying newer seats will give you the advantage of design advances that could make the seat easier to use or provide added protection.

DM— **We found in our research that it became a best practice starting in the 1990s that new parents should leave the hospital with a child safety seat.[2]**

FW— That is a strong recommendation from the American Academy of Pediatrics (AAP), and it's determined hospital by hospital as part of their discharge planning. Guidelines for car safety over the arc of a child's life were incorporated into well-child visits, telling parents when to move from a rear-facing car seat to a forward-facing one, a belt-positioning booster seat, and the vehicle seat belt. Car seats were—still are—a public health tactic in material form.

DM— **What special considerations are there for newborns in the car?**

FW— As is true for all children, the newborn should be placed in a car seat in the rear seat. For the newborn, the seat has to be rear facing to prevent spinal cord injuries. The reason why infants are at risk for these injuries is because their relatively heavy head leads their body's movement during a crash, focusing dangerous forces on their upper spine, which is not fully developed. Sitting rear facing spreads the crash forces over the entire back, supporting the child's head and protecting the brain, neck, and spine. We recommend rear facing for as long as your car seat will allow it. In fact, in Sweden children are usually rear facing until age four. And just look at supersonic pilots—all rear facing!

DM— Safety is really cultural. Different groups of people have different thresholds surrounding risk and safety. How does this play out in your work? You are in conversation with colleagues across the world, and your research is disseminated globally. How do different cultural contexts inform one another?

FW— Well, it's a pretty universal truth that parents want to do the right thing and protect their children. What's not universal is access to the correct devices and support for installing them correctly, although some states—Pennsylvania is one of them—have child safety seat loan programs and many fitting stations. We did a study years ago in the United States looking at why there was less use of booster seats among certain populations. We found that for some parents, even the slightest hint that they needed a law in order to protect their children was offensive. Behavior was really changed by whether or not parents had access to the right information—from people in their community who they respected—in order to protect their child. This perspective extends to other countries. We did a study in Beijing where we taught parents about the importance of belt-positioning booster seats. Even though it wasn't mandated by law, the parents—all of them—wanted to use a booster after the intervention.[3] Creating good habits early on is the best way to ensure safety, so we teach new parents the entire safety progression when the child is born—rear facing, then forward facing, then boosters, then seat belts—all in the rear seat. When we started our work, many people told me that parents wouldn't use booster seats for their older children. Look around now; if you're taking other kids home, don't their parents ask, "Where's the booster seat?"

DM— There's definitely a lot of booster-seat shifting and trading for play dates and rides home!

FW— That did not exist at all—*at all*—in 1995, even though they were available. It was very intentional on our part to convey that this is part of protecting your child. It bears repeating: I want to underscore that this is about design of behavior and social culture as much as it is about product design. You asked me why I stayed with this for so long, and I think this is the crux—safety is such an interesting behavior reflective of so much about us and our societies.

1 In 1986 the US Department of Transportation estimated that with 100 percent correct use, about 53,000 injuries and 500 deaths could be prevented each year in the United States among children from birth to four years of age. "An Evaluation of Child Passenger Safety: The Effectiveness and Benefits of Safety Seats," US Department of Transportation, National Highway Traffic Safety Administration Technical Report, DOT HS 806 890, February 1986, crash-stats.nhtsa.dot.gov.
2 The AAP wrote in 1990 that about a quarter of US hospitals with obstetric services had a car seat policy for discharging newborns, but about two-thirds of them waived the requirement if parents didn't have a seat. Another study at the time, which accounted for nine out of ten annual births in Michigan, showed that around a quarter of hospitals discussed the use of car safety seats with parents, but that only 4 percent demonstrated how to use them. American Academy of Pediatrics, Committee on Accident and Poison Prevention, "Safe Transportation of Newborns Discharged from the Hospital," *Pediatrics* 86, no. 3 (September 1, 1990): 486–87, pediatrics.aappublications.org/content/86/3/486.
3 For an excellent summary of US Child Passenger Safety (CPS) laws, see Sean Gugerty and Bradley Nolet, "Issue Brief: Hospitals' Role in Car Seat Safety," Legal Resource Center for Public Health Policy, University of Maryland, 2015, aw.umaryland.edu/.

STROLLER——Carriage, buggy, stroller, perambulator (or pram for short)—the nomenclature may shift with geography, history, idioms, and infant or child ages, but the desire for baby transport design has remained a constant for many parents and caregivers for centuries. A different proposition than babywearing, baby transport's exact design depends in modern times on the buyer, who must conquer choice anxiety in the face of myriad product permutations, with all their attendant accessories.

Prices of strollers can vary greatly, making this a design category in which economic and class status can be flaunted. While some basic foldable versions retail for less than $50, many models cost hundreds and sometimes thousands of dollars. Add-ons for storage, in-seat toys, matching diaper bags, cup holders, and decorative flourishes abound. And whether infants should face the caregiver or look out at the world is a fiercely debated topic. (Reversible seats now make both options possible on many models.)

In the 2009 film *Away We Go*, Maggie Gyllenhaal's character LN memorably rebuffs a well-intentioned gift of an outward-facing stroller with the exclamation, "I LOVE my babies. Why would I want to PUSH them away from me?" But for many this design offers a way for a carer to move with some level of independence, particularly while ferrying multiples or siblings.[1]

Patent for the Richardson baby carriage   In an address to a gathering of fellows at the Royal Society of Arts in London in 1923, Samuel J. Sewell, editor of a well-known trade journal, noted that he had not found a definitive design history for this product recognized as an "inestimable boon to both mother and child."[2] His potted chronology records all manner of ancient and early modern pull-cart-style contraptions for infants and invalids. Standouts include a pet-powered pram developed by the English architect William Kent for the 3rd Duke of Devonshire's children in 1773, and the first reversible-seating version, made of wicker and brass, patented by William H. Richardson, a Black Baltimorean, on June 18, 1889.[3]

Owen F. Maclaren's "Umbrella" Baby Stroller, 1966   Owen Finlay Maclaren, an Englishman and aeronautical designer with Scottish roots, applied his decades of experience designing fighter plane components to the problem of perambulating his young grandchild, Anne, while she was visiting him in the early 1960s. Maclaren's collapsible "folding baby carriage" B01 prototype is the infant-focused equivalent of Marcel Breuer's Bauhaus designs of four decades earlier. Like Breuer, Maclaren pared his product down to its essential components, using lightweight aluminum. The bare bones result weighed just six pounds, less than many newborns. Its simple fabric "chair" made a perfect canvas for bright, eye-catching graphics. Maclaren took the design to Silver Cross, which rejected the concept, thinking there would be little market interest. So Maclaren formed his own company. A decade after his stroller's debut, more than six hundred thousand were being produced annually.[4]

1   The CDC reports that in 2018 there were 123,536 twin births, 3,400 triplet births, and 125 quadruplet or higher order births in the United States alone. Centers for Disease Control and Prevention, National Center for Health Statistics: Multiple Births, 2018, www.cdc.gov/nchs/fastats/multiple.htm.
2   Samuel J. Sewell, "The History of Children's

and Invalids' Carriages," *Journal of the Royal Society of Arts* 71, no. 3694 (September 7, 1923): 716–28. Sewell asserts (716) that "a woman is not fitted by nature to carry a babe in her arms, on her back, nor on her head or shoulders…. Hence the need of a miniature carriage"— opinions to be taken with a healthy serving of salt.
3   W. H. Richardson,

Child's carriage, US Patent 405,600, filed December 27, 1888, issued June 18, 1889. Sewell notes that another American, Charles Burton, in 1852 joined a number of other inventors and manufacturers of baby carriages who had been active since the 1840s in London, "start[ing] a small factory in Hampstead…and open[ing] a showroom

in Oxford Street…which within three years became the centre of the trade. In 1856, there were four shops devoted to what were now called 'perambulators,' and all within a few hundred yards of Burton's showroom, and no fewer than 20 makers in all London." Sewell, "The History of Children's and Invalids' Carriages," 718.
4   See Colin Ward, *Silver

Cross: The Story of a Great British Brand* (Rossendale, UK: The History Writer, 2010).
5   Mark Dodgson, David Gann, Ammon Salter, *The Management of Technological Innovation: Strategy and Practice* (Oxford: Oxford University Press, 2008), 115.

William Wilson's Silver Cross Perambulator, 1877   William Wilson started out as a blacksmith in the Sunderland dockyards in England before founding the baby carriage company in Yorkshire that his sons would later take over and expand.[5] The instantly recognizable spring system, large wheels, and reversible hood of his Silver Cross pram conjure visions of Mary Poppins behind the handle. This "coach" has been the preferred baby transport of the British royal family since King George VI, born in 1895. Dubbed the "Rolls Royce of Prams," it was more recently the carriage of Prince William and Kate Middleton's three children, George, Charlotte, and Louis. Its relatively roomy accommodations allow space for multiples as well as different ages of siblings with the addition of an over-the-bassinet seat.

The Baby Class "eggcrate."   Parents of twins, triplets, or higher-order multiples may have to contend with a multi-passenger stroller daily. For everyone else, the sight of a gaggle of perambulating infants usually occurs when encoutering day-care groups of babies and toddlers on the move. Double strollers show up in fiction in the late nineteenth century—in the 1881 novel *What the Angels Saw on Christmas Eve*, a character finds the entrance to his home "blocked by a double baby carriage"[6]—and iterations of transport for twins emerged throughout the twentieth century, for example, Joseph B. Schaefer's 1917 model (essentially a wagon with two seats),[7] and those found in *Popular Mechanics*, which at midcentury featured a tandem "double decker" (1948) and triplet "suitcase stroller" (1951).[8] Tens of similar patents were filed in the intervening decades, and at the turn of the twenty-first century, a combination of women's high participation in the workforce and widely available fertility treatments meant childcare facilities had a need for moving mini-busloads of babies.[9] The result is the "eggcrate," sometimes of sturdy injection-molded plastic, sometimes more akin to Maclaren's skeletal frame—but inevitably an absolute beast to maneuver.

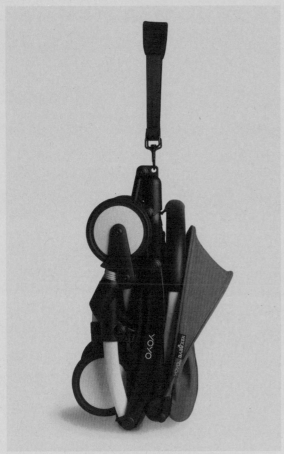

Jean-Michel Chaudeurge's Babyzen Yoyo, 2012 Mounting restrictions on carry-on luggage and security concerns led twenty-first century designers to create strollers that fold and fit into most airplane overhead bins. But capricious and ever-changing airline regulations have meant that the majority of strollers still must be checked at the gate. This makes models like the Yoyo, with a price tag nearing $500, better suited to subways and automobiles, where they're less likely to be lost or damaged in transit. Yet for all the focus on portability and minimized weight, strollers that can master stairs have yet to be designed. The death of a young mother, Malaysia Goodson, in New York on January 2019, when she fell carrying her one-year-old daughter in a stroller down the stairs to a subway platform, highlights the need for building greater accessibility into the urban infrastructure, not just into the products themselves.

Cindy Sjöblom's prototype for a wheelchair adaptive stroller, the Cursum, 2012 Parents who are wheelchair users find very few strollers on the market that are compatible with their needs. Cindy Sjöblom, a student in industrial design at the Umeå School of Design in Sweden, set out to fill this niche using the principles of universal design, whereby products and systems are created in ways that make them accessible for people of all abilities. The result is the Cursum, a stroller developed in close consultation with disabled parents. Its U-shaped swivel base and telescoping frame are designed to attach easily to a wheelchair and travel with the user, but can switch to freestanding when needed. The Cursum has yet to be mass-produced, suggesting an area of baby-transport design ripe for investment and innovation.

6 See "A Brief History of the Double Stroller," *Slate*, August 22, 2011, text for image 1 [of 7].
7 Joseph B. Schaefer, Baby-carriage, US Patent

1,256,379, filed March 30, 1917, issued February 12, 1918.
8 *Popular Mechanics*, August 1948, 120; *Popular Mechanics*, April 1951,

122.
9 See Geva Katz and Oron Lazarovich (Baby Jogger LLC), Convertible single and multi-seat stroller, US Patent

8,905,427 B2, filed April 30, 2008, issued December 9, 2014; Lukasz S. Poslowski, Joseph A. Lawlor, and David Stitchick

(Foundations Worldwide, Inc.), Stroller, US Patent D742,793 S, filed August 4, 2014, issued November 10, 2015.

GORDON PARKS

GORDON PARKS Born in Kansas in 1912, Gordon Parks was the youngest of fifteen children living in an era scarred by Jim Crow. As a photographer, he defined a generation, training his lens on poverty, the fight for civil rights, and ordinary lives. He worked for the Farm Security Administration (FSA) in the 1940s. An early series centered on Ella Watson, the cleaning lady at the FSA office, and her family, who eked out a life on her subsistence wage. He also documented the first (and so far, only) federally subsidized national childcare program, established through the US government's Lanham Act of 1941, which provided, among many other public services, $52 million (equal to more than $1 billion today) for child care for women participating in the war effort from August 1943 through February 1946.

1—— A young girl with her sister, Seaton Road, Washington, DC, June 1942

2—— Interracial activities at Camp Ellen Marvin, Arden, New York, summer 1943

3—— Story hour at a child care center in New Britain, Connecticut, June 1943

4—— Grandchildren of Ella Watson, a government charwoman, Washington, DC, August 1942

5—— Ella Watson reading the Bible to her household, Washington, DC, August 1942

6—— Washing up for lunch at a child care center in New Britain, Connecticut, June 1943

7—— Pouring lemonade at a birthday party on Seaton Road, Washington, DC, June 1942

2   3
4
5   6

ADOPTION——Families take all forms, and about two-fifths of families in the United States include children, whether biological, step, or adopted (this figure does not account for nieces, nephews, grandchildren, and others who might also share the same roof). While the vast majority of children live with one or two biological parents, many also live with stepparents, grandparents, aunts and uncles, or adoptive or foster parents.[1] These arrangements may be legally determined or informal—a "chosen family" or the result of unexpected circumstances—and exist across cultures, geographies, or within the same extended clan. Each represents a unique expression of kin, home, and identity.[2]

In the following pages, objects or photographs are shared by those who have adopted a child or were themselves adopted to tell an aspect of their story. Such things, the psychologist Mihaly Csikszentmihalyi explains, are umbilical cords of a different kind, "contain[ing] a symbolic ecology that represents both continuity and change."[3] For each of us, the familiarity and concreteness of objects help to organize our consciousness and experiences. Objects can invoke a sense of the maternal or of bloodline or identity, or they may provide a sense of equilibrium, providing a place where past, present, and future, belonging and separation, align. These stories remind us that dreams and anxieties about identity and belonging, origins and heritage, are a part of us all.

I've long been interested in the big white porcelain moon jars from the Joseon dynasty. With their sturdy bellies that swell outward, they're often talked about as wombs. But when I saw them at the museums in Seoul while looking for my birth mother, who'd gone missing, I was struck by their surfaces, which are blank and unyielding. This reminded me of the ways that the maternal can encompass gestures of refusal or withdrawal made in order to survive. Several years after that trip I would learn that my mother had left Korea long before I had gone there to find her. She had immigrated to the United States, and I thought of a different kind of evasiveness—the kind that's demanded of those who live un-documented—through which one escapes the gaze of the state but also one's own kin. The moon jar has helped me make sense of these realities.

——Caitlin Beach

I was born in 1958. My adoptive parents chose not to tell me I was adopted. I found out by accident at age thirty-one when the authenticity of my birth certificate was called into question by my employer. Although my original birth certificate was sealed by court order, I was able to obtain my baptismal certificate from the Catholic Church. See the asterisk following my name, Nancy Sue Craig? That asterisk turned out to be the key unlocking the reality that I was someone else before then. There was a before time I knew nothing about—a secret time when my name was Julie Rodelli. On the surface it represented a betrayal, but there was also another dimension. My adoptive mother drew her feelings of femininity and even her identity as a woman from the story that she had given birth to a child. As her lies began to close in on her and the story unraveled, she couldn't let go of the lie. Because for her being a woman meant being a mother.

——Julie Rodelli

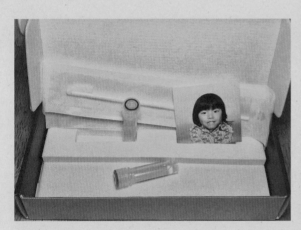

Who am I? What I know: As a newborn I was anonymously left at an orphanage in Kunsan, South Korea; at eighteen months I was adopted by a White American family. What I don't know: Everything else. But I never had a desire to find my biological family. For my most recent birthday my husband gave me a DNA test kit, and my reaction—mostly apprehension—surprised both of us. It has taken me a long time to find my place in this world, and a large part of the process was accepting the unanswerable questions. The kit sits on the hall table, where I pass it every day—still not ready. Can a DNA test tell me who I am?

——Tae Smith

My family was easily the poster child for Black adoption. Both maternal and paternal sides eschewed the formal adoption process and made binding decisions about who would raise their grandchildren. Their children had fallen prey to drugs, crime, and mental illness, and the next generation would not thrive without their intervention. So we remained within our family, maintained bonds with our parents, and were raised in a stable, loving environment without the assistance of lawyers or social workers. This African legacy of informal adoption meant their decision was made instinctively and shaped my idea of how to make a family. The ancestors positioned me to mother children I did not birth, and simultaneously to reach for my grandfather's prized thirty-pound Royal typewriter. Even as a child, I understood the power of words. They would come to define me, as I expressed joy, fear, racism, foster care, adoption, and Black single motherhood, first of a son and then a daughter. Though I was not allowed to touch Henry's typewriter, with ink that smudged if I touched freshly typed words before they dried on the page, I was destined to use his mode of communication to tell the world about the power of Black adoption.

——Nefertiti Austin

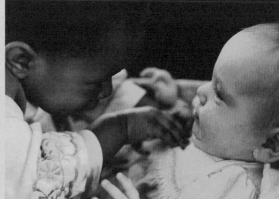

I was six months old when my parents first met me, and the official adoption was in October 1970, when I was one year and four months old. Mom had Mary not long after that. Mom was my mom, but she wasn't my mom, you know? I was forty-five years old when I met my birth mother for the first time, and I couldn't believe it. Her entire house was set up exactly like mine. It was like coming home. I loved my mom, but our relationship was complicated. But Mary was always my sister. She was my rock. These pictures tell some of the story.

——Nancy Taylor

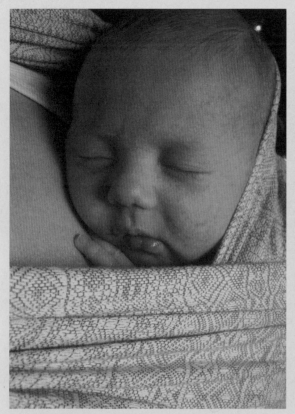

As a young woman I was fascinated by the bonds that form between a mother and her baby through pregnancy, childbirth, and nursing. So when my journey to motherhood did not follow that path, I felt the loss of those physical forms of bonding keenly. As my husband and I prepared to adopt our daughter, Lillian, I sought to understand and facilitate that physical bonding in every way possible, from skin-to-skin contact, to adoptive nursing, to baby wearing. I fell in love with this wrap the first time I saw it. Its softness in color and texture, delicate yet structured geometric design, durable woven fabric, and ability to literally wrap two bodies together captured the essence of the relationship I wanted to form: comforting, gentle, consistent, strong, and connected. From Lillian's newborn days into her toddler years, this wrap facilitated the physical connection I needed as I grew into becoming her mother.

——**Andrea Homer-McDonald**

I was adopted in 1978 when I was three months old. It was a closed process [meaning nothing was shared of the birth circumstances], and, following the protocol of the time, I was put in foster care for the first three months of my life, until my parents could be told that they would be allowed to adopt me. This is the only photo that exists from the time before my adoption. When I became a mother, I saw how much happens in those early months, and it made me think about how little I will ever know of that time in my own life. After my parents adopted me, they documented every moment of my life and took me for a portrait every month.

——**Karin Satrom**

The photograph on the right is of me and my "bio-mom" and documents the last time I would see her for thirty-five years. I was two
weeks old. I discovered these photos when I was twenty-one, while
cleaning the house after my mother died. My cousin told me who
the woman was. After my initial shock, I often wondered about her.
My search for her began years later, and we've since reunited.

——**Mike James**

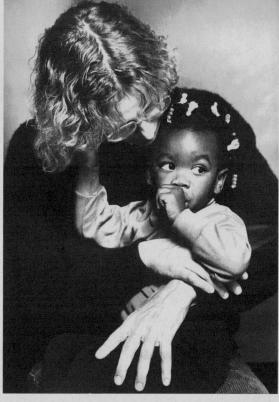

This is the first picture we received. We're assuming it was taken around 2003/4. We learned that her Chinese name was Lian Mo Li. *Lian* is the first four letters of Lianyungang, the name of the city where she was found as a young baby. Her actual birthplace will always remain a mystery. There are stories of birth families traveling miles to assure that the treasured babies they are abandoning are found safely and can be well cared for. We'll never know that pain, of course, but we'll forever honor the unimaginable loss of that heart-wrenching choice.

Mo Li means jasmine flower, and together with *Lian* our naming problem was solved! We added an I and she became our Molli Lian. We found this picture quite arresting and remember thinking how ready she seemed to get out of there—and, we hoped, to come home with us to her very own freshly painted room.

——Mark Mitchell

This portrait was taken when Kiani was about two. I love it because my hand symbolizes the roots I am offering for him to grow. Even though he is unsure, he's reaching up to my head as I lean down to comfort him. There is an intimacy and trust there that still captures our relationship even as he has grown into a very capable and confident young man.

——Ginger Mitchell

This is a photo of me and my biological mother on her wedding day. I feel very lucky to have built a relationship with her after meeting her at age thirteen. My adoptive parents were always open about the story, and I knew I wanted to find out who my biological parents were and that I had my adoptive parents' support. My birth mother had me when she was very young and didn't have any children after me. When I got in touch it was the first time she told her then partner about me. We had shy first letters, and later visits. This photo was taken a few years later at a point when she felt very much like family.

—Henrike Dreier

1   In 2010, 95 percent of US children under age eighteen lived with one or two biological parents. See Rose M. Kreider and Daphne A. Lofquist, "Adopted Children and Stepchildren: 2010," United States Census Bureau, April 2014, census.gov/prod/2014pubs/p20-572.pdf. **2**   "There is no single source for determining the total number of children adopted in the United States, and there is currently no straightforward way of determining the total number of adoptions, even when multiple data sources are used. No single agency is charged with compiling this national information." One of the only clear trends is that intercountry adoption to the United States has dropped precipitously in the last decade. Quoted from Child Welfare Information Gateway, "Trends in US Adoptions: 2008–2012," US Department of Health and Human Services, 2016, childwelfare.gov. **3**   Mihaly Csikszentmihalyi, "Why We Need Things," in *History from Things: Essays on Material Culture*, ed. Steven Lubar and W. David Kingery (Washington, DC: Smithsonian Institution Press, 1993), 25

FAMILIES

FAMILIES Family are bonded by love, by blood, by choice, by obligation, by trust, by flesh, by sacrifice, by proximity, by geography, by paperwork, and sometimes by name. Nuclear families, extended families, step families, adopted families, foster families, arranged families, blended families, surrogate families, legal families, interracial families, chosen families, broken families, mended families, reimagined families, off the map families.

1— Michelle's grandparents, aunt, and mum out for a walk in Glasgow, c. 1946
2— Amber and Tobi, from the 4th Trimester Bodies Project
3— A young mother bathes her baby
4— Michelle and Kelsey meet their new brother, Ross, with mum and adopted granny Queenie, March 8, 1985
5— Graham, Margot, Bruce, and Pauline in Prospect Park, Brooklyn, 1970s
6— *Four Generations*, 1986, from Mary Motley Kalergis's *Mother: A Collective Portrait* (1997)
7— Juliana's extended family gathers on a stoop in Brooklyn, c. 1992

2   3   4
5   6

Albert, Elisa. *After Birth*. London: Vintage Books, 2016.

Ariès, Philippe, and Adam Phillips. *Centuries of Childhood*. London: Pimlico, 1996.

Betterton, Rosemary. *Maternal Bodies in the Visual Arts*. Manchester, UK: Manchester University Press, 2018.

Block, Jennifer. *Pushed: The Painful Truth about Childbirth and Modern Maternity Care*. Cambridge: MA: Da Capo/Lifelong, 2008.

Boston Women's Health Book Collective. *Our Bodies, Ourselves: A Book by and for Women*. 2nd ed. New York: Simon and Schuster, 1976.

Brown, Jenny. *Birth Strike: The Hidden Fight over Women's Work*. Oakland, CA: PM Press, 2019.

Buller, Rachel Epp, and Charles Reeve. *Inappropriate Bodies: Art, Design, and Maternity*. Bradford, ON: Demeter Press, 2019.

Cassidy, Tina. *Birth: A History*. London: Vintage Digital, 2011.

Chalker, Rebecca, and Carol Downer. *A Woman's Book of Choices*. New York: Seven Stories Press, 2014.

Clark, Adele, and Donna Haraway. *Making Kin Not Population: Reconceiving Generations*. Chicago: Prickly Paradigm Press, 2018.

Cohen, Erica Chidi. *Nurture: A Modern Guide to Pregnancy, Birth, Early Motherhood—and Trusting Yourself and Your Body*. San Francisco: Chronicle Books, 2017.

Cooper Owens, Deirdre. *Medical Bondage: Race, Gender, and the Origins of American Gynecology*. Athens: University of Georgia Press, 2017.

Davey, Moyra. *Mother Reader: Essential Writings on Motherhood*. New York: Seven Stories Press, 2001.

Davis, Dána-Ain. *Reproductive Injustice: Racism, Pregnancy, and Premature Birth*. New York: New York University Press, 2019.

D'Ignazio, Catherine, and Lauren F. Klein. *Data Feminism*. Cambridge, MA: MIT Press, 2020.

DiGregorio, Sarah. *Early: An Intimate History of Premature Birth and What It Teaches Us about Being Human*. New York: Harper, 2020.

Ehrenreich, Barbara, and Deirdre English. *Witches, Midwives, and Nurses: A History of Women Healers*. [Place of publication unidentified]: Last Work Press, 2016.

Eig, Jonathan. *The Birth of the Pill: How Four Crusaders Reinvented Sex and Launched a Revolution*. London: Pan Books, 2016.

Erickson-Schroth, Laura. *Trans Bodies, Trans Selves: A Resource for the Transgender Community*. Oxford: Oxford University Press, 2014.

Federici, Silvia. *Revolution at Point Zero: Housework, Reproduction, and Feminist Struggle*. Oakland, CA: PM Press, 2012.

—. *Witches, Witch-Hunting, and Women*. Oakland, CA: PM Press, 2018.

Fessler, Ann. *The Girls Who Went Away: The Hidden History of Women Who Surrendered Children for Adoption in the Decades before Roe v. Wade*. New York: Penguin Press, 2007.

Firestone, Shulamith. *The Dialectic of Sex: The Case for Feminist Revolution*. London: Verso Books, 2015.

Friedmann, Jessica. *Things That Helped: On Postpartum Depression*. New York: FSG Originals, 2018.

Galchen, Rivka. *Little Labors*. New York: New Directions, 2019.

Garbes, Angela. *Like a Mother: A Feminist Journey through the Science and Culture of Pregnancy*. New York: HarperCollins, 2019.

Gaskin, Ina May. *Ina May's Guide to Childbirth*. New York: Bantam Books, 2019.

—. *Spiritual Midwifery*. 4th ed. Summertown, TN: Book Publishing Co., 2002.

Gibney, Shannon, and Kao Kalia Yang. *What God Is Honored Here?: Writings on Miscarriage and Infant Loss by and for Native Women and Women of Color*. Minneapolis: University of Minnesota Press, 2019.

Goldman, Kay. *Dressing Modern Maternity: The Frankfurt Sisters of Dallas and the Page Boy Label*. Lubbock: Texas Tech University Press, 2013.

Hardyment, Christina. *Dream Babies: Three Centuries of Good Advice on Child Care*. New York: Harper & Row, 1983.

Hearn, Karen. *Portraying Pregnancy: From Holbein to Social Media*. London: Paul Holberton Publishing, 2020.

Hendrickson-Jack, Lisa, and Lara Briden. *The Fifth Vital Sign: Master Your Cycles and Optimize Your Fertility*. [Place of publication unidentified]: Fertility Friday Publishing, 2019.

Heti, Sheila. *Motherhood*. Toronto: Vintage Canada, 2019.

Holden, Katherine. *The Shadow of Marriage: Singleness in England, 1914–60*. Manchester, UK: Manchester University Press, 2010.

Hooks, Bell. *Feminism Is for Everybody: Passionate Politics*. London: Pluto Press, 2000.

Hurley-Cronin, Johanna M. "The Experience of Childbirth". Master's thesis, National University of Ireland, 1985.

Kaplan, Laura. *The Story of Jane: The Legendary Underground Feminist Abortion Service*. Chicago: University of Chicago Press, 2019.

Kapsalis, Terri. *Public Privates: Performing Gynecology from Both Ends of the Speculum*. Durham, NC: Duke University Press, 1997.

Juliet Kinchin, Aidan O'Connor, et al. *Century of the Child: Growing by Design, 1900–2000*. New York: Museum of Modern Art, 2012.

Kitzinger, Sheila. *The Experience of Childbirth*. Rev. ed. London: Orion, 2004.

Knott, Sarah. *Mother Is a Verb: An Unconventional History*. [Place of publication unidentified]: Picador, 2020.

Lange, Alexandra. *The Design of Childhood: How the Material World Shapes Independent

Kids. New York: Bloomsbury, 2020.

Larson, Laura. *Hidden Mother*. Baltimore: Saint Lucy Books, 2016.

Layne, Linda L., Sharra L. Vostral, and Kate Boyer, eds. *Feminist Technology*. Urbana: University of Illinois Press, 2010.

Leavitt, Judith Walzer. *Brought to Bed: Childbearing in America, 1750 to 1950*. New York: Oxford University Press, 2016.

Leboyer, Frédérick. *Birth without Violence*. London: Pinter & Martin, 2011.

Lewis, Sophie. *Full Surrogacy Now: Feminism against Family*. London: Verso, 2020.

Logan, Onnie Lee, and Katherine Clark. *Motherwit: An Alabama Midwife's Story*. New York: Dutton, 1989.

Luke, Jenny M. *Delivered by Midwives: African American Midwifery in the Twentieth-Century South*. Jackson: University Press of Mississippi, 2018.

Lyerly, Anne D. *A Good Birth: Finding the Positive and Profound in Your Childbirth Experience*. New York: Penguin, 2013.

Martin, Emily. *The Woman in the Body: A Cultural Analysis of Reproduction; with a New Introduction*. Boston: Beacon Press, 2003.

Martucci, Jessica L. *Back to the Breast: Natural Motherhood and Breastfeeding in America*. Chicago: University of Chicago Press, 2015.

Mattes, Jane. *Single Mothers by Choice*. New York Random House, 1980.

Mead, Margaret. *Coming of Age in Samoa: A Psychological Study of Primitive Youth for Western Civilization*. New York: W. Morrow, 1928.

Mitford, Jessica. *The American Way of Birth*. New York: Dutton, 1992.

Murphy, Michelle. *Seizing the Means of Reproduction: Entanglements of Feminism, Health, and Technoscience*. Durham, NC: Duke University Press, 2013.

Oakley, Ann. *The Captured Womb: A History of the Medical Care of Pregnant Women*. Oxford: Basil Blackwell, 1986.

Odent, Michel. *Childbirth in the Age of Plastics*. London: Pinter & Martin, 2011.

Okamoto, Nadya. *Period Power: A Manifesto for the Menstrual Movement*. New York: Simon & Schuster, 2018.

O'Reilly, Andrea. *Toni Morrison and Motherhood: A Politics of the Heart*. Albany: State University of New York Press, 2004.

Ou, Heng, et al. *The First Forty Days: The Essential Art of Nourishing the New Mother*. New York: Stewart, Tabori & Chang, 2016.

Radl, Shirley L. *Mother's Day Is Over*. Rev. ed. New York: Arbor House, 1987.

Rapp, Rayna. *Testing Women, Testing the Fetus: The Social Impact of Amniocentesis in America*. New York: Routledge, 2000.

Rich, Adrienne. *Of Woman Born: Motherhood as Experience and Institution*. 10th ed. New York: W. W. Norton, 1986.

Romero, Jimena Acosta, and Michelle Millar Fisher. *Haré lo que deseo: Diseño y empoderamiento femenino = I Will What I Want: Women, Design, and Empowerment*. Mexico City: Toronja Ediciones, 2018.

Ross, Loretta J., et al. *Radical Reproductive Justice: Foundation, Theory, Practice, Critique*. New York: Feminist Press at the City University of New York, 2017.

Roth, Benita. *Separate Roads to Feminism: Black, Chicana, and White Feminist Movements in America's Second Wave*. Cambridge: Cambridge University Press, 2004.

Schreiber, Melody. *What We Didn't Expect: Personal Stories about Premature Birth*. Brooklyn: Melville House Publishing, 2021.

Sjöblom, Lisa Wool-Rim, Hanna Strömberg, and Richard Wyver. *Palimpsest: Documents from a Korean Adoption*. Montreal: Drawn & Quarterly, 2019.

Snitow, Ann. *The Feminism of Uncertainty: A Gender Diary*. Durham, NC: Duke University Press, 2015.

Solnit, Rebecca. *The Mother of All Questions*. Chicago: Haymarket Books, 2019.

Taylor, Janelle S., ed. *Consuming Motherhood*. New Brunswick, NJ: Rutgers University Press, 2004.

Taylor, Keeanga-Yamahtta, ed. *How We Get Free: Black Feminism and the Combahee River Collective*. Chicago: Haymarket Books, 2017.

Tone, Andrea. *Devices and Desires: A History of Contraceptives in America*. New York: Hill and Wang, 2002.

Traig, Jennifer. *Act Natural: A Cultural History of Parenting*. New York: Ecco, 2019.

Treichler, Paula, Lisa Cartwright, and Constance Penley. *The Visible Woman: Imaging Technologies, Gender, and Science*. New York: New York University Press, 1998.

Turner, Sasha. *Contested Bodies: Pregnancy, Childrearing, and Slavery in Jamaica*. Philadelphia: University of Pennsylvania Press, 2019.

Vergès, Françoise, and Kaiama L. Glover. *The Wombs of Women: Race, Capital, Feminism*. Durham, NC: Duke University Press, 2020.

Wertz, Richard W., and Dorothy C. Wertz. *Lying-In: A History of Childbirth in America*. New York: Free Press, 1990.

Weschler, Toni. *Taking Charge of Your Fertility: The Definitive Guide to Natural Birth Control, Pregnancy Achievement, and Reproductive Health*. 10th ed. New York: HarperCollins, 2006.

Westervelt, Amy. *Forget "Having It All": How America Messed Up Motherhood—and How to Fix It*. New York: Seal Press, 2018.

Withycombe, Shannon. *Lost Miscarriage in Nineteenth-Century America*. New Brunswick, NJ: Rutgers University Press, 2019.

Wong, Alice. *Disability Visibility: First-Person Stories from the Twentieth-First Century*. New York: Vintage Books, 2020.

Luz Argueta-Vogel is a Lenca Maya midwife, mystic, and muse. Based in the San Francisco Bay area, she plays and works seasonally and itinerantly, traveling often and throughout the continent, perpetually weaving relationships with varied land bases and relatives. As a ceremonialist and decolonization activist, she grounds her midwifery practice in principles of radical sovereignty and ecological stewardship and is guided by ancestral knowledge. She approaches birth humbly and with reverence and innovation while working as a guardian of transition to hold space for families as they grow and heal through the powerfully transformative process of life-bringing.

Zara Arshad is a curator and design historian specializing in twentieth- and twenty-first-century design from East Asia. She has previously held roles at the Victoria and Albert Museum (V&A) and the Design History Society in London, the Asia Culture Center in South Korea, and at Beijing Design Week and Icograda World Design Congress 2009 in Beijing. She has lived in the UK, South Korea, China, Syria, and Indonesia. Arshad is based at the University of Brighton and the V&A, is currently working on her PhD, and is a governing board member of China Residencies and half of the studio Geofictions.

Author and memoirist Nefertiti Austin writes about the erasure of diverse voices in motherhood in the critically acclaimed Motherhood So White: A Memoir of Race, Gender, and Parenting in America (2019). Her work on this topic has appeared in the New York Times, Washington Post, Huffington Post, MUTHA, GEN by Medium, and many other publications. She was the subject of an article on race and adoption in The Atlantic and has appeared on numerous shows/podcasts and radio programs, including the Today Show, 1A with Joshua Johnson, and NPR. Nefertiti is the proud adoptive mother of two children and lives in Los Angeles.

Juliana Rowen Barton is an architecture and design historian and curator who holds a PhD in art history from the University of Pennsylvania, Philadelphia. Her work centers on the intersections of design, domesticity, and the politics of display viewed through the lenses of race and gender. She has worked on exhibitions at the Center for Architecture and Design, Philadelphia, the Museum of Modern Art, New York, and the Philadelphia Museum of Art, where she co-organized Design in Revolution (2018)

and Designs for Different Futures (2019–20).

Caitlin Beach, born Kwon Meehye, is assistant professor of art history at Fordham University in New York, where her teaching and research focus on issues of subject formation, visibility, and racial capitalism across the nineteenth century. She is from Seoul and lives in New York, where she is an active member of and advocate for the transracial adoptee community.

Lindsey Beal is a photo-based artist in Providence, Rhode Island, whose work combines research about historical and contemporary women's lives with historical photographic processes, and often includes sculpture, papermaking, and artist's books. She teaches at the Rhode Island School of Design in Providence and at the Massachusetts College of Art and Design in Boston.

Speaker, author, and family man Thomas Beatie made international headlines as a man and husband who gave birth to three children in as many years while defending the validity of his marriage and identity in a precedent-setting court battle. He has been dubbed a pop-culture icon by People magazine and is known in the media as the world's first pregnant man. Thomas believes that through visibility it is possible to demystify harmful stereotypes and show that different is normal.

Maricela Becerra is a mother of two. She holds a PhD in Mexican literature and culture and is an assistant professor of Spanish at California State University at Channel Islands. She blogs about motherhood, academia, and everything in between.

Joan E. Biren, or JEB, is an internationally known photographer and documentary filmmaker who has chronicled the lives of lesbians and social justice movements for over four decades, making visible the often hidden histories of women and other marginalized people. A self-taught photographer, Biren began documenting lesbian lives because "I needed to see images of lesbians." Her first book, Eye to Eye: Portraits of Lesbians (1979), was a ground-breaking collection of intimate portraits of women at work, at home, making art, playing music, raising families, performing rituals, and loving each other. In 1987 she published Making a Way: Lesbians Out Front, a sequel of sorts.

Heather DeWolf Bowser serves women prenatally and postpartum, helping them to remember their innate wisdom, and offers

support in exploring fertility, wild pregnancy, birth choices, nutrition, and support after loss or pregnancy release. Her work centers on the intrinsic power of women to choose how to birth and mother their children—and the perfect wisdom of undisturbed, physiological birth that all mammals are programmed for. Her relationship with birthing women is one of wise woman support, council, and sisterhood. She believes that all women know how to birth and deeply trusts them to navigate their own journey bringing their babies into the world.

Megan Brandow-Faller is associate professor of history at the City University of New York, Kingsborough. Her research focuses on art and design in Secessionist and interwar Vienna, including children's art and artistic toys of the Vienna Secession; expressionist ceramics of the Wiener Werkstätte; folk art and modernism; and women's art education. She is the editor of Childhood by Design: Toys and the Material Culture of Childhood, 1700–Present (2018) and author of The Female Secession: Art and the Decorative at the Viennese Women's Academy (2020).

Khiara M. Bridges is a professor of law at UC Berkeley School of Law. Her scholarship focuses on race, class, reproductive rights, and the intersection of the three. She is also the author of three books: Reproducing Race: An Ethnography of Pregnancy as a Site of Racialization (2011); The Poverty of Privacy Rights (2017); and Critical Race Theory: A Primer (2019).

Sophie Cavoulacos is assistant curator in the film department at the Museum of Modern Art, New York, where she focuses on the moving image across the museum's cinemas, collections displays, and live programs.

Erica Chidi is an educator, author, doula, and cofounder and CEO of LOOM, a well-being brand empowering women/womxn through support of their reproductive, relationship, and sexual health. Her work, both as a doula and as author of Nurture: A Modern Guide to Pregnancy, Birth, Early Motherhood—and Trusting Yourself and Your Body (2017), has guided thousands of people in their transition from pregnancy to parenthood. Erica began her practice in San Francisco volunteering as a doula within the prison system. She went on to build a successful health-education practice in Los Angeles while continuing to work with organizations that serve marginalized communities. She has been featured in the magazines Women's Health, Vogue, Goop,

The Cut, and *Marie Claire*.

Meegan Daigler is an engineer and cofounder of Reia, a health care start-up focused on improving the treatment experience for people with pelvic organ prolapse (POP). Reia's first product is a nonsurgical treatment option for POP called a pessary. Reia's pessary design allows users to manage their pessary on their own and alleviates pain during insertion and removal.

Anna Dhody is curator and Gretchen Worden Chair of the Mütter Museum and director of the Mütter Research Institute at the College of Physicians of Philadelphia. She received her bachelor's in archaeology from Boston University and her master's in forensic science from the George Washington University. She has curated over twenty exhibitions at the Mütter Museum and has published papers in journals such as *Scientific Reports*, *Genome Biology*, and the *New England Journal of Medicine*. She lectures extensively both nationally and internationally. Dhody strives to provide an educational and "disturbingly informative" experience for the 180,000-plus visitors to the Mütter Museum each year.

Christine Dodson and former Bernie Sanders staffer **Sascha Mayer** founded Mamava, the leading expert in the design of lactation space, in 2006 after working together in a Vermont design studio, Solidarity of Unbridled Labour (formerly JDK). Mamava supports the twenty-first-century breastfeeding mother-on-the-go with freestanding lactation pods, a mobile locator app, and an engaged digital community. There are currently more than sixteen hundred Mamava suites across the United States and Canada. In 2018 Dodson and Mayer were named Vermont Small Business Persons of the Year.

Henrike Dreier, born in Lübeck, Germany, is a London-based graphic designer and art director. She codirects Studio Lindrei and designs with Graphic Thought Facility. She attended the London College of Communication and Central Saint Martins College of Art and Design, University of the Arts London.

Adam Dubrowski is a professor and the Canada Research Chair in Health care Simulation on the faculty of health sciences at Ontario Tech University. He studies factors that influence the acquisition of clinical skills, particularly the methods used for optimizing simulation in medical education and training. He draws on theories from other fields to evaluate and reshape existing medical edu-

cation programs, and to develop new ones.

Hailing from Scotland, **Michelle Millar Fisher** has worked as an educator, curator, and researcher in universities and museums including the Museum of Modern Art, New York, the Philadelphia Museum of Art, the Guggenheim, The Metropolitan Museum of Art, and the Museum of Fine Arts, Boston where she is currently the Wornick Curator of Contemporary Decorative Arts. Her work focuses on the intersections of people, power, design, and craft. She has co-authored many books, essays, and exhibitions including *Design and Violence* (2015), *Items: Is Fashion Modern?* (2017), and *Designs for Different Futures* (2019–20).

Claire Dion Fletcher is an Indigenous (Lenape-Potawatomi) and mixed settler Registered Midwife practicing in Toronto. An assistant professor at the Ryerson Midwifery Education Program, she focuses her teaching on Indigenous midwifery and social justice issues. Claire is currently co-chair of the National Aboriginal Council of Midwives. She completed her master of arts in gender, feminist, and women's studies at York University in Toronto, where her research focused on decolonized health care and Indigenous midwifery.

Tekara Gainey is a reproductive justice advocate and birth worker. She fuses her master's in anthropology with her reproductive work to acknowledge and address the systems of oppression that impact access to compassionate, nonjudgmental reproductive care for birthing persons and their families across the spectrum of their needs. Tekara is a birth doula and childbirth educator, and now serves as the program associate for Maternity Care Coalition's community doula and breastfeeding programs.

Lucy Gallun is associate curator in the Robert B. Menschel department of photography at the Museum of Modern Art in New York.

Angela Garbes is a writer based in Seattle, where she lives with her family on Beacon Hill. She is the author of *Like a Mother*, a narrative nonfiction book exploring the emerging science and cultural myths of pregnancy. *Like a Mother* was an NPR Best Book of 2018 and a finalist for the Washington State Book Award in Nonfiction. She is currently working on her next book, a collection of essays about human bodies. Her writing has appeared in the *New York Times*, *The Cut*, and *Bon Appétit*, and has been featured on NPR's Fresh Air. In a

previous life she was the staff food writer at the Seattle alt-weekly *The Stranger*.

Judy S. Gelles (1944–2020) was a multimedia artist who explored the interplay between art, sociology, and psychology using image and text. Over a forty-year career, she worked in photography, film and video, installation, and artist's books. Her photography is known for documenting family and domestic life, especially her own, and for its witty and frank reckoning with traditional roles for women as daughter, wife, and mother. She moved beyond her own family as subject, culminating in the decade-long Fourth Grade Project, a portrait study of the lives of three hundred children from around the world. Her incisive use of language overlaid on or under her images is a signature mark of her work.

Shoshana Batya Greenwald is the director of collections at Amud Aish Memorial Museum in Brooklyn. She is an Orthodox Jewish educator, writer, and design historian.

Robert D. Hicks is senior consulting scholar and William Maul Measey Chair for the History of Medicine of the College of Physicians of Philadelphia. For over a decade he served as director of the Mütter Museum and the Historical Medical Library at the college. He has worked with museum-based education and exhibitions for over three decades, primarily as a consultant to historic sites and museums.

Porsche Holland holds a master of science degree in ministerial leadership from Amridge University in Montgomery and a bachelor of science in biology from Tuskegee University, Alabama. Porsche is an AmeriCorps alum and national service advocate; as a consultant she supports national service program development from inception to sustainability. She is a community doula, peer counselor, birth worker mentor and trainer, and Black maternal health thought leader for the Maternity Care Coalition of Philadelphia, and an advisor to *Designing Motherhood*.

Andrea Homer-Macdonald is a dancer, movement educator, choreographer, and certified movement analyst (LABAN/Bartenieff Institute of Movement, Brooklyn). She is an adoptive mother who works and lives in New York City with her husband and two beloved children, Lillian and Felix.

Alexis Hope is an artist, designer, and researcher. She serves as design director for the "Make the Breast Pump Not Suck" project, as well as creative director of TEN

FWD, a design studio focused on creating playful, experimental objects and experiences. She is currently finishing her PhD at the MIT Media Lab in Cambridge, Massachusetts, where she investigates and creates participatory processes for technology design.

Karen Kleiman is a well-known international maternal mental health expert, practicing for over thirty-two years. As an advocate and author, she and her work have been featured on the internet and within the mental health community for decades. In 1988 she founded the Postpartum Stress Center, a treatment and training facility in Rosemont, Pennsylvania, for prenatal and postpartum depression/anxiety disorders, where she treats individuals and couples experiencing perinatal mood and anxiety disorders.

Alexandra Lange is a design critic and author of *The Design of Childhood: How the Material World Shapes Independent Kids* (2018).

Natalie Lira is an assistant professor of gender and women's studies in the Latina/Latino studies department at the University of Illinois at Urbana-Champaign. Her research uncovers the largely neglected racial aspects of California's eugenic sterilization program by providing evidence of the disproportionate institutionalization and sterilization of Mexican-origin women and men in state hospitals for the disabled during the first half of the twentieth century.

Devorah L Marrus lives in Columbia, South Carolina. She is the mother of five and helps codirect the Chabad programming in her city. She teaches women's classes and also in the Jewish preschool. Her passions include spearheading large events for the Jewish community and spreading love for the Jewish heritage.

Jessica Martucci is a historian of science, medicine, and technology. Her first book, *Back to the Breast* (2015), examines the story behind the return of breastfeeding in the United States at the end of the twentieth century. Her research has been published widely in both popular and academic outlets, including *Nursing CLIO* (blog), Distillations (podcast), the *AMA Journal of Ethics, the Journal of Women's History*, and the *Bulletin in the History of Medicine*, among others.

Ginger Mitchell is a Feldenkrais practitioner based in Denver who specializes in infants, children, rehabilitation, wellness, stress management, and awareness.

Mark Mitchell is a conductor, musical director, and musician and has performed off and on Broadway for decades. His wife, **Betsy Joslyn Mitchell**, is a former musical and dramatic actress who, among her many Broadway credits, originated the role of Nora in *A Doll's Life* and played leading roles in three Sondheim musicals. Their daughter is now a senior in high school.

Aidan O'Connor is an independent design curator, educator, and New Yorker newly based in Minneapolis (and loving it). She has worked in curatorial departments at the Museum of Modern Art, the Cooper-Hewitt, Smithsonian Design Museum, and the Metropolitan Museum of Art in New York, and at the Peabody Museum of Archaeology and Ethnology at Harvard University in Cambridge, Massachusetts. She has guest-curated exhibitions for the High Museum of Art in Atlanta; Vandalorum in Värnamo, Sweden; and the Hyundai Motorstudio Beijing. Aidan is mom to five-year-old Otis and two-year-old Casper.

Lauren Downing Peters is assistant professor of fashion studies and director of the historic Fashion Study Collection at Columbia College, Chicago. She holds a PhD in fashion studies from the Centre for Fashion Studies at Stockholm University and a master's in fashion studies from the Parsons School of Design, New York. She is also editor-in-chief of the Fashion Studies Journal and is currently finalizing the manuscript for her first book, *Fashioning the Flesh: Fashion, Fatness, and Femininity in Early 20th-Century America*.

Nicole Pihema, of Ngāpuhi and Te Rarawa descent, is the first Māori president of and is currently the chairperson for the Te Taitokerau region of the New Zealand College of Midwives. She has been a registered midwife since 2010 and is a Lead Maternity Carer (LMC) midwife in the Bay of Islands.

Alice Rawsthorn is an award-winning design critic and author whose most recent book is *Design as an Attitude* (2018). Her weekly design column for the *New York Times* was syndicated worldwide for over a decade. Born in Manchester and based in London, Alice chairs the boards of trustees at the Hepworth Wakefield art gallery in Yorkshire and the Chisenhale Gallery in London, and is a founding member of the Writers for Liberty campaign for human rights.

Helen Barchilon Redman is an artist who lives in San Diego but is still connected to Boulder, Colorado, where she spent a significant portion of her adult life enmeshed in that city's feminist art community. Her work in large-scale painting focuses on themes of matrilineage, maternity, and family. She has been a visiting artist at the University of Iowa, Iowa City, and an instructor at the University of Colorado, Boulder. She was awarded a bachelor's degree by the University of Miami and a master of fine arts by the University of Colorado. Her work is held in the collections of the Cornell Fine Arts Museum at Rollins College in Orlando, Florida, the Brooklyn Museum of Art, and the Museum of Fine Arts, Boston, as well as in other private collections.

Airyka Rockefeller is an artist, photographer, and writer based in San Francisco, known for her evocative, editorial style. In addition to documenting creative people, spaces, and gatherings across diverse fields of viticulture, food, art, and design, she is the founder of REALM, an interview-based project exploring concepts of home, and Amending, an annual pop-up shop that gathers modern and previously used items of beauty and function.

Julie Rodelli writes quirky, weird, fever-dream sci-fi, flash fiction, and microfiction stories. She lives in Seattle.

Raphaela Rosella is an Australian artist who works in the tradition of long-form documentary storytelling. Challenging bureaucratic narratives (for example, case files and criminal records), she has spent over a decade co-creating photo-based projects alongside several friends and family members to unveil the interlocking structural systems, institutions, biased media representations, relentless bureaucratic processes, and violent histories that feed intergenerational trauma, poverty, violence, addiction, the forced removal of children, incarceration, and the burden of low expectations. Her artistic practice draws heavily on relational exchanges and a collaborative ethos to resist tropes of victimhood by presenting everyday stories of women's connectedness, belonging, and kinship.

Loretta J. Ross started her career in the women's movement in the 1970s at the DC Rape Crisis Center, National Organization for Women, the National Black Women's Health Project, and SisterSong Women of Color Reproductive Justice Collective. She is one of the co-creators of the reproductive justice framework. Her most recent publication is *Reproductive Justice: An Introduction*, co-written with Rickie Solinger in 2017; her next book is on calling in the calling out culture.

Ofelia Pérez Ruiz is an Indigenous registered midwife and spokesperson for the Chiapas Nich Ixim Movement of Traditional Midwives.

Hannah Ryan is assistant professor of art history at St. Olaf College in Northfield, Minnesota, where she teaches modern and contemporary art history. Her primary area of research has been the art that reveals women's lived experiences, particularly maternity and lactation, with attention to issues of race, gender, and labor. Employing a decolonial and feminist approach, her dissertation, and current book project, is a sociopolitical history of infant feeding in the Americas told through visual culture, situating human milk as a substance of particular value. As a researcher and curator, Hannah is also engaged with photography, trauma, and resilience, as well as the intersections between art history, intersectional feminism, and food studies.

Karin Satrom currently leads the in-house design team at the Metropolitan Opera, New York. As design director, she oversees and creates the concepts and designs of all print and digital materials to promote more than twenty-six operas each season. She has created an in-house agency, the Metropolitan Opera Studio, and implemented a digital project management system.

Tae Smith is a costume and textile expert specializing in creating exhibitions. Her fifteen years of experience, which includes current museum-level knowledge of conservation, has made her one of the most sought-after experts in the field of exhibiting costumes and textiles in the United States. She has a bachelor of science in fashion design and went to graduate school at New York's Fashion Institute of Technology in their Fashion and Textile Studies master's program. She has also been a part-time faculty member in the Fashion Studies graduate program at the Parsons School of Design in New York.

Orkan Telhan is an interdisciplinary artist, designer, and researcher whose investigations focus on the design of interrogative objects, interfaces, and media, engaging with critical issues in social, cultural, and environmental responsibility. Telhan is associate professor of Fine Arts (Emerging Design Practices) at the University of Pennsylvania, Stuart Weitzman School of Design, in Philadelphia. He holds a PhD in design and computation from MIT's

architecture department and was part of the Sociable Media Group at the MIT Media Lab and a researcher at the MIT Design Lab in Cambridge, Massachusetts. His work has been exhibited at the Istanbul Design Biennial, Milano Design Week, Vienna Design Week, and Ars Electronica in Linz, Austria, among other venues.

Stephanie Tillman (she/her) is a midwife, writer, and activist in Chicago. She completed her undergraduate degree in global health and medical anthropology at the University of Michigan, and her graduate degree in Nurse-Midwifery at Yale University, New Haven. Stephanie is a Clinical Medical Ethics Fellow at the University of Chicago, where she is focusing on consent in pelvic care. She is on the Board of Directors of the Midwest Access Project, is Immediate Past Chair of the Board of Directors of Nurses for Sexual and Reproductive Health, and an Advisory Committee member of the Queer and Transgender Midwives Association. Stephanie is the founder of @FeministMidwife, where she seeks to engage providers and consumers in conversations about consent in health provision, queer care, sex positivity, abortion care, equalized power dynamics, reproductive justice, and trauma-informed frameworks.

Sandra Oyarzo Torres is a midwife, educator, and advocate. She has paved the way for midwifery regulation in Latin America by educating her fellow midwives about the vital need for every midwife to deliver high-quality, respectful, evidence-based maternity care. She is an associate professor in the Department of Education in Health Sciences in the College of Midwives at the University of Chile, Santiago; serves as vice president of the International Confederation of Midwives; and is a Women in Global Health (WGH) board member.

Malika Verma's work intersects craft, cultural identity, and aesthetics. Engaged with evolving design languages, she is a vocal advocate for India's design and craft communities, and the founder of Border&Fall, a strategic and creative agency shifting perceptions of "Made in India." She created and produced The Sari Series: An Anthology of Drape, a digital cultural documentation of India's regional sari drapes.

Erin Weisbart is a mad scientist (biochemist turned computational biologist), designer, and seamstress. She runs the popular sewing blog *Tuesday Stitches,* and together with her friend and business partner, Lisa Kievits, developed the website *Maternity*

Sewing: Your Source for Maternity and Nursing Sewing Patterns.

Artist, author, and curator **Deb Willis**'s art and pioneering research focuses on cultural histories envisioning the Black body, women, and gender. She is a celebrated photographer, acclaimed historian of photography, MacArthur and Guggenheim Fellow, and university professor and chair of the Photography & Imaging department at the Tisch School of the Arts at New York University.

Carmen Winant is an artist and writer based in Columbus, Ohio, where she is the Roy Lichtenstein Endowed Chair of Studio Art at the Ohio State University. Her work utilizes installation and collage strategies to examine feminist modes of survival and revolt. Winant's recent projects have been shown at the Museum of Modern Art, Sculpture Center (New York), Henie Onsted Kunstsenter (Oslo), the Wexner Center of the Arts, Kunsthal Charlottenborg (Copenhagen), and through the CONTACT Photography festival (Toronto), which mounted twenty-six of her billboards across Canada. Winant's recent artists' books, *My Birth* and *Notes on Fundamental Joy*, were published by SPBH Editions, ITI Press, and Printed Matter Inc. Winant's work is included in the collections of the Museum of Modern Art, New York; the Minneapolis Institute of Art; and the Henie Onstad Art Center, Sandvika, Norway. She is a 2019 Guggenheim Fellow in photography. Winant is the mother of two sons, Carlo and Rafa, whom she shares with her partner Luke Stettner.

Amber Winick is a writer and design historian based in New York's Hudson Valley. She is the recipient of two Fulbright awards and has lived and researched design around the world. She holds a master's in design history, decorative arts, and material culture from the Bard Graduate Center in New York, and studied anthropology and child development at Sarah Lawrence College in Bronxville, New York. She holds regular study groups around child development and respectful caregiving. Her two young daughters serve as research subjects for their design-loving, better-pregnancy-birth-and-postpartum-championing, slow-childhood-advocating mother. *Designing Motherhood* is her first book.

Brendan Winick is an award-winning, Brooklyn-based illustrator and musician. He is also Amber's beloved younger brother.

Dr. Flaura Koplin Winston is the Distinguished Chair in the Department of Pediatrics at the Children's Hospital of Philadelphia

(CHOP) and a tenured professor of pediatrics at the Perelman School of Medicine at the University of Pennsylvania. At CHOP she is the founder and Scientific Director of the National Science Foundation Center for Child Injury Prevention Studies and the Center for Injury Research and Prevention, and she leads the CHOP Innovation Ecosystem Initiative. Her interdisciplinary background in medicine, engineering, and public health has allowed her to conduct research at the interface of child and adolescent health, injury, technology, and behavior, which led her to establish the scientific foundation dedicated to the principal cause of child death and injury, while also building and leading effective multi-stakeholder health care and prevention teams. Her "research-to-action-to-impact" approach to academic entrepreneurship has led to new patents, products, programs, policies, and laws, as well as a CHOP spin-out technology company called Diagnostic Driving, Inc. For her scientifically rigorous and impactful work, she was elected in 2017 to the National Academy of Medicine.

The cultural anthropologist and home birth advocate Sheila Kitzinger wrote in her 2013 book *Birth and Sex* that "the only thing that compares with having your first baby is having your first book!" Let's just say this one had a long gestation. And while it was not an easy or quick birth, it was a good birth (a concept introduced by Dr. Anne Lyerly). This positivity was entirely due to our family, collaborators, and colleagues.

If it takes a village to raise a child, we found that it takes a medium-sized country to make a book like this one, especially during a pandemic. We are endlessly grateful to so many people who were essential in the birthing of this book. It has been a collaborative endeavor from the very beginning, and the meager thanks we can offer here do not adequately compensate for the great effort so many people have gone to on behalf of this project, for which we are profoundly grateful.

We must thank at the outset the contributors to this book, both those who authored their own chapters and those who consented to interviews. This project would not be half as rich without the varied and deep expertise of these voices: Luz Argueta-Vogel, Zara Arshad, Anjoo Aradhya Bahadur, Juliana Rowen Barton, Lindsey Beal, Thomas Beatie, Maricela Becerra, Joan E. Biren, Khiara Bridges, Sophie Cavoulacos, Erica Chidi, Meegan Daigler, Anna Dhody, Christine Dodson, Adam Dubrowski, Claire Dion Fletcher, Tekara Gainey, Lucy Gallun, Angela Garbes, the late Judy S. Gelles, Shoshana Batya Greenwald, Robert Hicks, Porsche M. Holland, Alexis Hope, Malika Verma, Karen Kleiman, Alexandra Lange, Natalie Lira, Devorah Leah Marrus, Jessica Martucci, Sascha Mayer, Aidan O'Connor, Lauren Downing Peters, Nicole Pihema, Alice Rawsthorn, Helen Redman, Raphaela Rosella, Loretta Ross, Ofelia Pérez Ruiz, Hannah Ryan, Orkan Telhan, Stephanie Tillman, Sandra Oyarzo Torres, Erin Weisbart, Deb Willis, Carmen Winant, and Flaura Winston.

In particular chapters, we asked people to share very personal stories, and we owe them special thanks for the gracious ways they opened up to us: Nefertiti Austin, Caitlin Beach, Ruth Blue, Heather DeWolf Bowser, Megan Brandow-Faller, Julie Cirelli, Henrike Dreier, Geraldine Freeman, Katrina Gardner, Leigh Gath, Angelica Gunn, Ulla Huopaniemi-Sirén, Dorte Hvidtjørn and the kind team at Aarhus University Hospital's perinatal loss unit, Mike James, Paige Johnston, Lisa M. Palmer, Kiersten Peterson, Maggie Preston, Andrea Homer-McDonald, Ginger Mitchell, Mark, Betsy, and Molli Mitchell, Jacqueline Neubauer, Julie Rodelli, Karin Satrom, Tae Smith, Mary and Nancy Taylor, and many more who remain anonymous.

When we sought partnerships for this project, we encountered many "noes"— years of them, in fact. But when we turned up on the doorstep of the Maternity Care Coalition in Philadelphia in 2019 (thanks for the generous tip, Erike De Vreya!), MCC immediately welcomed us with open arms. The very first person to do so was Karen Pollack, executive vice president of programs and operations, who for over twenty years had been working tirelessly to support pregnant people and their children. Karen had no need of two neophytes, yet she gladly welcomed us. She introduced us to Marianne Fray, MCC's chief executive officer, and the rest of her amazing team, which includes Gabriella Nelson, associate director of policy, Deanna Galer, director of development, and Katherine Mitchell, director of communications. We say it often, and it is true: we are riding on their coattails and are extremely lucky to be able to connect our research to their profound professional experience. We must also highlight the group of MCC advisors who were instrumental to the formation of the entire project—book, exhibition, and public programs—and who taught us new ways of engaging with the scholarship and practice of maternal health and reproductive justice. Words cannot adequately express the life-changing experiences we had in our many meetings with doula Tekara Gainey, early childhood education expert and author Sabrina Taylor, doula and lactation specialist Porsche M. Holland, and culturally appropriate care specialist Adrianne Edwards. We also enthusiastically and sincerely thank MCC staff emerita Bette Begleiter, who read through every word of every chapter of this book from her viewpoint as a specialist in culturally appropriate care and social work on the ground.

There is a running theme to this project: brilliant women with whom we are fortunate to have collaborated. Two deserve special mention: MCC executive assistant Zoë Greggs has arranged and attended countless *Designing Motherhood* meetings, tirelessly coordinated book permissions and myriad aspects of the exhibition, and generally leapt into curatorial practice like she was born for it. She is also responsible for the beautiful "Emergence" image spread in the book. Our other interlocutor on this project (among so many others) is the indefatigable Juliana Rowen Barton. In addition to graciously lending her scholarly superpowers to several chapters of this book, she led the crucial image research that deepened and expanded the themes and ideas presented here. She also rolled up her sleeves to handle the grunt work of gathering image permissions and countless other administrative tasks alongside us with unfailing goodwill. Simultaneously, she successfully defended her doctoral dissertation and was awarded a prestigious postdoctoral placement.

We will forever appreciate the folks at the Pew Center for Arts and Heritage in Philadelphia, including the anonymous reviewers of our proposal, who awarded us a substantial grant to make this project a reality. Thanks go to Kelly Shindler, director of exhibitions and public interpretation, who was our doula throughout the process; Amaka Eze, program assistant for exhibitions and public interpretation; and Paula Marincola, executive director.

We are forever grateful to the angels who supported the project financially and emotionally, including the incomparably kind Diana Limbach Lempel, companies Binto, Nyssa, Mamava, LOOM, Storq, the Art Mamas Alliance, Petra Slinkard, and the many incredibly kind donors via the project's website, including the artists (Sol Calero, Lena Corwin, Jack Halten Fahnestock, Awol Erizku, Harvey Finkle, Anna K.E., Roberto Lugo, Caitlin Mociun, Mary Ping, Helen Redman, Alexandre Singh, and Gerri Spilka) and purchasers who participated in the DM x MCC Art Sale.

Natasha Chandani and Lana Cavar of Clanada, the designers of this book, have been an unbridled joy to work with. The result is masterful, and it has been an absolute honor to collaborate with them. At times the circumstances around our collaboration were truly biblical—with deaths in our families, power outages, plagues, and more—but the laughter and respect shared during our meetings kept the project vital and pleasurable. Thanks are also owed to Miho and Tamara Karoly of Kaligraf for the great prepress work and to the production team at Kerschoffset. Kathleen Krattenmaker was our editor par excellence, and a kind, steady, precise, and wonderfully thoughtful presence during our writing process. We also deeply appreciate all the efforts of the team at MIT Press, including Victoria Hindley, our commissioning editor; Janet Rossi, our production manager; Gabriela Bueno Gibbs, assistant acquisitions editor; and Nicholas DiSabatino, global publicity manager and senior publicist. Thanks are also owed to Sarah Brown McLeod, who has been our fearless press and communications champion across all our partner institutions. And we want to make special mention of Romy St. Hilaire, who contributed brilliantly to the curatorial team.

We are grateful beyond measure for our enthusiastic and collaborative colleagues at the two exhibition venues in Philadelphia, the Mütter Museum and the Center for Architecture and Design. At the former, we thank Robert Hicks, senior consulting scholar and William Maul Measey Chair for the History of Medicine; Anna Dhody, acting co-director and the Gretchen Worden Curatorial Chair, and director of the Mütter Research Institute; Nancy Hill, museum manager; Natalie Howard, director of communications; Michael Keys, exhibition manager; and Hanna Polasky, project researcher, all of whom have deep expertise that, at the risk of sounding like a broken record, was indelibly important to the success of this project. And at the Center for Architecture and Design, we sincerely thank Rebecca Johnson, executive director, and Elizabeth Paul, communications director. Special thanks go to Erike De Veyra for making so many wonderful connections for us. And we must heap praise on Helen Cahng, the exhibition designer who so brilliantly planned and oversaw the installations at both venues. We are also infinitely grateful to commissioned artists Helina Metaferia, Michelle Angela Ortiz, and Alison Croney Moses, whose work with us was just beginning to unfold as this book went to press. We thank each of these wonderful exhibition partners and participants from the bottom of our hearts.

Part of the genesis of this project was our inability to find the material covered in these pages in the design histories that we were taught and that we went on to teach, and so it has been a particular joy to work with the wonderful Orkan Telhan, a longtime friend and associate professor of fine arts, emerging design practices, in the University of Pennsylvania's School of Design, on creating a design studio curriculum. We were able to test the curriculum in the fall of 2020 in Orkan's classes for design students, who produced fantastic, nuanced, personal work.

So many people helped us at every juncture of our research. The following list was frightening to write because we knew we would surely miss some who should be here, for which we beg forgiveness: Kate Abercrombie, Tracy Abney, Glenn Adamson, Sarah B. Barnes at the Wilson Center, Simon Barton and Rachel Holdsworth at Bourn Hall Clinic, Emily Bates at Gavin Brown Enterprises, Siobhán Bohnacker, Dee Burn and her colleagues at Norland College, Charlotte Burns, Dan Byers, Dugald Cameron, Elsa Chahin, Wei Hung Chen, Julie Cirelli, Nikki Columbus, Margaret "Meg" Crane, Anja Aronowsky Cronberg, Gitte Dalberg-Larsen and Ida Thygesen Gjørup of OrganiCup, Jamie Diamond, Catherine D'Ignazio, Sarah DiGregorio, the Dittrick Medical History Center of Case Western Reserve University, Carol Downer, Claudette Dunn, Ruth Erickson, Lynne Farrington at the Kislak Center for Special Collections at the University of Pennsylvania, Harry Finley at the Museum of Menstruation, Catriona Fisk, Tom Fitzgerald, the Florida State Archives, LaToya Ruby Frazier, David Gelles, Tricia Gesner at the Associated Press, Carly Gieseler, Aimee Gilmore, Glasgow School of Art archives, Andrew Goodhouse, Hendrik-Jan Grievink at Next Nature Network, Cassandra Hatton, Karen Hearn, Chris Hudson, Steve Huggins of CuddleCot, Lauren F. Klein, Kate Kraczon, Alison Lapper, Debbie Laurin, Susan Lennon at Alamy, Edan Lepucki, Emily Liebert, Catherine Losing, Ellen Lupton at the Cooper-Hewitt, Alastair Macdonald, Lee Marks, Emma McClendon, Stiliyana Minkovska, Sara Moe, Jack Mord of the Thanatos Archive, Amelia Morris, Dani Murano, Aisling Murray, Anna Ruth Myers, Elisa Nadel at Artbook/D.A.P., Judy Norsigian and her colleagues at Our Bodies Ourselves, Ksenia Nouril, Kelly O'Donnell, Bárbara Oñate, Natalie Oppenheimer at the Children's Hospital of Philadelphia, Karen Paterson, the Planned Parenthood Federation of America, Martha Poggioli, Soumeya Bendimerad Roberts, Airyka Rockefeller, Meg Rotzel and her colleagues at the Schlesinger Library at the Radcliffe Institute for Advanced Study at Harvard University, Priscilla "PJ" Ryland, Sveva Costa Sanseverino, Clare Sauro, Gregory and Maggie Scott, Yutong Shi, Deborah Carlisle Solomon, Luise Stauss, Dane Strom, Ronit Sukenick, Beth DeFrancis Sun at the American College of Obstetricians and Gynecologists, Jodi Throckmorton, Barrie Underwood of Science Photo Library, Fran Wang and Rachel Hobart of Yona, Brendan Winick (our wonderful and fearless illustrator), and Ayla Yavin Acupuncture and Herbs. Thanks always to the midwives in our corner: Cathy Gallagher, Janice Heller, Cara Muhlhan, Nuranisa Rae, Susan Schmidt, and Jo Zasloff and her sister, Dr. Eva Zasloff, who kindly acted as a peer reviewer for this book.

We tested some of our ideas about designs for motherhood in public as a springboard for this project. Paola Antonelli, mentor and curator extraordinaire, and our dear friends Anna Burckhardt, Stephanie Kramer, and Kristina Parsons welcomed maternity as a theme in *Items: Is Fashion Modern?*, an exhibition at MoMA in 2017. Curator Jimena Acosta Romero was a wonderful partner on *I Will What I Want: Design, Women, and Empowerment* at Parsons the New School in New York and at muca-Roma in Mexico City in 2018. And we must also thank the collaborators for the 2019 exhibition *Designs for Different Futures*, most especially Liz Baill, Caitlin Deutsch, and Emily Schreiner, for embracing ideas about public health as museum programming. The original northstar of this project was our beloved Juliet Kinchin, who inspired us with her groundbreaking 2012 MoMA exhibition *Century of the Child: Growing by Design, 1900–2000*, and her brilliant coorganizer of that project, Aidan O'Connor, who is a contributor to this book (see the chapter on the hospital bag).

Our project was further supported and fine-tuned by public discourse in a range of venues. We are thankful for the many classes, conferences, and public programs that hosted us as we sorted through the ideas that have found space in these pages, as well as the many that we will have to roll over to the second (and third) book, for which we have ample material. We are especially fortunate for the many folks who follow @designingmotherhood on Instagram, and who comment, message, and share their own experiences and ideas. We cannot underscore how much this interaction has helped refine our own ideas and sustain us in community as we prepared this project.

This book is about the material culture that shapes reproductive experiences, and we owe thanks to the people who have been formative in our lives along these lines. For Amber, these people are Charlotte Doyle, Margery Franklin, Aaron Glass, David Jaffee, Michele Majer, Amy Ogata, Gilberto Perez, Karen Rader, Paul Stirton (for Michelle too), David Valentine, Catherine and Whalen. For Michelle, they include her amazing, kind, warm colleagues in the Contemporary Art department at the Museum of Fine Arts, Boston, Debra Lennard, Liz Munsell, Daniela Sierra, Reto Thuring, Akili Tommasino, and Marina Tyquiengco who have long indulged her enthusiastic sharing of new discoveries in this project at every turn, as well as her professors and friends at the CUNY Graduate Center in New York.

This is also a book about communities of mothers, mother figures, and sisters, and we are both blessed to have had so very many of those. They include Michelle's late mum, Ellie; her mother-in-law, Deb; her adopted grandmother, Queenie; her special aunts, Panda and Sensifer; her best-friends-from-home, Penny Norman, Oliva Reeves, Rebecca Bell, Helen Nisbet, Tamsin Clarke, and Laura Bennison, and her best-friends-from-here, Caitlin Mociun, Meredith Brown, and Natalie Musteata; her cousin Sharon Hoover; family-in-law Pat and Claire Bennett; and her beloved families-by-nannying, most especially Rena, Rob, Ella, and Hannah of the Krasnow-Marx family, and the Gusick-Giersdorf family of Jens, Ned, and Emma. They also include Amber's great-aunts Helen and Millie DeMeo and dear friends Lise Registre, Ana Abramcyk, Sofiya Akilova, Tara Anderson, Sarah Bachelier, Nicole Cloutier, Stephanie Diamond, Caitlin Dover, Cara Fraver, Lindsey Heddleston, Leah Kaminski, Nomi Kleinman, Anna McDonald Norman, Lindsey Norris, Daphne Revie, Helen Sansone, Sveva Costa Severino, Sarah and Naomi Sorkin, Ashley Steele, Saukok Chu Tiampo, Danel Trisi, Graham Winick, Bruce Winick, and Margot Winick. And special mention goes to Jessica Warner, the wonderful human who introduced us to each other around a dinner table somewhere in Brooklyn around 2014. Jessica has been a rock for us both for years.

In the time it took us to create this book, a lot happened. Michelle moved cities three times for her work—each time hoping that the research for this project might fit into her institutional day job. It didn't, but that didn't stop us. Her beloved mum, Ellie, died and was much missed as we wrote about motherhood. Michelle's biggest thanks go to her husband, Austin, who has consistently made space for her career, desires, and bodily autonomy around reproductive choices, and has made her toast and countless cups of tea early each morning during her writing and research for years. He is an unparalleled partner, friend, and the love of her life. She is also deeply grateful for the presence and support of her sister, Kelsey, her brother, Ross, and her sister-in-law, Kathryn.

Meanwhile, Amber gave birth and settled into a new home down the road from her wonderful parents-in-law, who were early supporters of the book. Pooa and Tony made a work space for her in their basement and lovingly cared for Amber's youngest, Cosima, while her eldest, Alice, was at nursery school. Her own mom, Terry, moved to an apartment nearby so she could join them for family meals and help care for the girls while Amber worked. "It'll be fun!" Amber promised her. And, as he always does, her husband, Daniel, supported every dream she had for this book. He read every single first draft, fearlessly co-parented, and kept her grounded, laughing, and well loved throughout the process. She counts herself so lucky to have the support of her family. Thank you, Daniel, Alice, Cosima, Terry, Tony, and Pooa. She could not have done it without you.

And we are grateful for each other. As with marriage or co-parenting, it hasn't always been easy (though it mostly was), but it was always in pursuit of joy, adventure, care (of ourselves and each other), and new personal and professional horizons. We have loved having this experience together, learned from and with each other, and emerged with a lifelong bond.

Michelle Millar Fisher and Amber Winick
October 2020

Kuwabara, Yoshinori, 79

labor and birth
  clean birth kit, 167–68
  doula role in, 185–88
  films of, 227–32
  in home births, 209–12
  pain management during, 213–16
  perineal repair, 221–22
  photography of, 205–8, 217–20, 225–26
  positions during, 163–66
Lamaze method, 213–14
Lang, Raven, 224
Lange, Alexandra, 9–11
Lasker, Edward, 260
laughing gas, 215
Leboyer, Frédérick, 210, 214
Le Guin, Ursula, 60n16
Lepuki, Edan, 252
lesbian culture, 50–51
Lessing, Doris, 58
Lewis, Sophie, 78
LIA pregnancy test, 82
Liebig, Justus von, 264
life forms, origins of, 29–30
LifeWrap, 168
Lindbergh, Charles, Jr., 287
Lindo Wing, St. Mary's Hospital, London, 233, 234
Lira, Natalie, 65–66
Lishko, Polina, 34
Livingstone, Ken, 150
Lochia (uterine discharge), 252
London Transport, Baby on Board button of, 149–50
Lopez, Antonio, 113, 114
Lotus Project, 248

Maclaren, Owen F., 310
MacVicar, John, 89–90
Madrigal v. Quilligan, 66
Mamava pod, 261–62
Marin, Sanna, 286
marketing, digital, 127–28
Marmite, 83–84
Marrus, Devorah Leah, 276
Martucci, Jessica, 257–58
masculine birth, 141–44
masturbation, during labor, 215
maternal mortality, 20–21, 168, 190, 210, 211, 212n19
Maternity Care Coalition (MCC), 22–23, 181–85, 186
maternity clothing
  anti-radiation, 95–96
  business sector, 105–6
  corsets, 101–2, 104
  sari, 107–8
  sewing patterns, 115–18
  showing pregnancy in, 97–99

tie-waist skirt, 24n10, 103–5, 131
Mauriceau, François, 162
Mayer, Sascha, 261–62
McClain, Dani, 24n11
McDonald, Eugene, 287–88
McGlasson and Perkins, 35
Medicaid, 23, 192, 211
medicalization of childbirth, 191
Medline, 249, 250
menstrual cup, 35–36
menstrual cycle, 41–42
menstrual evacuation kit (Del-Em device), 20, 47–48
menstrual hygiene products, 35–40
Merrell (William S.) Company, 54
midwives
  Black, 179–80, 191, 210–12
  direct-entry, 212n13
  Indigenous, 137–40, 210, 224, 281–82
  new generation of, 71–72
  obstetrical tools, 56
  regulation of, 133–36, 203, 210, 211, 250
milk glass beads, for identification, 245–46
Miller, Suellen, 168
Miller, Wayne, 226
Mills, A. L., 249
Mills, Victor, 295, 296n2, 296n8
Minkovska, Stiliyana, 166
miscarriage, 145–48, 152
Mitchell, Ginger, 323
Mitchell, Mark, 323
Miyake, Issey, 284
Model Arrows (Ari Fitz), 132
Mongan, Mickey, 214
monitor, baby, 287–88
monitoring, fetal, 93–94, 173–74
Moore, Demi, 102, 105, 114, 130, 131
Morgenthaler, H. J. W., 245–46
Morrison, Toni, 58
mortality. *See* death
motherhood
  and adoption, 58, 317–24
  cultural attitudes toward, 20–22
  photographic portrait of, 241–44, 301–4
  products of, 10, 15–20
Mumsnet, 24n11, 149, 150
Murray, Jenni, 126
Museum of Modern Art (MoMA), 18–19, 24n7, 10, 226, 260

Nanfu Wang, 68
nannies, 269–70
National Childbirth Trust (NCT), 125–26, 252
natural childbirth, 125–26, 178, 216
Neel, Alice, 131
Nelson, Gabriella, 23
Nelson, Gunvor, *Kirsa Nicholina*, 228
Nelson, Maggie, *The Argonauts*, 24n11
Nestlé baby formula, 264

neural tube defects (NDTs), 84
newborns. *See* infants and babies
Newland, Colleen, 248
Next Nation Network (NNN), 78
Nilsson, Lennart, 29, 79, 85–88
nitrous oxide, 215
Noguchi, Isamu, 287, 288
Norland College, nanny uniform of, 269–70
Norris, Vic, 30
Northrup, Christiane, 215
nutrition
  postpartum, 273, 275
  prenatal, 83–84
Nyssa Care, 252

obstetrical tools, 56
O'Connor, Aiden C., 155–56
Odent, Michel, 166, 214
Offen, J. Allen, *Adventure to Motherhood*, 193–96
one-child policy, 67–68
Oreck, Robert, 36
Organon pharmaceutical company, 81
orgasmic birthing methods, 215
Our Bodies, Ourselves, 16, 31–36, 92

pain management, during labor, 213–16
paintings, pregnancy portrait, 130, 131, 169–72
Paleolithic pregnancy portrait, 130
Palopoli, Frank, 53, 54
Paoletti, Jo B., 154
Papenek, Victor, 155
parental leave, paid, 22, 24n16, 248, 285
parenting manuals, 237–38
Parks, Gordon, 313–16
Par-tu-ri-ent Pod, 78
Pascall-Bonaro, Debra, 215
patient rights/responsibilities, 76
Peck, Ellen, 57–58
pelvic exams, 71–75
pelvic floor exercise, 240
pelvic prolapse, 275
Pérez Ruiz, Ofelia, 138–40
perineal irrigation bottle, 252
perineal repair simulator, 221–22
perineometer, 239–40
Perry, Samuel M., 257
pessaries, 275
Peters, Lauren Downing, 101–2
Petit Pli children's clothing, 283, 284
Petrucci, Daniele, 79
Phillips, Kameelah, 56
Pick, Frank, 150
Piercy, Marge, 78
Pihema, Nicole, 138–40
Pikler, Emmi, 297–98
pill, the, 33–34
pillow, pregnancy, 119–20
Pinard horns (fetoscopes), 94

In reproducing the images contained in this publication, the authors obtained the permission of the rights holders whenever possible. If the authors could not locate the rights holders, notwithstanding good faith efforts, they request that any contact information concerning such rights holders be forwarded so that they may be contacted for further editions.

Front Matter Sophia Harris, CPM, LM, sophiaharrismidwife.com; Wellcome Collection Library, London

REPRODUCTION Pregnancy in Print. Alamy; Feminist Majority Foundation; The Portal to Texas History, Texas Fashion Collection, University of North Texas Libraries, Denton; Nieman Reports/ Pentagram; Getty Images; Special Collections Research Center, University of Michigan, Ann Arbor. **Cell.** Lennart Nilsson, TT/Science Photo Library, London. *Our Bodies, Ourselves.* Our Bodies Ourselves. **The Pill.** The Percy Skuy Collection, Dittrick Medical History Center, Case Western Reserve University, Cleveland. **Menstrual Cup.** Photograph by Carrie Eisert; OrganiCup. **Blood.** Collection of the authors; © Janice Rubin; Thinx; © 2020 Judy Chicago / Artists Rights Society (ARS), New York; UltuCup; Museum of Menstruation (images 6-8). **Charting the Menstrual Cycle.** Collection of Cooper Hewitt, Smithsonian Design Museum, New York. Museum purchase through gift of the Taub Foundation, 2016-54-378 © 2020 Artists Rights Society (ARS), New York / VG Bild-Kunst, Bonn. **Dalkon Shield.** Photograph by Constance Mensh for The College of Physicians of Philadelphia. **Del-Em Device.** Wikipedia/ Creative Commons and the Feminist Women's Health Center, Atlanta; Carol Downer. **Joan E. Biren.** All images © 2020 JEB (Joan E. Biren). **Clomid.** Public domain. **Speculum.** frog design, Inc. **Childfree.** Collection of Michelle Millar Fisher. **Protest.** Arthur and Elizabeth Schlesinger Library on the History of Women in America, Radcliffe Institute for Advanced Study, Harvard University, Cambridge, Massachusetts; Jjumba Martin; British Library, London; © Ellen Shub; Agencja Gazeta/Jakub Wlodek; Arthur and Elizabeth Schlesinger Library on the History of Women in America, Radcliffe Institute for Advanced Study, Harvard University, Cambridge, Massachusetts; Alamy/Keval Bharadia; Maggie Preston. **Sterilization Abuse.** Rachel Romero/San Francisco Poster Brigade. Library of

Congress Prints and Photographs Division Washington, DC, 2015647473. **Population Policy Posters.** IISH/Stefan R. Landsberger/ private collection. **Test-Tube Baby.** Bourn Hall Clinic, Bourn, England; Granger Historical Picture Archive. **Table Manners.** Planned Parenthood of San Francisco, Susan Ferreyra, Katrine Hughes, and Anne Waltzer. **Artificial Womb.** Photograph by Bram Saeys/Next Nature Network.

PREGNANCY Home Pregnancy Test. Brendan McCabe; Photograph by Jino Lee. LIA Diagnostics, Inc., Philadelphia. **Prenatal Vitamins.** The Museum of Applied Arts and Sciences, Australia; Public domain. **Lennart Nilsson.** All images © Lennart Nilsson, TT / Science Photo Library, London. **Sonogram.** Dugald Cameron. **Amniocentesis.** Illustration by Brendan Winick; Alamy. **Pinard Horn.** Photograph by Allan Gichigi. **Anti-Radiation Clothing.** Beijing Zhongyuankejian Technology Co., Ltd. **Showing.** Arrows. Porsche Holland. Sarah Sorkin. Jamie Diamond. Collection of Michelle Millar Fisher (images 5 and 6). Collection of Amber Winick. **Pregnancy Corset.** Lane Bryant Archives. **Tie-Waist Skirt.** Everett Collection, Newark, New Jersey; Public domain. **Sari.** Philippe McLean. **Deb Willis.** Deb Willis (images 1 and 3). Brandywine Workshop and Archives and LLILAS Benson Latin American Collection, University of Texas at Austin. Photograph by Mark Doroba, Visual Resources Collection, University of Texas Libraries (image 2). **Maternity Mega-Dress.** © Jean-Paul Goude. **Patterns for Pregnancy.** Wei Hung Chen. **Pregnancy Pillow.** Photographs by Airyka Rockefeller. **Exercise for Pregnancy.** Alysia Montaño and Cadenshae; Wellcome Collection Library, London (images 2 and 5); Tara-Brigitte Bhavnani; Doretta Davanzo Poli; AP/Chikako Yatabe; Alamy/Angela Hampton Picture Library; © Warner Brothers/ Madeline Lewis. **National Childbirth Trust.** Wellcome Collection Library, London. **Algorithms for Pregnancy.** Talia Shadwell. **Pregnancy Portraits.** Alamy/UB40 with permission of Alison Lapper. **Midwifery in Transition.** All images courtesy of The State Archives of Florida. **Midwives.** Amber Bracken. **Masculine Birth.** Photograph by David McNew/Getty Images with permission of Thomas Beatie. **Loss.** Alamy; Wellcome Collection Library, London; © Dianne Yudelson; Kiersten Peterson; Wellcome Collection Library, London; Jacqueline Neubauer; David Jones/Flickr

CC; Courtesy of anonymous; Lisa M. Palmer. **Baby on Board Button.** Photograph by Catherine Losing. **Baby Showers.** Claudette Dunn; Shoshana Greenwald. **Gender Reveal.** Alamy/AB Forces News Collection.

BIRTH Hospital Bag. WaterAid. **Lindsey Beal.** All images courtesy of Lindsey Beal. **Forceps.** Wellcome Collection Library, London, ESTC T135372; Photograph by Constance Mensh for The College of Physicians of Philadelphia. **Birthing Furniture.** Illustration by Brendan Winick; Wellcome Collection Library, London (image 2 and 3); Science Gallery Dublin; Jote Khalsa and Lindsey Heddleston; Stiliyana Minkovska. **Safe Delivery App.** Ayzh. **Helen Redman.** All images courtesy of Helen Redman. **Electronic Fetal Monitoring.** Collection of Michelle Millar Fisher. **C-Section Curtains.** Photograph by Tracy Abney of Rocket City Doulas. **Baby Drawer.** Kaiser Permanente Heritage Resources. *All My Babies.* Georgia Department of Health, Atlanta. **Maternity Care Coalition.** All images courtesy of Maternity Care Coalition and the Kislak Center for Special Collections, Rare Books, and Manuscripts, University of Pennsylvania, Philadelphia. **Doulas and Birth Companions.** Maternity Care Coalition and the University of Pennsylvania Library Archives, Philadelphia (MSColl760, box 44, folder 56). **#ListenToBlackWomen.** The State Archives of Florida, Tallahassee. *Adventure to Motherhood.* Copyright 1960 by Audio Visual Educational Co. of America, Inc., Miami. All rights reserved under the International and Pan-American Conventions and the International Copyright Union. **Designs for Grief.** Día de los Angelitos series courtesy of Dane Strom; The Thanatos Archive; Flexmort; Megan Brandow-Faller; Grief Watch; Heather DeWolf Bowser; Amber Winick; Tonny Foghmar. **Carmen Winant.** Images courtesy of Carmen Winant, published by ITI Press and Self Publish, Be Happy Editions. **Home Birth.** From the family archive of Amber Winick. **Pain.** Judith Elaine Halek. **Emergence.** Samantha Noel of Samantha Noel Photography; Greta Rico; Elaine Baca; Stephanie Entin Little Plum Photography www.littleplumphoto.com; Monet Nicole Moutrie; Jote Khalsa and Lindsey Heddleston. **Placenta.** Melissa Jean Photography. **Birth Photography.** © LaToya Ruby Frazier/Courtesy of the artist and Gavin Brown's enterprise, New York/Rome.

Birth in Film. Filmform. **Mother's Gaze.** Marthe Rowen and Nathalie Barton; Karina Bishop; Arthur and Elizabeth Schlesinger Library on the History of Women in America, Radcliffe Institute for Advanced Study, Harvard University, Cambridge, Massachusetts; Amber Winick; Zoe Greggs; Arthur and Elizabeth Schlesinger Library on the History of Women in America, Radcliffe Institute for Advanced Study, Harvard University, Cambridge, Massachusetts; Courtesy of the State Archives of Florida, Tallahassee; © ash luna | 4th Trimester Bodies Project. **Lindo Steps.** Getty Images/Manchester Daily Express/SSPL. **Thalidomide.** Geraldine Freeman.

POSTPARTUM   Dr. Spock. (c) Pocket Books. **Perineometer.** John Wiley & Sons, Ltd.; Illustration by Brendan Winick. **Raphaela Rosella.** All images © Raphaela Rosella 2017. This project was assisted by the Australian Government through the Australia Council for the Arts. **Newborn ID.** Science Museum Group Collection, UK © The Board of Trustees of the Science Museum. **Incubator.** Library of Congress Prints and Photographs Division, Washington, DC; New York Public Library. **Kuddle-Up.** Photograph by Jennifer Mason Photography. **Car Seat.** Collections of the Henry Ford Museum, Dearborn, Michigan. **Postpartum Mesh Underwear.** Jamie Diamond. **Feeding.** Jazmyne Futrell/@mixedmombrownbabies; © ash luna | 4th Trimester Bodies Project; Photograph by Malika Pham, courtesy of Gabriella Nelson; Smithsonian American Art Museum, Washington, DC; Gift of the Harmon Foundation; Lourdes Grobet; Collection of Amber Winick; Vincent Ferrané; Little, Brown, and Company. **Nursing Bra.** Bendon/Naked Brand Group. **Breast Pump.** Photograph by Bengt Backlund/Upplandsmuseet, Uppsala, Sweden; Medela LLC. **Baby Formula.** Photograph by Fritz Henle. Library of Congress Prints and Photographs Division, Washington, DC. **Carers.** Collection of Amber Winick (images 1, 5, and 8); Photograph by Amber Bracken; © Jamel Shabazz; Loira Limbal/Through the Night; Alex Huanfa Cheng; Sveva Costa Sanseverino. **Norland Nanny Uniform.** Norland College, Bath, England. *Kraamzorg.* MAI (Maria Austria Instituut), Amsterdam; Karen Kleiman and Molly McIntyre for the Postpartum Stress Center, Rosemont, Pennsylvania; and *Good Moms Have Scary Thoughts*, Familius LLC, all rights reserved Public domain; Sophia Harris, CPM, LM/www.sophiaharrismidwife.com; Maternity Care Coalition and the Kislak Center for Special Collections, Rare Books, and Manuscripts, University of Pennsylvania, Philadelphia; Justin Chauncey Photography; Asian American Pacific Islander Health Research Group (AAPIHRG)/Postpartum Folklore Project at UC Berkeley; Reia Health; Devorah Leah Marrus. **Baby Carrying.** Alamy/Ray Evans; Alejandro Linares Garcia; Ann Moore; Bernardo de Niz; Suzanne Shahar via Flickr; Hogan via Flickr; Collection of Amber Winick. **Petit Pli.** Photograph by Sun Lee. Peti Pli. *Äitiyspakkaus.* Photograph by Atte Hyvärinen. Finnish Labor Museum Werstas, Tampere. **Baby Monitor.** © 2020 Artists Rights Society (ARS), New York/The Isamu Noguchi Foundation and Garden Museum. **Hidden Mothers.** Collection of Lee Marks and John C. DePrez Jr., Shelbyville, Indiana. Photographs digitized by Laura Larson. **Family Leave.** Photograph by Vanessa Simmons (top) and by Ken Richardson (bottom)/MIT Media Lab/Breastpump Hackathon. **Diapers.** Marion O'Brien Donovan Papers, Archives Center, National Museum of American History, Philadelphia © Smithsonian Institution. **Emmi Pikler.** Illustration by Brendan Winick. **Crib.** Found photograph, Collection of Amber Winick. **Judy Gelles.** All photographs © Judy Gelles, courtesy of Pentimenti Gallery, Philadelphia. **The Stroller.** Public domain; © 2020 Artists Rights Society (ARS), New York; Collection of Michelle Millar Fisher; Public domain; Babyzen; Cindy Sjöblom. **Gordon Parks.** Farm Security Administration/Office of War Information Photograph Collection, Library of Congress, Washington, DC. All photographs by Gordon Parks, courtesy of the Library of Congress and the Gordon Parks Foundation. **Adoption.** Korea Open Government License Type 1/Cultural Heritage Administration of Korea; Julie Rodelli; Tae Smith; Nefertiti Austin; Photograph by Caroline Carlson/Nancy Taylor; Andrea Homer-Macdonald; Karin Satrom; Mike James; Molli, Mark, and Betsy Mitchell; Photograph by Katie Tartakoff/Ginger Mitchell; Henrike Dreier. **Families.** Collection of Michelle Millar Fisher (images 1 and 4); © ash luna | 4th Trimester Bodies Project; Collection of Amber Winick (images 3 and 5); © Mary Motley Kalergis; Collection of Juliana Barton.